C. C. Everett

ANCIENT HISTORY

FOR

COLLEGES AND HIGH SCHOOLS.

BY

WILLIAM F. ALLEN

AND

P. V. N. MYERS.

Part II.

A SHORT HISTORY OF THE ROMAN PEOPLE.

BY

WILLIAM F. ALLEN,

Late Professor of History in the University of Wisconsin.

BOSTON, U.S.A.:

PUBLISHED BY GINN & COMPANY.

1900

Entered according to Act of Congress, in the year 1890, by
GINN & COMPANY,
in the Office of the Librarian of Congress, at Washington.

ALL RIGHTS RESERVED.

TYPOGRAPHY BY J. S. CUSHING & CO., BOSTON, U.S.A.
PRESSWORK BY GINN & CO., BOSTON, U.S.A.

To

PROFESSOR HENRY W. TORREY,

WHO FIRST AWAKENED ME TO AN INTEREST

IN HISTORICAL STUDY.

NOTE.

On December 8, 1889, the last night of my husband's life, he made the final corrections in the proof sheets of the history, and pronounced the work ready for the public. The preface still, however, remained to be prepared, and at my request, Professor Turner, first his pupil and later his friend and assistant, with whom he has had daily conversations in regard to his history, has prepared a preface, embodying my husband's aims and plans for the work.

MARGARET ANDREWS ALLEN.

MADISON, WISCONSIN,
Jan. 1, 1890.

PREFACE.

In this book Professor Allen desired briefly to relate the history of the Roman people. To him Roman society presented itself as an entirety, so that the political, economic, literary, and religious elements in the life of the Roman people could not be understood in isolation, but only in relation with each other. While thus he considered society as a whole, he found in Roman history two fundamentally important series of events, each of which influenced the other; first, the policy and process by which the Roman Dominion was secured and organized during the Republic, its reorganization under the Empire, and final disruption at the time of the German migrations; and secondly, the social and economic causes of the failure of self-government among the Romans, and the working of the same forces under the Empire. In connection with these fundamental considerations, the land question is treated, and the history of literature and religion is carefully traced.

To illustrate and revivify more fully the life of the times, references have been made throughout the book to carefully selected historical novels, and to popular works for collateral reading. Professor Allen's conception of history, and the estimate which he placed upon the historical novel is shown by the following quotation from his paper upon "Historical Fiction," read shortly before his death, at a meeting of the Madison Literary Club: —

"The outline of events — dates, dynastic changes, decisive battles, wars of conquest, rise and fall of empires — must be learned as history. But when we have learned these, what, after all, do we possess? Only a skeleton, to be clothed with the flesh and blood of history. These facts have no more value in themselves than the names and positions of the stars to one who has no knowledge of the constitution and movements of the heavenly bodies; or the minute description of every variety of beetle or lichen, apart from the laws of growth and classification. Except for the gratification of intellectual curiosity, enabling us to understand the allusions in literature to historical names and events, the value of historical study consists entirely in two things: first, it teaches the relations of cause and effect, as they are exemplified in the working of historical forces, the interplay of human passions and interests; secondly, it introduces us to the life of a past generation, so that its thoughts, its emotions, its habits, its concerns, may in a measure become as real to us as that of the age in which we live, and the people whom we meet every day. These we may call the philosophical and the picturesque aspects of history; and I do not know of any other benefit conferred by historical study. No historical fact is of any value except so far as it helps us to understand human nature or the working of historic forces.

"Now the first of these, the study of historical causes and effects, lies out of the range of historical fiction as completely as is the case with the systematic study of events. Both of these — events and their interpretation — may come incidentally into historical fiction, but only incidentally. The methods are totally different. These subjects, especially the relation of cause and effect, must be treated with a degree of abstraction, and almost wholly by analysis; but fiction, as far as it is skilful, avoids abstractions, eschews analysis. Its method is synthetic and concrete. It is plain that this concrete method of fiction is exactly adapted to the second of the two objects specified, — the picturesque aspect of history, the delineations of life and society. But what I want especially to point out is that this is precisely what formal instruction in history, or formal historical treatises, cannot do at all, or can do very imperfectly."

Teachers will notice that the more important dates are incorporated in the text, while the free use of dates in the margin serves to give more detailed guidance to the reader.

Particular care was taken in the selection of maps and illustrations. The colored maps are reproductions of the charts accompanying Professor Freeman's *Historical Geography of Europe*. The cuts are from Prang's *Illustrations of the History of Art*, Jaeger's *Weltgeschichte*, and other equally good authorities.

Professor Allen had a strong admiration for Theodor Mommsen as the master of Roman history. To him, more than to any other authority, would he have acknowledged his indebtedness. He seldom differed with Mommsen, and then only after most careful consideration; but he was an earnest student of the original sources, and he did not hesitate to use his own judgment and to avail himself of the researches of all the best authorities. This acknowledgment, the only one possible under the circumstances, is gratefully made in Professor Allen's name.

F. J. T.

PREFACE

Particular care was taken in the selection of maps and illustrations. The colored maps are reproductions of the charts accompanying Professor Freeman's *Historical Geography of Europe*. The cuts are from Prang's *Illustrations of the History of Art*, Lübke's *Kunstgeschichte*, and other equally good authorities.

Professor Allen had a strong admiration for Theodor Mommsen as the master of Roman history. To him, more than to any other authority, would he have acknowledged his indebtedness. He seldom differed with Mommsen, and then only after most careful consideration; but he was an earnest student of the original sources, and he did not hesitate to use his own judgment and to avail himself of the researches of all the best authorities. This acknowledgment, the only one possible under the circumstances, is gratefully made in Professor Allen's name.

F. J. T.

TABLE OF CONTENTS.

                                                    PAGE

CHAPTER I. — Italy.. 1

PERIOD I. — THE MONARCHY (to B.C. 509).

CHAPTER II. — Patrician Rome.
    I. History and Tradition................................... 10
   II. Institutions... 18
  III. Religion 22
CHAPTER III. — The Tarquins...................................... 29

PERIOD II. — THE EARLY REPUBLIC (B.C. 509-367).

CHAPTER IV. — Social Controversies.
    I. The Tribunate of the Plebs: to 494[1]................... 38
   II. The Agrarian Laws: to 471............................. 44
CHAPTER V. — The Contest between the Orders.
    I. The Contest for Civil Rights: to 445................... 52
   II. The Contest for Political Rights: to 396................ 61
  III. The Triumph of the Plebs: to 367...................... 68

PERIOD III. — THE ITALIAN WARS (B.C. 367-266).

CHAPTER VI. — The Conquest of Latium: to 338................. 77
CHAPTER VII. — The Conquest of Italy.
    I. The Second Samnite War: to 304...................... 84
   II. The Third Samnite War: to 286......................... 92
  III. The War with Pyrrhus: to 266.......................... 96

PERIOD IV. — OF FOREIGN CONQUEST (B.C. 266-133).

CHAPTER VIII. — The First Punic War: to 218 104

[1] The dates mark the period covered in the text by the Part to which they are affixed, and are, therefore, not always that of the termination of the event which gives a name to the Part: see the Chronological Synopsis, *post*.

CONTENTS.

	PAGE
CHAPTER IX.— The Second Punic War.	
I. To the Revolt of Capua: to 216	115
II. To the End of the War: to 201	122
CHAPTER X.— The Wars in the East.	
I. The Second Macedonian War: to 197	131
II. The Wars with Antiochus and Perseus: to 168	134
CHAPTER XI.— The Supremacy of Rome: to 133	138

PERIOD V.— OF CIVIL DISSENSIONS (B.C. 133–27).

CHAPTER XII.— The Gracchi: to 121.	
I. The Social and Economical Condition of Italy	147
II. Tiberius Gracchus	154
III. Caius Gracchus	158
CHAPTER XIII.— Marius.	
I. The Contest of Parties: to 100	166
II. The Social War: to 90	172
CHAPTER XIV.— Sulla.	
I. The First Civil War: to 82	176
II. The Constitution of Sulla: to 79	181
CHAPTER XV.— Pompey.	
I. The Roman People	186
II. The Conquest of the East: to 63	191
III. The First Triumvirate: to 54	197
CHAPTER XVI.— Cæsar.	
I. The Conquest of Gaul: to 51	205
II. The Second Civil War: to 44	210
III. The Death of Cæsar	220
CHAPTER XVII.— Octavian: to 27	226

PERIOD VI.— THE EARLY EMPIRE (B.C. 27–A.D. 193).

CHAPTER XVIII.— Augustus.	
I. The Reign of Augustus: to A.D. 14	231
II. The Augustan Age	238
CHAPTER XIX.— The Julian and Claudian Emperors.	
I. The Julian Cæsars: to 41	243
II. The Claudian Cæsars: to 68	250
CHAPTER XX.— The Flavian House: to 96	255
CHAPTER XXI.— The Five Good Emperors.	
I. Trajan: to 138	261
II. The Antonines: to 193	269

PERIOD VII.—THE CENTURY OF TRANSITION (A.D. 193–284).

CHAPTER XXII. — The Severi.
    I. The Dynasty: to 235 276
    II. The Government 279
    III. The Religion 282
    IV. Foreign Relations 284
CHAPTER XXIII. — The Third Century: to 284 287
CHAPTER XXIV. — Affairs in the East: to 284 289

PERIOD VIII.—THE LATER EMPIRE (A.D. 284-476)

CHAPTER XXV. — Reorganization of the Empire.
    I. Diocletian: to 314 296
    II. Constantine the Great: to 337 302
CHAPTER XXVI. — The Triumph of Christianity: to 391 311
CHAPTER XXVII. — The Barbarian Invasions: to 419.
    I. The Visigoths upon the Danube 316
    II. Stilicho 322
    III. Alaric 325
CHAPTER XXVIII. — Aetius: to 454 329
CHAPTER XXIX. — The Fall of the Empire: to 476 336

LIST OF ILLUSTRATIONS.

	PAGE
Mystic Deities of Etruria	7
Gate at Volaterræ	8
The Roman *As*	12
Plan of Rome under the Kings	16
Reverse of the *As*	24
A Vestal Virgin	25
Restoration of Capitol and Cloaca Maxima	31
Walls of Signia	46
The Curule Chair	63
Etruscan Archer	67
Samnite Warrior	85
Sarcophagus of Scipio Barbatus	103
Column of Duilius	107
Portrait of Marcellus (coin)	123
Portrait of Scipio Africanus	126
Etruscan Tomb at Corneto	130
Philip V. (coin)	132
Antiochus the Great (coin)	134
Perseus (coin)	136
The Wounded Gaul	137
Suovetaurilia	146
Marius	170
Italian Coin in the Social War	174
Mithradates VI. (coin)	176
Sulla	181
Pompey (statue)	192

xiv   *LIST OF ILLUSTRATIONS.*

	PAGE
Cicero	197
Roman Rider and Sueve	207
Cæsar	214
Gladiators	225
The Young Cæsar	226
Lictors	230
Augustus (statue)	234
Street in Pompeii	242
Agrippina (coin)	243
Tiberius	245
Germanicus	247
Vespasian (coin)	256
Arch of Titus	257
Roman Soldier	260
Trajan	262
Siege of a Dacian Stronghold	266
Hadrian	268
Antoninus Pius (coin)	269
Marcus Aurelius receiving the Submission of Germans	274
Commodus as Hercules	275
Septimius Severus (coin)	277
Caracalla	278
Prætorians	286
Triumph of Sapor	290
Aurelian (coin)	292
Ruins of Temple of the Sun	293
Diocletian	296
Christ as the Good Shepherd	300
Arch of Constantine	303
Constantine	305
Aetius	331

LIST OF MAPS.

COLORED.

	PAGE
I. Italy before the Growth of the Roman Power	10
II. The Mediterranean Lands, at the Beginning of the Second Punic War	114
III. The Roman Dominions, at the End of the Mithradatic War	196
IV. The Roman Empire, at the Death of Augustus	236
V. The Roman Empire under Trajan	260
VI. The Roman Empire Divided into Præfectures	308

BLACK.

I. Rome under the Kings	16
II. The Ager Romanus, B.C. 450	66
III. The Ager Romanus, B.C. 338	81
IV. Central Italy, at the Time of the Second Punic War	118
V. Plan of the Battle of Cannæ	121
VI. Rome under the Empire	293

PART II.

ROME.

CHAPTER I.

ITALY.

The Mediterranean Lands. — The Roman Empire is the great central fact in the history of nations. All the nations of the ancient world, except those in the far east, were one after another conquered by Rome, and incorporated in her empire; and the nations of the modern world began with the disruption of this empire. The nations of antiquity, which were thus gathered under the dominion of Rome, occupied the lands which bordered the Mediterranean Sea — the "circle of lands known to the ancients," *orbis terrarum veteribus notus.* In this Mediterranean circle of lands, bounded by an impassable desert on the south, and a succession of almost equally impassable mountain ranges on the north, the events of ancient history took place.

Natural Entrances into the Basin of the Mediterranean. — There were only five points at which these natural limits could be easily passed, and at which therefore ancient history went outside of the circle of Mediterranean lands. These were: in the far East, where the river Euphrates approaches so near the sea as to afford a natural channel of intercourse with the countries of the Orient; in Egypt, where the Nile and the Red Sea, parallel to each other for a long distance, make an easy passage to the East, either by caravan or by the Isthmus of Suez; by the waters which connect the Black Sea with the Mediterranean; by the pass of the Julian Alps, at the head of the Adriatic Sea, into the valley of the Save, the only easy passage through the Alps; and west of Italy, where the river Rhone, flowing southerly into the sea, gives a ready entrance into the countries of the north. The three first of these have at all times been the great routes of oriental commerce; by the Julian Alps the Germanic invaders reached Italy; by the Rhone Cæsar made his way into inner Gaul, Germany, and Britain. These five points are marked by the five great commercial cities of Antioch, Alexandria, Constantinople, Trieste (in ancient times, Aquileia), and Marseilles.

The Coasts of the Mediterranean. — The Mediterranean Sea is long and narrow, stretching from east to west. The northern and southern coasts differ widely in character. The African coast is in general devoid of prominent features, whether promontories or bays. There are only two points upon this coast which are by nature well designed for commerce: first, where the great river Nile flows from the south, creating the fertile land of Egypt, and again where, west of the shallow Syrtis, a bold headland thrusts itself into the sea, directly opposite Italy. On this headland stood the rich commercial city of Carthage, the chief rival and enemy of Rome; at the mouth of the Nile the
B.C. 332. great emporium of Alexandria was founded by Alexander the Great.

Northern Coast of the Mediterranean. — The northern coast of the Mediterranean, on the other hand, is broken into four large peninsulas, — Asia Minor, Greece, Italy, and Spain. These peninsulas have been the scene of illustrious events through the whole course of history. As the earliest recorded history of mankind was in the countries of the East, and civilization moved from the east to the west, the four peninsulas came in this order into the field of history. Asia Minor played an important part in the annals of the great oriental empires; then Greece took the lead; after Greece, Rome; the greatness of the Spanish peninsula belongs to modern times.

The Peninsula of Italy. — Italy differs from the three other peninsulas in being long and narrow in shape. It stretches into the sea in a general southeasterly direction, at its extremity bending sharply to the south, so as to present rudely the shape of a boot, the heel of which is turned towards Greece.[1] This southeasterly direction brings it very near to Greece and Illyricum, so that the Adriatic Sea, which separates it from them, is long and narrow, like the peninsula itself. To the west of it are three large islands, Sicily, Sardinia, and Corsica, so situated that the waters between them and Italy are almost enclosed by them; these waters are called the Tyrrhenian Sea. A long stretch of water separates these islands from the westernmost peninsula, that of Spain. This easterly trend of the Italian peninsula gives it an almost central position in the Mediterranean Sea.

The Mountain Systems. — Italy is separated from the countries to the north by the highest range of mountains in Europe, the Alps. These mountains form a sort of semicircle, coming down quite to the sea upon the west (the Maritime Alps), and thus separating Italy from Gaul as well as Germany by a barrier of great difficulty; but on the east (the Julian Alps) they open by a low and easy pass into the valleys of the Save and Danube. This pass of the Julian Alps was the principal highway into Italy at the time of the barbarian invasions. The great mountain chain of Italy, upon which the peninsula is built, is that of the Apennines, which, starting from the Maritime Alps in an easterly direction, bends by degrees to the southeast and then to south, along the whole extent of the peninsula: the mountains of Sicily are a continuation of this chain. This island was once no doubt a part of the mainland, but was torn from it by some convulsion of nature. This mountain chain presents in its general course the form of a flattened arc, with its convex side towards the northeast: the longest stretches of land, and therefore the largest rivers, are of course upon the inside of the arc, or the western coast of Italy.

---

[1] The illustration has been carried out further by comparing the island of Sicily to a foot-ball.

Cisalpine Gaul. — The great basin between the Alps and the northern Apennines is drained by the river Padus (*Po*), which flows into the Adriatic Sea. This region was in early times not considered a part of Italy, but was known as Cisalpine Gaul, or " Gaul-this-side-of-the-Alps," being inhabited by settlers from Gaul: it is now known as Lombardy.

The River Systems. — In Italy proper there are west of the Apennines three principal river systems, the seat in modern times of the three great cities of Florence, Rome, and Naples, and in ancient times of the territories of Etruria, Latium, and Campania. The northernmost of these rivers is the Arnus (*Arno*); the central, much the largest, is the Tiber, occupying nearly a central position in the peninsula; in Campania, a level region of remarkable fertility, there are two important rivers, — the Liris, flowing from the north, parallel with the coast, and the Vulturnus, which rises among the high mountains of Central Italy. The valley of the Liris, with its confluent the Trerus, serves to connect Campania directly with Rome; through this valley ran the so-called Latin Way (*Via Latina*), and it is at present the route of the railroad from Naples to Rome. The Vulturnus affords a passage into the heart of the Samnite country. The only river necessary to mention on the eastern coast of Italy is the Aufidus, which flows through the broad pasture land of Apulia: upon its banks was fought the disastrous battle of Cannæ.

B.C. 216.

The Italian Race. — Italy was chiefly occupied by nations of the so-called Italian race, a branch of the Aryan family of nations, to which the Germans, Slavs, and Celts also belong. There were two principal branches of the Italian race, the Latins and the Umbro-Sabellians. The Latins (to which race also the natives of Sicily belonged in part) occupied a rather limited territory south of the Tiber, between the mountains and the sea: Rome was a Latin city. The Umbro-Sabellian race embraced a large number of nations spread widely through the peninsula: of these the most important were the Umbrians, furthest north; then the Sabines near to Latium, the Samnites upon the upper waters of the Vulturnus, and further south the Lucanians. Of all these the Samnites were the most powerful and important.

The Remnants of Earlier Nations. — Besides these nations of Italian race, there are found other nations of foreign stock: part of them earlier inhabitants who had been pushed into out-of-the-way corners of the land when the Italians entered the peninsula — like the Britons in Wales; part of them invaders of a later date. Of the earlier inhabitants we count the Japygians, in Calabria,[1] the extreme southeastern corner (the *heel*) of Italy; the Venetians, in the northeast, who have given their name to the modern city of Venice; and the Ligurians in the northwest. The Japygians and Venetians were probably of the Aryan race, distantly related to the Italians: the Ligurians appear to have been akin to the Iberians of Spain and Gaul. They were subdued by the Romans in the third and second centuries before Christ, — in the period of the Punic Wars, — in a long series of obstinate contests. The city of Genoa is situated in the Ligurian territory, and when it was reorganized in the time of the French Revolution, it took the name of the Ligurian Republic.

The Intruding Nations. — 1. *The Etruscans*. The intruding nations are of more importance. Chief among these were the Etruscans, who occupied the extensive country north of the Tiber, between the mountains and the sea; their chief seat was in the valley of the Arno. It is not known with certainty what was their origin; but there are indications that they entered Italy from the north, occupied the valley of the Po for a while, and then conquered the region which is known by their name, Etruria. This region had before been occupied by the Umbrians, the northernmost of the Italian peoples; but they were now crowded back into the mountain region east of the upper Tiber, which river separated them from the Etruscans.

The Etruscan Confederacy. — The Etruscans formed a con-

---

[1] The name *Calabria* has in modern times been shifted to a completely different region, the *toe* of the boot.

federacy of twelve cities, the names of which are not known with certainty. Among them were probably Fæsulæ (now *Fiesole* near Florence); Arretium and "lordly Volaterræ," also in the valley of the Arno; Clusium, at a point which commands alike the valleys of the Tiber and the Arno (now *Chiusi*, an important railroad junction); Veii, about ten miles from Rome — the most formidable enemy of Rome in the first century of the republic; and Cære and Tarquinii, also near Rome, on the seacoast. The chief city of the confederacy was Volsinii.

Etruscans in Other Parts of Italy. — There was another confederacy of twelve cities in the valley of the Po, probably older, but less important, as the Gauls conquered this region from them: the capital of this group was Felsina (*Bologna*); other towns were Mantua and Ravenna. South of the Tiber the Etruscans never got a permanent foothold. When they were at the height of their power, in the sixth century B.C., an Etruscan family ruled for a while in Rome, and even established its dominion over Latium; but this came to an end with the Roman republic. In Campania they laid the foundations of a third confederacy, of which the chief city was Capua; but this was captured
B.C. 420. by the Samnites, not long before the conquest of the Po valley by the Gauls. With the growth of the Roman republic the power of the Etruscans decayed, and after
B.C. 396. the conquest of Veii by Rome they played no large part in history.

Civilization of the Etruscans. — At the commencement of the Roman republic the Etruscans were far the most powerful people of Italy. In alliance with the Carthaginians they had
B.C. 537. defeated the Greeks in the earliest sea-fight on record, near Corsica, and had taken possession of that island, the Carthaginians occupying the neighboring island of Sardinia and the western half of Sicily. The government of the Etruscans was aristocratic, but with elected kings, called *Lucumos*. They were a wealthy people, more advanced in civilization than their neighbors of Italian race, but of a gross and barbaric taste. Their religion was a sombre

superstition. In every city special reverence was paid to Jupiter, Juno, and Minerva. The Etruscan kings of Rome introduced this worship into that city, and this group of deities is known from their temple on the Capitoline Mount as the "Capitoline Triad."

MYSTIC DEITIES OF ETRURIA.

Their Language. — The Etruscans used an alphabet derived from that of the Greeks, and have left an abundance of inscriptions; but the most laborious and long-continued labors of philologists have not yet succeeded in deciphering the inscriptions, or even in determining positively to what race the Etruscans belonged. Their monuments, in the form of walls, tombs, etc., are numerous and well preserved. It has been generally believed that the civilization of the Romans was largely influenced by that of the Etruscans; but, although there is no doubt that the Romans received from them the trappings and ceremonial of royalty, the institutions and civilization of Rome appear to have been mainly of independent growth, but influenced powerfully by the Greeks. The Etruscans were great builders, and in the time of their domination in Rome, they adorned the city with splendid temples and other public works.

GATE AT VOLATERRÆ, SHOWING THE PRINCIPLE OF THE ARCH.

2. *The Gauls.* The Gauls, of Celtic race, crossed the Alps in successive streams in the first century of the republic (the fifth century before Christ), and took possession of the valley of the Po, expelling from it the Etruscans. This region was from this time known as Cisalpine Gaul (p. 4), this name extending as far as the first great bend of the peninsula upon the Adriatic, where the city of Sinigaglia (*Sena Gallica*) preserves the memory of their name. After the conquest of this region the Gauls proceeded to invade Etruria proper, even advancing as far as Rome, which they captured and burned; for many years after this their raids were a constant terror to the inhabitants of Latium.

B.C. 390.

They were organized in five tribes or nations,[1] and their chief city

---

[1] The Insubrians, about Milan; the Cenomāni, east of them; the Lingŏnes, south of the Po and upon the coast; the Boii, west of them; and the Senŏnes, south of the Lingones.

PERIOD I.—THE MONARCHY.

CHAPTER II.

PATRICIAN ROME.

I. HISTORY AND TRADITION.

Latium. — We have seen that the Tiber was the largest and most central river of the Italian peninsula. South of the Tiber, between the Apennines and the sea, stretched Latium, the "flat land," about half as large as the state of Rhode Island.[1] In the centre of Latium is the Alban Mount, a volcanic group, nearly circular in shape, wholly surrounded by the low country of Latium. Many of the towns of the Latins were situated upon spurs of the Alban Mount; for the low lands (now known as the *Campagna*) were exceedingly unhealthy, and the inhabitants settled upon elevated spots, both for health and for security against attack.

The Latin Confederacy. — The Latin towns formed a confederacy, which at first consisted of thirty towns; but in the course of time the strongest of these conquered and annexed their weaker neighbors, so that when we reach historical times there were not more than twelve or fifteen of these which remained independent. The chief town of the confederacy was Alba Longa, the "long white town"; but this town was conquered by Rome, which now succeeded to the presidency of the league. Every year the so-called Latin Festival was celebrated by the Roman magistrates upon the summit of the Alban Mount; and for the purposes of this festival the league always continued to consist

---

[1] This was the original Latium; the name was afterwards extended to the country south of it, as far as the Vulturnus.

was Mediolanum (*Milan*). They were conquered by the Romans at about the time of the Second Punic War.

3. *The Greeks.* The third intruding nation — earlier, however, than the Gauls — was the Greeks, who established colonies along the southern and western coasts of Italy in the eighth and seventh centuries before Christ. These colonies were so rich and prosperous that this region of country was known as Great Greece (*Magna Graecia*); its chief city was Tarentum. The most important Greek colonies were in Sicily, where their principal city, Syracuse, was one of the largest and most splendid in the world.

The Early Industry of Italy. — The nations of Italy were cultivators of the soil when they entered the peninsula, but they had not wholly outgrown the pastoral stage, and the care of cattle still continued to form a leading part of their industry. All the institutions and the manners and customs of the early period are those of peasants dwelling on their own lands and cultivating them with their own hands. Barley and spelt were their principal crops; they cultivated the vine at a very early date, and received the olive from the Greeks. Cattle made a large part of their wealth, and values were reckoned in cattle until some time after the establishment of the republic. Pasturage was at all times an important part of their industry, especially east of the mountains. The plains of Apulia supported great herds of cattle during the winter, which were then driven in the summer to the mountain regions of Samnium and Lucania. The Greeks in the south were supported principally by commerce. The Etruscans, too, being more highly civilized than the nations of Italian race, had an active foreign trade; and it was the admirable commercial situation of Rome, with the commerce which grew out of it, that gave this city its first impulse to greatness.

ITALY BEFORE THE GROWTH OF THE ROMAN EMPIRE

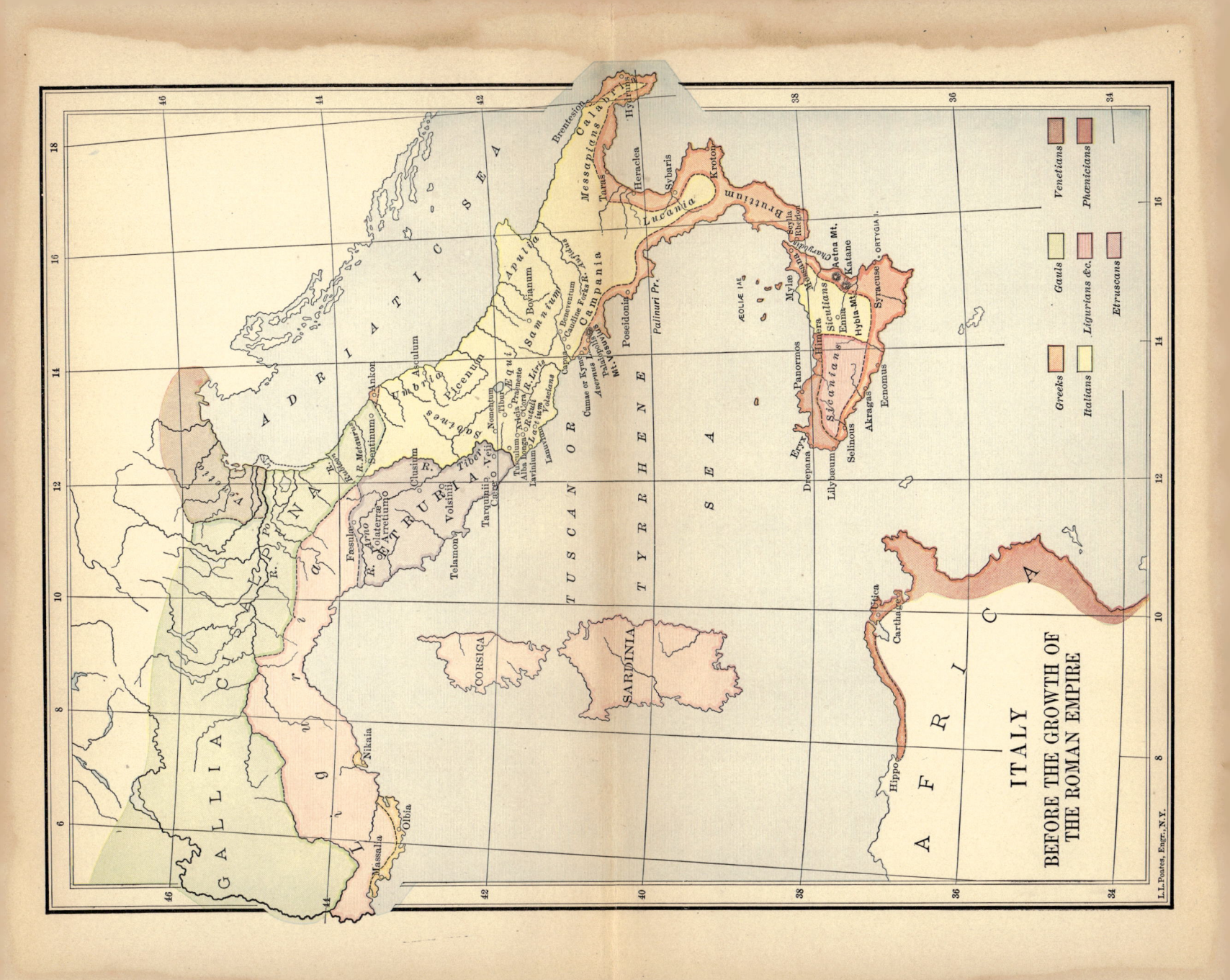

THE SITUATION OF ROME. 11

of thirty members. By the conquest of Alba Longa and other towns Rome came into possession of about one-third of the territory of Latium.

The Surrounding Nations. — The Latins were surrounded on all sides by nations of foreign race. North of the Tiber were the Etruscans, of whom we have already spoken (p. 5) as being the most powerful nation of Italy. The wars with the Etruscan city of Veii were the most serious in the early history of the republic; and the capture of this town, B.C. 396, forms the most important turning-point in the growth of the power of Rome. Among the Apennines east of Rome were the Sabines, a simple and hardy people of Italian race. It is believed that the city of Rome was formed by the union of a Sabine settlement with a Latin town upon the Tiber. Further east, among the mountains, were the Æquians in the interior and the Volscians near the sea; and in the valley between them, watered by the river Trerus, a branch of the Liris, dwelt the Hernicans. The Sabines, Æquians, Volscians, and Hernicans all belonged to the Umbro-Sabellian branch of the Italian race; but the Hernicans, being lowlanders like the Latins, united with them in an alliance to repel the raids of the Sabine, Æquian, and Volscian mountaineers (see Chap. IV.).

Rome. — The city of Rome was situated upon a group of low hills upon the left bank of the Tiber, about fourteen miles from its mouth: it thus occupied very nearly a central position in Italy, and upon the largest and most important river of the peninsula. The hills upon which it was built were low, but sufficiently elevated to be healthy and easily defended.[1] It was a Latin town, probably a colony of Alba Longa; but at a very early date it was united with a Sabine community.

Situation of Rome: Its Military Importance. — The situation of Rome upon the river gave it two great advantages over all the other towns of Latium. First, there is a high hill upon the Etruscan side of the river, directly opposite, which formed a natural

[1] The Esquiline, the highest of the hills, is about 218 feet above the level of the sea; the Janiculum, upon the other bank of the river, is 273 feet.

fortress to protect Latium against the powerful city of Veii, only ten miles away. This hill, the Janiculum, was held by the Romans, and connected with the city by a wooden bridge (the *pons sublicius*). The Romans were thus the chief champions of the Latins against their most formidable enemies; and this fact kept them in a constant state of warlike preparation and activity. All free men were soldiers in those days, but the Romans surpassed all the nations of antiquity in military prowess.

Its Commercial Importance. — The second advantage that Rome possessed came from its central situation, on the largest

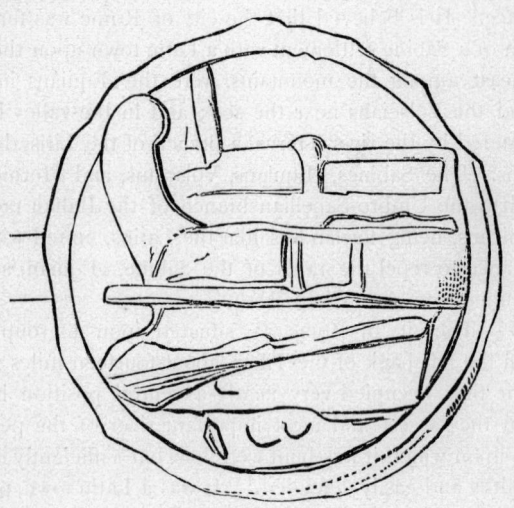

THE ROMAN *AS*. (Size of the Original.)

navigable river of Italy. Just above the bridge was an island in the Tiber, and this point was naturally the head of navigation for larger craft. So Rome became an active commercial town, not merely for trade up the river, but for foreign trade; and when the Romans had conquered the lower course of the river they founded the colony of Ostia at its mouth, for the purpose of carrying on their foreign commerce. As the military position of Rome made the Romans the most warlike people of antiquity, so the commercial advantages of its situation made them the most careful accountants and the most business-like in their administration. Their greatness was built upon these two qualities. The importance of commerce and navigation to the early Romans is shown by the fact that the device upon their coins is the prow of a ship.

Rapid Growth of Rome. — The commercial and military advantages arising from the situation of Rome gave it a rapid growth in wealth and power.[1] The first settlers were no doubt peasants, like the rest of their countrymen, living by the care of flocks and the cultivation of the ground; but their early prosperity came from trade, and at the time at which we become acquainted with them they were already distinguished warriors.

History and Tradition. — The authentic history of Rome begins at about the beginning of the fifth century before the Christian era. From this time on, that is, from the establishment of the republic, we have a list of magistrates, and an account of events, very meagre and incomplete, it is true, but derived from contemporary records, and therefore serving as a basis for chronology. Before this time we have only tradition, handed down by word of mouth from generation to generation. Not but that the Romans possessed the art of writing during this earlier period; but that they left no continuous record of contemporaneous origin, — only a few isolated monuments. But there can be no chronology, and therefore no genuine history, unless the record is continuous as well as contemporaneous. Nevertheless, the value of oral tradition is, so far as it goes, very great. We cannot rely upon it for an accurate outline of events, but it may preserve the memory of individual names and occurrences as well as of institutions and customs. Much, therefore, that has come down to us from this pre-historic period, is no doubt historical in character, although it cannot be assigned to any definite date.

[1] Read article by Goldwin Smith, "The Greatness of Rome," in the *Contemporary Review*, May, 1878.

Mythical Period. — As we go back in the narration of events, we come at last to a time when even tradition deserts us, and what has come down to us as history is really nothing but the product of the imagination, or even of conscious invention. This is the mythical period. In the history of all primitive nations the earliest narrated events must be understood to be mythical; they may contain some germs of historical truth, but are for the most part pure fable. Then follow the traditions handed down by oral memory, incomplete, but truthful in their substance; only with contemporaneous written records begins genuine history.

Early Roman History. — At the commencement of the historical period Rome was a republic, and it continued under a republican form of government for nearly five hundred years. But according to the tradition, which was very recent and positive, and which there is no reason to doubt, Rome had shortly before been governed by kings, and the names of seven of these kings were preserved in memory. The reigns of the kings belong to the traditionary period, and the names and many of the events of the reigns of all but the two earliest may be accepted as genuine; the first two kings belong to the realm of pure fable. During the last part of the monarchy the kings were of an Etruscan family of the name of Tarquin; it was the tyranny of the last of this

B.C. 509. family, Tarquin the Proud, that drove the Romans to rise in rebellion, overthrow the kingly rule, and set up a republic.

The Mythical Kings. — There were more than twenty different accounts of the way in which Rome was founded, but

B.C. 753.[1] they all agree in representing its founder and first king as Romulus, who was believed to be a son of the god Mars. It is common for primitive nations to believe that their founders were of divine origin. For example, Cedric, the first king of Wessex, from whom the kings of England down to the present time have been descended, was believed to be sprung from the

[1] These dates are those handed down by tradition, and must not be taken to be historically accurate.

god Odin; and even Alexander the Great, in the full light of history, claimed to be the son of Zeus. Romulus was associated during a part of his reign with Titus Tatius, king of the Sabine settlement upon the Quirinal; in the joint reign of these two kings we have the memory of the union of the Latin and Sabine communities. Romulus was regarded as not only the founder of the city, but as the creator of its political and military institutions; while his successor, the Sabine Numa B.C. 715. Pompilius, a mild and peace-loving sovereign, was the organizer of the religious institutions. In these two kings, therefore, wholly mythical in character, were impersonated the fundamental institutions of the city.

The Kings of the Patrician Period. — The kings who follow Romulus and Numa Pompilius may be considered as belonging to genuine tradition, and as having a certain historical character. Tullus Hostilius was a warlike king, who B.C. 672. conquered Alba Longa, and made Rome the head of the Latin confederacy. Even before his time the Romans had conquered the towns upon the Tiber to a distance of about twelve miles above the city; and his successor Ancus Marcius extended these conquests to the mouth of the river, B.C. 640. where he founded the sea-port colony of Ostia. By these conquests the Roman territory, the *Ager Romanus*, which had at first extended only from two to five miles in each direction, was made to include about one-third of Latium. Upon the death of Ancus Marcius, an Etruscan by the name B.C. 616. of Lucius Tarquinius was made king, and his family continued on the throne until the overthrow of the monarchy. There is no reason to doubt that kings of these names ruled in Rome, and performed some of the actions that are related of them; but it cannot be supposed that the dates of their accession are correctly handed down by memory, and it is altogether likely that there were other kings whose names have been forgotten, either because they did nothing deserving to be remembered, or because their actions have been ascribed to the more distinguished rulers.

According to the traditional dates, the reigns of these kings averaged nearly thirty-five years, not an impossible thing, but a very unusual average for seven successive rulers.[1]

The Early City. — The original city was upon the Palatine Hill, the most isolated of the hills of Rome, and therefore the one best fitted for an independent settlement. The Palatine city was called

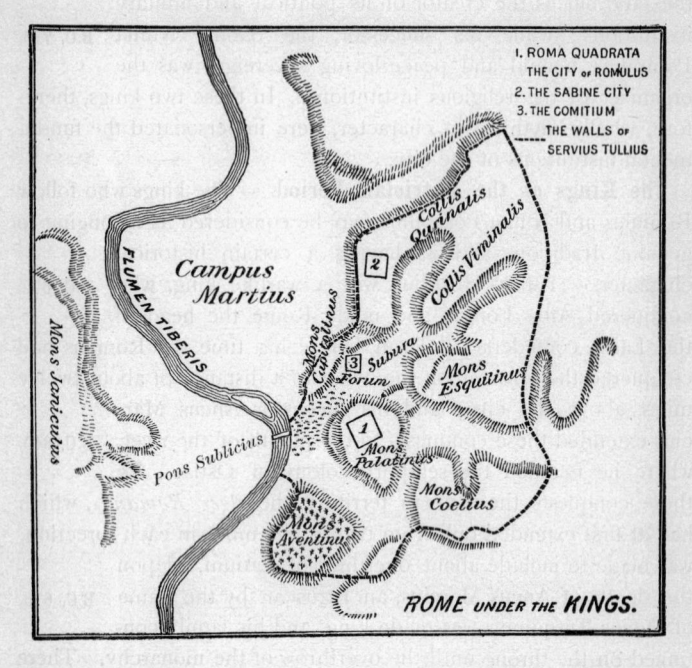

Roma Quadrata, or "Square Rome"; some massive walls of this early town have been discovered in recent years. By degrees the town outgrew its walls and spread over the surrounding heights, and then, as we have seen, united with a Sabine city upon the

---

[1] The seven first Capetian rulers of France reigned 267 years (from 956 to 1223), an average of 38 years, in every case son succeeding father; but I know no other case of so large an average.

Quirinal. The original Romans now formed the tribe of *Ramnes*, while the Sabines were known as *Tities*. A third tribe, the *Luceres*, was added afterwards, perhaps when Tullus Hostilius conquered Alba Longa and transferred its citizens to Rome, settling them upon the Cœlian Hill. In the valley between the Palatine and the Quirinal, swampy and subject to overflow, was the *Forum* or market-place, and beside it, upon a spot somewhat more elevated and dryer, a space was enclosed called the *Comitium*, for assemblies and other public purposes. The citadel of the new city was upon a precipitous spur of the Quirinal, called the Capitoline.[1]

The Ager Romanus. — The original territory of Rome was probably of about the same dimensions as that of most of the other Latin towns, and appears to have extended about two miles to the north and west, and five or six miles to the east and south, being thus of nearly the size of a Western "township." It outgrew these limits, however, long before the historical period. Romulus, as we have already said, is related to have conquered the towns to a distance of twelve or fifteen miles up the river, and to have annexed their territory; some of these towns, if not all, were probably Sabine. Tullus Hostilius conquered Alba Longa, to the southeast, and annexed its territory, including the summit of the Alban Mount, and Ancus Marcius subdued the towns along the lower course of the river, as far as its mouth.

The Enlarged Domain. — At this period, therefore, the Roman domain extended about fifteen miles to the northeast, the southeast, and the southwest, and comprised the entire course of the Tiber to a distance of twenty-five or thirty miles from its mouth, except the stronghold of Fidenæ, about five miles above Rome, which served as a base of operations upon the Latin side of the river for the neighboring Etruscan city of Veii, just as the Janiculum did for the Romans upon the Etruscan side of the river. The *ager Romanus* was, however, very irregular in shape. The course of the Anio, the principal branch of the Tiber upon the east, was occupied by the powerful cities of Gabii and Tibur, while Tusculum

[1] See plan, p. 16.

held the northern slopes of the Alban Mount, and to the south the Roman territory bordered upon those of Aricia, Ardea, and Laurentum. The *ager Romanus* at this epoch comprised about one-third of Latium, and it was not permanently enlarged after this time until about a hundred years after the establishment of the republic, except by the annexation of Gabii by the last Tarquin.

II. INSTITUTIONS.

Patrician Rome. — The reigns of these first four kings of Roman tradition mark a distinct period of time, which must have continued much longer than tradition has it, and which we may call *Patrician Rome*, because the only citizens at this period were the members of those families which were afterwards known as patrician. There were other inhabitants, but these were either held in servitude, or were wholly without political rights.

The Gentile System. — In this period the Roman people, like all primitive communities, consisted of a number of family groups called *gentes* ("clans"), the members of each of which believed themselves to be descended from a common ancestor.[1] Each *gens* consisted of a number of families, each under the authority of the "father of the family" (*pater-familias*), who ruled with absolute sway over his wife and children, even having the right to put them to death. The members of these families were called *patricians*, or "sons of the fathers" (*patres*); and no one but those who belonged to these patrician families had any share in the government. Each clan belonged to one of the three tribes of which the Roman people were composed (p. 17), and each tribe was divided into ten curies (*curiae*), groups intermediate between the tribes and the clans. Every Roman citizen thus belonged at once to a family, a *gens*, a *curia*, and a tribe.

---

[1] The name of the *gens* was a patronymic, indicating descent from this ancestor; *e.g.*, the Julian *gens* (*gens Iulia*) claimed to have derived their name from that of Iulus, son of Æneas.

Divisions of Land. — It is believed that when the several branches of the Italian race, in their migration, moved into the peninsula from the north, they were already organized in these family groups or clans, each settling by itself in a territory of its own. They afterwards associated themselves into larger organizations, but each clan still continued to occupy its own district of land. The names of the early divisions of the Roman domain, so far as they are preserved, are derived from those of patrician clans; and we are informed that each curia and each tribe also had a territory of its own.

The Government of Rome. — The Romans were governed by an elected king,[1] who was also the chief priest of the people, their judge, and their commander in war. The people were a collection of families, each under its *pater-familias*, and the king was the *pater-familias* of the whole people. These heads of families, who had absolute power, each in his own household, composed a Senate, or Council of Elders (*senior* means "elder"), which served as a council to the king. The senators, being all heads of families, or *patres-familias*, were called the *patres*, "fathers." Afterwards — indeed, in the earliest historical times, — the senators were appointed by the king.[2] Their number was three hundred, and this continued to be the regular number of senators until the last century of the republic. Besides the Senate, there was an assembly, composed of the body of citizens; that is, of all capable of bearing arms, whether they were heads of families or not. This assembly met and voted by curies; a vote was never taken of the people a whole, but each curia voted by itself, and the majority of the curies decided the question. The assembly thus organized was called *comitia curiata*.

---

[1] In the elective character of the monarchy the Romans differed from the Greeks, whose kings reigned by hereditary title. Under the Tarquinian dynasty the Roman monarchy also appears to have become hereditary.

[2] In the republic the appointment of senators was made at first by the consuls and then by the censors; in the last century of the republic all who had held certain offices became members of the Senate without formal appointment.

The Auspices. — The Romans believed that their city was under the immediate care and protection of the gods, and that the gods would express their will to them by signs, called *auspices*. These auspices were interpreted by a body of priests, called *augurs*, and no public action was ever entered upon without consulting the gods by auspices. The auspices therefore formed the foundation of the public authority, and were regarded as belonging to the Senate, because the Senate was composed of all persons who had authority in their families. But although the auspices belonged to the Senate, they were temporarily lodged in the hands of the king, or (under the republic) of the elected magistrate, and he alone had the right to consult the gods in behalf of the state. When there were no magistrates, as on the death of the king, or a failure to elect consuls, the auspices returned to the Senate, where they belonged (*auspicia ad patres redierunt*) ; this was called an *interregnum*, and the city was governed by an *interrex* until the vacancy was filled by a new election.[1] In virtue of the auspices the Senate possessed the right to nullify any action of the assembly which appeared to conflict with the religion or constitution of the state.

The Army. — The army, or "levy" (*legio*), was composed of one thousand men from each tribe (*milites*, from *mille*, "thousand"), and the commander of each tribe was called tribune (*tribunus*). There was also a body of cavalry, consisting of three companies ("centuries") of one hundred men each, one from each tribe. This number was afterwards doubled, and subsequently raised to eighteen.

The Dependent Classes. — The Romans also had slaves, for the most part persons who had been captured in war. Each *gens* had likewise a number of serfs, called *clients*, who cultivated the lands of the gens, bore its name and took part in its sacrifices. The clients probably belonged to some foreign race which had been subjugated by the Latins, but not reduced to slavery. They were personally free, but had no legal or political rights; each client had to be

---

[1] The interrex governed for only five days, and there was sometimes a long succession of *interreges* before the vacancy could be filled.

represented by some patrician head of a family, who was called his *patron*. When a slave was emancipated, he became the client of his former master, and was known as a *freedman* (*libertus*). A second dependent class consisted of traders and handicraftsmen, of foreign birth, who, like the clients, had to be represented by a patrician patron. This class became very numerous with the growth of foreign commerce, especially after the foundation of the seaport colony of Ostia (p. 15).

The Rural Plebeians. — There was another class, more important than either the clients or the resident foreigners; — the inhabitants of the conquered Latin towns, who had not been admitted to the patriciate. These were, unlike the clients, of the same race with the Romans, and had the same fundamental institutions. They were peasants, as the Romans were originally, and when they had lost their political independence, they had retained their personal freedom, a part of their land, and full rights of property and trade (*commercium*). Many of them were prosperous and wealthy farmers. Being foreigners in Rome, however, they had not the right of intermarriage (*conubium*) with patricians; for in early society this right exists only by special agreement. Their legal status was that of the clients, and they have been called the clients of the state. This class was known as *plebeians;* but they were distinguished on one hand from the clients by being freeholders, and on the other from the resident foreigners by being peasants; in the course of time these other two classes were associated with them, and the name plebeian was applied to all who were not patricians. It was this class of free peasants, whom we may call the rural plebeians, that carried on the long contest for social and political equality during the first century of the republic.

The Patrician Gentes. — It will be seen by this description that each patrician gens formed a little community by itself, the state being an association of these communities. No doubt at first the lands of the gens belonged to the gens as a community: but in the very earliest historical accounts we find every man owning his own land. Perhaps each gens was originally under a single head: but when we come to the knowledge of them they appear rather as aristocracies, each containing several powerful noblemen. They of course differed greatly in number and wealth; but one of these clans, with its slaves and clients, must have been a powerful and formidable body.

Power of the Gentes. — The patrician noblemen remind us, in their turbulent independence, of the barons of the Middle Ages.

B.C. 479. It is related that the Fabian gens voluntarily carried on a war against Veii by its own resources; the number of its members at this time is given as three hundred and six, besides three or four thousand clients. Appius Claudius, the founder of the Claudian gens, emigrated from the Sabine country with over five thousand clients, from which it appears that the Sabines also had a nobility like the Roman patriciate. We find a similar nobility in other Latin towns; but the Roman patricians differed from the others in having made large fortunes by foreign commerce. We shall better understand the importance of this fact when we come to the economic disturbances of the early republic. The Roman patricians may therefore be described as a rich landed and commercial nobility, with a large body of serfs (clients) and slaves. The rural plebeians, on the other hand, were free peasants, the common freemen of the Italian race; while the clients were, in all probability, the remains of a subjugated population of foreign stock.

III. RELIGION.

Religion. — The religion of the Romans was a form of nature-worship. They believed in the existence of special spirits (*numina*) who controlled the several departments and operations of nature. To these they gave names, conceiving of them as male and female; thus Vulcan was the god of fire, and Neptune of the sea, while every process of growth in plants or in the human body had its special deity.[1] But, although they personified the powers of nature

---

[1] *E.g.*, Ossipāgo, who knits the joints of the child's body; Carna, who strengthens his flesh; Nodōtus, who forms the joints in the growing plant;

in this way, and gave them names, they did not, like the Greeks, imagine them as like human beings, living together in a world by themselves, and from time to time taking part in the affairs of men. Rather, they looked upon them as abstract powers, whose only function it was to direct the operations of nature. They had no statues of their gods in the earliest times, but worshipped them in symbolic forms or "fetishes." Thus Jupiter was symbolized by a piece of flint, Mars by a spear, Vesta by the sacred flame. They also personified the abstract qualities themselves, such as Honor, Modesty, Panic, Harmony: to these deified qualities they built temples and offered sacrifices. In a religion like this there could be very few myths, or stories about the actions of their gods, such as the Greeks delighted in. On the other hand, they had very elaborate and solemn forms of worship, which they exercised with the greatest formality and precision.

The Chief Gods of Rome. — Their chief god was Jupiter, god of the sky and the atmosphere; he was the special guardian of the vine, which depends so much upon the weather for its fruitfulness. In the time of the Tarquins, Jupiter was associated with Juno and Minerva to form what is known as the Capitoline Triad (p. 7). Mars,[1] the god of heroic strength, was the special protecting deity of the Italian race, especially of the Romans; and when the Romans grew into a great military nation, they identified him with the Greek Ares, and made him the special god of war. The original goddess of war was Bellona (from *bellum*, "war"). The Sabine Romans had also their god of war, Quirinus, a counterpart of Mars. Jupiter, Mars, and Quirinus were distinguished above all other gods in the primitive religion, and each had a priest of his own, called a *flamen*.[2] Mars also had a company of priests called "leapers" (*Salii*), young men of noble birth, who every

---

Volutina, who wraps the leaves in folds. Saturnus (of sowing), Minerva (of memory), Flora (of flowers), were originally divinities of this class.

[1] The name is probably from the same root as *mors*, "death," and perhaps *mas*, "male."

[2] There were also twelve inferior flamens, of Vulcan, Flora, Pomona, etc.

year, in his month (*March*), went in a procession through the city, leaping and dancing, and beating their shields with spears. Janus (*Dianus*) and Diana were the god and goddess of the sun and moon; but Janus became especially the god of beginnings. Every prayer began with an invocation to him, and the first month of the year, *January*, was named for him. He was represented as having two faces turned in opposite directions. Many gods and goddesses of great importance in this early time afterwards became

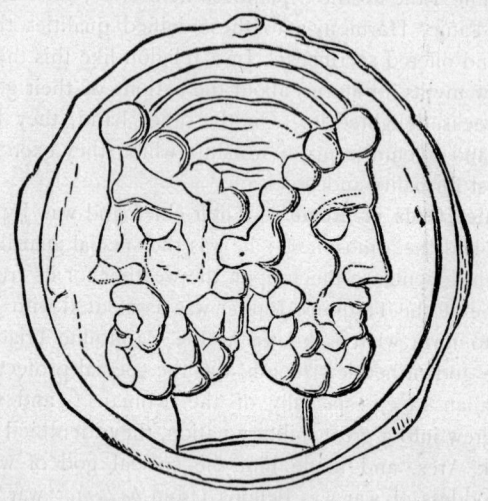

HEAD OF JANUS, UPON THE REVERSE OF THE ROMAN *AS*.

insignificant; others, like Ceres and Minerva, rose in importance; while others, such as Apollo, Æsculapius, Bacchus, and Isis were, in the course of time, introduced from Greece and other countries.

The Worship of Vesta. — Vesta (Ἑστία), goddess of the hearth, is the only deity common to both Greeks and Romans, except Jupiter ("father Zeus"). The family altar, with its worship of the household gods and deified ancestors, was the centre of the life of every household. Every household had its *lar familiaris*[1] (house-

[1] In later times there were always two *lares*.

hold god of the family), who was worshipped in company with Vesta. In these sacred rights (*sacra*) was the life of the family. Each of the larger outgrowths of the family — the gens, the tribe, and the city itself — had its altar and its domestic worship, under the patronage of Vesta; the clients of the gens also participated in these *sacra*. The sacred hearth of the city was in the round temple of Vesta, near the Forum.[1] Here she was served by the Vestal Virgins, at first four, afterwards six in number, maidens of free birth, whose duty it was to keep the fire always burning upon the altar. If it should be extinguished by any accident, it must be lighted from a "pure flame," which had not served human purposes, either by striking a spark with flint, or by rubbing together two dry sticks; and if any one of the virgins should break her vows, it was a portent of dreadful meaning.

A VESTAL VIRGIN.

The Festivals. — The Romans being a community of peasants, all their festivals in early times were such as belonged to the life of shepherds and husbandmen. Among these were the *Palilia*, April 21, to Pales, the goddess of flocks: on this day it was believed

[1] The foundations of this temple and the remains of the residence of the Vestals have been recently excavated. The portrait of the Vestal, given in the text, is from a statue discovered here.

that the city had been founded by Romulus. On April 28 was the procession, on the farms, to propitiate *Robigo* (rust or mildew), the chief enemy of the growing crops. Towards the end of May were the *Ambarvalia*,[1] or procession to purify and bless the fields; it ended with the *Suovetaurilia*, or lustratory sacrifice of a bull, a swine, and a sheep. A similar celebration in behalf of the city was made at the same season by an association (*collegium*) of noble young men, called the Arval Brothers (*Fratres Arvales*). This institution was kept up with great devotion, even during the empire; and a number of inscriptions, describing the ceremony in all details, have been discovered in their sacred grove, in a spot near the Tiber, about five miles from the city. In August were the *Consualia*, or festival to Consus, the god of the granary (from *condo*, to store away), sometimes called the Equestrian Neptune. It was at this festival that the Romans, under Romulus, were believed to have provided themselves wives by seizing the Sabine maidens, who had come as spectators of the games. On December 17 was the festival of Saturn, the god of sowing : the *Saturnalia*. On this occasion slaves were allowed their freedom for the day, and indulged themselves in boisterous merriment. In September were the Great or Roman Games, — horse-races and such-like. These were held in the Circus Maximus, in the valley between the Palatine and the Aventine.

The Priesthoods. — The public exercises of religion were under the management of the king, who was the chief priest of the city, assisted by a board (*collegium*) of "pontiffs," at this time four in number, afterwards fifteen. A similar board, called the *Augurs*, had the duty of interpreting the auspices or signs sent by the gods to the king or other magistrate in behalf of the city. A company of Heralds (*Fetiales*) had the duty of performing the ceremonies in the declaration of war, and other offices of an international character. The *Luperci*, of whom there were two companies, performed, on the fifteenth of February, a strange ceremony, running

---

[1] See an interesting description of this festival in Pater's *Marius the Epicurean.*

nearly naked through the city, and striking whomever they met with thongs made of the hides of newly slaughtered goats. Their course followed the enclosure of the earliest city, around the Palatine.

The Calendar. — The Romans reckoned time by the course of the moon; the appearance of the new moon was proclaimed (*calare*) by the pontiffs, and this first day of the month was known as the *Kalends*. A cycle (*annus*) of ten months was employed for contracts and treaties, but at a very early period a year of twelve months was adopted, to bring the reckoning by moons into correspondence with the course of the sun.

Money. — As a standard of weight they employed the *as* (pound), divided into twelve *unciæ* (ounces).[1] The Romans coined no money until about the time of the Decemvirs, but copper was cast in pound bars, and in all purchases the copper was weighed. As late as the time of the Decemvirs fines were imposed in oxen and sheep instead of money. B.C. 451.

Art. — There are no indications among the early Romans of the fine artistic sense which distinguished their kinsmen the Greeks at the same stage of advancement. The æsthetic qualities were not absent from the Italian peoples, as has been shown at more than one epoch since; but they were held in check by the severe and practical turn which the Roman mind took in every department. No doubt, like every body of peasants, they had their simple tunes and their popular songs, celebrating the brave deeds of their fathers. From such songs, handed down in family circles, are derived the legends of Coriolanus, Camillus, and other worthies of the olden time.[2]

The Roman Character. — The Roman religion, which was at bottom identical with that of the Greeks, had received a totally different bent, and came to consist almost exclusively in observ-

---

[1] The ounce was divided into 24 scruples: from this our table of Apothecaries' Weight is derived.

[2] See Macaulay's *Lays of Ancient Rome*.

ance and ceremonial. It was, therefore, excessively formal and mechanical. But if their religion was devoid of beauty, it exerted a wholesome influence on character. The Romans were a serious, just people, although stern and severe; and their religion, in its primitive condition, was almost wholly free from the indecencies and excitements which are found even among the Greeks, and still more in the religions of Asia. In the best time of the republic they had the simple manners and homely virtues of peasants. At a later period they lost their seriousness, while their sternness degenerated into wanton cruelty, and the native simplicity of their religion was obscured by immoralities and orgies, mostly of oriental origin.

In short, the genius of the Romans was essentially practical. Their religion consisted wholly in works; art and literature were foreign to their genius: but even in their earliest estate we note, in their military achievements, their political contests, and their system of law, the three fields in which they were destined to make their greatest contributions to civilization, — war, government, and jurisprudence.

CHAPTER III.

THE TARQUINS.

The Tarquinian Dynasty. — According to tradition, Ancus Marcius, the fourth king, was followed by three successive kings of Etruscan origin, belonging to the family of Tarquin, — Lucius Tarquinius the Elder (*Priscus*); his son-in-law, Servius Tullius; and son, Lucius Tarquinius the Proud (*Superbus*). It is evident that the story in this form is impossible, for the younger Tarquin is represented to have been still a young man after the long reign (forty-four years) of the alleged usurper, Servius Tullius. There is no reason to doubt, however, that a line of kings of this name reigned in Rome, and that it was of Etruscan origin. The last Tarquin was expelled, on the ground of tyranny, at about the beginning of the fifth century before Christ,[1] and a republican government established.

B.C. 616.
B.C. 578.
B.C. 534.

Achievements of the Tarquins. — The rule of the Tarquins is marked by three principal achievements: the establishment of their power over all Latium, the construction of great public works, and the abolition of the exclusive privileges of the patricians.

1. The Tarquinian Empire. — We have seen (p. 17) that the Roman territory, *ager Romanus*, at the accession of this dynasty, had been extended by the conquests of Tullus Hostilius, Ancus Marcius, and earlier kings, so as to reach from the mouth of the Tiber to a point about thirty miles up the river, and also in a southeasterly direction to the Alban Mount, including the summit of this mountain: making in all about a third of Latium. On the river the Romans did not succeed in permanently holding the stronghold of Fidenae, about five miles from Rome, near to Veii and generally in alliance with it. Below the city, on the other

---

[1] The traditionary date was B.C. 509.

hand, they held both banks of the river. On the Alban Mount the Roman territory thrust itself like a wedge between that of two Latin towns, Tusculum and Aricia.

The Conquests of the Tarquins. — To this extensive territory the Tarquins added nearly all the rest of Latium; not, however, annexing it to the Roman domain, but holding it as tributary. In the confusion of the revolution which put an end to the monarchy, the Latins regained their independence, and the Roman territory had nearly the same extent at the commencement of the republic which it had had under Ancus Marcius.

2. The Public Works of the Tarquins. — The most important of the public works of this period were three in number. First, the splendid temple of Jupiter, with side chapels to Juno and Minerva,[1] upon the Capitoline Hill. This building was known as the Capitolium, or Temple of Jupiter Capitolinus, and was regarded as the seat of the Roman dominion.[2] Secondly, a magnificent set of sewers, the principal of which was the great sewer, *Cloaca Maxima*, which drained the marshy valley between the hills, and rendered the ground fit for the purposes of the market-place (*Forum*) and the place of public assemblies (*Comitium*). In this structure the principle of the arch was employed, which was in use in other parts of Italy also at this early period.[3] These sewers are still in

---

[1] Until this time Minerva, the goddess of memory or mind, does not seem to have been one of the chief deities.

[2] The foundations of this building have been recently discovered. As this temple was the central seat of the Roman religion and nationality, and was frequently used for meetings of the Senate, the name *capitol* has come to be applied very generally to buildings which are the seat of government. Thus Shakespeare makes Julius Cæsar assassinated in the *Capitol*. But the Roman capitol did not correspond in any respect with the capitol at Washington, except in these occasional sessions of the Senate.

[3] The round arch, with its extension into the vault and dome, is, as we shall see, the distinctive feature of ancient Italian architecture. The Greeks employed horizontal beams resting upon columns; the pointed arch is the characteristic feature of the architecture of the middle ages. See the arched gateway of Volaterræ, p. 8.

use. Thirdly, the city walls, which were now for the first time made to include both the Sabine and the Roman towns (p. 16), as well as the Aventine, an extensive hill at this time uninhabited, but afterwards assigned to the plebeians, and the fortified hill, Janiculum, on the opposite bank of the river. These walls were the work of Servius Tullius, the greatest king of this dynasty, although, according to a tradition, a usurper.

THE CAPITOLINE AND CLOACA MAXIMA. A RESTORATION.

3. The Reforms of Servius Tullius. — The extension of civil rights to the plebeians was also the work of this king, although the elder Tarquin is said to have planned some such reform, but to have been prevented by religious obstacles. The idea of the constitution of Servius Tullius, as it is called, was perhaps borrowed from the Greeks, for it is in many features the same as that of Solon, established in Athens a few years before the traditionary date of Servius Tullius. The principle of the reform is what is known as *timocracy*, according to which the

B.C. 594.

power is lodged in the hands of the rich, instead of those of high birth. By the patrician constitution, the members of the original families possessed all the power in the state: by the timocratic reforms of Servius Tullius a certain preponderance was given to the richest citizens.

The Classes and Centuries. — The original object of this reform was to increase the military force of the city, and to equalize the public burdens, by imposing military service upon all owners of land (*locupletes*), whereas these had before rested upon the patricians alone. The reform applied, therefore, only to the rural plebeians, or free peasants, not to the clients or to the city plebs. For this purpose the landowners (patricians and plebeians alike) were divided into five "classes," according to the amount of their landed property, and each of these classes again was divided into a number of "centuries." The centuries of each class were in two equal groups: the *juniores*, containing the citizens of military age (below forty-six), and the *seniores*, composed of those above the age of active service.

Military Service. — Military service was an exclusive privilege of citizens, as is the case in all early communities: therefore the admission of the plebeians to military service was in effect to recognize them as citizens, although not fully qualified citizens. From this the right to vote followed necessarily, although not at once. Each soldier equipped and provided himself at his own expense, and the armor and equipment of each class was more complete and costly than that of the class next below.[1] Besides the one

[1] The centuriate organization was as follows:

First class: 40 centuries each of active and reserve	80
18 centuries of cavalry	18
Second, third, and fourth classes, 20 centuries each	60
Fifth class, 30; mechanics, musicians, etc., 5	35
	193

The three first classes were heavy-armed, and composed the phalanx: the first class (with leather helmet, round shield (*clipeus*), breastplate, greaves, spear, and sword) composing four ranks; the second class (omitting the

hundred and seventy centuries of infantry, there were also eighteen centuries of cavalry, composed of young men of the first class, who received a horse, and provision for its keeping, from the state (*equites equo publico*). These centuries, like those of the infantry, were open to patricians and plebeians alike; but it is reasonable to suppose that this privileged service was practically confined to the patricians. As these eighteen centuries, when added to the eighty centuries of infantry of the first class, made a majority of the whole number of centuries, it is easy to see that, when the centuries were used as a voting organization, the first class was able to outvote all the others. The smiths, carpenters, musicians, and citizens below the rating of the fifth class made five additional centuries.

The Local Tribes. — Servius Tullius also divided the city into four districts, called "tribes,"[1] for administrative and financial purposes. The names of these — *Suburana, Palatina, Esquilina,* and *Collina* — were derived from those of the principal hills of the city, and the valley between. The territory outside of the city walls also fell into a number of smaller districts (*pagi*), which were afterwards formed into sixteen so-called "rural" tribes; and in the course of time the whole number of tribes was brought to thirty-five.[2] These tribes were made the basis for the military levy, each furnishing an equal number of men to each century of the army. From the tribes also was levied a land-tax, *tributum*, when required by the exigencies of the state, to be repaid when the treasury should be full.

---

breastplate) and the third (omitting also the greaves) composing one rank each. Behind these stood the fourth class, armed with spear and darts, and the fifth, who had nothing but slings.

[1] The tribes of Servius Tullius, in their origin purely territorial, must not be confounded with the three patrician tribes, which were primarily divisions of the people, although each tribe was resident in a definite district.

[2] It is Mommsen's view that the rural districts were formed into tribes at the time that the land was made private property; ownership in severalty being at first confined, as in the German village communities, to the homestead, while the cultivated fields were held in common.

The Comitia Centuriata. — Servius Tullius did not interfere with the patrician institutions, — the three tribes, the curies, and the *comitia curiata;* the new arrangement was only for military purposes. But those that support the state with their contributions, and defend it with their blood, cannot be prevented from having a voice in its management; and in the course of time the custom grew up of summoning all the citizens, instead of the patricians alone, to vote on public questions. For this purpose the organization by centuries was well suited, and the assembly thus organized was called *comitia centuriata*. We cannot tell certainly whether this assembly was used under the monarchy, but during the republic it was the regular organ of public action.

The Relation of Rome to Latium. — In the reign of Servius Tullius a temple of Diana was built upon Mount Aventine, as a common sanctuary for Romans and Latins. The Aventine was at this time unoccupied, and although it was within the walls of the city, like the Capitoline or citadel, it was not included in either of the four city tribes; it was afterwards assigned to the plebeians for their special residence. The regulations for the festival and markets held at this temple, and the treaties with the cities which combined to build it, were carved in Greek letters upon a bronze pillar set up in the temple; this pillar was still in existence at the close of the republic. That this temple was erected in Rome shows that this city was now regarded as the head of the Latin nationality. Tarquin the Proud established a still more complete authority over the whole of Latium; but it was the personal dominion of the king, not an enlargement of the power and territory of the city, and when the kingly power was overthrown, the empire over Latium was lost.

B.C. 456.

Conquests of Tarquin the Proud. — The only permanent acquisition of territory made by the city under the Tarquins, was that of the neighboring city of Gabii, which entered into a treaty with Tarquin the Proud by which its citizens became Roman citizens, and its territory a part of the *ager Romanus*, while the city still continued to govern itself in local concerns. This treaty too was in existence at the Christian era, inscribed upon an ox-hide stretched over a wooden shield. Two colonies were also planted by this king as military posts in the furthest part of Latium — Circeii upon the coast, and Signia on a spur of the Volscian mountains, commanding the valley of the Trerus; but authority over both was lost when the Latins regained their independence, at the expulsion of the Tarquins.

The Republic. — The revolution by which the kingly office was abolished is placed by tradition in the year B.C. 509. But the chronicles of these years are so confused and incomplete, that all we can say with certainty is that it took place at about the end of the sixth century before Christ. The Romans were acquainted with the art of writing at this epoch, as is shown by the two treaties mentioned in the last section; there was also a commercial treaty with Cârthage, made in the first year of the republic, and extant in the later republic, which illustrates the commercial importance of Rome at this time.[1] But although the Romans possessed the art of writing, they do not appear to have kept a regular chronicle of events until the time of the republic, and even then the records for a long time consisted of hardly more than lists of magistrates, battles and triumphs, disasters and portents.

War with the Etruscans. — The revolution which overthrew the monarchy led to a war with the Etruscans and Latins, which, according to the account, lasted fourteen years, and brought Rome to the verge of destruction. Lars Porsena, king of Clusium — at this time the leading Etruscan city, — gained a decisive victory, and compelled the Romans to an ignominious peace, by which they ceded a considerable tract of territory to the Etruscan city of Veii, gave up their weapons, and agreed in future to use no iron except for purposes of agriculture.[2] The Romans would not,

[1] The date of the several treaties with Carthage is subject to great controversy, the two highest authorities, Polybius and Diodorus, being directly in contradiction with each other; but I cannot see sufficient reason to reject with Mommsen the express statement of Polybius in relation to a document which he had probably seen with his own eyes.

[2] An agreement similar in object to those by which modern nations bind themselves to dismantle their fortresses.

however, consent to receive back the Tarquins, and the banished family remained in exile; the tomb of the family was discovered a few years ago in the Etruscan city of Cære. The war was at last ended by the decisive victory of the Romans at Lake Regillus; by this the independence of the Roman republic was secured.

B.C. 496.

Greek Influence. — It was a tradition among the Romans that the battle of Lake Regillus was saved to them by the aid of the Greek gods Castor and Pollux, and that these gods brought to the city the first tidings of the victory. In gratitude for this assistance they built a temple to Castor and Pollux on the spot, near the temple of Vesta, where they had made their appearance.[1] This is only one out of a number of evidences of an early and active intercourse of the Romans with the Greeks of Magna Græcia and Sicily. The Roman alphabet is derived from that of the Greeks, and the method of reckoning time and the system of weights and measures were modified by intercourse with the Greeks. We have seen too that the institutions of Servius Tullius bore a Greek stamp, and we shall find strong indications of the same influence in the decemviral legislation.

The Sibylline Books. — Still more important, as an agency in introducing Greek forms of worship, was the purchase of the Sibylline books by Tarquin the Proud, and the appointment of a special "college" or board of priests to take charge of them. These books were in Greek, and contained prophecies in reference to Rome. The commissioners who had charge of them (known afterwards as the "Board of Fifteen in charge of sacred rites," *Quindecimviri sacris faciundis*), consulted these books in times of public danger or embarrassment, and by their direction many Greek forms of worship were from time to time introduced into Rome.

Etruscan Influence. — But while the Greek influence upon the

[1] Three columns are still standing of the Temple of Castor. They mark the spot of the original temple, but themselves belong to a later edifice, built in the time of the empire.

civilization of the Romans was early and powerful, that of the Etruscans does not appear to have been very marked. The Etruscans were nearer than the Greeks, and they were the richest and most powerful people of Italy. But they were of wholly foreign race, while the Greeks were a people nearly related to the Romans. The trappings and ceremonial of royalty: the lictors with their axes and bundles of rods (*fasces*), the purple robe, and the curule chair, were introduced into Rome by the Etruscan kings, and these were retained by the chief magistrates of the republic.

Public Works. — The great buildings and other public works of the Tarquinian period were constructed, it is true, by the forced labor of the poorer citizens, but under the direction of Etruscan architects and builders. The name of a street opening into the Forum, *Vicus Tuscus*, is evidence of an Etruscan settlement, probably made at this time. As it led through a low and marshy quarter, it cannot have been occupied by the upper classes; but was probably the residence of Etruscan workmen. The era of great public works came suddenly to an end with the expulsion of the Etruscan dynasty of kings, and it is many a year before we meet with a renewed activity in this line. Even in buildings, therefore, the Etruscan influence was not permanent; and in the language, religion, and institutions of the early Romans, we find few traces of any foreign influence except that of the Greeks.

PERIOD II. — THE EARLY REPUBLIC.

CHAPTER IV.

SOCIAL CONTROVERSIES.

I. THE TRIBUNATE OF THE PLEBS.

The Magistrates. — The government established at Rome, after the expulsion of the kings, was an aristocratic republic, in which the controlling power was in the hands of the patricians. Two consuls were elected every year as chief magistrates, and these consuls must be patricians. These magistrates exercised the full powers of the king, only that they were obliged to allow an appeal to be taken from their decisions in criminal cases,[1] to the assembly of the people: in this way it came about that the Assembly became the supreme criminal court. This was, however, only within the limits of the city, and, as a symbol of this limitation of their power, the axes were within these limits removed from the bundles of rods carried by their attendants, the lictors: beyond these limits the axes were replaced in the *fasces*, and the consuls resumed their full authority. In times of great public danger either of the consuls could appoint a dictator, who, for a term of six months, exercised the full and unlimited power of king; and he, too, must be a patrician.

The Assemblies. — But although the patricians kept the substance of power in their own hands, they could not undo the work of Servius Tullius, who had incorporated the plebeians in the military force; neither would it have been safe to attempt to carry

[1] "Where sentence of capital or corporal punishment had been pronounced otherwise than by martial law, — a regulation which by a later law (of uncertain date, but passed before 451) was extended to heavy fines." — MOMMSEN.

on the new republic without the aid of the plebeians. They therefore took the assembly of centuries, the *comitia centuriata*, in which patricians and plebeians voted on an equality, and made it the regular organ of popular action, the "great assembly." This assembly received the power to elect magistrates, make laws, declare war, and pass judgment in criminal cases. It must not be supposed, however, that the plebeians were fully on an equality with the patricians even in this assembly. It will be remembered that the first class, composed of the richest citizens, could outvote all the rest. Now the patricians were, with hardly an exception, rich, while the plebeians were mostly poor. The patricians therefore really controlled the votes of the assembly. The old assembly by curies was not abolished, but became now entirely unimportant.

The Senate. — Another privilege granted to the plebeians was that some of their leading men — the richest among the rural plebeians — were allowed to sit in the Senate, but without the right to debate, and with powers inferior to those of the patrician members of the Senate.[1] Out of this there grew up an aristocracy among the plebeians, which in the course of time associated itself with the patrician aristocracy, and formed a new nobility.

Civil Dissensions. — Hardly were the wars at an end which established the independence of the republic, when we find the Roman people in a condition of extreme distress and destitution, and torn by dissensions. We have seen (p. 35) that the revolution which expelled the Tarquins also brought to an end the domination which they had established over the Latin cities; for a hundred years after this time the Romans were engaged in a constant struggle to regain this lost ascendancy. At the same time the commerce, which had been the foundation of their power, was cut off, or at least seriously crippled: it is long before Roman commerce revived, and it never again became relatively as important as it appears to have been in the early patrician state.[2] From this

[1] The auspices, with the right to cancel the action of the comitia, and to assume power in an interregnum (p. 20), belonged to the patrician senators alone.

[2] In the later republic senators were prohibited by law from engaging in commerce.

time the Romans were an essentially military people. Now when we consider that, besides the loss of empire and of commercial preponderance, they had seen their land laid waste and their property destroyed by the ravages of war, and that the burden of incessant military service forced them to neglect the cultivation of their fields, we find it easy to understand how there followed a degree of impoverishment and distress which caused social convulsions of the most formidable character. It was a condition of things like that which caused Shay's rebellion after the American Revolution.

Sufferings of the Poorer Classes. — These calamities fell principally upon the poorer classes, and as the poorer classes were all plebeians, while the patricians were a wealthy aristocracy, the disturbances which followed are usually spoken of as if they arose out of the political disqualifications of the plebeians. But as a matter of fact they had very little to do with these political disqualifications, or with the great struggle between patricians and plebeians, which began a generation later. The plebeians were peasants, and there were among them rich peasants, who, as we have seen (p. 39), were admitted to the Senate, and thus in part associated with the governing class. It was the poor among the plebeians — that is, the small peasants, owners of little freeholds, which they cultivated with their own hands — upon whom the burden fell. The condition of the poor was a hard one at any rate, because the times were hard; but now the distress of the hard times was brought to a crisis by the harsh and abusive execution of the laws by the magistrates.

A Characteristic Incident of the Times. — There were two ways in which the poor peasants were exposed to abuses on the part of the magistrates: in the requisition of military service, and in the enforcement of the law of debt. Both of these abuses find illustration in an incident which, whether historically true or not, depicts accurately the condition of the peasants. "An old man, dressed in rags, with long tangled hair and beard, screaming and calling for help, rushed into the market-place. The crowd having gathered around him, he stood in full sight, and said: 'I was born free; I served my full time in my youth, fought in twenty-eight battles, and often received testimonials of bravery in the wars; but in the troublous times which came upon the city I was obliged to incur debt, in order to pay the taxes which were levied upon me, because my fields had been laid waste and my property consumed in the hard times. Then when I could not pay my debt, I was seized as a slave by my creditor, with my two sons; my master laying hard tasks upon me, which I refused to perform, I was beaten with many stripes.' At the same time he showed his breast marked with scars, and his back covered with blood."[1]

The Condition of the Debtors. — The treatment inflicted upon this man was wholly within the lawful powers of creditors towards delinquent debtors. They even had the right, when there were several creditors, to cut the debtor in pieces, and each take a share proportioned to his debt.[2] They did not have these powers, however, until after a formal judgment by the consul. This harsh law of debt, giving the creditor absolute power over the body of the debtor, is found in other early nations,[3] but was nowhere so severe as in Rome. In Athens, just a hundred years before this time, the evil had reached such a height that the great statesman, Solon, was appointed commissioner, with extraordinary authority, to devise some remedy for it. Solon wisely abolished the law which gave the creditor this power; but the Romans had not the foresight to do this, and the laws of debt continued to be a source of contention and abuses for nearly two hundred years.[4]

Importance of this Question in Roman History. — We shall better understand the importance of this question in Roman history if we bear in mind that Rome, like Athens, was an active

---

[1] Dion. Hal., vi. 26. The same story is related by Livy, ii. 23.

[2] "Cut him to pieces like a butcher," Dio says; but he adds that this right was never exercised as a matter of fact. Before judgment the debtor was known as *nexus*, after judgment as *addictus*.

[3] See, for example, 2 Kings iv. 1.

[4] Their worst features were abolished B.C. 326.

commercial city, and that its commercial prosperity had been greatly impaired by the disturbed condition of things at the establishment of the republic. The law of debt could not work much harm so long as the Romans were a simple community of peasants, or so long as they enjoyed the brilliant prosperity which was brought in by foreign commerce. But with the crippling of this commerce all classes in the community were cramped in their resources; and the peasants were the ones, as is always the case, who felt it first and most severely.

Military Service. — The plebeians were not only the sufferers from the law of debt: they were the ones upon whom fell the chief burdens of military service. In all countries it is the peasants who form the rank and file of the army. The plebeians stood, it is true, nominally upon an equality with the patricians in this respect, since the levy for the army was made from the classes and centuries (p. 32), which consisted of both orders alike. But the levy for each year was made at the discretion of the consuls, and as a matter of course fell chiefly upon the plebeians. The patrician young men served in the cavalry, while the old men were in the centuries of reserves. It is mentioned as an unusual thing, that a certain patrician served on foot in the legion.[1]

The Powers of the Magistrates. — In two ways, therefore, the peasants were subject to abuses of authority by the consul. First, in the conscription for the year he had it in his power to be harsh or considerate, fair or unfair. Cases are often mentioned of plebeians who were forced into the army when they had already rendered all the military service that was due from them, or were obliged to serve in the ranks when they had a right to a higher position. Secondly, it was the consul who, in the exercise of his judicial powers, decided the cases of delinquent debtors; and here, too, a severe magistrate would hold strictly to the letter of the law, while one of kindly disposition was able to temper justice with mercy. It is related that at this very time a dictator who tried to administer justice mercifully, found himself so thwarted

[1] Livy, iii. 27.

THE SECESSION OF THE PLEBS. 43

by the relentless temper of the creditors, that he abdicated his office, rather than lend himself to its abuse.[1] The poor plebeians could not look for aid to the wealthier members of their own order, because the magistrates were exclusively patricians, while the creditors were those members of the patrician order who had made themselves rich by commerce.

The First Secession of the Plebs. — Soon matters came to a crisis. The Latin war had been ended by the battle of Lake Regillus, and Latins and Romans alike were en- B.C. 496. gaged in a war with the Sabines, Æquians, and Volscians. The plebeians composing the army seized this oppor- B.C. 494. tunity for vindicating their rights. They marched out of the city to a hill about three miles distant, just beyond the river Anio, and encamped there, refusing to fight the battles of the patricians until their wrongs should be redressed. This is known as the First Secession of the Plebs, and the hill which they occupied was thereafter called the Sacred Mount. There was talk among them of never returning to Rome, but of sending for their wives and children, and building a new city upon this spot. This would have been a fatal blow to the prosperity of the city, for the plebeians were the tillers of the soil and the rank and file of the army, and could not be spared. The patricians therefore offered a compromise, which was accepted after some hesitation. No change was made in the laws. Those suffering from debt or its consequences were relieved for the present; and for the future a novel guaranty was offered them against the abuses of the law.

The Tribunate of the Plebs. — This guaranty was the right to appoint officers from their own number, called *tribunes*, to protect them against abuses at the hands of the magistrates. These abuses, it will be remembered, were of two kinds: the unjust imposition of military duties and the harsh execution of the laws of debt. As it was only the acts of magistrates which were subjects of complaint, the remedy consisted in allowing the newly appointed tribunes to interfere and prevent such acts. This power of the tribunes was

[1] Livy, ii. 31.

called *jus auxili*, "power of assistance." The tribunes were at first two in number, then five, and afterwards ten. Whenever the consul, or his assistant, the quæstor, undertook to enforce the law of debt with undue severity, or to compel a citizen to serve in the army when no service was due from him, or in any other way to treat him unjustly or oppressively, the tribunes had the right absolutely to nullify this action. This power of protection was extended to patricians as well as plebeians.[1] In order to ensure its free exercise, the persons of the tribunes were made sacred; the whole people bound themselves by oath to protect them in the exercise of their office, and any one who violated this sanctity was outlawed and could lawfully be put to death.

The Plebeian Assembly. — Besides the *jus auxili*, or power to protect against abuses of magisterial authority, the tribunes had the right to call meetings of the plebeians, in order to take action in matters which concerned their collective interests. By the establishment of this assembly, presided over by the tribunes, the *Plebs* became a separate organized body, a state within the state. It elected its own officers, managed its own collective concerns, punished the misdemeanors of its members, and very soon found itself, with a compact organization and able and determined leaders, a controlling force in the state.

II. The Agrarian Laws.

The Triple Alliance. — The year after the secession to the Sacred Mount, a treaty of alliance was made by the consul Spurius Cassius with the Latin Confederacy, and a few years later the Confederacy of the Hernicans joined the league. The object of this alliance was the protection of these three nations of lowlanders against the raids of the Sabine, Æquian and Volscian mountaineers. It continued in force about one hundred and fifty years, until B.C. 338. By the terms of this treaty all three members of the league were on a

B.C. 493.
B.C. 486.

[1] See, for an example, Livy, iii. 13.

footing of entire equality. They agreed to "have peace with one another as long as the heavens and the earth shall endure"; they were to assist each other in all defensive wars, and to divide booty and spoils equally. But although the league was in form one of equality, it was a matter of course that a rich and populous city like Rome should have the leadership or "hegemony" over a multitude of small towns, just as Athens had done in the case of the Confederacy of Delos; and, just as Athens had turned her hegemony into an empire, so in like manner Rome soon came to treat her Latin and Hernican allies as dependents, and at last converted them into subjects.

The Latin Confederacy. — The Latin Confederacy consisted at this time of twelve or fifteen independent cities, of which Aricia was the chief, although Tusculum was the nearest and most closely connected with Rome. Like Rome, it had at its head two Prætors.[1] Of the Hernicans there were only five or six cities.

The Latin Colonies. — For the purpose of common defence the allied powers established at this time two military posts, Norba and Signia,[2] in strong positions upon the Volscian frontier. These towns were called Latin colonies, because the colonists, in case they were Roman citizens, lost their Roman citizenship by going to the colonies, and became Latins, while the towns themselves were made members of the Latin Confederacy. Each settler received two *jugera* of land (about one acre), with rights of pasture, etc., in the common field. Thus, while belonging to a garrison of soldiers upon the borders of a hostile land, the colonist was at the same time a husbandman, with a lot of land and a household of his own. When the Romans entered upon their great career of conquest, about a hundred years after this time, they made use of military posts of this class, — the Latin colonies, — to secure their conquests, establishing a number of them after every success-

---

[1] The Roman magistrates whom we know as *consuls* were at first called *prætors*.

[2] The colony of Signia was said to have been founded by the last Tarquin (p. 35); but its possession was lost in the early years of the republic.

ful war. The massive walls of Norba and Signia, the earliest, and for many years the only Latin colonies,[1] are still in large part preserved.[2]

WALLS OF SIGNIA.

Spurius Cassius. — Spurius Cassius, the statesman who negotiated both these treaties, with the Latins and with the Hernicans,
B.C. 485. fell under the suspicion of aiming to make himself king, and was put to death for treason by vote of the people.

[1] Circeii (p. 35), was lost shortly after the expulsion of the Tarquins, and was not re-established until 393.
[2] These walls were probably standing long before the founding of the Roman colony. They are what are known as *Cyclopean* walls, built of huge blocks of unhewn stone, without cement. They are sometimes called *Pelasgic;* but there is no sufficient evidence that the Pelasgians were ever in Italy.

It is not certain what was the precise nature of the charges against him, but they are represented as having some connection with the controversies about the public lands, which began at this time. Spurius Cassius was the first man who proposed an agrarian law in Rome.

The Public Lands. — It was the practice of the ancients, when they had carried on a war successfully, to punish the vanquished nation by taking from it a part of its territory, generally one-third. By this policy the Romans had come into possession of large tracts of land, which were the property of the city, and were known as public land, *ager publicus*. This public land of the Romans may be compared to the public land of the United States, and, like that, it could be sold, rented, or given as homesteads to actual settlers. If it was sold or given away, it ceased to be *ager publicus*, and became *ager privatus*. But all these methods required that the land should be accurately surveyed and registered; and when the lands were distant, or exposed to hostile raids, or when, for any other reason, it was not convenient to make a permanent disposition of them, another method was adopted, which was convenient as a temporary arrangement, but became the source of great injustice and dissensions.

Occupation. — The method in question was, to allow it to be occupied, under the general supervision of the magistrates, by any person who cared to make use of it. The occupier took as much vacant land as he pleased, within such natural limits as were found suitable, very much like an American " squatter," only that it was done by authority of law. For this he paid to the city, not a fixed sum of money, as in the case of leasehold land, but a fixed proportion of the produce (a tenth of cultivated land, a fifth of orchards and vineyards), or so much a head for cattle pastured upon the land. Land thus occupied, which was the property of the state, but in the possession of individuals, was called *ager occupatus*, and the tenure was called *possessio*.

Patrician Occupation. — Only patricians were allowed to occupy land in this manner, because they alone were fully qualified citizens. The plebeians had been made citizens by the laws of Servius Tullius (p. 31), but they had not yet the full rights of citizenship, and were in certain respects still regarded as foreigners. It was not until more than a hundred years after this time, B.C. 367, that the Licinian Laws gave them the full rights of citizenship, and along with these the right to occupy the public lands.

Possession a New Form of Property. — As the magistrates, who had charge of the public lands, were all patricians, it came about that the greater part of the lands fell into the occupation of wealthy patricians, who added them to their private estates, and cultivated them by means of their slaves and clients. The quæstors, whose business it was, were slack in collecting the dues, and the state, which had the right to resume the property, neglected to do so. The occupiers had no legal title, and could not maintain their possession by any regular legal process; but the consul (afterwards the prætor [1]), who administered the law in civil cases, would always protect them against any third party; and thus possession came to be a species of legal estate almost as valid as true ownership. The occupied lands were bought and sold, and passed by inheritance; so that at last the possessors regarded them as to all intents and purposes their own.

The Agrarian Laws. — It followed from this system of occupation that there was placed upon the plebeians more than their share of the public burdens. We have seen that they formed the rank and file of the army, and were the chief sufferers from the invasions and raids of the neighboring nations (p. 42); moreover, when a land-tax (*tributum*) was imposed, in order to meet the needs of war, it fell in undue proportion upon the plebeians, because the "occupied" lands were not subject to this tax. We do not hear of this exclusion from the public lands as one of the grievances which led to the secession of B.C. 494; but after order was restored, it appears to have occurred to Spurius Cassius, the most eminent statesman of his time, that the public lands afforded

---

[1] The administration of civil justice was transferred from the consuls to a new magistrate, called prætor, by the Licinian laws, B.C. 367.

a means of remedying the evils, and preventing future distress. He brought forward a proposition that the state should take into its possession the occupied lands, as it had a right to do, and parcel them out among the poorer citizens, — a measure very similar in its object to our homestead law. According to tradition it was on the charge of seeking to gain popularity with the plebeians by this measure, that Spurius Cassius was accused of treason. However just and beneficent his proposition was, it brought upon him the opposition and enmity of his own class, and was probably the cause of his condemnation and death.

B.C. 486.

Distributions of Land. (1) **Colonies.** — There were two ways of giving land to poor citizens. One was that of establishing military colonies, which has been already described (p. 45). This method made provision for a number of poor plebeians, by giving them land and a home; but it required them to move to a distance from their old homes, and to give up their Roman citizenship and become foreigners (Latins). This method was therefore unacceptable: and at any rate it was not until a hundred years after this time that it became common.

(2) **Assignment.** — The other method was to assign lots of land in full property to individuals (*viritim, i.e.* "man by man"): this was known as *Assignatio*. This was the aim of the agrarian laws of Spurius Cassius, and it will be easily understood that the patrician occupiers resisted the measure with the greatest determination. For the present they succeeded in preventing its passage, and the agrarian demands were not satisfied until Rome entered upon her great career of conquest, about a hundred years later; then portions of the conquered land were distributed by assignment, and a great number of Latin colonies were established.

The Agrarian Contests. — The contest upon the agrarian law continued with the greatest bitterness and persistency for about thirty years, and brought the city to the verge of civil war. It was indeed rather a contest between two hostile nations than a controversy between two parties in the same nation; for the patricians were the only fully qualified Roman citizens, and controlled the magistrates and assemblies of the city, while the plebeians were now an independently organized body, with officers and assemblies of their own. Probably the plebeians were already the strongest in numbers, even counting the clients of the patrician clans as a part of the patrician forces; and at any rate the veto power of the tribunes, giving them the right of almost unlimited obstruction, joined with their sacred character, which made it sacrilege to injure or obstruct them, gave the plebeians an enormous advantage.

Usurpation of Power by the Tribunes. — It was easy for officers in possession of such privileges as those of the tribunes, to stretch their right of self-protection into a right of punishing any who should stand in their way. They began to carry things with a high hand, and even summoned consuls before them, threatening them with chastisement or death. On several occasions patricians were heavily fined or driven into exile, and soon the plebeian assembly was in practical possession of a power not unlike that of the *comitia*. This was, it is true, a usurped and illegal power, — an "organized lynch-law" it has been called; but the patricians were unable to resist it. The dissensions became so violent that it sometimes seemed as if the machinery of government would come to a stop. It can be well imagined that a city torn by such internal contests as these rapidly lost strength and energy in military relations also.

Wars with Neighboring Nations. — All this time the Romans were harassed by a succession of petty wars with the Sabines, Æquians, and Volscians on the south of the Tiber, and the Etruscans of Veii on the other side of the river. They were so seriously weakened by the dissensions within the walls and the loss of foreign commerce, that even with the alliance of the Latins and the Hernicans, the contest often seemed hopeless. The well-known story of Coriolanus, which belongs to this period, is a lively illustration of the civil discord of the time, and the disasters resulting from it.[1]

[1] The story of Coriolanus has very little historical foundation in fact, but is of great value as a picture of the times.

The Destruction of the Fabian Gens. — Another incident, somewhat later in time, and better authenticated, affords a striking example, at once of the power and coherence of a patrician class, and of the spirit of heroic patriotism that inspires its members. At one time, when the city was in great straits, in the war against Veii, the Fabian gens offered to carry on the war by its own resources. This was one of the proudest and most powerful clans among the Romans, and one of the most active in the contest of the orders. Like the followers of a mediæval baron or a Highland chieftain, they gathered, three hundred and six in number, "all patricians," with three or four thousand clients, and marched to the attack of Veii. But their strength was not equal to their spirit; they were taken in ambuscade and cut off almost to a man. The arch of the gate by which they had marched out, between the Capitoline and the river, was ever after regarded as unlucky (called *Porta Scelerata*).

B.C. 479.

CHAPTER V.

THE CONTEST BETWEEN THE ORDERS.

I. THE CONTEST FOR CIVIL RIGHTS.

The New Leaders of the Plebeians.—In the early republic, as we have seen, the contests were social rather than political. It was the poor peasants that suffered from the abuses of magisterial power in exacting military service and executing the laws of debt, and that felt as a hardship the engrossment of the public lands by the patricians. The rich plebeians, the better class of peasants, had little interest personally in these controversies. But they, no less than the poorer members of their order, began to feel as a grievance their exclusion from the full rights of citizenship, and they soon saw that they could use the new organization, with its officials and assembly, as an instrument for the attainment of full political equality. The contest which now ensued was carried on with a persistency and a far-seeing sagacity which show these rural plebeians to have been a class possessed of high political capacities. It lasted for more than a hundred years, and ended B.C. 367. with a complete victory, by which they obtained a full equality with the patricians in all essential particulars. In this contest the rich plebeians placed themselves at the head of their order as its champions and leaders.

The Publilian Law.—The first object of the new leaders was to obtain a better organization of their order. The assembly of the plebeians for the first twenty years was organized by curies (p. 18); for as the curies were local divisions they afforded a convenient basis for assemblies of the plebeians residing within their limits. But in the curies the clients of the patricians, and the traders and handicraftsmen of the city, voted on an equality with the free peasants; and the patricians were able to influence the action of

THE PUBLILIAN LAW.

the assembly through their clients. It was resolved, therefore, that in future the plebeian assembly should be organized by the local tribes (p. 33), which had been formed for the purposes of military and financial administration, and in which, therefore, only freeholders were taken into account. The new Tribal Assembly of the plebeians was established by the so-called Publilian Law,[1] and shortly afterwards the number of tribunes was raised to ten. This assembly, with its ten tribunes, became in time one of the most important institutions in the state, taking upon itself to pass ordinances for the whole body of citizens; while the tribunes stretched their veto power into a right to nullify almost any action of any magistrate. B.C. 471.

Disastrous Wars. — A few years after the passage of the Publilian Law, the patricians undertook to partially satisfy the agrarian demands by establishing a colony at Antium, a Volscian town upon the sea-coast, which the fortunes of war had just put in their power. But the colony was unpopular (see p. 49), and the city was soon re-conquered by the Volscians. Indeed these were years of disaster. The Volscians not only reconquered Antium, but got possession of Velitræ, on the southern slope of the Alban Mount. The Æquians, the most active of their enemies at this period, gained even more important advantages. They seized Mount Algidus, the pass which commanded the road afterwards known as the *Latin Way*, which led from Rome to the country of the Hernicans in the valley of the Trerus. The triple alliance was thus cut in two. The Hernicans, as well as the more distant of the Latin towns, were cut off from communication with Rome, and this important stronghold served as a base of operation for the Æquians in a succession of predatory raids. Even the great Latin cities of Tibur and Præneste, neighbors of the Æquians, withdrew from alliance with Rome, and stood neutral in the contest. B.C. 467.

---

[1] All laws during the Roman Republic must be passed by an assembly of the people, upon the proposition of the presiding magistrate, and they took the name of the magistrate who proposed them. The law in question was proposed by the tribune Publilius Volero.

Change of Policy by the Plebeian Leaders.—The agrarian agitation had now been kept up for nearly thirty years without result, and the plebeian leaders saw that it was time to change their policy. From this time on their efforts were directed no longer to secure a merely remedial measure which could benefit only a few, but to remove the disabilities under which the entire body of the plebeians rested, and which were the real source of their hardships. What enabled the patricians to engross the public lands, was the fact that they were the only citizens with full rights; it would be of very little advantage to procure assignments of land for this man and that man, so long as the legal and constitutional relation of the two orders was not fundamentally changed. The contest for the agrarian law was quietly dropped, and new and more vital issues were presented. The great struggle which now began, and which ended, after about a hundred years, in the so-called "equalization of the orders," may be divided into two distinct periods. During the first of these the efforts of the plebeians were especially directed towards equality in civil rights; in the second their aim was political equality.

The Terentilian Rogation.[1]—The new contest began
B.C. 461. with a proposition by the tribune Gaius Terentilius Harsa, that the laws should be written down, or, as we should call it, codified. In all early communities law is derived from custom, and is interpreted by tradition. In Rome the custom upon which law rested was of course that of the patricians, the only fully qualified citizens, and the tradition was that of the patrician magistrates. The plebeians, enjoying only a partial and incomplete citizenship, were subject to an administration of law which was wholly at the discretion of the patrician magistrates. More than this: as the law was *customary* law, and had never been written down, the plebeians were judged by laws and rules of pro-

---

[1] A proposition of law was called a "rogation," from *rogo*, "ask," because the presiding magistrate asked the people if they would order it (*jubere*), to take effect. The Terentilian rogation never became a law, although the substance of it was adopted.

cedure which were not understood by themselves, and which were interpreted and executed by patrician magistrates. So long as the knowledge and the administration of the laws were the exclusive possession of the patricians, there was no security for justice, even in the simplest controversies of property and contract.[1]

Opposition to the Law. — This demand for the codification of the laws seems to us perfectly fair and reasonable; but it was a blow struck at the fundamental institutions of the state, and the patricians saw clearly that this first step towards destroying their exclusive privileges would in time necessarily lead to a radical revolution in the principles of the government. They met it, therefore, with a most furious and determined opposition, which they kept up for nearly ten years.

Kæso Quinctius. — The opposition was led by a party of young bloods, of patrician families, at the head of whom was Kæso Quinctius, son of the famous Lucius Quinctius Cincinnatus, a handsome, high-spirited young man, of remarkable bodily strength and prowess in war. Under his lead the hot-headed young patricians resisted the passage of the law by breaking up the plebeian assemblies, beating and otherwise maltreating their officers, even laying violent hands on the tribunes in contempt of their sacred character. The tribunes, driven to desperation, disregarded the law in their turn, and stretched the power of their assembly far beyond its lawful limits. Kæso was summoned before it on a capital charge requiring enormous bail; and when he escaped by night and went into exile, the bail was exacted from his father with such severity that he was obliged to sell his property and retire to a little farm beyond the Tiber, where he lived with his wife in a poor cottage, cultivating his fields with his own hands.

Appius Herdonius. — The next year, while the city was still divided into two hostile camps, and the agitation for the Terentilian Law was at its height, an event occurred of the most startling character. A Sabine nobleman, Appius

B.C. 460.

---

[1] On this point consult the first chapter of Maine's *Ancient Law*.

Herdonius by name, with a band of followers and a company of Roman exiles, floated down the Tiber by night, landed just above the city, and entering it by an unguarded gate, took possession of the citadel[1] overlooking the Forum. It is probable that the banished Roman patricians had associated themselves with the enemy of their country, just as is related in the case of Coriolanus. Probably Kæso Quinctius was among them; for although his name is not mentioned on the occasion, it disappears from this time, and he is spoken of a year or two later as being already dead. Herdonius expected to be joined by the disaffected party in the city, and by the slaves, whom he called upon to rise. But the moderate party among the patricians, at their head the consul Publius Valerius, were patriotic Romans; and the plebeians, although perplexed and suspicious, were on the alert. Herdonius was caught in a trap. With the help of a body of troops from the friendly city of Tusculum, Valerius and the plebeians stormed the citadel and put to death the whole party. Valerius was himself killed in the assault.

Cincinnatus. — It was a perilous season for Rome. The political quarrels had reached the dimensions of civil war, and the foreign enemies were every day growing stronger and bolder.

Appius Herdonius was a Sabine; the occupation of Mount Algidus by the Æquians was a more permanent and disastrous loss. It gave the Æquians a base of operations from which they were able even to capture Tusculum; the Romans, by helping in its recovery, requited the good service which the Tusculans had done them in recapturing the Roman citadel from Herdonius. The following year a Roman army was attacked in its camp near Mount Algidus and nearly brought to destruction. The panic at Rome was great. For a moment party strifes were forgotten, and the veteran Cincinnatus, the father of Kæso Quinctius, was called from his retirement and made dictator. In sixteen

B.C. 460.
B.C. 459.
B.C. 458.

---

[1] The height now occupied by the church of Sta. Maria in Araceli; they seem also to have occupied the neighboring height of the Capitolium.

COMPROMISE MEASURES. 57

days, as the story goes, he had relieved the beleaguered army, recaptured Mount Algidus, and defeated the army of the enemy, and sent it under the yoke. But the success, if it was ever gained in reality,[1] was of short duration. The Æquians soon recovered the pass, and the confederacy was for several years actually cut in two (see p. 53). From this time for about forty years it was all that the Romans could do to hold their own; and during this interval the petty wars with Sabines, Æquians, Volscians, and Etruscans cease to possess any interest or importance for us.

Compromises. — Both parties were now weary of their long controversies, and, we may suppose, both parties saw with alarm that while the city was distracted with their dissensions, the enemy were growing stronger and more active. The years that followed were marked by compromises upon all the points of dispute. The attempt to resume the occupied lands was dropped, and the district of the Aventine, within the walls, but unoccupied, and therefore not included in any of the local tribes, was given to the plebeians;[2] it was divided up into building lots, and became the distinctively plebeian quarter. Two years afterwards the jurisdiction of the tribunes was regulated by a law[3] which gave them authority to pass judgment in cases punishable by fine. On the other hand they lost the power which they had illegally exercised of punishing by death or banishment; offences which were subject to these penalties were reserved for the centuriate assembly, which consisted of the entire people.[4] The law made two sheep and thirty kine the maximum of fines to be imposed by the tribunes.[5] By a law passed a few years later these values

B.C. 456.

B.C. 454.

B.C. 430.

---

[1] In all the events of this period, and indeed long after, it is impossible to draw a hard and fast line between history and tradition. The substance is no doubt true, but the details are largely poetic creation.

[2] This was by the Icilian Law.   [3] The Aternian-Tarpeian Law.

[4] This rule was fixed by the law of the Twelve Tables (p. 59).

[5] This probably means that small offences were fined one or two sheep, and that the next highest penalty was one beeve, and so on to thirty.

THE CONTEST BETWEEN THE ORDERS.

were commuted into money, at the rate of one hundred *asses* for each head of cattle, and ten *asses* for a sheep.[1] If a higher fine was imposed by a magistrate, an appeal could be taken to the assembly.

Commission to Greece. — As a part of the compromise policy, the proposition of the Terentilian Law was laid aside, and it was agreed to send a commission of three patricians to Greece, in order to examine the laws of Athens and other cities, and report at home such changes as might be desirable in those of Rome. Athens was at this time at the height of its power and splendor. Its institutions had been radically reformed by Solon about one hundred and fifty years before, and had since then been remodelled from time to time in a more democratic spirit. This epoch is known as the Age of Pericles, when, under the inspiration of this great statesman, the art and literature, as well as the power of Athens, were at their height.

The Decemvirate. — The commissioners returned in B.C. 452. two years, bringing with them a Greek named Hermodorus, a native of Ephesus, to assist in compiling the code; a statue was afterwards erected in his honor upon the comitium. The Romans now elected a board of ten commissioners, all patricians, known as the *Decemviri* ("ten men"), to revise and codify the laws; and, as was the usual practice among the ancients,[2] placed the government of the city in their hands while B.C. 451. they were engaged in the work. All the regular magistrates, as well plebeian as patrician, — consuls, quæstors, tribunes, and ædiles, — were suspended for the time; and the right of appeal to the public assembly in criminal cases, no less than the right of the tribunes to assist against abuses of magisterial power, was also suspended.[3]

---

[1] This was the Julian-Papirian Law. The *as* was a pound of copper (p. 27); the estimated value of neat cattle was therefore one hundred pounds of copper each, which would be, at the present value of copper, about $15.00.

[2] Other examples are those of Solon in Athens (B.C. 594), and Sulla (B.C. 82), and the Triumvirs (B.C. 41), in Rome.

[3] Niebuhr and many other scholars have been of the opinion that it was part of the scheme to have this board of ten (like the nine Archons in Athens)

Second Year of the Decemvirate. — The work of codification was not completed the first year; a second board of ten commissioners (three of whom were plebeians) were therefore elected, who finished the work and made it public. The new code was engraved upon twelve columns (ten of them being the work of the first board), and was known as the Law of the Twelve Tables.[1] The Twelve Tables formed the basis of all Roman law, and were regularly committed to memory by Roman school-boys, as the most essential part of their education.

B.C. 450.

Its Overthrow. — When the second year of the Decemvirate was at an end, the commissioners did not lay down their office, but continued to hold it illegally for several months. They are accused also of gross tyranny and cruelty; the odium falling chiefly upon Appius Claudius, the most active and influential among them.[2] By their oppression the plebeians were driven to secede a second time, — first gathering in the plebeian quarter, the Aventine, and thence marching out, as before, to the Sacred Mount. The Decemvirs were forced to abdicate, and were punished with death, after which the regular machinery of government was again put in operation. The new consuls, Lucius Valerius and Marcus Horatius, carried a law making it an offence punishable with death to procure the election of any magistrate without the right of appeal from his decisions.[3] Other laws of these consuls will be spoken of in the next chapter.

B.C. 449.

take the place of the magistrates as a permanent form of government. It is hard to believe, however, in view of the contests of the next seventy-five years, that the patricians were now ready to share the substance of power with the plebeians.

[1] *Tabulae* (Tablets or Tables) was the name given to any flat surface used for writing or engraving; usually of wood, spread with wax, but in the case of inscriptions, of bronze or marble.

[2] The legend tells of two gross cases of abuse: the unjust judgment of Appius Claudius, decreeing a plebeian girl, named Virginia, to be the slave of his client, from which fate her father rescued her by stabbing her to the heart; and the death of a brave soldier, Sicinius Dentatus.

[3] This did not apply to the dictators, who were not elected, but appointed, and who were not subject to appeal for nearly two centuries after this time.

The Twelve Tables. — Only fragments of the Twelve Tables have come down to us, and we know very little of their details. The code was largely occupied with describing and regulating the legal procedure, so as to put an end to the capricious administration of law by the magistrates : this was probably the principal object of the Terentilian rogation. The Twelve Tables did not merely codify the old customary law, but altered and ameliorated it so as to make it better suited to the needs of an advancing civilization. The law of debt was not abolished, but its harshness was somewhat mitigated. The death penalty, which had been lawlessly exercised by the tribunes, was now reserved to the centuriate assembly,[1] while the plebeian assembly, presided over by the tribunes and ædiles, became the regular organ for the punishment of inferior offences.

Changes in Family Law. — The most significant work of the new code was in relaxing the family organization upon which the patrician institutions had rested, and thus preparing the way for a modern organization of society. It contained provisions for freeing both wife and sons from the absolute power of the head of the family, *pater-familias*. What is even more important, it laid the foundation for the social assimilation of patricians and plebeians. Until this time the patricians alone had a recognized system of *gentes*. The clients belonged to the *gentes* of their patrons, as dependent members, but the plebeian family organization, of precisely the same nature as the patrician, had not been recognized by Roman law. The law of the Twelve Tables gave recognition to the gentile system of the plebeians, and at the same time, by granting to the clients the right of holding property and some independence of action in relation to their patrons, it relaxed and gradually abolished the institution of clientage. From this time the clients appear no longer as unqualified adherents of the patricians, but are by degrees merged in the great body of the plebeians.

---

[1] This was presided over by the consuls, but the tribunes might bring prosecutions before it.

The Canuleian Law. — The laws of the Twelve Tables mark a turning point of vital importance in the social history of the Romans. Not only the strict organization of the patrician families, but their exclusive privileges, are now at an end. The next step, completing the civil equality of the two orders, followed much more rapidly than could have been expected. Only four years after the overthrow of the decemvirate, B.C. 445, the tribune, Gaius Canuleius, carried a law to extend to the plebeians the *conubium*, or right of marriage with patricians.

Right of Intermarriage. — Primitive nations, as a rule, prohibit intermarriage with foreigners : and the plebeians, being citizens of Latin towns which were originally independent of Rome, were foreigners to the patricians. It is true, the Servian constitution had made them citizens, but citizens with inferior rights ; and even the law of the Twelve Tables had contained the prohibition of intermarriage. But the plebeians had now been admitted step by step, not into the patrician organization, but into a permanent political association with the patricians. They had even received the right to have a gentile organization of their own similar to that of the patricians. It was therefore only a short step further to allow the families to intermarry. By the passage of the Canuleian Law, the plebeians secured entire equality in civil rights, and the two orders were rapidly merged into one people. Having now secured civil equality, the sagacious plebeian leaders next proceeded to contend for political equality.

II. THE CONTEST FOR POLITICAL RIGHTS.

The Roman Constitution. — After the overthrow of the decemvirate the old form of government was restored, with some changes.

I. The Magistrates : two consuls, elected yearly in the centuriate assembly, with chief executive and military authority, and jurisdiction in civil cases. They were assisted by two quæstors, whose powers had originally been judicial, but who now had the treasury as their special charge. The quæstors had formerly been appointed by the consuls, but were now elected in a newly organized assembly of the tribes, the *comitia tributa* — not to be confounded with the plebeian assembly — in which patricians and plebeians voted alike. All magistrates must be patricians.

II. The Senate, consisting of three hundred members, appointed by the consuls, chiefly patricians, but with a few plebeians. Its powers were chiefly advisory; but the patrician members had the right of nullifying laws on the ground of unconstitutionality, and of assuming the government if at any time the city was left without regular magistrates (*interregnum*).

III. The Assemblies, three in number, composed of patricians and plebeians without distinction. The principal assembly was the *comitia centuriata* (p. 34), organized according to age and property. This assembly elected the consuls and afterwards other higher magistrates, passed laws, declared war, and exercised criminal jurisdiction in all cases involving the punishment of death, bodily chastisement or exile. The newly formed *comitia tributa*, organized by tribes or local districts, elected the quæstors and the other inferior magistrates afterwards introduced, and had the power of making laws. The old patrician *comitia curiata* (p. 19), to which the plebeians had now been admitted, were kept up for certain formalities, especially for granting the *imperium*, or power to command, to the newly elected consuls.

IV. The Plebs, consisting of all who were not patricians — rural plebeians, clients, and city plebs; presided over by two tribunes, assisted by two ædiles. Its assembly,[1] composed exclusively of plebeians, was organized by tribes, and had full power to regulate the affairs of the plebeians. The tribunes had also not merely the *jus auxili* (p. 43), but also the power of vetoing the action of any magistrate, unless specially exempted by law; especially of forbidding the adoption of ordinances of the Senate (*senatus consulta*), and the presentation of rogations (p. 54) to the people. The ædiles had the charge of the streets and markets. The assembly had the power of imposing fines upon

[1] Often known as *comitia tributa*, but properly *concilium tributum plebis*.

any citizen, and its ordinances (called *plebiscita*) appear to have had the force of laws when the Senate gave its approval.

The New Demands of the Plebeians. — The plebeians were now in possession of three out of the four essential rights of citizenship. The *commercium*, or right of property, they, as being Latins, had always enjoyed; the *suffragium*, or right of voting, had been extended to them at the establishment of the republic; the *conubium*, or right of intermarriage, they had just obtained by the Canuleian Law. They now proceeded to demand the only remaining right, the *honores*, or right of holding magistracies. The contest upon this issue, forming the second stage of the Contest of the Orders, continued for about eighty years, until it was determined by the Licinian laws, B.C. 367.

Privileges of the Consulate. — The office of consul carried with it, for the year of its tenure, the complete exercise of the kingly power, except so far as this power had been limited by the right of appeal to the people in criminal cases (p. 38). During his term of office the consul was distinguished by the royal insignia (p. 37): and after retiring from office he enjoyed, as a *consularis*, or man of consular rank, an especial dignity in the state, with the right to wear the consular dress on public occasions, to speak among the first in the Senate, and to set up in the hall of his house waxen masks of his ancestors, as tokens of nobility (the *jus imaginum*). These privileges, which were derived from the religious preëminence of their order, the patricians were not disposed to yield to the plebeians, even after they had consented to ally themselves with them in marriage. The executive and military authority of the office, on the other hand, could hardly be refused to the class which composed the rank and file of the army.

THE CURULE CHAIR.[1]

The Military Tribunate. — It was readily agreed, there- B.C. 444. fore, in the very year after the passage of the Canuleian Law, to grant the plebeians the substance of magisterial authority,

---

[1] On the reverse of a denarius of the Furian gens.

while still withholding from them all the privileges which conferred nobility. This was accomplished by temporarily suspending the office of consul, and placing the consular power in the hands of the military tribunes, six in number, who were the regular officers of the legion. These officers had heretofore been appointed by the consuls, from the two orders indifferently. Now they were to be elected by the people: but it usually happened that only three or four were chosen by the people, the rest being probably appointed as before, and not having consular power. Each year it was decided by a popular vote whether to elect consuls or military tribunes, and this compromise was continued for more than fifty years. The influence of the patricians was still so great in the elections, however, that it was forty-four years before a plebeian was elected military tribune with consular power.

B.C. 443. **The Censorship.** — The year after the establishment of the military tribunate, it was decided to withdraw from the consular magistrates a portion of their duties, and place them in the hands of a pair of new patrician magistrates, called *Censors*, elected for five years. The duties of this new office were to make out a list of the citizens, and distribute them into classes according to their property, as a basis for the military levy and taxation, as well as of voting; also the general superintendence of public works and contracts. Thus the patricians kept these important powers in their own hands. After the schedule of citizens and property was completed, a purifying ceremony or *lustrum* was accomplished, from which the name *lustrum* was given to the five-years interval. The work of the censors, it was found, could be completed in a year and a half; for the remainder of the lustrum, therefore, this office was left vacant.[1]

---

[1] These original powers of the censors were afterwards enlarged so as to make their office the most dignified and powerful in the state. Especially they exercised the *lectio senatus*, or right of making out the list of senators, and the *regimen morum*, or right of punishing immoral and indecent acts: it is this function that has given the word *censor* its familiar meaning.

Quæstorship. — The quæstors, two in number, were originally assistants of the kings and the consuls, appointed by them, and having principally judicial functions. Now that the administration of criminal justice had passed completely to the public assemblies, the duties of the quæstors became chiefly fiscal, they having the charge of the treasury under the direction of the Senate and higher magistrates. After the decemvirate they were elected by the people in the newly organized *comitia tributa* (p. 62), and a few years later the office was thrown open to the plebeians; as the quæstors did not have the use of the curule chair[1] or the *jus imaginum*, this concession was readily made by the patricians. At the same time two new quæstors were added, as quartermasters in the army; and the number was increased from time to time as there was need. B.C. 421.

Renewed Strength of Rome. — The harmony established through these compromises infused great vigor into the administration of the republic. During the quarter of a century which followed the decemvirate there was a decided advance in the power of Rome. The old Latin city of Ardea was subdued on the occasion of some disturbances, and organized as a military colony. Soon after, the dictator, Aulus Postumius, gained a signal victory at Mt. Algidus over the Æquians and Volscians, and recovered this important post, thus restoring the territorial unity of the confederacy (p. 53). It is related that the victorious general put to death his own son, for leaving his post without orders during the battle in order to gain an unforeseen advantage. A similar occurrence is related in other wars, and we must believe that the stern Roman discipline and sense of duty was carried on occasion even to this extreme. B.C. 442. B.C. 431.

New Conquests. — There now followed a rapid succession of conquests, and a great extension of the Roman territory. The

---

[1] The magistrates who had the right to use the curule chair (of the regular magistrates, the consul, prætor, censor, and curule ædile) were known as *curule magistrates;* the tenure of these magistracies conferred nobility upon the descendants.

THE AGER ROMANUS AND THE LATIN CONFEDERACY

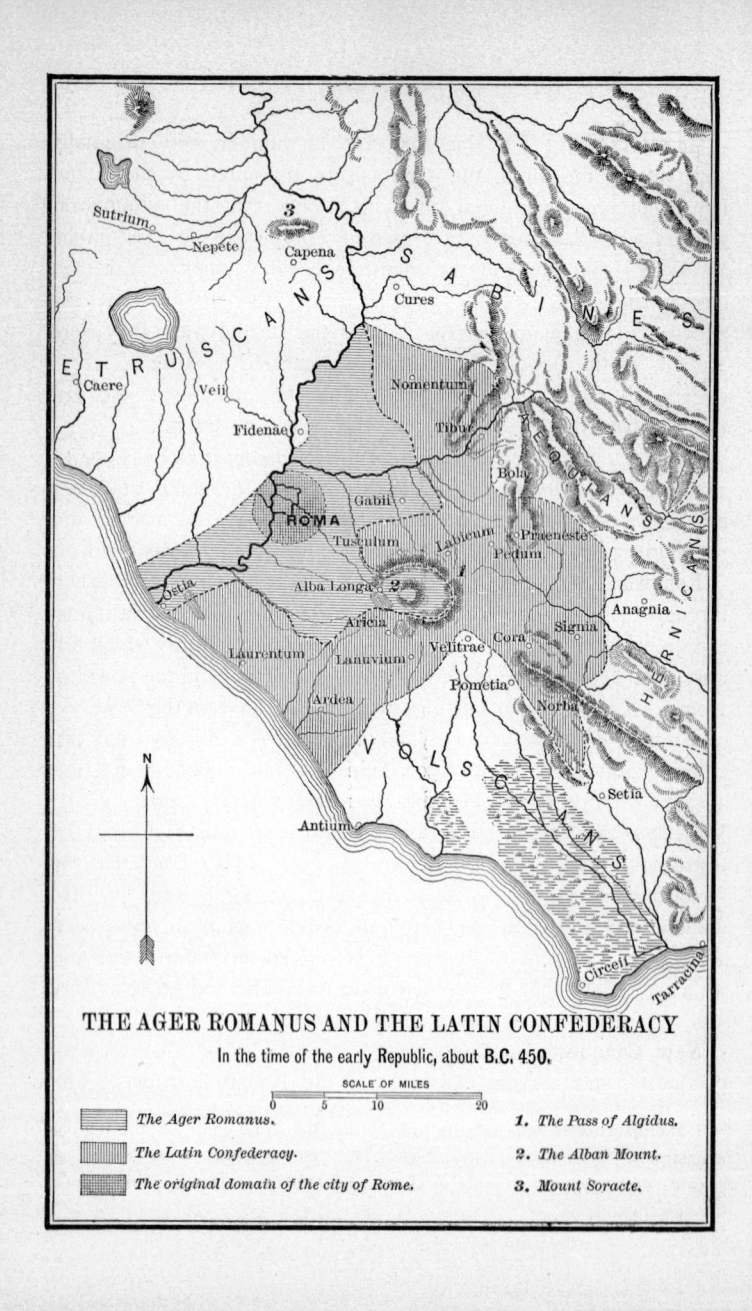

In the time of the early Republic, about B.C. 450.

- The Ager Romanus.
- The Latin Confederacy.
- The original domain of the city of Rome.

1. The Pass of Algidus.
2. The Alban Mount.
3. Mount Soracte.

capture of Fidenæ, the outpost of Veii, on the left bank B.C. 426. of the Tiber, completed for Rome the occupation of that bank, and was the necessary step to the conquest of Veii. The defeat of the Æquians at Mt. Algidus had restored communication with the Hernican country (p. 53); the city of Labicum, in this neighborhood, was now annexed by Rome, B.C. 418. and soon after the Æquian town of Bola. The Romans B.C. 415. also captured the Volscian town of Anxur (afterwards B.C. 406. known as Terracina).

Siege of Veii. — Inspired by these successes and by the consciousness of growing strength, the Romans now determined to rid themselves of their most powerful and formidable rival, the Etruscan city of Veii. This city, only ten miles distant from Rome, was the advance-guard of Etruscan power, as Rome was the outpost of the Latin nationality. If the Etruscans had been at this time as strong and as united as they had once been, it is not likely that they would have allowed the fall of Veii. But there were dissensions among them, and the other Etruscan cities refused to aid their confederate. Moreover the Etruscan power was itself upon the wane. The Gallic tribes from beyond the Alps had invaded the valley of the Po, and were at this moment engaged in the overthrow of the northern Etruscan empire; while in the south the city of Capua, the capital of the

ETRUSCAN ARCHER.

Etruscan possessions in Campania, had just been cap- B.C. 424. tured by the Samnites. The undertaking to conquer Veii was not as hopeless as it would have seemed a half century earlier; and, at any rate, Rome could not hope for wide empire, or even for permanent possession of her present conquests, so long as this inveterate enemy was at her gates.

Conquest of Veii. — The siege of Veii was kept up with various fortunes for ten years, and was at last brought to a triumphant conclusion in B.C. 396 by the Dictator Marcus Furius Camillus. The city was captured by means of a mine carried into its citadel. The contest had been one of life and death, and the vengeance inflicted by the victors upon their defeated enemies was terrible. The people of Veii were exterminated; the men were put to the sword, and the women and children sold into slavery. A portion of the peasant population became Roman citizens, retaining their estates; the rest of the land was divided up among the Roman people, while the walls and buildings of the city were left empty and deserted. The worship of Juno, the patron deity of Veii, was transferred to Rome, where a temple was built for her upon the Aventine. It was said that the soldier who first entered her temple after the capture of the city asked the image of the goddess whether she would go to Rome,[1] and that she answered by a nod.

Enlargement of the Roman Domain. — The next year the neighboring city of Capena was also conquered and annexed. By these annexations the Roman territory was greatly enlarged: four new tribes were made, bringing the number to twenty-five, and two military colonies, Nepete and Sutrium, were established upon the Etruscan frontier.

B.C. 395.

B.C. 383.

III. Triumph of the Plebs.

Reform in Military Organization. — The war with Veii was a critical event in the territorial growth of Rome. The removal of this rival left Rome without any obstacle to its growth, and from this time on there was a steady advance in its possessions and power. The larger enterprises which she now undertook demanded a greater concentration of resources, and a more efficient military organization; and at about this time a reform was made in the military system, which is generally believed to have been the work of the great commander of this age, Marcus Camillus. In the

[1] *Visne Romam ire, Juno?* — LIVY, v. 22.

first place, the siege of Veii itself was an enterprise wholly different from any previous one. Heretofore the army had been a militia, levied every year for a summer campaign, and serving without pay. But when a regular siege was commenced, to continue year in and year out until the city fell, it was necessary to have permanent works and troops in uninterrupted service, and these could not be had without pay. From this time the Roman army, without ceasing to be a militia — for every citizen, and none but citizens, must serve — was a body of paid troops.

The Phalangal Order. — Still more important was the change in organization and tactics. The early Roman army, like that of the Greeks, was a *phalanx;* that is, a compact body of troops, forming a continuous line without breaks or intervals: the centuries of the early army appear to have been only administrative divisions, of no consequence in the line of battle. An army drawn up in this order, and armed with long spears, was almost invincible in defence; but it could not move with ease or precision except upon level ground, and was unsuited to attack. The Greeks developed the phalanx to its highest degree of efficiency, by combining with it a large body of cavalry and light infantry. The Macedonian phalanx was a military organization of wonderful power, but proved no match for the Roman legion.

The Manipular Order. — The Romans developed their military system in precisely the opposite direction, securing a high degree of flexibility and individuality of action by surrendering the compactness and mass of the phalanx. This change was made by successive steps at various periods, but appears to have been begun at the present time, under the influence of Camillus. The legion was divided into thirty companies, called *maniples*, the average strength of which may be reckoned as one hundred and twenty heavy-armed men, and twenty light-armed, making 4200 in all.[1] Each maniple was commanded by two centurions, the legion being commanded by six military tribunes, two exercising com-

[1] The maniples were afterwards combined into ten battalions, called *cohorts*, and on the other hand subdivided each into two platoons, called *centuries*.

mand at a time. The division by classes was given up, and all the heavy armed troops were equipped alike, an oblong wooden shield covered with leather and protecting the whole body (*scutum*), being now substituted for the round brass *clipeus*.

Order of Battle. — The arrangement of the maniples when in order of battle was what was known as the *quincunx*. The army was formed in three ranks, the maniples of one standing behind the spaces of that in front; by this it was possible to withdraw the front line and advance those in the rear through the spaces between the maniples. The three ranks were distinguished from one another in age and equipment, and a regular system of reserves was adopted, the three lines coming successively into action.[1]

The Cavalry. — The cavalry was always a secondary concern with the Romans, except in the very earliest period; but at the time of the war with Veii the practice came up of having a corps of volunteer cavalry (*equites equo privato*), composed of wealthy young men who had not found admittance into the eighteen centuries of public cavalry. In the course of time both bodies of cavalry became mere parade corps, while the Romans depended upon their auxiliaries for an active cavalry force.

The Battle of the Allia. — Six years after the conquest of Veii a terrible disaster befell the Roman people. Their city was captured and burned by an army of Gauls, who had come into collision with the Romans in the following manner. These Gauls had attacked the Etruscan city of Clusium, which was friendly to Rome, and the Romans had sent ambassadors to intercede for their allies. But the ambassadors, in contempt of their sacred character and obligations, took part in the battle on the side of the Etruscans, and one of them even slew a Gallic leader. At this the Gauls were so incensed that they turned their assault from Clusium against the nation of the faithless ambassadors. The two armies met, July 18, 390,[2] upon the River Allia, about eleven

---

[1] The soldiers of the first rank were called *hastati*, the second *principes*, the third *triarii*. This is the organization found in the Samnite and Punic Wars.

[2] This is the date usually given; really it was about three years later.

miles from Rome; and the Romans sustained a defeat so unexpected and overwhelming, that this day (*dies Alliensis*) was always afterwards regarded as one of ill omen. The Roman army was destroyed. The survivors mostly escaped to the abandoned city of Veii near by, the fortifications of which were still standing, and here maintained themselves; the magistrates and able-bodied men within the city withdrew into the Capitol, while the rest of the population scattered into the country and the neighboring towns.

Capture of the City. — The Gauls advanced slowly and cautiously into the city. They could not believe that it would be taken without another battle, and they feared an ambuscade. But they met no resistance. The streets and houses were deserted. At last they found their way to the Senate-house; and here they found the senators, who had disdained to fly, seated in their usual order. At first they stood and gazed upon them with awe. Then a Gallic soldier laid his hand upon the white beard of a senator and stroked it. The senator, regarding it as an indignity, raised his ivory staff, and struck him upon the head. This broke the spell which the sight of the dignified assembly seemed to have cast over the invaders; the senators were speedily massacred, and the city given up to pillage. The victors burned all parts of it within their reach, and in this conflagration perished most of the records of the earlier history.

Siege of the Capitol. — The Capitol still held out, and was stoutly besieged for seven months. At one time the besiegers nearly succeeded in capturing the garrison. A messenger from the Roman army at Veii scaled the rocky sides of the hill by night. His tracks were seen, and the next night the Gauls followed his footprints, and made their way nearly to the top. But the garrison were waked by the cackling of the sacred geese in the temple of Juno, and under the lead of Marcus Manlius, a distinguished patrician, repulsed the invaders. Another incident of the siege is the daring act of Kæso Fabius, a young man who passed in open day from the Capitol to the Quirinal Hill, in order to accomplish a certain religious ceremony which was due at that date, and then returned to the garrison. It would seem that the Gauls were so impressed by his boldness and his sanctity, that they allowed him to pass without question.

End of the Siege. — The Gauls, as is well known, were a people prompt and courageous in attack, but lacking in persistence; and it could hardly have been expected that they should keep up the siege without discouragement for so long a time. At last news came to them that the Venetians, a tribe of northeastern Italy, were invading their territory, and they readily agreed to a treaty, by which they withdrew from the city upon the payment of one thousand pounds of gold. To raise this sum the women contributed their jewels and ornaments, and received as a recompense the right to ride in carriages in the streets of the city.

Rebuilding of the City. — Rome was now in ruins, and a few miles distant stood a large, well-built city, empty of inhabitants. It is not surprising that many of the plebeians wished to abandon the desolated spot, and transfer their government and residences to the site of Veii. But attachment to their fatherland, regard for the sacred auspices of the city, and the consideration of the peculiar advantages of the situation of Rome, prevailed; an inland town, like Veii, could never have attained to the imperial greatness of the city upon the Tiber. As soon as it was decided that they should remain in their old home, they energetically went to work to rebuild their houses. The city provided bricks without cost, and in the haste of building no pains were taken to observe carefully the course of the streets and sewers, or even the precise boundary lines of property, but every man was allowed to build very much as he pleased. The consequence was that Rome was a network of narrow, crooked streets, with very high houses; and no remedy was found for the irregularity until after the ground was burned over again in the great conflagration of
A.D. 64.   Nero.

Advance of the Roman Power. — It is one of the marvels of history that this great calamity appears hardly to have checked for a moment the advance of the Roman power. Her enemies rose on all sides, expecting to crush her in her distress: the Volscians, the Æquians, and the Etruscans all at once assailed her. But the hero Camillus was again made dictator, and by rapid and masterly movements defeated the three enemies, one after the other. The wars continued, however, at intervals, for several years, and even the old allies of Rome, the Latins, now united themselves with their old enemies. Out of it all Rome came victorious. The fertile territory of Pometia, now the *Pontine Marshes*, was conquered from the Volscians; B.C. 386. new military colonies were established,[1] more dependent upon Rome than the older ones; and the nearest Latin town, Tusculum, an old and faithful ally, whose timely succor had saved the city when surprised by Appius Herdonius B.C. 381. (p. 56), was annexed to Rome. In this period of glory we see a new activity in public works, for the first time since the age of the Tarquins. Part of the walls were rebuilt of hewn stone, and the Capitoline Hill was faced in the same material.

Camillus. — This period may be fitly called the age of Camillus, for this great general lived to an advanced age, the most conspicuous character among his countrymen, and closely connected with every important event. He was a man of genius and of unquestionable integrity. To him is no doubt due the reform in military organization which laid the foundation of the great empire of Rome (p. 67); he was at the same time the leading champion of patrician privileges, and near the end of his life took an active part in resisting the innovations of the Licinian laws. He has been compared to the Duke of Wellington, who, like him, gained his reputation in the field, and then distinguished himself as the leader of the conservatives in an unsuccessful resistance to reform. The chief faults of Camillus were arrogance and ostentation. One of his numerous triumphs he celebrated in a chariot drawn by white horses, an honor which properly belonged only to Jupiter and the sun-god. On this account he incurred the displeasure of the common people, who condemned him on some pretext to

---

[1] B.C. 393, Circeii; 383, Sutrium and Nepete; 382, Setia.

pay a heavy fine — either for neglect of their interests in disposing of the plunder of Veii, or for the impiety displayed in his triumph.[1]

Distress of the Common People. — But in all the splendor and glory which surrounded Rome and her aristocracy, the common people were reduced to extreme distress by the devastations of the wars. At no time were the exactions of the money-lenders, and the horrors of the law of debt, so keenly felt as in the years which followed the burning of the city by the Gauls. It is related that a leading patrician, Marcus Manlius — the most conspicuous person in Rome next to Camillus — tried to remedy the distress of the poor, just as had been done by Spurius Cassius, exactly a hundred years before. By his own means he redeemed numbers of unfortunate debtors, paying off their debts, and restoring them to freedom. It would seem that he was not contented with this, but was excited by his sympathy into actual sedition; however this may be, he was, like Cassius, accused of aiming at royal power, and was put to death for treason.[2]

B.C. 384.

Renewal of Civil Contests. — Thus, after a long interval of calm, the social dissensions broke out again, — a twofold contest this time, poor against rich, plebeians against patricians. The contest was begun by two eminent plebeians, — Lucius Sextius and Gaius Licinius Stolo, a member of the same distinguished family as the first plebeian military tribune,[3] and also connected by marriage with patricians of the highest rank. These two men, as tribunes, proposed a series of laws, a kind of "Omnibus

---

[1] The annals of these years are exceedingly confused, and the story of Camillus, as well as of the capture of Rome, is full of fabulous incidents, among which we may probably count his exile to Ardea, his rescue of Rome from the Gauls, and his recovery from them of the tribute money.

[2] There was a third "demagogue," who ranked in tradition with Cassius and Manlius — Spurius Mælius, who in the year B.C. 439, in a time of great scarcity, relieved the necessities of the poor from his own means, and was put to death on the charge of treasonable designs — not by legal trial, like the two others, but by the authority of the dictator.

[3] This family also produced two of the most distinguished nobles of the last century of the republic, — Crassus and Lucullus.

Bill," which aimed to satisfy by one act of legislation the interests of all classes of plebeians, — at once relieving the debtors, remedying the abuses connected with the public lands, and admitting the plebeians to the magistracies.

Triumph of the Plebs. — The contest was long and bitter. For ten years in succession Licinius and Sextius were re-elected to the tribunate; the obstructive power of the tribunes and the imperial authority of consuls and dictators were pitted against each other, and more than once brought the state to actual anarchy.[1] At last the patricians were forced to yield, and a compromise was made, the chief advantage of which was with the plebeians. The Licinian rogations were passed, with some amendments, and, in celebration of the era of good feeling thus brought B.C. 367. about, the aged Camillus vowed and dedicated a temple to Harmony (*Concordia*),[2] at the head of the Forum.

The Licinian Laws. — The provisions of the Licinian laws were six in number:

1. Consuls were in future to be elected, one of whom must be a plebeian; legally both might be, but in practice one was regularly a patrician.

2. The college of priests having charge of the Sibylline books was divided between the two orders.

3. The interest already paid upon debts was to be deducted from the principal, and the balance to be paid up in three years.

4. The occupation of the public land was thrown open to plebeians, but no person was to occupy more than 500 *jugera* (about 250 acres).

5. No person should have upon the public pasture more than 100 head of large cattle and 500 head of sheep or goats.

6. In the cultivation of great estates it was required that only

---

[1] The annals of this period show an interregnum of five years, not historically to be depended upon, but an indication of the anarchy of the times.

[2] The foundations of this temple are still preserved, between the Arch of Septimius Severus and the Tabularium.

a certain proportion of slave labor should be employed; for the rest there must be free laborers.

The Magistracies. — The chief magistracy was thus thrown open to the plebeians, and with this the long contest between the orders came to an end. It is true that, as a concession to the patricians, the consulship, when thrown open to the plebeians, was deprived for a second time of an important part of its functions, which were given to a new patrician magistrate. The administration of justice in civil cases was put into the hands of a new magistrate known as *Prætor;* and the prætor, as well as the censor, dictator, and interrex, must be patricians. Also two patrician ædiles (called *curule ædiles*) were elected, to match the plebeian ædiles. But now that plebeians had been admitted to the highest regular magistracy, it was impossible to exclude them long from the inferior ones. Within half a century all these offices, except that of interrex, which was patrician in its very nature, were thrown open to the plebeians, and shortly after all the priesthoods of importance were also open to them.[1]

The Social Legislation. — The social provisions of the Licinian laws were less effective. The unjust law of debt was not abolished or amended, but a temporary amelioration was applied to the present distresses. The three last provisions of the law were wisely devised, and showed a correct understanding of the social dangers; but no machinery was provided for their execution, and they rapidly became a dead letter. One of the first who was punished for occupying more land than the law permitted, was the first proposer of the law, Gaius Licinius. But notwithstanding the inadequacy of these laws, so far as the causes of social evils were concerned, the Roman people now entered upon so rapid and triumphant a career of victory and economic prosperity, that it was nearly two hundred years before social questions again became a large factor in political controversies.

---

[1] These were the offices of pontifex, augur, and *epulones*. The *rex sacrificulus*, chief flamens, etc., were always patricians.

PERIOD OF ITALIAN WARS.

CHAPTER VI.

THE CONQUEST OF LATIUM.

Relations of the Orders. — The relations between the patricians and plebeians during the thirty years which followed the passage of the Licinian laws were jealous and uneasy, but free from any open disturbance. It was natural that the patricians should continue to resist the advance of plebeian privileges, and on the other hand it is not surprising that the plebeians were timid in the exercise of their new powers. More than once the patrician magistrates, by sheer audacity — refusing to receive votes for plebeian candidates[1] — succeeded in preventing the election of plebeian magistrates; the plebeians were indignant, but helpless. But they grew bolder and acquired political experience; B.C. 339. and at last, to the horror of the patricians, a plebeian dictator was appointed, with a plebeian master of the horse.

The Publilian Laws of Philo. — The decisive victory of the plebeians, definitely securing the advantages gained by the Licinian Laws, came in the year 339, when the plebeian dictator, Quintus Publilius Philo, procured the passage of three laws of the greatest importance to his order. The first enlarged the powers of the plebeian assembly in some way not definitely known; the second took from the patrician members of the Senate the power of nullifying laws on the ground of unconstitutionality (p. 39); the third required that one of the two censors should be a plebeian. From this time, as will readily appear, the plebeians possessed even greater privileges than the patricians: for they had an assembly and officers of their own from which patricians were excluded, while they were themselves admitted to all the patrician offices.

---

[1] The presiding magistrate had a large and undefined power in this direction.

Usury Laws. — The Licinian legislation had not altered the unjust laws of debt, but had only offered a temporary remedy for its abuses; and the years which followed were full of complaints of usurers, and attempts to regulate the trade of money-lending. The legal rate of interest was reduced from ten to five per cent, and at last the business of money-lending was forbidden.[1] This was one of those well-meaning but impracticable enactments of which the history of legislation is full; it was probably never executed, and at any rate it soon became a dead letter.

Growth of Territory. — Meantime the Roman power was steadily growing, and the Roman territory steadily enlarging. The most important acquisition of territory during this period was the Etruscan city of Cære. As its Etruscan inhabitants were of foreign blood and speech, they did not receive full Roman citizenship. They were allowed to govern themselves in local concerns, but not to take part in the public affairs of Rome. This inferior form of citizenship was entitled "citizenship without suffrage," or "Cæritan rights," and was afterwards bestowed upon a number of other towns.

B.C. 353.

The Gallic Wars. — During this period the Gauls resumed their invasions, and for many years gave much annoyance to the Romans and other Latins. The accounts of these Gallic wars are enlivened by many heroic and romantic incidents, which are no doubt derived from family chronicles and popular songs. Thus the name of the hero Marcus Valerius Corvus is said to have been derived from the fact that he fought in single combat with a gigantic Gaul, and was assisted by a raven (*corvus*), which fluttered in the face of his antagonist, pecked at his eyes, etc., and thus distracted his attention. Titus Manlius Torquatus received his name, too, from a Gaul whom he slew, and whose necklace (*torques*) he stripped from the dead body and placed around his own neck.[2]

---

[1] By the Genucian Law, B.C. 342.

[2] The twisted chain which the Gauls wore about the neck is seen on the famous statue known as the Dying Gladiator, but which is now recognized to have represented a wounded Gaul, a work of the Pergamene period of art.

Treaty with the Samnites. — The growing power of Rome is evidenced by the treaties of equal alliance which she framed in these years with two powerful neighbors, both of whom afterwards became her most bitter enemies. These were the Samnites and the Carthaginians. The Samnite Confederacy, occupying the mountain region of central Italy, was now the most powerful nation of the Italian race. The Samnites had not long before conquered the Etruscan settlements in Campania, B.C. 424. of which the chief town was Capua, thus giving the first blow to the Etruscan ascendancy in Italy. On the other hand, by the conquest of the Pomptine territory, the B.C. 386. Romans became neighbors of the Samnites in Campania, and the two nations, in B.C. 354, now entered into a treaty of friendship and alliance.

Treaty with Carthage. — A few years later a treaty B.C. 348. was made with the Carthaginians, at this time the greatest maritime power in the western Mediterranean. A treaty had once before been made between Rome and Carthage (p. 35), when Rome was at the height of its commercial activity, just after the expulsion of the kings; but for long years the attention of the Romans had been engrossed by affairs nearer home, and the treaty now made was to all intents and purposes a new compact. By this treaty the authority of Rome over the Latin cities was recognized, and they were allowed to trade with Carthage and the Carthaginian possessions in Sicily, Sardinia, and Corsica, but were forbidden to sail beyond the bay of Carthage, or to trade in Spain.

First Samnite War. — The treaty with the Samnites did not prevent a war between the two nations, which broke out only eleven years later. It was a short war, and our B.C. 343. accounts of it are too confused and fragmentary to enable us to understand its events in detail. Its most important result was to bring the city of Capua under the power of Rome. The territory of this great city was annexed to the Roman domain, and its inhabitants received the same rights as those of Cære (p. 78).

This war was immediately followed by another of much greater moment, but extremely obscure in its causes and incidents.

The Latin War. — The cities which composed the Latin Confederacy had long been dissatisfied at the growing preponderance of Rome, and its arrogant treatment of its allies. The conquest of Veii had inured only to the advantage of Rome, and had been followed by the conquest of the Pomptine territory, the annexation of Tusculum, Capena, and Cære, and the establishment of Latin colonies (Sutrium and Nepete), which were connected only with Rome.[1] The triumph of Rome over the Samnites, and the annexations of territory in Campania, excited still greater alarm among the Latins, and they made an effort to secure fair treatment before it should be too late. First they demanded that half the Senate and one of the two consuls should be Latins; and when this demand was rejected, they tried to enforce it by war. This war, too, was short and decisive; the principal battle was fought at Trifanum in Campania, and the war was ended two years later, B.C. 338.

Dissolution of the Latin Confederacy. — The Latin War, short and obscure as it was, marks the most important era in the development of the Roman policy. By it the *hegemony* or leadership of Rome was converted into an *empire* (*imperium*). The Latin Confederacy was dissolved: four of its members — Tibur, Præneste, Cora, and Laurentum — were left independent, but forbidden to enter into any alliances with one another, while Aricia, Lanuvium, Pedum, and Nomentum lost their independence and were annexed to Rome.[2] But the treatment which these received was liberal and magnanimous. They were associated with Rome on terms of perfect equality; their territory became part of the Ager Romanus, and their citizens became Roman plebeians; while in their own towns they continued to exercise full powers of self-government in

---

[1] These later colonies did not belong to the Latin Confederacy.

[2] Labicum, Pometia, and Tusculum had been annexed before, and Ardea had been made a Latin colony; Velitræ, originally a Volscian town, received *Cæritan rights*.

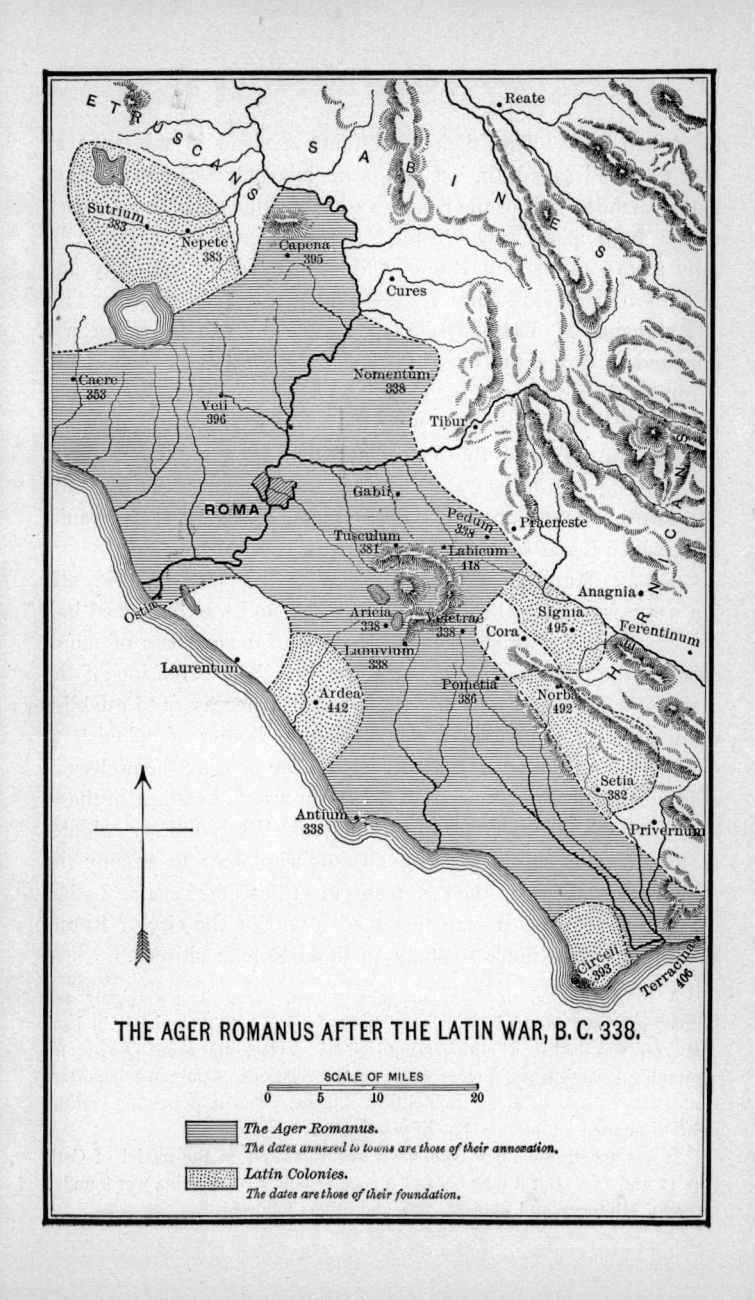

THE AGER ROMANUS AFTER THE LATIN WAR, B.C. 338.

local concerns.[1] Thus their inhabitants received in substance all that they had asked for, but in a more advantageous form. They had demanded half of the Senate and half of the magistrates, which would have made a two-headed state. It was far better to be fully incorporated with Rome, and thus maintain the unity and integrity of the body politic.

Extension of Latium. — At the same time that Latium was annexed to Rome, the towns further along the coast — Fundi and Formiæ — were also annexed as *municipia* of the second grade, possessing Cæritan rights — with local self-government, but without Roman suffrage. By this the territory of Rome was made to extend unbroken to its Campanian possessions, and from this time the name Latium embraced the whole country as far as Campania, from which it was separated by the river Vulturnus.

Maritime Colonies. — Antium was treated differently from the other conquered towns, and was organized in a manner which became the type of a new class of municipality, the *Maritime* or *Roman Colony*. The extension of the Roman possessions along the coast made it necessary to establish naval stations, by planting at suitable points bodies of colonists to occupy the soil as settlers, at the same time holding themselves in readiness to defend the coast.[2] Antium was the earliest of these. The maritime colonies thus formed resembled the military colonies of the inland; only, while the citizens who went to occupy the military posts gave up their Roman citizenship and became Latins, the maritime colonies were reckoned a part of the city of Rome, and the colonists remained fully qualified Roman citizens.

B.C. 338.

---

[1] A town annexed to Rome on these terms, losing its sovereignty and becoming a part of the Roman state, but retaining self-government in local concerns, was called a *municipium*. This device, the *municipality*, for combining local self-government with imperial relations, is the most important contribution made by Rome to political science. Towns possessing Cæritan rights composed an inferior class of *municipia*.

[2] It was not strictly a new type, for it was organized on the model of Ostia (pp. 12 and 17). But it now became a regular policy. Tarracina was founded B.C. 329, Minturnæ and Sinuessa 296, and others followed.

THE ROMAN FORUM.

Adornment of the Forum. — The sea-port of Antium was thus converted into a maritime colony of Rome; and in token of the victory and of the new policy of which it was an example, the ships of its navy were broken up and their beaks (*rostra*) conveyed to Rome, where they were used to ornament the speaker's stand, opposite the Senate-house, on the line between the Comitium and the Forum. From this time the speaker's stand was known as the *Rostra*. This was the work of the plebeian consul Gaius Mænius, who also erected a column B.C. 339. upon the Comitium, known as the Mænian column, at which the police officers punished wrong-dealers, and which also came to be used as an advertising board, to post the names of delinquent debtors.

Relief of the Forum. — This same Mænius appears to have been the first who, in his censorship, undertook B.C. 318. systematically to give the Forum some regularity and elegance as a public square. It was at first a bare open space, where country people brought their produce to sell, and the prætor sat on his curule chair to administer justice in the midst of the crowd. In the course of time the cattle market (*Forum Boarium*) and vegetable market (*Forum Holitorium*) had been established near the river, and the Great Forum left for more reputable trade. Booths had been built along both sides of it, which rudely enclosed the space; and now Mænius required these booths to be made more regular and shapely, and constructed upon their tops some stagings called *maenianae*, which commanded a view of the Forum, and were let to spectators when games and other exhibitions were given in the Forum. The Forum became from this time more and more the centre of political life, as well as of judicial proceedings, and of such branches of business as those of brokers, bankers, and jewellers.

CHAPTER VII.

THE CONQUEST OF ITALY.

I. THE SECOND SAMNITE WAR.

The Samnite Wars. — The First Samnite War and the Latin War, by very greatly enlarging the territory of the republic, by dissolving the Latin Confederacy, and by converting the leadership of Rome in Latium into a sovereignty over Latium, form the most important era which we have yet reached in tracing the growth of the Roman empire. There now followed a series of three wars, known as the Second and Third Samnite Wars, and the War with Pyrrhus, the result of which was to expand the sovereignty over Latium into a sovereignty over all Italy. These three wars occupied, with brief intervals of peace, a period of more than fifty years; and with the final defeat of Pyrrhus in the battle of Beneventum, the conquest of Italy may be said to have been completed.

B.C. 275.

Romans and Samnites. — The events which we have described had made Rome one of the two foremost powers of Italy, having no formidable rival left but Samnium; for Etruria had been losing strength for nearly a century, and was no longer a match for her warlike neighbor. The annexations of territory made by Rome had brought her into immediate contact with the Samnites, and war could hardly fail to follow. In this war the combatants were nearly matched. In ambition, vigor, and martial qualities they were perhaps equal. In population and extent of territory, and therefore in warlike resources, the Samnites were superior; but this superiority was more than counterbalanced by the advantages which the Romans derived from their greater power of concentration. The Samnites formed a loosely knit confederacy, spread over a large surface of territory, and incapable of prompt and sustained co-operation. All the resources of Rome, on the other hand, were concentrated within the walls of the city, and lodged in the hands of magistrates who for the time being exercised almost absolute authority. At a later time, when the Romans were confronted with generals like Pyrrhus and Hannibal, who held command uninterruptedly year after year, their annual change of magistrates proved a source of great weakness; but their present antagonists were in this respect no better off than themselves. With this advantage of centralized power, it is no wonder that Rome triumphed in the Samnite Wars.

SAMNITE WARRIOR. (From a Vase.)

Second Samnite War.—The Second Samnite War began B.C. 327 and ended 304, when a peace was made which was hardly more than a truce, for war broke out again in six years. By this peace the Romans gained no new territory, although they had from time to time, in the course of the hostilities, founded military posts (Latin colonies) in the enemies' country; but these towns were of Latin nationality, not subject to Rome, although closely allied with it. In 306 the Hernican confederacy, which had joined the alliance against Rome, was dissolved, as that of the Latins had been a few years before, and most of its towns were annexed to Rome; but three of them,[1] when offered the privilege of complete Roman citizenship, declined it with thanks, preferring their humble independence.

Quintus Fabius Maximus. — The greatest Roman of this period was Quintus Fabius, called Maximus (greatest) because of his services to the state. He was a bitter personal enemy of Papirius Cursor, and a warm friend of Decius Mus, whom he had as colleague in several high offices. The hostility between Papirius and Fabius came about in this way. In one of the early years B.C. 325. of the war Papirius, then the foremost man in Rome, was dictator, and the youthful Fabius was his master of horse.[2] It happened that the dictator was called to Rome on some necessary business, and before leaving gave strict orders that there should be no fighting in his absence. This order the high-spirited Fabius disobeyed, and gained a signal victory over the enemy. Papirius was a strict disciplinarian. When he learned of the disobedience of Fabius he promptly hastened to the camp, leaving his business at Rome unfinished, sternly summoned the offender before him and sentenced him to immediate execution. The army, elated with its victory, and proud of its gallant young commander, rose in mutiny; Fabius was rescued and carried to Rome where, after long and stubborn resistance, Papirius at last, at the entreaty of the Senate, agreed that the ends of justice had been reached by the condemnation of Fabius, and consented to exercise his prerogative of mercy by sparing his life.

Lucius Papirius Cursor. — But the two men were B.C. 310. never afterwards friends. A few years later Fabius, as consul, was called upon to appoint Papirius dictator; he neither answered the messengers of the Senate, nor even looked at them, and when he had performed the required duty, gloomily rejected their thanks. Papirius was a typical Roman of his time,

---

[1] These were Aletrium, Ferentinum, and Verulæ.

[2] The master of horse (*magister equitum*) was second in command to the dictator.

— of mighty physical strength, untiring, never defeated, inexorable, and at the same time with a certain grim humor. On one occasion a body of contingents from Præneste had not supported him to his mind. He summoned their commander to his tent, and called to the lictor to bring an axe; and as the officer stood pale and trembling, expecting immediate execution, he ordered a troublesome stump to be hewn away; then dismissed the offender with severe reproof.

The Caudine Forks. — The most striking incident of this war was the capture of the entire Roman army, in the year 321, at the Caudine Forks, a pass in the Apennines, a few miles beyond Capua.[1] The successful Samnite general, it is said, Gaius Pontius, sent to ask the advice of his father, an aged and experienced commander, as to what he should do with the captured army. His advice was to dismiss it unharmed; and, when this was rejected, he recommended that every man should be put to death, — by the first course he would earn their gratitude, by the other deprive them of the power of vengeance. But Pontius, neglecting his father's advice, determined to subject his captives to the deepest humiliation, by sending them under the yoke,[2] the greatest disgrace which could be inflicted; then forced the leaders to agree to a disadvantageous peace, and sent them home. But by the Roman law no treaty was valid unless accepted by a vote of the people. The Senate therefore refused to recognize the agreement, and ordered the consuls to be surrendered to the enemy, as amends for the violation of the agreement which they had personally made. Pontius, as was natural, indignantly refused to accept such an atonement for a broken engagement, and the war went on with increased bitterness.

[1] The locality of this event has been a subject of great controversy. The *Furculæ Caudinæ* were probably at the pass of Arpaja, where the village of *Forchia* still preserves the name; and the army was entrapped in the valley beyond this and Montesarchio, which town is upon the site of the ancient Caudium.

[2] The yoke was constructed by fixing two spears in the ground, and laying a third over their top; under this the whole army was obliged to pass.

War with the Etruscans. — After the war with the Samnites had continued for a number of years, hostilities broke out with the Etruscans also. This once powerful nation was now in a state of decline, and had even suffered its two southernmost cities, Veii and Cære, to be conquered by Rome. The conquest of these cities had extended the Roman frontier about thirty miles to the north, where a rugged mountain range, known as the Ciminian Forest, separated the two nations. This frontier was protected by the military colonies of Sutrium and Nepete, founded just after the conquest of Veii (p. 68).

B.C. 311.

The Ciminian Forest. — The Etruscans, passing through the forest, undertook the siege of Sutrium. The consul Quintus Fabius, advancing against them, relieved the city, drove the enemy before him, and then pursued them with all his forces through the forest, — a region almost unknown to the Romans, — gained a brilliant victory, and then returned in triumph. There was great consternation and almost a panic at Rome when the daring consul disappeared with his army in this unknown wilderness; but his audacity was justified by the results. This was the last campaign of any moment ever carried on by the Romans against the Etruscans.

B.C. 310.

The Disqualified Classes. — The period of this war is marked by political changes of great importance. The Publilian Laws (p. 77) had gained for the rural plebeians nearly all the rights which they needed, and placed them practically on an equality with the patricians. But the plebeians of the city were still under great disqualifications. None but land-owners could belong to the tribes, and therefore to the tribal assemblies: by this not only the rabble of the city, but the well-to-do and reputable traders and handicraftsmen, were excluded from political privileges. In the centuriate assembly five centuries were provided for these; but the tribal organization made no provision for them at all. Worst of all was the condition of the freedmen, or emancipated slaves, a class which rendered the chief part of those professional and administrative services which are among the most important

B.C. 338.

and highly paid at the present day, such as teachers, physicians, secretaries, and stewards. For it must be understood that the slaves of the Romans were not an inferior, semi-barbarous class, but contained many persons superior to their masters in education and culture, — Greeks, Sicilians, Carthaginians, and, perhaps already, Asiatics.

Censorship of Appius Claudius: 1. The Senate. — Appius Claudius, a patrician of high rank, came forward as the champion of these disqualified classes, and by his innovations made his censorship an epoch in the history of the city. The censors had been recently entrusted with the duty of drawing up the Senate-list, which had before devolved upon the consuls. In preparing his list Appius included the names of some sons of freedmen. It struck the conservative and aristocratic Romans with horror, and his colleague in the censorship refused to act with him; so that, by a stretch of audacity, Appius conducted his censorship alone, in violation of all the principles of the constitution.[1] He even continued to exercise the office after the expiration of the eighteen months, on the ground that the election was properly (as it had been originally) for the entire *lustrum*, of five years. But while the censor had the power to draw up the list of senators, he could not oblige the consul to accept it. The consuls of the following year refused to recognize the validity of the changes made by Appius, and convened the senate by the list of the previous year.

B.C. 312.

2. Reorganization of the Tribes. — A second revolutionary measure of this censorship was almost as short lived. By a single act of authority as censor, he deprived landed property of its exclusive right to determine political qualifications, and based these qualifications upon the possession of property of any kind; the right of every citizen to vote and to bear arms was to be determined by the entire amount of his property, not by his landed property

---

[1] The principle of *collegiality*, by which two colleagues exercised co-equal powers — as consuls, censors, military tribunes, etc. — was fundamental in the institutions of the republic.

alone. This rule continued in operation until the censorship of Quintus Fabius, eight years later, who left all the citizens in the enjoyment of the suffrage which they had obtained, but for future citizenship established a distinction between the four city and the twenty-seven[1] rural tribes. The rural tribes were, as heretofore, to contain only land-owners; all other citizens were to be rated and to vote in the city tribes, which now came to be regarded as inferior in rank to the others. By this conservative act Fabius earned the title of Maximus (greatest).

B.C. 304.

3. Public Works. — Appius Claudius was equally distinguished for the system of public works inaugurated in his censorship. He brought to Rome the first regular supply of water, from a point seven or eight miles distant, by the so-called Appian Aqueduct. The system thus begun was carried out by his successors at various times, so that Rome became in antiquity, as it is still, distinguished for the excellence and abundance of its water supply. He also built the first military road, the famous Appian Way, from Rome to Capua, most of the way along the coast, the whole of the intervening country being now Roman territory. This road was so solidly and substantially built that long stretches of it are still preserved in good condition. The system of military roads commenced by Appius Claudius was also continued and extended by his successors, until all Italy, and, indeed, the provinces also,[2] were covered with a network of well-built highways connecting with the city the chief colonies and allied towns.

4. Religious Innovations. — Appius Claudius was no less an innovator in religious matters. The worship of Hercules was until his time a gentile cult, conducted by the two families of the Potitii and Pinarii; at his solicitation the Potitii sold the ritual, and it was made a public cult administered by slaves. It was believed that, as a consequence of this act of impiety, the Potitian

---

[1] This was the present number of tribes; two were added after the Second Samnite War, and two after the First Punic.

[2] Roman milestones, marking a Roman military road, have recently been discovered in the Syrian desert.

gens speedily died out. In his censorship the guild of pipers was deprived of an old privilege of banqueting in the temple of Jupiter. Indignant at the affront, the entire guild retired to Tibur, and refused to return. As its services were indispensable in the religious ceremonies, the magistrates were in great embarrassment. No nation was ever more precise than the Romans in the exercise of religious formalities, and now, as in a mediæval interdict, neither festival, nor sacrifice, nor funeral could be duly performed. At last the Tiburtines devised the plan of making the pipers drunk, loading them in carts, and conveying them in this condition to Rome. When they woke from their debauch and found themselves upon the Forum, they readily agreed to remain, but upon conditions which their recent experience forced the Romans to accept. Their former privilege was restored to the pipers, and they also received the right every 13th of June to go through the streets in a procession like a carnival, — tipsy, disguised with masks and grotesque garments, and making all the noise they pleased.

Gnæus Flavius. — Another important innovation of this period was the publication of the formulas of legal procedure, together with the calendar of court days, by Gnæus Flavius, a freedman of Appius Claudius. This information had been until this time in the sole possession of the patricians, who, by this exclusive knowledge, had a great advantage in the administration of the law. Flavius, being a clerk in the employ of the ædiles, had an opportunity to make himself acquainted with these secrets; and in the year of the peace he was himself chosen B.C. 304. curule ædile, the first person of his rank ever elected to a curule office. In all these things Appius Claudius showed himself indifferent to precedent and privilege, and a favorer of the disqualified classes in the city. As to the rural plebeians, on the other hand, who were now rapidly becoming the most powerful body in the state, he was their active opponent; his controversy with their leader, Manius Curius Dentatus, was the last incident in the long struggle between patricians and plebeians.

II. The Third Samnite War.

Union of Italy against Rome. — The Third Samnite
B.C. 298. War was an uprising of the Italian nations to prevent, if
not too late, the threatening domination of Rome, which
the last war had proved to be the strongest power in Italy. The
Etruscans, Umbrians, and Gauls, as well as the lesser nations of
central Italy, united under the lead of the Samnites; only the
Lucanians stood with Rome. The war was short, ending in 290
with the complete discomfiture of the Samnites. By the treaty
of peace now made, as by that of 304, the Romans abstained from
adding any large amount of Samnite territory to their domain,
contenting themselves with planting Latin colonies at important
military points. The colony of Venusia, established at the close
of the war on the borders of Apulia, was of unprecedented proportions,
consisting of 20,000 settlers. Its size and its situation,
in the rear of Samnium, made it the chief agency in holding the
Samnites in subjection, and it was an important strategic point
in the war with Hannibal.

Battle of Sentinum. — The chief battle of the war was fought
at Sentinum, in Umbria, in the year 295. The consuls of this
year were the tried friends and colleagues, Quintus Fabius Maximus
and Publius Decius Mus. Fortunately for the Romans, a
diversion in Etruria had led the Etruscan troops to abandon their
allies and hasten to protect their homes; for some reason the
Umbrians too took no part in the battle, and the Samnites and
Gauls were left alone. Even as it was, the battle was for a long
time doubtful. Fabius held his own against the Samnites, but the
impetuous Gauls threw into confusion the left wing, commanded
by Decius. The defeated consul then resolved, according to
ancestral custom, to devote himself to the infernal gods, and thus
by the sacrifice of himself to gain a victory for his country. Calling
upon the pontiff, Marcus Livius, who was present, to dictate to
him the formula of self-devotion, he repeated the words in due

order, calling down the wrath of the gods upon himself and also upon the enemy; then spurred his horse into the thickest of the enemy, and fell pierced by their weapons. His death had the desired effect. His soldiers were incited to renewed efforts, and soon drove the Gauls before them in flight.[1]

Annexations of Territory. — The battle of Sentinum was the most considerable in the whole course of the Samnite wars. Hostilities continued, however, for five years longer. In the year 290 the consulship was held by the distinguished Manius Curius Dentatus, who inflicted a final defeat upon the Samnites, and afterwards subdued the Sabines, who had joined with the enemies of Rome. For these victories he celebrated two triumphs in the same year. The Samnites were left in possession of their independence, and became allies of Rome. The Sabines were forced to become Roman citizens, although they did not receive the right of suffrage until several years later: their territory became a part of the *ager Romanus*, which was now extended to the Adriatic Sea. Thus the Roman territory, stretching in a broad belt from sea to sea, wholly cut off the Samnites and allied nations to the south from the Umbrians, Gauls, and Etruscans to the north.[2] The Latin colony of Hatria was founded at this point upon the Adriatic Sea, and a few years later another large district upon this sea, the Picene territory (*Picenum*), was annexed by Rome.

B.C. 268.

Manius Curius Dentatus. — Manius Curius was a peasant by birth, and may be taken as a typical example of a Roman of the old stamp. During the generation in which he was the leading statesman and general of Rome, he never abandoned the interests

---

[1] It is related that the father of Decius had devoted himself in a similar manner in a battle in the Latin War, B.C. 340. There is no impossibility, but on the other hand a high degree of probability, that the son was inspired to his heroic act by his father's example; but the accounts of the Latin War are confused and full of fabulous detail, while the battle of Sentinum is a thoroughly authentic event.

[2] See map of Central Italy at the time of the Second Punic War.

of his class, which he defended, at the very beginning of his public career, against Appius Claudius, the champion of patrician privileges (p. 91). When territory was annexed by Rome, he secured a large amount for the purpose of assignments (p. 49) to the soldiers of the war, refusing to take for himself more than the share of a common soldier. Like Appius Claudius, he distinguished himself by the extent and beneficence of his public works. Among these was the canal which drained a swampy district in the neighborhood of Reate, conducting its waters into the river Nar by a precipitous descent which we know as the beautiful waterfall of Terni; also the second Roman aqueduct, the *Anio Vetus*, forty-three miles long. He brought to a triumphant end not only the war with the Samnites, but also that with Pyrrhus. After this crowning victory, he retired to his farm in the Sabine country, where he lived the life of a common peasant.

B.C. 275.

Gaius Fabricius. — Next to Dentatus as a typical Roman, and perhaps even more distinguished, was Gaius Fabricius, a Hernican peasant, who by ability and integrity raised himself to a foremost place among the public men of his time. He was younger than Curius, the period of his activity being that of the war with Pyrrhus; and, while a skilful and successful soldier, he achieved his principal distinction a statesman and diplomatist. The straightforward and incorruptible republican proved himself (like Franklin and Jay at the court of Paris), a match for the subtle Greeks.

The Hortensian Law. — The long succession of wars, lasting with intervals over fifty years, had brought the Roman peasantry to a state of suffering and destitution similar to that which followed the Gallic invasion, and this was not adequately relieved even by the numerous colonies and the assignments of land made by Dentatus. Our knowledge of these events is very scanty.[1] All that is certain is that in the year 286 a third secession of the Plebs took place, this time to Mount Janiculum. By the influence of Dentatus, Quintus Hortensius was made dictator, and proposed

[1] There is a gap in Livy's history from near the end of the Second Samnite to the beginning of the Second Punic War.

the so-called Hortensian Law, by which the plebeian assembly received full and uncontrolled power to pass laws which should be valid for the whole body of citizens. Henceforth this assembly, presided over by the tribunes, became the usual law-making body.

The Roman Institutions. — The institutions of the republic had now reached their highest point of energy and efficiency. The contest between patricians and plebeians was at an end, and the two orders were on a practical equality. The patricians, it is true, were still alone eligible to certain priesthoods of great dignity and antiquity; but on the other hand the plebeians had what was far more important, the sole right to hold the offices of tribune and plebeian ædile, and to vote in their tribal assembly. The assembly of citizens — whether organized by tribes or by centuries — was by law the controlling authority in the state, and the magistrates exercised in their terms of office an almost unlimited executive and administrative power. But these assemblies and magistrates were themselves hardly more than the organs of the Senate, a body which, by unwritten law, was gradually gathering all power into its own hands.

The Senate. — The Senate was composed of three hundred members, the list being made out by the censors from *lustrum* to *lustrum*, and containing first the names of all who had held high office, and then of such others as were deemed competent.[1] They held their position for life, unless degraded by succeeding censors; and it is clear that a body of men like this, which embodied all the experience and tried statesmanship of the community, would exhibit a clearness of purpose and a persistency of policy which would easily control the yearly changing magistrates, and through them the assemblies of the people.

The Worship of Æsculapius. — In spite of the elevation of the city above the unhealthy country around, and the draining of its

[1] Only those who had held office were fully qualified senators; the others, relatively inexperienced in public business, had a right to vote, but not to debate. As voting was done by going into the lobbies (*pedibus ire*), these were known as *pedarii*.

low-lying parts by the great sewers, it was exposed to numerous pestilences, by the closeness of the streets, the want of systematic cleansing, and the habit of burying the dead within the walls.[1]

B.C. 291. After one of the severest of these, just before the close of the Third Samnite War, the Sibylline books advised that Æsculapius, the god of healing, should be invited from Epidaurus in Greece. The commissioners who were sent for this purpose were received courteously, and conducted to the famous shrine; here the legend says that the serpent, sacred to Æsculapius, at once followed them through the city and on board their ship, in which he was conveyed to Italy. Arrived at Rome, the serpent glided to the island in the Tiber, and here a temple was erected, which became a chief seat of the worship of the god. This is the fourth important Greek cult naturalized in Rome; Castor and Pollux, Apollo, and the Eleusinian Triad — Ceres, Liber, and Libera — had already been established there.

III. THE WAR WITH PYRRHUS.

Tarentum. — The authority of Rome was now established over the entire peninsula, with the exception of the northern portions occupied by Gauls, Ligurians, and Venetians (which were not reckoned properly a part of Italy), and the cities of Magna Græcia in the south. At the head of these Greek cities was Tarentum (the modern *Taranto*), a colony of Sparta, a commercial city of great wealth and enterprise, under democratic government. This city, probably the richest, and, next to Rome and Capua, the largest city of Italy, now made a last effort to check the domination of Rome over the peninsula; this was with the co-operation of Pyrrhus, king of Epirus, the greatest general of his time.

Outbreak of the War. — There was a treaty of peace between

---

[1] See Lanciani's *Ancient Rome in the Light of Recent Discoveries*, p. 64. It should be understood that the Romans in early times buried their dead, as many families did even after cremation had become usual; and that the poor, victims of pestilence, etc., were hurriedly thrown into huge pits.

Rome and Tarentum, similar to that with Carthage (p. 79), prohibiting the Romans from sending ships beyond the Lacinian promontory, on the southern coast of Italy. The Tarentines (like the Carthaginians in their treaty), wished to reserve this lucrative field of traffic to themselves. But the Romans, in the consciousness of their new power, were not to be checked in their natural expansion. Communication by sea with the Adriatic was essential to the security of their new possessions upon that sea. In deliberate violation of the treaty a Roman fleet appeared off the harbor of Tarentum.[1] War followed, and the Tarentines invited Pyrrhus to place himself at the head of an Italian coalition. B.C. 281.

Pyrrhus. — The oriental world was at this time in a state of turmoil and perpetual warfare. The empire of Alexander the Great had, since his death, broken into a number of fragments, and Pyrrhus was perhaps the ablest and most ambitious of the princes who at this time ruled over a part of these dominions. This invasion of Italy was in the very year of the defeat and death of the aged Lysimachus, king of Thrace, and of the final division of Alexander's empire. Pyrrhus brought with him to Italy a large body of soldiers, and twenty elephants — a new and strange antagonist to an Italian army, and one which, to a certain extent, served the purpose of modern field artillery. For a hundred years after this time the elephants played a large, and often a decisive, part in Roman warfare. B.C. 281.

Battle of Heraclea. — The first battle of the war was fought at Heraclea. In this battle the Roman cavalry gained the first advantage; but the compact phalanx of Pyrrhus was more than a match for the Roman legion, which was not skilfully handled; and the elephants, with their strange appearance and formidable advance, put the Romans to flight. But the losses of Pyrrhus were very great, and he was so impressed with the sturdiness and fighting qualities of his enemies, that he B.C. 280.

[1] This act was, in its intent, not unlike the violation by Russia of the provision of the Treaty of Paris, restricting its naval force in the Black Sea.

sent his most skilful diplomatist, Cineas, as an ambassador to Rome, to offer terms of peace.

Embassy of Cineas. — The embassy of Cineas made a deep impression upon the imagination and memory of the Romans. He was an orator of persuasive eloquence, who possessed the art of winning men to his friendship and confidence. His gifts were rejected, but his arguments were powerful, and the Senate was upon the point of voting to accept his terms, when the aged and blind Appius Claudius caused himself to be led into the assemblage, and declared that Rome should never treat for peace so long as a foreign enemy stood upon the soil of Italy. This speech was preserved as the earliest example of Roman eloquence, and was still read in the time of Cicero. It had its effect, and Cineas returned to his master with his work unaccomplished. Deeply impressed by the dignity and incorruptibility of the Roman statesmen, he pronounced Rome a temple, and the Senate an assembly of kings.

End of the War. — Pyrrhus was now joined by many of the Italian nations, and the following year gained another victory at Asculum. But this victory was followed by no decisive advantages, and in the same year he passed over to Sicily to defend his ally, the Greek city of Syracuse, against the Carthaginians who were in alliance with Rome. During the three years of his absence the Romans were engaged in chastising the Samnites and others who had joined with Pyrrhus. Upon his return to Italy the final and decisive battle of the war was fought in 275 at Beneventum, where Manius Curius gained a complete victory and brought the war to an end. Pyrrhus returned to Greece, where he shortly after lost his life.

B.C. 279.

The Roman Empire. — The result of this war was that the cities of Magna Græcia were brought within the empire of Rome, by entering into treaty relations, which bound them, like the Italian states, to furnish contingents in war to the Roman armies. The power of Rome now extended over the whole of Italy proper, and was organized as follows:

THE ITALIAN STATES.

I. The *Ager Romanus*, comprising about one-fourth of Italy, and consisting of:

1. The city of Rome and its territory, divided into thirty-three tribes (shortly afterwards increased to thirty-five), which formed the basis of voting and of financial administration. This territory and its tribes were scattered in all parts of Italy, wherever the citizens had received assignments of land.

2. The so-called Roman colonies (p. 82), consisting of Roman citizens, scattered along the sea-coast for its defence.[1] The colonists possessed full rights as citizens, and were members of the tribes, but were called on for no military duties except defence of the coast.

3. The *municipia* of best standing (p. 82). These had been admitted to full Roman citizenship, still retaining the rights of local self-government. These *municipia*, like the colonies mentioned above, were assigned to the several tribes.

4. The *municipia* of Cæritan rights (p. 78). The inhabitants of these communities had full civil rights, and local self-government, but had not the right of voting in Rome. The territories of towns of this class, as well as of that which follows (the præfectures), were of course not included in the tribes.

5. The præfectures (*præfecturae*); subject communities, which did not even retain local self-government, but were under præfects sent from Rome.

II. The independent communities, which were not in law subject to Rome, but which by treaty or by the terms of their foundation were required to support Rome with their military forces. These were:

1. The Latin colonies, at this time twenty-two in number.[2]

---

[1] There were at this time only seven of these, but the number was gradually raised to thirty-five, many of which were not upon the sea-coast.

[2] Thirteen others were afterwards founded, with inferior privileges. After the Second Punic War, it appears to have been difficult to persuade citizens to go to Latin colonies, thereby forfeiting their citizenship; they cease therefore from the year 180, and the colonies established after this date, whether on the coast or in the interior, received full Roman citizenship.

These were founded by Rome as permanent garrisons, and the colonists possessed certain important privileges, such as the right of acquiring Roman citizenship; they were however independent states, with the right of coining money, of harboring Roman exiles (*jus exili*), etc.

2. The allies (*socii* or *civitates foederatae*) : cities which, either individually or in confederacies,[1] had entered into formal treaty relations with Rome, by which they bound themselves to contribute regular contingents to the Roman army. The communities of this class composed more than half of Italy. They were entirely independent in their government, and were never called upon for tribute.

B.C. 90.

The political organization thus described continued without material change until the last century of the republic, when, as a result of the Social War, the Roman domain (*Ager Romanus*) and Roman citizenship were made to comprehend the whole of Italy.

Social Condition. — The period which we have now reached is that in which the Roman people were at their greatest height of vigor and prosperity. There were a few rich families — plebeian as well as patrician — which owned great estates, and held also large amounts of public land (see p. 47) by occupation; but the enormous acquisitions of territory by conquest had made sufficient provision for the poor, and the growth of great estates was not yet felt as an evil. A hundred years later, these great estates, cultivated by slave labor, had engrossed most of the peninsula, and their owners had become an arrogant and grasping oligarchy. But at present the Roman people were still in the main a body of peasants, living in the simple and frugal style of their ancestors. It was a maxim of Manius Curius, himself a Sabine peasant, that seven *jugera* (about three and a half acres) were enough for the support of a family;[2] and he refused any larger share for himself

[1] For example, the Samnite Confederacy.

[2] It must be understood that the peasant had, besides this estate, certain rights of pasturage, etc., in the common field.

in the allotment of land. The cultivation of the soil with their own hands was still the occupation of Roman citizens, and their well-directed industry had made into a garden many a tract of land which has since become a desert.[1] An illustration of the simple manners of the time is found in the expulsion from the Senate by Fabricius of a patrician of consular rank, because he owned ten pounds of silver plate.

Commencement of Economic Decay. — The period upon which we now enter, that of foreign wars, waged for conquest and spoliation, worked a speedy change in this condition of society. The change indeed had already begun. The system of great landed estates had already invaded considerable parts of Italy, and the enormous treasures suddenly acquired by the victory over the Samnites and the conquest of the Greek cities brought about a rapid revolution in the style and expense of living.[2] Wealth acquired by industry works only good; but wealth acquired by plunder, fraud, and the spirit of gaming, always corrupts: of this truth Roman history, from this time on, is a conspicuous witness. The Romans had now tasted the sweets of ill-gotten riches, and the plunder of foreign lands became more and more their governing motive. By fair means and by foul, great estates were built up at the expense of the free peasantry; slave labor, that form of labor which is the most immediately profitable, crowded out free labor; the cultivation of the soil itself was neglected, and what had been well-tilled fields became desert or swamp or expanse of pasture-land. From this point of time commences the decay of the Italian peasantry, and along with it of Italian agriculture.

Changes in Currency. — The economical revolution which now began was twofold; a rapid rise of prices, resulting from the great additions made to the circulating medium, and a spirit of

[1] The region of the Pontine marshes, for example, now a malarious wilderness, was thickly populated and well cultivated, being rendered healthy and cultivable by an elaborate system of drainage, of which remains still exist.

[2] In the triumphal procession in the year B.C. 293, 1380 pounds of silver were carried, which were afterwards deposited in the treasury.

eager speculation, which tended still further to raise prices and to change fundamentally the habits of the community. The critical point of time in this movement was the year B.C. 269, in which silver currency was first introduced. The money of Rome had until now been exclusively of copper, the unit being the *as*, nominally a pound in weight, but really only about ten ounces: this was divided into twelve *unciae* (p. 27).

The Silver Standard. — Silver was now made the standard. A mint was established in the temple of Juno Moneta upon the Arx,[1] and the spoils of Tarentum were coined into pieces of nearly the value of the Greek drachma (about eighteen cents[2]), which were to stand towards the copper coins as having the value of ten *asses;* hence they were called *denarii*,[3] and an intermediate piece of one-fourth (two and a half *asses*) was named *sestertius* (*semis-tertius*). The ratio thus established between silver and copper was soon changed. The abundance of silver currency rapidly lowered its value, while at the same time there was a general rise in prices, caused by the growth of commerce and of luxury. By successive steps the *as* was reduced in weight, until at last, it had fallen to one ounce, at which standard it remained; four *asses* of this weight were equal to a *sesterce*, and sixteen to a *denarius*.

B.C. 217.

Germs of Art. — It is commonly said that the Roman people were deficient in artistic capacity. It is true that they never developed an original school of art, and they certainly did not possess the wonderful power of creative art which distinguished the Greeks. Their minds were exclusively set upon practical problems of life, government, and law, so that their æsthetic nature was held in abeyance, only to find ripe expression in modern times. But at this period of the culmination of national character and powers, we find promising germs of art and

---

[1] The spot until recently occupied by the church of Santa Maria in Araceli. From the epithet *Moneta* the word *money* is derived.

[2] Afterwards reduced to a little over sixteen cents.

[3] From *deni*, "ten apiece."

culture. The ballads, sung at family gatherings and banquets, extolling the deeds of some Fabius or Valerius or Horatius, have been a source of tradition which long passed as history. Even plastic art was not wanting. The sarcophagus of Scipio Barbatus (*the Bearded*), one of the commanders in the Second Samnite war, has been preserved to this day, and is a model of chaste and elegant workmanship.

SARCOPHAGUS OF SCIPIO BARBATUS.

Loss of Creative Power in Art. — The tremendous wars upon which Rome now entered, the feverish grasping after power and wealth, the growing disregard of everything but power and wealth, and the rapid corruption of character which inevitably followed, destroyed all the healthier growth of a finer civilization; and the Romans, given up to the pursuit of power and pleasure, were content to look to the despised Greeks for forms of art which should minister to their craving for ostentation and sensuous luxury.

PERIOD OF FOREIGN CONQUEST.

CHAPTER VIII.

THE FIRST PUNIC WAR.

Carthage. — Carthage was a rich and populous city upon the northern coast of Africa; its ruins are only about ten miles from the modern city of Tunis. It was a colony, founded by the Phœnician city of Tyre, at the time when the Phœnicians were the principal sea-faring nation of the Mediterranean. As Phœnicia sank in importance, this colony, situated upon a magnificent harbor, took its place as an emporium of commerce. The other Phœnician colonies, as Utica, Gades (*Cadiz*) and Tartessus (the biblical *Tarshish*), submitted to its lead, and its power was extended over the northern coast of Africa and the island of Sardinia, while Corsica and a part of Spain were tributary to it; it had also, by a long and hard contest, established its rule over all the western part of Sicily. This beautiful island was now divided between Carthage and Syracuse, the two greatest cities of the West; and the contest between them was not yet at an end.

Rome and Carthage. — Carthage was a republic, like Rome, and the power and resources of the two republics were not very different. But they were unlike in one important respect: Carthage controlled the resources of subject nations of a foreign and inferior race, while Rome was at the head of a great nationality, of sturdy qualities and homogeneous in blood. Carthage was never anything more than Carthage, and her armies were made up of barbarian subjects, — Numidians, Libyans, and Iberians. Rome was now identified with Italy, and her armies were composed of Roman and Sabellian peasants — every one of them citizens of Rome, or of some town in alliance with Rome.

Contrast in Character. — Moreover the Carthaginians, even at their best, stood on a lower plane of character than the Romans. The Romans were severe and inflexible, but they had not yet developed that cruelty of temper to which they were afterwards educated by their wars of conquest and gladiatorial shows. The Carthaginians were cruel by nature. Their gods were not the genial deities of Greece, nor the serious and ethical gods of Rome: they had brought with them from Phœnicia the cruel rites of Moloch and the profligate rites of Astarte. The Romans, after they became corrupted, punished their slaves with the lingering tortures of crucifixion; but this punishment the Carthaginians constantly inflicted upon captive enemies and unsuccessful generals.

Relations of Rome and Carthage. — The Romans and Carthaginians were old friends; even in the wars of Pyrrhus they had stood together against the Greek cities and their allies. Their separate interests had not yet brought them into collision. But it was with the Carthaginians as it had been with the Samnites. As soon as the extension of the Roman empire had brought the two friendly states into close neighborhood, their interests became antagonistic, and hostilities soon followed. The First Punic[1] War began barely ten years after the end of the war with Pyrrhus.

Origin of the War. — The First Punic War was in its origin almost an accident. A contest of centuries had been going on between Carthage and Syracuse for the possession of Sicily. Into this contest Rome was drawn by a single act of bad faith; and, once involved in the struggle, it did not lay down its arms until the Carthaginians were expelled from Sicily, and all their possessions in that island transferred to Rome. This war is therefore properly called "The War for Sicily," although the possession of Sicily was not its original motive.

---

[1] *Punic* is another form of *Phœnician*. The Carthaginians were Phœnicians, just as the inhabitants of the French and English colonies in America were Frenchmen and Englishmen; and the wars with Carthage, three in number, were known as the Punic Wars.

THE FIRST PUNIC WAR.

The Mamertines. — Hiero, king of Syracuse, had taken into his pay a body of Campanian mercenaries. These men had mutinied, and under the name of Mamertines, "Sons of Mars,"[1] had seized the city of Messana and held it, in defiance of both Syracusans and Carthaginians. Finding themselves hard pressed, they sent an embassy to Rome, offering to place themselves and their city under its authority and protection. Now a few years before a body of Campanian troops in the Roman service had, in like unlawful manner, seized and held the Italian city of Rhegium; and had been punished with prompt and terrible severity as soon as the city was brought under the Roman power. The mutineers, three hundred at a time, were scourged and beheaded upon the Roman Forum, and the city was restored to its lawful owners. But now a spirit of lawless ambition prevailed, and, under the influence of the consul Appius Claudius (son of the blind statesman), the Romans voted to accept the offer of the Mamertines. This was in the year 264.

B.C. 271.

Creation of a Navy by the Romans. — The Romans commenced the war with prompt and successful operations. Hiero was compelled to enter into a treaty of alliance, which he kept loyally during the remainder of his long reign. The Romans then captured the important stronghold of Agrigentum, and soon were masters of the entire island, with the exception of a few maritime ports. More than this they could not accomplish as long as the Carthaginians were masters of the sea. For the maritime activity of the Romans had always been in the way of commerce. They had no navy, and had never conducted a war by sea. They were even ignorant of the construction of war ships. But their native energy was aided by fortune. A Carthaginian quinquereme[2] had been stranded upon their shore. Taking this as a model, they built with great rapidity a number of galleys, trained the oarsmen in the use of the oars by practising the strokes on land, while the ships were still building, and astonished their

---

[1] *Mamers* is another form for *Mars*.

[2] A war-galley with five banks of oars.

enemies with the appearance of a numerous and well-equipped fleet.

Battle of Mylæ. — The Romans still lacked experience and skill in naval warfare. They were beaten in their first engagement. But their new commander, Gaius Duilius, seeing that his countrymen were inferior in naval tactics, but invincible on land, determined to foil the tactics of his enemy by giving to the engagement on ship-board the character of an engagement on land. Naval tactics in antiquity consisted chiefly in manœuvring; the aim was to bring the sharp beak upon the prow in contact with the side of the enemy's vessel, and thus disable or sink it. This action he aimed to prevent, by providing his ships with grapples which, when fastened upon the enemy's vessel, should at once prevent independent movement, and serve as boarding-bridges. The plan succeeded perfectly. The Carthaginian ships were seized by the grapples and held fast, while the Roman soldiers poured upon the decks and gained a decisive victory. B.C. 260. For this achievement Duilius was rewarded by the erection of a column in his honor upon the Forum, adorned with the beaks of the captured vessels (*columna rostrata*), and by the permission to be accompanied by the music of flute-players when returning home at night from banquets.

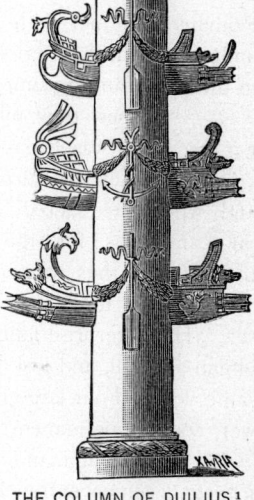

THE COLUMN OF DUILIUS.[1]
(A Restoration.)

Marcus Atilius Regulus. — By these successes on land and sea the Romans seemed to be secure in the possession of Sicily, and the consul Regulus, a few years later, thought B.C. 256.

[1] The inscription of this column is in part preserved, although probably belonging to a later copy.

that the time had come to "carry the war into Africa," and there strike a final and decisive blow. For a time he carried everything before him, and the Carthaginians were forced to sue for peace. The arrogance of Regulus, in first proposing unreasonably hard terms, and then, when these were rejected, in unduly despising his antagonists, and neglecting to take the most necessary precautions, worked his own ruin, and came near being fatal to his country's cause. His defeat and capture the next year formed a turning point in the history of the war.[1]

War in Sicily. — The defeat of this expedition was followed by the evacuation of Africa and the renewal of the war in Sicily. The Romans now met with disaster after disaster. Their principal undertaking in this period of the war was the siege of Lilybæum, in the westernmost point of the island. Here too, after some successes, they miscarried. The consul Publius Claudius,

B.C. 249. who was engaged in the siege, made up his mind to attack by surprise the Carthaginian fleet at Drepana : and when the sacred chickens, which were regularly carried on campaigns for the purpose of taking auspices, refused to eat, and thus warned against the undertaking, he remarked, "If they will not eat, they shall drink," and tossed them in the sea. His enterprise failed; he was out-generalled by the Carthaginian admiral, and lost his fleet. Another fleet was wrecked the same year. Four large fleets had been lost in the course of the war, and no permanent advantage had yet been gained. A new Carthaginian commander, Hamilcar Barca, a man of

B.C. 247. genius, entrenched himself on Mt. Ercte[2] near Panormos, and afterwards upon Mt. Eryx. From these strongholds he harassed the Romans, and made their possession of Sicily insecure.

B.C. 241. **The Last Year of the War.** — Twenty-three years had passed in war, and the end seemed no nearer than ever.

---

[1] The story, related by some ancient writers, of his embassy to Rome and return to a death of torture, is not credited by modern historians.

[2] Now known as Monte Pellegrino, the noble height close to Palermo.

Since the disasters at Lilybæum, the Romans had ceased to contend by sea, and the successes of Hamilcar threatened to deprive them of the land also. Even the Senate, for almost the only time in its history, lost heart; but the heroic nation did not know what it was to despair. By a supreme effort, through the voluntary contributions of citizens, to be repaid in the event of victory, a new fleet of two hundred vessels was built, manned by sixty thousand sailors, and placed under the command of the consul Gaius Lutatius Catulus, a man prompt in decision and of indomitable courage.

Battle of the Ægates. — The appearance of this new fleet took the Carthaginians by surprise; for of late years naval warfare had been suspended, and they as well as the Romans had neglected this arm of the service. Catulus left them no time to make up for their neglect. A Carthaginian fleet was on its way to Sicily heavily laden with supplies. It was the intention of its commander to land the cargo, take troops on board, and thus be prepared to fight. These designs were assisted by the weather; the sea was very rough, and many commanders would have allowed the vessels to pass, waiting for calmer weather. But Catulus left nothing to chance. In spite of the storm he boldly sailed out of the harbor, engaged the enemy, and gained a complete and overwhelming victory. The Carthaginian navy was destroyed, and Hamilcar with his army was left without support or supplies. This battle, ending the First Punic War, was fought off the Ægates Islands, west of Sicily. Upon news of this defeat, B.C. 241. Hamilcar immediately agreed to a peace, the conditions of which were the cession of Sicily and the islands about it, and the payment of 3200 talents (about $3,500,000) in ten yearly instalments.

Mutiny of the Carthaginian Mercenaries. — Immediately after peace was made, Carthage was involved in a formidable war by the mutiny of her mercenary troops. They were at last reduced by Hamilcar, after a war of over three years, marked by the most savage cruelties on both sides. While the Carthaginians were engaged in this death struggle, the Romans basely took advantage of their distress to seize upon the islands of Sardinia and Corsica; and when the Carthaginians protested, they required them to pay an additional tribute of 1200 talents.

Foreign Acquisitions. — The three great islands which the Romans had now acquired are so near to Italy, and stand in such relation to it, that they may be almost considered as belonging to it; as we have before shown (p. 3), they serve, with the Italian mainland, to make the Tyrrhenian Sea an enclosed body of water. Their possession may therefore be regarded as a natural and almost necessary result of the possession of Italy. Nevertheless they were not politically united with Italy. A new system of government was applied to them, which was afterwards extended to other foreign conquests, and is known as the Provincial System.

The Provincial System. — The difference between the provincial system and the system which prevailed in Italy was this. All lands in Italy were either a part of the Roman domain, or were independent communities in alliance with Rome. If there were certain communities which could be regarded as subject, such as the præfectures (p. 99), they were nevertheless Roman communities, and their inhabitants Roman citizens, although under certain disqualifications. But outside of Italy the conquered states were held strictly as subjects. Their lands were not regarded as their own, but as belonging to Rome, and it was only by sufferance that their former proprietors retained them; on this ground a heavy tribute was imposed upon them.

Government of the Provinces. — A Roman governor was appointed to administer each province, and for this purpose two new prætors were now elected.[1] These governors had absolute and practically irresponsible powers, and, as the gradual deterioration of the Roman character went on, these prætors or proconsuls[2]

---

[1] Two others were added after the Second Punic War. A second had been already elected, for the administration of justice with foreigners.

[2] When there were not enough prætors to administer all the provinces, some of these were assigned to prætors or consuls with extended powers (*imperium prorogatum*); such an officer was known as *pro-prætor* or *pro-consul*.

CONQUEST OF CISALPINE GAUL.

became notorious for avarice and cruelty. Besides the subject territories, the area of a province might embrace free cities and kingdoms which were in alliance with Rome and were not legally subject to the governor,[1] although of course this independence was in reality only nominal. Syracuse also was independent until after the death of King Hiero. It will be well B.C. 215. understood that the provincial system was a fruitful source of corruption and misgovernment; for the provinces soon became an object of plunder and profit to the governor, the Roman people, and individual citizens.

War with the Gauls. — The First Punic War lasted twenty-three years (264-241), just the duration of the Second Samnite War (327-304); and another period of twenty-three years (241-218) separated it from the Second Punic War. The principal part of this interval was spent by the Romans in the conquest of the country between the Apennines and the Alps, at this time occupied by Gauls. The war with the Gauls began shortly B.C. 238. after the peace with Carthage, but did not assume large proportions until the passage of a law proposed by the B.C. 232. tribune Gaius Flaminius, making assignments to citizens (p. 49) of lands recently taken from the Senonian Gauls. It was easy to see that this was only the first step to the occupation of the whole Gallic country; and all the Gallic tribes, except the Cenomani in the northeast, took up arms against Rome.

Conquest of Gaul. — The war continued ten years longer, culminating in a formidable invasion of Etruria B.C. 225. by a Gallic army of 70,000 men. To avert the peril two Gauls, male and female, were buried alive on the Forum, in accordance with the popular superstition; the well-trained legions were a more effective resource, and the Gauls were defeated with great slaughter. Three years later the B.C. 222. war was ended by a battle in which the consul Marcus Claudius Marcellus gained the *spolia opima* — the third recorded occasion — by slaying the Gallic king with his own hand.

---

[1] For example, Messana in Sicily.

The North of Italy. — Rome now ruled the entire peninsula of Italy, with the exception of some mountain tribes, chiefly Ligurians. The Latin colonies of Placentia (*Piacenza*) and Cremona were founded in the conquered territory, and a military road, the Flaminian Way, carried across the Apennines as far as Ariminum (*Rimini*), which now became the headquarters of Roman administration north of the Apennines. But the newly conquered peoples were by no means willing or submissive subjects. Wholly foreign to the Romans in race, character, and institutions, not incorporated in the political system of their conquerors, but held down with the strong hand, the Gauls only waited for an opportunity to throw off the hated yoke. With good judgment Hannibal made them the basis of his operations against Rome in the great war which followed.

The Illyrians. — While the war was going on with the
B.C. 229. Gauls, the Romans were drawn into hostilities also with the Illyrian pirates, on the eastern coast of the Adriatic Sea, and entered into alliance with Corcyra and other Greek cities of that region, — the beginning of their intercourse with the nations of the East.

Gaius Flaminius. — The law by which Gaius Flaminius distributed the Gallic lands among the citizens (p. 111) was a significant event in Roman history, inasmuch as it was the first occasion on which the popular assembly was called upon to decide matters which were regularly managed by the Senate. Flaminius has been called the first Roman demagogue; and this act was the first step towards the legislative anarchy of the last century of the republic. But he was not a demagogue of the type of Cleon or Clodius.

He was an intelligent reformer and an able administra-
B.C. 227. tor; and as first governor of Sicily he won a reputation for integrity and humanity which long preserved his name in the grateful remembrance of the inhabitants of the province. His violation of constitutional procedure in carrying his agrarian law avenged itself in the bitter hostility of the nobles which pursued him through life, and in the vindictiveness with which the

Gauls in Hannibal's army hunted him to death at Lake
Trasimenus. B.C. 217.

Reform of the Comitia. — Flaminius was the typical
reformer of this age, and we can probably ascribe to his B.C. 220.
censorship the most important constitutional change of
this epoch, which was made at some time between the First and
Second Punic Wars. By this measure the centuriate assembly
(p. 33) was reorganized and brought into connection with the
thirty-five local tribes, which now became the basis of this assembly as well as of the tribal assemblies proper.[1] As the preponderance of the first or most wealthy class appears to have been taken
away by this reform, it may without hesitation be regarded as one
of the steps in democratic progress.

Beginnings of Roman Literature. — At this period we mark
the first beginnings of Roman literature — neither vigorous in
themselves, nor distinctly national. It was rather a reflection of
Greek literature than an original creation. The writer, indeed,
who ranks as the earliest of Roman authors, Livius Andronicus,
was a Greek by birth. He was a wretched poetaster, but his
translations of Homer long served as text-books in the schools
of Rome. The most distinguished writer of the time, Quintus
Ennius, was also the native of a Greek city; his works — epics,
dramas, and satires — had great merit, and continued to rank as
the chief creations of Roman literature, until eclipsed by the
writings of Virgil and Horace. The earliest Roman historian,
Quintus Fabius Pictor, — a member of the distinguished Fabian
gens, and the author of a work of great merit, — wrote, neverthe-

---

[1] We possess no definite statement as to this reform, but it is pretty well
agreed that it consisted in making the number of centuries of each class equal:
each of the thirty-five tribes having now two centuries (one of *seniores* and
one of *juniores*) from each of the five classes. This made 350 centuries, to
which must be added the eighteen centuries of cavalry, and five of workmen
and musicians, 373 in all. It is the opinion of Mommsen, however, that the
280 centuries of the four lower classes were grouped into 100 voting divisions,
so that the entire number of votes was 193, as before.

less, in the Greek language; while the comedies of Plautus and Cæcilius were nothing but free translations from the Greek comedians. The only writer of the time who can be called a genuine Roman was the poet Gnæus Nævius. He was a Roman citizen, and a writer of some original power; and his independent spirit made him enemies among the nobility.[1] His principal work was a history in verse of the First Punic War, in which he had himself taken part.

Germs of the Drama. — After these feeble beginnings more than a century passed before Rome can be said to have had any school of literature. There were germs, in the rude songs and sports of peasants, out of which a native drama might have been developed: beginnings which may be compared with the corresponding creation of Thespis in Athens, out of which the Attic drama sprung. But the fashionable taste craved nothing but imitations of the Greek, and in this department the next generation witnessed the creation of a literature of much merit;[2] while the native mimes and fables, abandoned to the lower classes, preserved their original coarseness and grossness.

---

[1] His verse *Fato Metelli fiunt consules* (The Metelli receive consulships by fate) not only called out from the consul of B.C. 206 the rejoinder *Dabunt malum Metelli Naevio poetae* (The Metelli will make the poet Nævius smart), but also procured him imprisonment and exile.

[2] See Chap. X.

COLONIAL SCHOOL

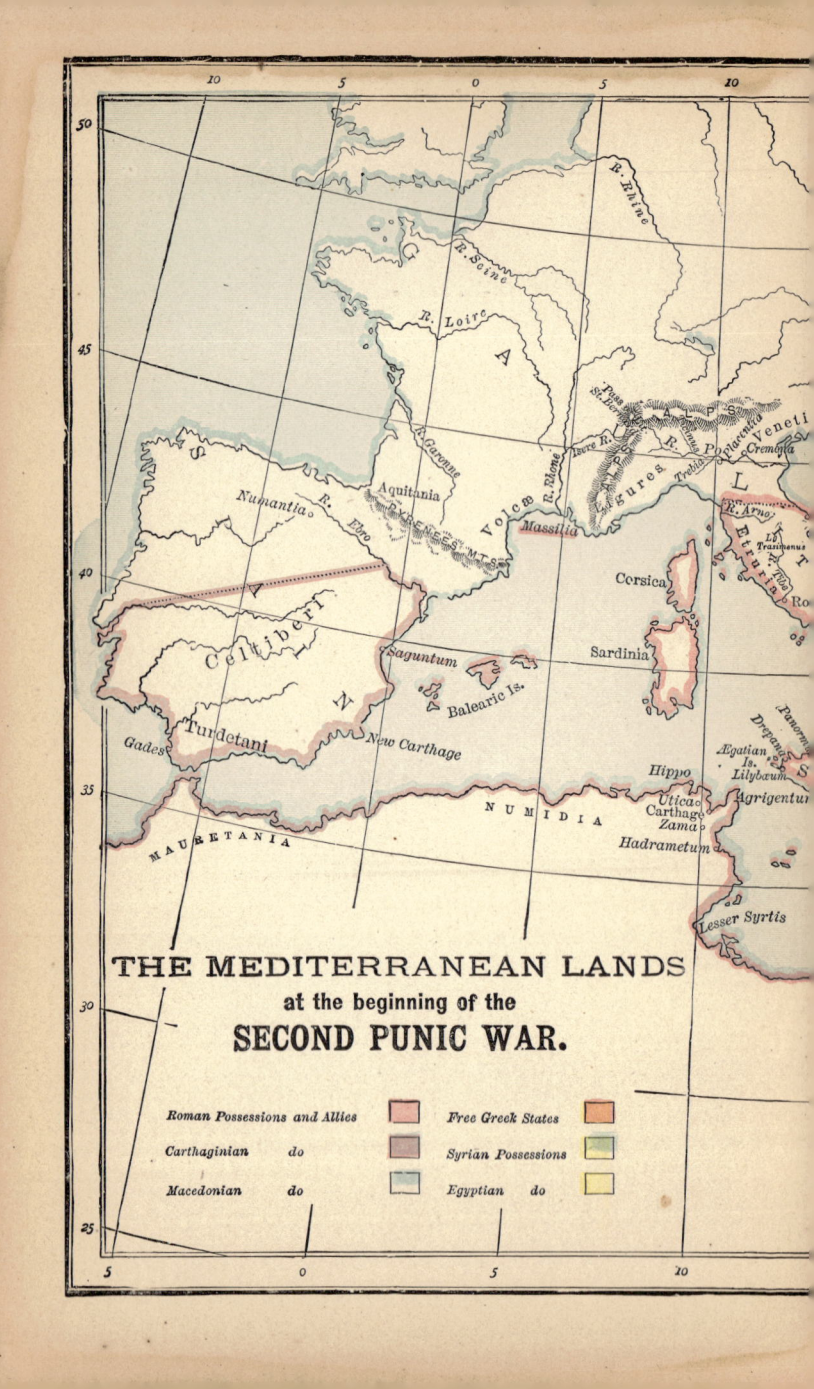

THE MEDITERRANEAN LANDS
at the beginning of the
SECOND PUNIC WAR.

Roman Possessions and Allies
Carthaginian do
Macedonian do
Free Greek States
Syrian Possessions
Egyptian do

R. Ister or Danube
ILLYRIA
Pharos
THRACE
Olbia
K. Bosporus
Chersonesus
Byzantium
Heraclea
Paphlagonia
Nicæa
Galatia
KINGDOM OF THE SELEUCIDÆ
MACEDONIA
R. Axios
R. Strymon
Epidamnos
Apollonia
Cannæ
Tarentum
Crotona
Messana
Rhegium
Syracuse
Corcyra
Epiros
Thessaly
Pydna
Cynoscephalæ
Lemnos
Lesbos
Pergamus
Magnesia
Chios
Ephesus
Samos
R. Mæander
Ætolia
Elis
Corinth
Athens
Megalopolis
Sparta
CARIA
Lycia
Rhodes
Crete
Cilicia
Tarsus
Antioch
Cyprus
Salamis
Paphus
SYRIA
Cyrene
Barca
CYRENAICA
Greater Syrtis
Altars of Philainoi
Alexandria
EGYPT
R. Nile

CHAPTER IX.

THE SECOND PUNIC WAR.

I. TO THE REVOLT OF CAPUA, B.C. 216.

The War with Hannibal.[1] — The war which now followed was the greatest and most perilous in the annals of Rome; a war in which one of the great generals of history, inspired with a bitter animosity against Rome, brought her very near to destruction. What saved her in this crisis was the vigor and patriotism of her people, the homogeneous character of the people of Italy, and the generous policy which the conquering city had pursued towards her Italian allies.

Cause of the War. — Both nations were conscious that the contest was to come, and prepared for it to the best of their ability. The loss of Sicily was the fortune of war; but the seizure of Sardinia and the extortion of an additional tribute were acts of cupidity and bad faith which rankled in the heart of every Carthaginian. When Hamilcar Barca, after suppressing the war of the mercenaries, set out for Spain, to establish a new empire there in place of that which had been lost, he took with him his nine-year-old son, Hannibal, and trained him to be his successor in command, first making him take an oath of eternal hostility to Rome. The family of Barca incorporated in themselves the sentiment of the patriotic party in Carthage.

The Barcas in Spain. — Taking as his starting-point the old Phœnician colonies, Gades and Tartessus, in the south of Spain, Hamilcar proceeded to conquer the peninsula. At his death

---

[1] The best history of this war is Arnold's *The Second Punic War* (Macmillan). For an entertaining work of fiction read *The Carthaginian Boy*, by Henty.

B.C. 228. he was succeeded by his son-in-law, Hasdrubal, who carried on his work with equal zeal and ability, and founded the city of New Carthage (*Cartagena*), as capital of the new empire. The Romans, engrossed in their wars with the Gauls and Illyrians (p. 111), watched jealously the growth of the Carthaginian power, but were not in a condition to resist it.

B.C. 225. They nevertheless entered into a treaty with Hasdrubal, by which he bound himself not to pass the Ebro with an

B.C. 220. armed force. When Hasdrubal, shortly after, was assassinated, Hannibal, now about twenty-six years old, succeeded to his command, and at once began preparations for war. The Romans, still involved in Illyrian affairs, and believing that the peace party in Carthage would have the upper hand, were taken unprepared.

Beginning of the War. — The first act of Hannibal, after completing the subjugation of the native tribes as far as the Ebro, was to attack the Greek city of Saguntum, an ally of

B.C. 219. Rome. This he captured and destroyed after a siege of eight months. War was at once declared, and Hannibal immediately set out with his army, passed the Ebro and the Pyrenees, traversed Southern Gaul, and had already crossed the Rhone when the consul, Publius Scipio, on his way to Spain, landed at Massilia. On learning this astonishing news, that the war was to be waged in Italy, not in Spain and Africa, Scipio promptly changed his plans, despatched his brother Gnæus to Spain, — where he afterwards joined him as proconsul, — and returned to Pisæ. Here he took command of the Italian forces, and summoning his colleague, Sempronius, from Sicily, where he was on his way to attack Carthage, hastened to Cisalpine Gaul to meet the invader in the valley of the Po.

The Passage of the Alps. — Hannibal meanwhile had made his way over the Alps with enormous loss and suffering, and reached the valley of the Po at about the same time as Scipio.[1] His

---

[1] It has generally been held that he crossed by the route of the Little St. Bernard; it seems probable, however, that it was by a more southern pass, probably Mont Cenis or Genèvre.

reasons for taking this difficult route were well founded, although he seems to have underrated the difficulties and hardships of the march, and to have undertaken it too late in the season. His army was reduced to less than half its number, and was in a terrible state of exhaustion. But he knew that the Roman power in Gaul was not yet firmly established, and he reckoned with confidence upon making the Gauls his auxiliaries. In this he was not deceived. Cisalpine Gaul was at once lost to Rome, and its people composed a constant and reliable part of Hannibal's army throughout his Italian campaigns.[1]

Operations in the Valley of the Po. — Hannibal ended this eventful year with a brilliant victory. The newly founded colony of Placentia, upon the Po, was the base of operations for the Roman commander. In a cavalry skirmish upon the river Ticinus, Scipio was repulsed and severely wounded, after which he encamped upon the river Trebia, about six miles from Placentia. Here he was shortly joined by the army of his colleague Sempronius, who now took command, Scipio being still disabled by his wound. Hannibal was encamped on the other side of the Trebia, about five miles distant.[2]

Battle of the Trebia. — Hannibal, like all great commanders, understood thoroughly how to reckon with his antagonists, and had no difficulty in drawing the rash and impatient Sempronius into an ambuscade. It was already December, and the river — a mere mountain stream — was swollen with rains. Early one morning, before the Roman soldiers had breakfasted, the Numidian cavalry of Hannibal appeared before the camp, and by skilful manoeuvring and feigned flight, succeeded in enticing the Romans across the river. The water was icy cold, and almost up to their necks; they were hungry as well as chilled to the bone;

---

[1] The Cenomani, however, in the country about Verona, held with Rome.

[2] The accounts of the battle, given by Livy and Polybius, do not allow it to be determined absolutely on which side of the river each army was encamped. It is probable that the Romans were on the right bank, and that the battle took place upon the left.

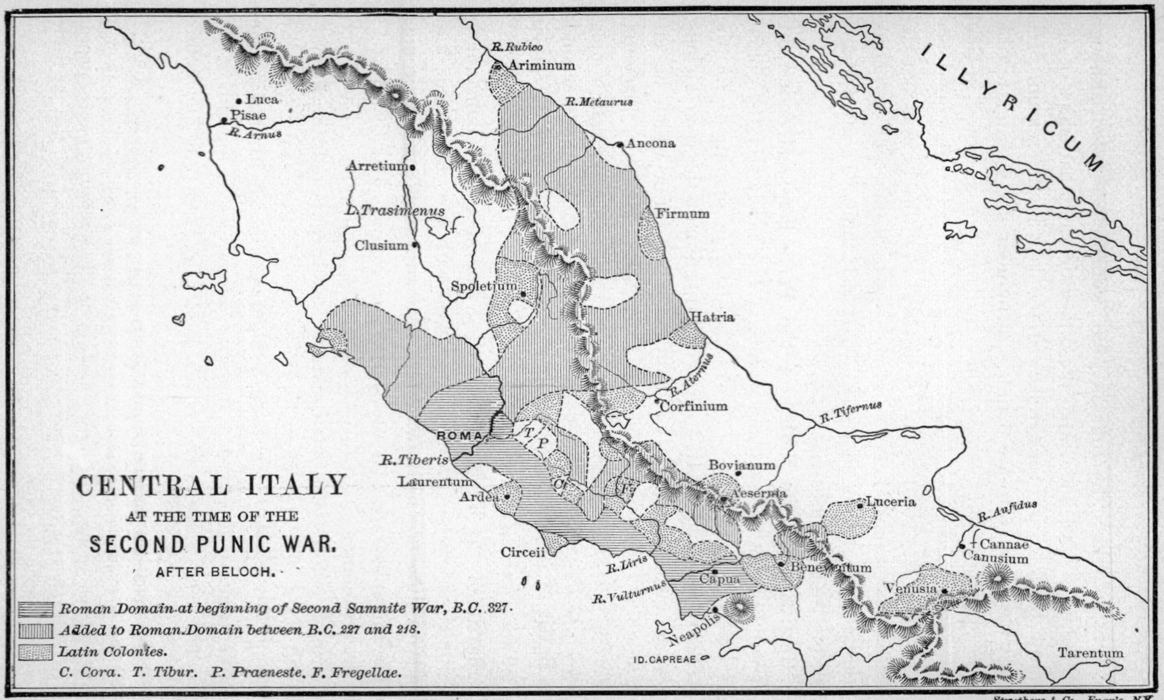

Struthers & Co., Engr's, N.Y.

and then, while engaged in an unequal fight with Hannibal's well-fed and well-cared-for soldiers, they were suddenly assailed in the flank and rear by fresh troops, who had been placed in ambuscade. The army was cut to pieces, only a remnant escaping to Placentia. The year of Scipio's consulship being now at an end, he repaired to Spain, to join his brother Gnæus.

Invasion of Etruria. — The following year Hannibal B.C. 217. gained a still greater victory. The new consul, Gaius Flaminius (p. 112), had stationed himself at Arretium (*Arezzo*) in the upper valley of the Arno, in order to block Hannibal's passage into Etruria. The position seemed every way a favorable one. But Hannibal always did what was unexpected. Crossing the Apennines early in the spring, long before the passage was thought practicable, he made his way with severe suffering and losses through the marshy region of the lower Arno, and then by a bold flank march placed himself between Flaminius and Rome, giving notice of his position by burning and destroying everything around him. In the passage of the marshes he lost one eye.

Battle of Lake Trasimenus. — Without waiting for his colleague, who was at Ariminum, Flaminius hastily set out in pursuit, only to fall into the trap set for him by the wily Carthaginian. His road led through a narrow defile upon the northern shore of Lake Trasimenus. Here Hannibal prepared his ambuscade, and when the Roman lines, in the early morning, emerged from the defile into the open space beyond, they were furiously assaulted in front, in the rear, and on the flank. A heavy fog prevented them from even seeing their assailants, and they had no escape except into the lake, in which many of them were drowned. The Roman army was annihilated: Flaminius himself was slain by one of those Gauls whose enmity he had incurred by his agrarian law fifteen years before.

Hannibal in Southern Italy. — After this crushing victory, Hannibal proceeded to Southern Italy, expecting to rally to his support the Sabellian nations of that region, as he had the Gallic tribes of the north. He gave himself out as the champion of the oppressed Italians against their Roman conquerors: whatever Romans or Latins fell into his hands he slew or put in chains, but the citizens of the allied cities he dismissed to their homes, hoping thus to secure their friendship. But he made a mistake similar to that of Napoleon III., when he reckoned upon the support or the neutrality of the southern Germans in his war against Prussia. "Blood is thicker than water." The Sabellian tribes were kinsmen of the Romans, and had no fellowship with the Phœnician invaders. Moreover, they did not feel themselves oppressed. Except for their contributions of troops to the Roman army, they were left to govern themselves as they pleased. Not a city opened its gates to Hannibal; not a tribe allied itself with him.

Fabius Maximus. — In Rome no attempt was made to conceal the extent of the disaster. "We have been beaten in a great battle" was the announcement made by the prætor to the assembled people. It was decided to appoint a dictator and — in the absence of the surviving consul — the people by a formal vote designated Quintus Fabius Maximus for this office. Fabius Maximus was descended from the hero of the Second Samnite War — a man equally illustrious, but of a very different type. The grandfather was distinguished for boldness and enterprise, amounting sometimes to rashness; the dictator was slow and cautious, and by these qualities earned the surname *Cunctator* — "delayer." The "Fabian" policy, which he adopted, was to avoid a general engagement, watch his enemy assiduously, and weary him out with resultless manœuvring. Knowing very well that there was nothing that Hannibal so much desired as a pitched battle, he determined that in this at least he should be disappointed; and in this policy he persisted in spite of the remonstrances of his officers and the people of Rome.

Operations upon the Aufidus. — So the year 217 came to an end with no further decisive actions. The dictator's term of office had expired, and the consuls of the following year were divided in temper and policy. The patrician consul, Lucius Æmilius Paulus, an able and experienced officer, had been taught by the

THE BATTLE OF CANNÆ.

disasters of former years to recognize Hannibal's genius,
as well as the superiority of his troops, especially in   B.C. 216.
cavalry. His plebeian colleague, Gaius Terentius Varro,
rash and inexperienced, considered only that his army was twice as
large as that of Hannibal, and was determined to force an engagement. The consuls commanded on alternate days, and Hannibal
knew very well when it was Varro's day. He had captured the
Roman magazines at Cannæ, on the right bank of the Aufidus
near its mouth, and the consular army hastened to the spot,

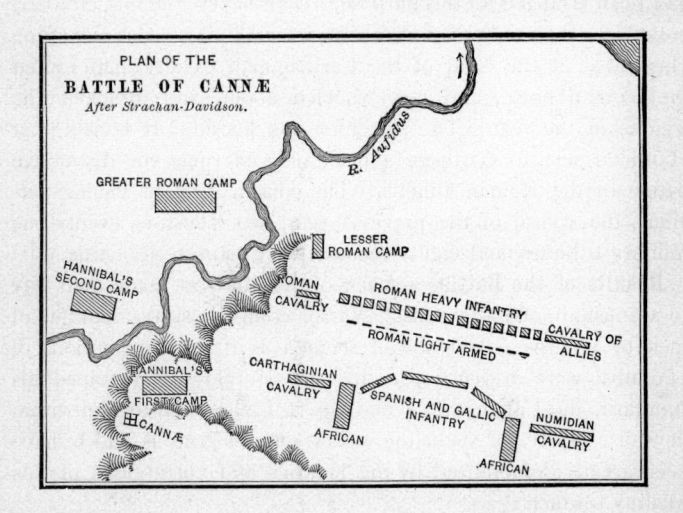

PLAN OF THE
BATTLE OF CANNÆ
After Strachan-Davidson.

encamping on the left bank of the river, nearer the sea. They
established also a smaller camp upon the right bank, for the purpose of watching Hannibal, and preventing foraging. This division
of their forces was made safe by their superiority in numbers.

Battle of Cannæ. — On his day of command Varro led his
troops from the larger camp and crossed the river, drawing up all
his forces in line of battle, facing the south: the Roman cavalry
occupied his right wing; that of the allies, the left. The infantry,
in the centre, were formed in heavy columns, by which they lost the

special advantage of the manipular arrangement, and there appear to have been no reserves. Hannibal, too, had his cavalry upon the two wings, and his centre was composed of his Spanish and Gallic infantry, arranged in the form of a crescent, with its convex side towards the Romans. Between these and the cavalry were the Libyan troops, his chief reliance, drawn up in heavy columns. Thus, when the Roman infantry had easily driven in the Spanish and Gallic troops, and were eagerly pursuing them, they found themselves suddenly attacked on both flanks by the Libyans, who had been arranged for this purpose. Their heavy columns, crowded in between the two lines of assailants, were helpless; and meantime Hasdrubal, at the head of the Carthaginian cavalry, had routed the Roman horse, and now wheeled about, and attacked the legions in the rear. The slaughter was fearful. It is said that Hannibal sent to Carthage a peck of gold rings, the distinctive badge of the Roman knights. The consul, Æmilius Paulus, Servilius, the consul of the previous year, two quæstors, twenty-one military tribunes, and eighty senators were slain in the battle.

Results of the Battle. — A few of the survivors made their way to Canusium, and the consul, Varro, escaped with a handful of men to Venusia. And now it seemed as if the expectations of Hannibal were at last justified. All Southern Italy joined his standard, and Capua, the second city in Italy, received him within its walls. Here he spent the winter, and his army is said to have been greatly demoralized by the luxuries and corruptions of this wealthy town.

II. To the End of the War, b.c. 201.

News of the Defeat in Rome. — It can be imagined what was the consternation at Rome when the news of this third and most crushing defeat was brought. The city was so full of mourning that the festival of Ceres, celebrated by women, had to be omitted, because it was not lawful for persons in mourning to take part in it, and there were no matrons who were not in mourning: by an ordinance of the Senate it was directed that mourning should not continue longer than a month. But there was no panic or thought of submission. The Senate refused to ransom the soldiers who had allowed themselves to be captured, but raised new levies, even arming slaves and persons of no repute. The prætor, Marcus Claudius Marcellus, — the best soldier that Rome now had, — was at once despatched to the support of Varro with fresh troops; and never did the Senate display its staunch patriotism more nobly than in voting to thank the consul Varro — its bitter enemy, and the author of the disaster — "because he had not despaired of the republic."

The Years after Cannæ. — Hannibal, for his part, was now, by the victory of Cannæ and the occupation of Capua, at the summit of his prosperity. For two or three years longer he continued to gain. The year after Cannæ the venerable Hiero, king of Syracuse, the faithful ally of Rome, died, and his worthless successor carried his city over to alliance with Carthage. Two years later Tarentum, the third city of Italy, was gained by treachery, and in the same year Hannibal made a treaty with Philip V., king of Macedonia, by which the Romans were drawn into the brief and unimportant contest known as the First Macedonian War. But the great object of his hostility, the Roman empire in Italy, stood as firm as a rock. Rome never relaxed its efforts, but under the leadership of Marcellus, the "sword of Rome,"

B.C. 215.

B.C. 213.

MARCELLUS, THE SWORD OF ROME.

and Fabius Maximus, its "shield," held its own, and began slowly to win back what it had lost. The Latin colonies never swerved for a moment from their loyalty.

Capture of Syracuse. — In the year 212 Syracuse was captured by Marcellus, after a siege of several months. It had been defended chiefly by the genius of the celebrated mathematician

Archimedes, whose mechanical contrivances foiled all the efforts of the besiegers, so that they were at last forced to reduce it by blockade. According to the savage custom of the ancients the city was given up to pillage, and in the confusion Archimedes perished. Marcellus had wished to spare his life; but he was slain in a passion by an ignorant soldier, who found him engaged in studying diagrams drawn in the sand, and to whom he only cried out "Don't disturb my circles."[1] Syracuse, with its territory, was now annexed to the Roman province of Sicily.

Capture of Capua and Tarentum. — Before the fall of Syracuse, the Romans had laid siege to Capua, and Hannibal, whose strength was in cavalry, and who was weak in the means of assaulting fortified places, could not succeed in drawing the besieging army from its intrenchments. As a last means of raising the siege, he marched upon Rome, hoping that the besiegers would follow him, in order to defend the city. But the city was found provided with defenders, and the army at Capua never relaxed its grip. Capua was taken, its leading men were executed, and the city itself deprived of all political rights, being reduced to the rank of a village, and governed by Roman præfects. Two years later Tarentum fell into the hands of the Romans, and Hannibal's venture was plainly doomed to failure, unless speedy assistance should come.

B.C. 211.

B.C. 209.

Affairs in Spain. — Hannibal had left his brother Hasdrubal in Spain, and the war had been waged in that country with varying fortunes. At first the brothers Publius and Gnæus Scipio, "two thunderbolts of war," had gained great successes; then both had been defeated and killed within a month of each other, and the young Publius Scipio, son of the consul of 218, was elected by the people to command in their place. He soon regained the entire peninsula; but Hasdrubal, after the loss of a great battle, succeeded in eluding the victor, made his way across the Pyrenees, and hastened to the relief of his brother in Italy. In 207 he appeared in the valley of the Po at the head of a large and well-trained army.

[1] *Noli turbare circulos meos!*

THE WAR IN AFRICA.

Battle of the Metaurus. — Hannibal was at this time B.C. 207. in the neighborhood of Venusia, in Apulia, watched by the consul Gaius Claudius Nero, while his colleague Marcus Livius was watching for Hasdrubal in the north. Nero waylaid some messengers sent to Hannibal by his brother, and having thus learned of the approach of the invading army, adopted a sudden and bold plan. Leaving the principal part of his army in an intrenched camp, he hastened with a few cohorts of choice troops, succeeded in uniting with Livius before the arrival of Hasdrubal's army, and attacked the enemy at the river Metaurus. This decisive battle was determined by Nero's prompt sagacity. Seeing that on the right wing, where he was placed, the nature of the ground did not allow the free manœuvring of all his troops, he withdrew a portion of them, passed round the rear unnoticed, and fell upon the right flank of the enemy with overwhelming force. The victory was complete, the Carthaginians losing almost as heavily as the Romans at Cannæ. Hasdrubal himself fell in the battle.

Failure of Hannibal. — As soon as the battle was over Nero rapidly led his cohorts back to Venusia, carrying with him the head of Hasdrubal, which was thrown into the camp of Hannibal, and gave him the first news of the disaster. The last hope of success was now gone : it only remained for him to retire into the southern recesses of the peninsula, where he remained until summoned by his country to protect her in turn against invasion.

War in Africa. — The Romans had learned by the experience of this war the folly of constantly changing their commanders. By re-elections and extraordinary commands they had used the services of Fabius and Marcellus for successive years in the critical period of the war. The young Scipio, too, had been kept year after year in Spain, where he learned thoroughly the art of command ; and after his consulship his command was B.C. 205. continued to him by the Senate year after year[1] until he

---

[1] The device of proroguing commands, which might be continued indefinitely, was a salutary corrective to the practice of annual commands.

brought the war to a close. Spain was now thoroughly subdued, and the policy of Scipio was to "carry the war into Africa." Here he was assisted by the Numidian king Masinissa, whose rival, Syphax, was the ally of Carthage. After two years of warfare between these antagonists, Hannibal was summoned home from Italy, and the war was finished upon the soil of Africa.

Battle of Zama. — The final battle of the war was fought at Zama, in B.C. 202. Scipio, a general of original genius, in this

SCIPIO AFRICANUS.[1]

battle took the final step in the development of the legion.[2] Instead of arranging the army in the usual order of the *quincunx* (p. 70), by which the maniples of the second rank or line stood behind the spaces of the first, he left these spaces open, in order

[1] From a bust in the Vatican Museum.

[2] This is Delbrück's view. It is at any rate certain that at Cannæ, fourteen years before, the Roman troops were in a crowded mass, incapable of manœuvring, while in the Macedonian wars, which follow immediately after Zama, the legion was in its highest condition of flexibility and efficiency.

THE BATTLE OF ZAMA.

that the elephants, of which Hannibal had an unusual number, might not trample upon the close masses of troops, but might find a passage between the divisions. A still more important innovation was to draw up the three lines at a considerable interval from one another. By this the close order of the phalanx was completely abandoned, and the legion acquired its characteristic flexibility, since not only each of the three lines, but each maniple or group of maniples (three maniples making a cohort), had now room to manœuvre independently. The result justified his calculations. The light-armed troops, pouring through the open spaces, drove back the elephants in disorder upon the Carthaginian ranks; and at the same time Hannibal's cavalry was routed and driven in flight by the Roman horsemen, aided efficiently by those of Masinissa. Scipio then moved his second and third lines to the right and left, and threw them upon the flanks of the enemy, while his cavalry, returning from the pursuit, assaulted them in the rear, and completed the victory.

The Roman Legion. — The legion remained essentially unaltered from the time of Scipio to that of Marius, a century later. The three lines, the *hastati*, the *principes*, and *triarii*, were, in this period, drawn up at a distance apart, and brought successively into action; but such was the prowess of the Roman soldiers, and the skill with which they were handled, that the *triarii*, or reserves, were seldom called for. The armament too was changed. The short heavy javelin (*pilum*) had already taken the place of the long spear characteristic of the phalanx; and it appears to have been Scipio who armed his troops with the short Spanish sword, with which he had become acquainted in his Spanish wars. The soldier first hurled his javelins (*eminus*) with tremendous force into the ranks of the enemy, and then, drawing his sword, followed up with a hand-to-hand assault (*comminus*) — like a volley of musketry followed by a bayonet charge.

Terms of Peace. — Peace was at once made (201). Spain, with its islands, was surrendered to Rome, and was organized into two provinces, Hither and Farther. Syphax was carried captive to

Rome, and Masinissa recognized as independent king of Numidia, with territories enclosing those of Carthage on the south as well as the west: from this time, for more than fifty years, he was a steadfast and serviceable ally of Rome. Carthage gave up all her war-vessels except twenty, and paid a war indemnity of 4000 talents ($5,000,000), besides 200 talents ($250,000) annually for fifty years. Rome was now the only power in the Western Mediterranean. Scipio, from his conquest of Africa, received the surname *Africanus*.

Hannibal. — Hannibal's career was not ended by the battle of Zama. He proved himself as great in peace and in the field of administration, as in the conduct of war. His financial reforms and economical administration enabled his countrymen not only to pay the indemnity to Rome, but rapidly to regain their old prosperity. Again the animosity of Hannibal appeared a menace to Rome, and the Senate sent an embassy to Carthage, probably to demand his surrender. He escaped and took refuge in the court of King Antiochus, where he became the leading counsellor of that monarch in taking up war against Rome.

B.C. 195.

Livius and Nero. — Livius and Nero, the victors upon the Metaurus, were personal enemies. Livius had been condemned and heavily fined by the popular assembly, shortly before the war, for some offence, the precise nature of which is not known, and had retired in dudgeon to his country estate, where he lived in solitude, a morose and misanthropic life. The censors had forced him to return to the city, to shave his beard and put on decent clothes, and to take his seat again in the Senate. He was then elected consul, and did a man's duty in the office. But he had not forgotten his grievance. Three years later the caprice of the elections made the two men colleagues again, in the censorship. In the exercise of their duties their enmity broke out in spiteful and unseemly factiousness. In the review of the cavalry each censor ordered his colleague to sell his horse (*equum vendere*), the technical expression for removal from that

B.C. 204.

honorable corps. Then, in drawing up the list of citizens, first, Nero declared Livius an *aerarius*,[1] thus depriving him of his vote in the tribes; and Livius capped the climax of absurdity by degrading the entire Roman people to the same rank, with the exception of the single tribe (*Maecia*) which had voted for his acquittal, giving as his reasons that they had condemned him unjustly, and afterwards, without any new evidence, had made him consul and censor. Of this action, the effect of which would have been to destroy the very framework of government, the consuls of course took no account.

The Worship of the Great Mother. — While Hannibal was still in Italy, it was read in the Sibylline books B.C. 205. (p. 36) that a foreign invader would be obliged to leave the soil of Italy if the Great Mother should be brought to the city; and commissioners were sent to Asia for this purpose. Cybele, the mother of the gods, was the special deity of the Phrygians of Asia Minor, worshipped at Pessinus with noisy and frantic rites. The prophecy directed that the goddess, when brought to Rome, should be formally received by "the best Roman"; and while the commissioners were absent upon their errand, the Senate decided that the best Roman was Publius Scipio,[2] cousin of Africanus. The chief ally of Rome at this time in Asia was Attalus, king of Pergamus, and by his intervention the priests at Pessinus were persuaded to deliver to the Roman envoys the meteoric stone which symbolized the goddess. It was brought in a ship to Ostia, at the mouth of the Tiber, where it was delivered to Scipio, and then reverently conveyed to Rome by the matrons who had gathered at Ostia to receive it. The worship of the Great Mother, at about the season of the Vernal Equinox, became one of the favorite cults of the Roman populace, and her processions of priests, clad in Asiatic costume, with noisy chants and beating

---

[1] This term was applied to those who had no land, and consequently no vote in the tribes (pp. 88-90). For an account of these incidents, see Livy, xxvii. 34; xxix. 37.

[2] Called *Nasica*, from his prominent nose.

130   *THE SECOND PUNIC WAR.*

of tambourines, begging from the by-standers money for the support of the ritual,[1] was a novel sight in the streets of Rome, by no means acceptable to the sober-minded votaries of the old religion.

[1] All the forms of worship which belonged regularly to the religion of the State were maintained by appropriations of money made by the Senate out of the treasury.

ETRUSCAN TOMB AT CORNETO,
Showing the Construction of the Roof with the Impluvium.

CHAPTER X.

THE WARS IN THE EAST.

I. THE SECOND MACEDONIAN WAR.

Foreign Conquest. — The war with Hannibal was followed by a period of about fifty years, occupied with foreign wars, chiefly in the East. In these wars Rome gained many brilliant victories, and acquired an enormous increase of power and territory, so that at the end of the period, B.C. 146, she stood without rival as the first power in the world. But along with the acquisition of foreign dominion and of private treasures, there came deterioration of character and a rapid loss of public spirit. These years, which witnessed the building up of the Roman empire, were the period in which the causes of corruption and downfall were most rapidly developed. Power and wealth became more and more the sole object.

The East: Egypt. — There were at this time three great empires in the East, one in each continent.[1] Egypt, under the Ptolemies, was in friendly relations with Rome, and made the Senate the guardian of its youthful king. It took no active part in the great wars of the age, but the two other great empires, of Asia and Macedonia, were its constant rivals and enemies.

Asia. — All of Western Asia was nominally under the rule of the dynasty of the Seleucidæ,[2] now under its most powerful king, Antiochus III., the Great: in his time came the collapse of this

---

[1] See map of the Mediterranean Lands at the beginning of the Second Punic War (p. 114).

[2] The descendants of Seleucus Nicator (d. B.C. 280), one of the generals of Alexander the Great. At the disruption of Alexander's empire he secured the largest and most important share.

empire. In the far East, upon the Caspian Sea, the Parthians had already achieved their independence: in time they grew to be the great Asiatic power. In Asia Minor Antiochus ruled over the shores of the Mediterranean and the fertile regions of the interior, while the Greek cities upon the Ægean paid him tribute. But in the mountainous regions of the north a group of petty states — Bithynia, Pontus, Cappadocia, Galatia, etc. — were practically independent; at Pergamus, in the west, King Attalus ruled over a small but prosperous and well-ordered state; while the island of Rhodes — "the Venice of antiquity" — was a flourishing commercial republic. Both Rhodes and Pergamus, being naturally hostile to Antiochus, were steadfast allies of Rome.

Greece. — The kingdom of Macedonia, now under Philip V., was the third of the great powers of the East. A considerable portion of Greece was subject to him, while other Grecian states maintained their isolation and independence. But the feeling of the necessity of union had gathered most of the Greek states into two confederacies, — the Achæan league, embracing most of the Peloponnesus, and the Ætolian league in Northern Greece.[1] The rude and predatory Ætolians were allies of Rome from the first; the cautious and conservative Achæans were for a time neutral, but afterwards united with Rome. Thus in the wars which followed, Philip and Antiochus were natural allies, while the independent states of Greece, as well as Rhodes and Pergamus, joined with Rome. By the supineness and preoccupation of Antiochus, Philip was left to contend single-handed against Rome and her allies; and, after the defeat of Philip, Antiochus in his turn was easily overpowered.

PHILIP V.

Second Macedonian War. — The first of the great series of wars in this period was waged against Philip of Macedon. In this war the decisive battle was fought by Titus Quinctius Flamininus

[1] These leagues had existed for a long time, but were reorganized about the middle of the third century before Christ.

at Cynoscephalæ (*Dog's Heads*), a range of low steep hills in Thessaly, in the year 197. In this battle the Roman legion and the Macedonian phalanx were for the first time brought into conflict with one another. The Roman legion, as we have seen (p. 69), consisted of thirty independent companies (maniples), in which each man was trained to act promptly and efficiently by himself, and the openness of the order gave space for individual prowess. It had now attained its greatest efficiency.

The Macedonian Phalanx. — The Macedonian phalanx consisted of sixteen ranks of men, arranged in close order — each man having only half the space of the Roman legionary — and armed with spears over twenty feet long. The five front ranks couched their spears so as to present to the enemy an unbroken wall of five rows of points, while those in the rear rested theirs upon the shoulders of those in front. A mass of men thus armed, and closely knit together, was impregnable against assault, and irresistible when moving upon level ground; but it had no power to adapt itself to a change of circumstances, and when once disturbed by irregularities of ground, or assaulted in the rear, was powerless. Both of these defects were seen in the battle of Cynoscephalæ.

Battle of Cynoscephalæ. — In this battle, which was brought on unexpectedly upon a stormy day, the battle was opened by a cavalry skirmish unfavorable to the Romans, who were protected by the efficient cavalry of the Ætolians. Philip, flushed by his success, brought his phalanx rapidly over the range of hills. The right wing maintained its order, and carried all before it; but the left wing fell into confusion from the rapid march, and was easily routed, upon which the victorious Romans promptly swung round to the left, and took the victorious phalanx in the rear, where it had no power of resistance. This victory ended the war.

Congress at Corinth. — The following spring Flamininus convened a congress of the Greek states at Corinth, where, amid the enthusiastic applause of the Assembly, he declared Greece free of Macedonian rule. Rome, satisfied with having placed a check upon the formidable power of Macedonia, and not having as yet any desire to gain territory east of the Adriatic, took nothing for herself; but the Ætolian and Achæan leagues each received considerable accessions of territory.

II. THE WARS WITH ANTIOCHUS AND PERSEUS.

The Asiatic War. — It was not long before the Romans
B.C. 192. were drawn into another war in defence of their allies, the republic of Rhodes and Eumenes, the new king of Pergamus, against Antiochus of Asia. It became a general war, in which the independent states of Asia Minor and Greece were divided against one another. Philip of Macedonia, true to the

ANTIOCHUS THE GREAT.

terms of peace, aided the Romans, and so did the Achæans and the king of Bithynia; while the Ætolians, disappointed with their share of the conquests of the last war, espoused the party of Antiochus. At their invitation Antiochus even crossed
B.C. 191. into Greece, but was defeated at Thermopylæ, and forced to retire to Asia Minor. Here he was defeated the following year in the battle of Magnesia.

B.C. 190. **Battle of Magnesia.** — The Roman commander in this battle was Lucius Scipio, called *Asiaticus*, brother of the conqueror of Hannibal. As his brother accompanied him as aid (*legatus*), and really directed the operations of the campaign,

BATTLE OF MAGNESIA.

the merit of the victory is ascribed to him. In the battle of Magnesia the weakness of the phalanx was again manifested. The legions could do nothing against it by direct assault, as long as it remained stationary, or moved steadily over suitable ground. The Roman commander, therefore, held the legions back, and indeed they took no part in the battle; but the cavalry and the light-armed troops assaulted the phalanx with showers of missiles, which broke up the solidity of their array, and threw them into confusion. After this they were speedily routed.

Terms of Peace. — As a result of this battle, Antiochus agreed to surrender all of Asia Minor north of Mt. Taurus, most of which was added to the dominions of Pergamus, which now became a powerful kingdom. Rhodes received the territory on the mainland as far north as the river Mæander, and from this time for more than two hundred years was the chief maritime power of the Eastern Mediterranean; it did not lose its independence until the time of the Emperor Claudius. The petty kingdoms upon the Black Sea (p. 132) continued independent.

Death of Hannibal. — In this war Antiochus had been assisted and counselled by Hannibal, who had taken refuge with him after his exile from Carthage. If Hannibal had been trusted with the entire conduct of the war, instead of being employed in only subordinate operations, the result might have been different. When peace was made, Hannibal had nothing to hope for. Compelled to flee from the court of Antiochus, he took refuge with Prusias, king of Bithynia, and escaped surrender to the Romans by taking poison. He was sixty-seven years B.C. 183. old.

Collapse of the Empire of the Seleucidæ. — The battle of Magnesia forms a crisis in the history of the Orient. With the loss of Asia Minor the direct relations of Antiochus with Europe were at an end, and he became a purely Oriental sovereign. But the power of his empire was broken. Not long after his death the Parthian king, Mithradates the Great, conquered as far west as the Euphrates. Even before this, the Jews, B.C. 163.

under the heroic race of the Maccabees, had achieved virtual independence; and now the mighty empire of the Seleucidæ, which had once stretched from the Ægean to the Indus, was reduced to the dimensions and name of Kingdom of Syria.

Wars in the West. — In the fifty years which followed, the Romans were continually engaged in petty campaigns to strengthen their authority in Spain and in Northern Italy, the country of the Gauls and Ligurians. By degrees the whole of Italy up to the Alps was brought firmly under their power. Spain was not fully subdued until later. At the same time a series of contests was carried on in Illyricum, where at last the foundations of
B.C. 167. a provincial government were laid, although the countries were not completely subdued and organized as a province until a long time after.

The Third Macedonian War. — Notwithstanding the Romans had taken nothing for themselves in the Eastern wars, their allies began to feel jealous and suspicious of their growing strength. The loyalty of Philip of Macedon began to waver, and after his death his son Perseus
B.C. 179. became actively hostile. In the
B.C. 172. war that followed the Rhodians remained neutral, but unfriendly; and even Eumenes of Pergamus appeared estranged. This Third Macedonian War was ended by the battle of Pydna,

PERSEUS.

B.C. 168. in which the Romans were commanded by Lucius Æmilius Paulus, son of the one who was killed at Cannæ, a man now advanced in years, but of the best Roman type, indomitable and active, and of unblemished integrity. Paulus, bareheaded and lightly armed, was everywhere present, directing and inspiring his troops. Here, as at Cynoscephalæ and Magnesia, the phalanx showed its weakness. It lost its compactness on the uneven ground, and was broken to pieces by the assaults of the Roman cohorts.

The Kingdom of Macedonia overthrown.

Even now, in spite of the growing demoralization of the Roman people, they still refrained from adding to their own dominions. Perseus was carried a prisoner to Rome, where he graced the triumphal procession of Æmilius Paulus. His kingdom ceased to exist; and its territories were divided into four republics, which for about twenty years enjoyed a show of independence under the protection of Rome.

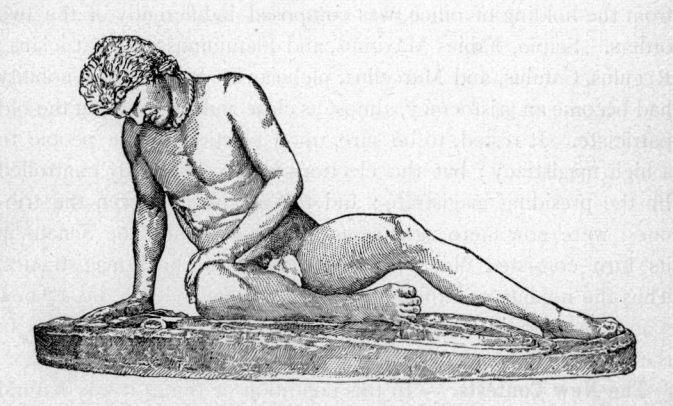

THE SO-CALLED DYING GLADIATOR.

In reality a wounded Gaul: a work of Pergamene art, showing the *torques* about the neck (p. 78).

CHAPTER XI.

SUPREMACY OF ROME.

The New Nobility. — The contest between the patricians and plebeians — that is, between the original body of citizens and the new citizens — had now been at an end for more than a hundred years; and the new nobility (p. 65), whose rights were derived from the holding of office, was composed indifferently of the two orders. Scipio, Fabius Maximus, and Flamininus were patricians; Regulus, Catulus, and Marcellus, plebeians. But this new nobility had become an aristocracy, almost as close and exclusive as the old patriciate. It rested, to be sure, upon election by the people to a high magistracy; but the elections were very greatly controlled by the presiding magistrate; and the magistrates, even the tribunes, were now mere agents of the Senate, while the Senate in its turn consisted chiefly of those who had held magistracies. Thus the nobility controlled the elections, and seldom did a "new man" succeed in raising himself to any of the higher offices in the state.

The New Contests. — In this condition of things it was natural that a new party antagonism should arise between the nobility, represented by the Senate, and the members of families which had not yet arrived at nobility. We see the beginning of this antagonism in the early years of the Second Punic War, when Flaminius and Varro were elected as consuls against the opposition of the Senate and in the interests of a policy opposed to that of the Senate. The disasters at Trasimenus and Cannæ discredited this party, and the still active spirit of patriotism maintained union of action as long as the danger lasted. Now that the danger was over, and the republic entered upon its great career of prosperity and glory, party spirit began to show itself again, and reached a pitch of unscrupulous violence which at last tore the republic in pieces.

Scipio. — The leading representative of the nobility in its best estate was Scipio Africanus (B.C. 234–183), one of the few men of genius whom the republic produced, the one to whom was due the successful conduct of the wars against Hannibal and Antiochus. He was a man of magnanimous temper, honorable in his dealings, and temperate in his life, but proud in the consciousness of integrity and the intuitions of genius. In public affairs he favored the policy of limiting the empire to its natural boundaries, Italy and the neighboring coasts and islands, leaving the more distant lands independent, but under the leadership of Rome.

Cato. — The most conspicuous leader of the opposition was Marcus Porcius Cato (B.C. 232–147), better known as Cato the Censor, for the severity with which he exercised the functions of this office. Cato was a peasant by birth, and his Sabine farm was near that of the great peasant-statesman of a century before, Manius Curius; and he took him for his type. But while he resembled his model in personal integrity, energy, and ability in war and statesmanship, adding to these a shrewdness and homely wit which distinguish him among all Romans, he was devoid of generosity and nobility of character. For nearly half a century he was the leading politician of Rome; and it is during these fifty years that the changed character of the Romans, the predominance of low and self-seeking motives, both in public and private life, becomes apparent. Cato contended vigorously against these tendencies; but he fought against symptoms rather than against the disease itself, and the indirect influence of his character was to emphasize more and more the selfish and ungenerous features of Roman policy. In opposition to the policy of Scipio, he favored the subjugation of foreign states and the extension of the mischievous provincial system — the chief cause of Roman deterioration; and his last public act was to hound on his countrymen to the destruction of Carthage.

B.C. 184.

Exile of Scipio. — This spirit of faction found its first expression in a charge brought against the two Scipios of misappropriating the public funds, in failing to account for the treasures gained in the war against Antiochus. Of the facts of the case we know very little. Africanus proudly refused to render an account (which he was under no legal obligation to do), tore the papers in pieces in the presence of the people, and, reminding them that it was the anniversary of the battle of Zama, invited them to follow him to the Capitol, and offer thanks to the gods. He then withdrew to his estate at Liternum, where he died four years later, forbidding his body to be taken to his native city for burial. The condemnation of Asiaticus was prevented by the intercession of the tribune Gracchus, a personal enemy.

B.C. 187.

Greek Influence. — It was at this period of the earliest close connection between Rome and Greece that the Romans first felt strongly the charm of Greek art and literature and the power of Greek speculation. As was natural, it was among the nobles, men like Scipio and Flamininus, that this influence was most strongly felt; and we can well believe that men of their type brought home with them what was best and most ennobling of Grecian creations. But it was not so with all. The Greeks were not what they had once been; and their art, literature, and philosophy at this age possessed no elevating or ennobling power, but were positive sources of corruption. Men like Cato, partly from narrow prejudice, partly from a clear vision of the dangers, set themselves against the fashionable Greek culture of the day: of course without effect. Their opposition was speedily justified by the discovery of gross indecencies and crimes connected with the secret worship of Bacchus, a degradation of the religious sentiment even below the standard of the noisy and orgiastic rites of the Great Mother (p. 129). An inquiry was set on foot by the Senate, numerous persons were punished, and severe laws were passed; but without much effect, for the cause of the evil was in the growing debasement of character.

B.C. 184.

The Roman Comedy. — One phase of this Greek influence has left a permanent record in works of literature, — the earliest works of Roman literature which we possess in any completeness. The Romans displayed little originality or creative power; but they attained great success in translating from the Greek, and these translations from the Greek comedians are partly preserved. The principal Roman comedian of this period was Plautus (B.C. 254–184), twenty of whose plays, free translations from Menander and other Greeks, are extant. These comedies present a picture of life which is neither Greek nor Roman, but a mixture of the two, lively and graphic, full of fun, sometimes gross. As a treasure of pure Latinity these plays of Plautus are invaluable. A generation later came Terence (B.C. 195–159), six of whose plays are preserved. These too are translated from the Greek, and they no doubt present the elegance and geniality of the original more truthfully than the coarse and rollicking plays of Plautus.

Cato's Treatise upon Agriculture. — Another work which has come down to us entire from this period deserves special mention, both as the earliest specimen of Latin prose, as the composition of a very distinguished man, and as a work very characteristic of the Roman genius. This is Cato's treatise upon agriculture; he composed a number of other works, especially the *Origines*, upon early Italian history, but this is the only one extant. As we have seen (p. 100), agriculture was held in great honor among the Romans. A treatise upon this subject by the Carthaginian Mago had been translated into Latin by order of the Senate. Cato's work upon agriculture is a short and dry treatise, of no literary merit, and so purely technical in its details that its value to us is chiefly in indicating the bent of the Roman mind at this period and the general character of Roman industry.

The Basilica Porcia. — The construction of a new court-house by Cato was an important event in the architectural history of Rome. The law-courts had hitherto been held upon the Forum, wherever the praetor saw fit to set up his tribunal. But the Forum was now becoming crowded, and the business of the courts was liable to be interrupted by bad weather or out-door noises. Cato therefore, in his censorship, bought land upon the comitium, between the Senate-house and the Capitoline, and on it erected a hall for the courts of justice, called *Basilica Porcia*. The style of building was that of a long hall divided lengthwise by two rows of columns.[1] Several other basilicas were in the course of time erected upon the unoccupied sides of the Forum and elsewhere, and this form of building was afterwards adopted for the Christian churches.

B.C. 184.

Wars with Greece and Africa. — By the three great wars in the East, Rome had gained prestige and wealth, but no increase of territory. But the time had now come when she was to seize into her hands the dominion over the whole Mediterranean. The capture and destruction of two cities in the same year, Carthage and Corinth, mark the sudden advance of the great republic to the summit of power.

B.C. 146.

Province of Macedonia. — The order of things established in Macedonia after the battle of Pydna (p. 136) did not long continue. An impostor, calling himself Philip, son of Perseus, excited an insurrection which was easily suppressed; and Macedonia, in the year 146, was converted into a Roman province. In the same year a war, into which the Achæan cities had rashly entered, was brought to an end by the consul Lucius Mummius. The war had been caused in part by insults offered to Roman ambassadors in Corinth; and now the Senate showed how far it had degenerated from the ancient Roman character, by ordering the complete destruction of this city, the most populous in Greece, and the seat of the most flourishing commerce. An enormous quantity of works of art were carried to Rome. The city ceased to exist, and its commercial preponderance was transferred to the Islands of Rhodes and Delos. The states and cities of Greece were left to govern themselves, but were required to pay an annual tribute,

[1] It is seen in the oldest churches of Rome, such as that of Santa Maria Maggiore; the foundations of the Basilica Julia, built by Julius and Augustus Cæsar on the south side of the Forum, are well preserved.

and were placed under the administration of the governor of Macedonia.[1]

Third Punic War. — In the same year as the destruction of Corinth, the Senate committed an even greater crime in the destruction of the ancient rival of Rome, Carthage. The prosperity and steadily increasing wealth of Carthage excited the jealousy and hatred of a party at Rome, of which the aged Cato was the leader; his hatred of Carthage was so bitter that he ended every speech, on whatever subject, with the words, "It is my judgment that Carthage should be blotted out."[2] With the connivance of the Roman government, the Numidian king, Masinissa, now nearly ninety years old, but as active and energetic as a young man, picked a quarrel with Carthage; and in the war that followed he gained a decided victory. B.C. 152.

Bad Faith of the Romans. — War with an ally of Rome was a breach of the treaty of peace, and the Romans did not hesitate to seize upon this pretext for the destruction of their rival. All the old spirit of magnanimity and good faith had disappeared from the public policy of Rome, and nothing in the whole course of its history displays a more cold-blooded brutality than its treatment of Carthage now. War was declared; but the Carthaginians, weakened and humbled, B.C. 149. were anxious to avert war by any concession. They were ordered first to give three hundred hostages, young men of their noblest families. When these had been delivered, they were commanded further to give over all their engines and munitions of war. These were brought to Utica, the Roman headquarters, and delivered, — more than 200,000 sets of armor, 2000 war engines, and an enormous amount of stores. Then they were informed that their city must be destroyed: their liberties and their municipal independence were preserved to them, they were to continue in possession of their territory, and they might build

---

[1] In the time of Augustus Greece was separated from Macedonia, and organized as an independent province by the name of Achaia.

[2] "*Censeo Karthaginem esse delendam.*"

a new city, but it must be at least ten miles from the sea. There must be no more commercial rivalry.

Siege of Carthage. — This announcement filled the people of Carthage with indignation and fury. They laid aside all dissensions, and united in the defence of their country. Every forge and workshop was busy night and day. The women cut off their hair for bow-strings, the public buildings were stripped of timber and metal for material, and when, after a month's delay, the Romans appeared before the walls, they were astonished to find the city in a complete state of defence.

Scipio Æmilianus. — The Carthaginians, excited to a fiery energy, were more than a match for their assailants; and the siege was protracted for three years. It was not until the young Scipio took command that the contest began to turn in favor of the Romans. Publius Cornelius Scipio was the son of Æmilius Paulus, the victor at Pydna, but had been adopted by the son of the elder Africanus, whose name he took. He is known by the surname Æmilianus, denoting his birth; also as Africanus, from his conquest of Africa. He was not a man of the genius of the elder Africanus; but by his uprightness of character, well-balanced powers, and moderation of temper, he deserves to be regarded as the leading Roman of his time. Like others of his family, he was not in sympathy with the vindictive spirit of Cato, but would have been glad to preserve Carthage as a worthy rival of Rome. In the spirit of an obedient citizen, he carried out a policy of destruction which he did not approve. Knowing that Scipio alone was capable of carrying the war to a successful issue, the Roman people, in spite of his being under the legal age, elected him to the consulship, and gave him sole command in Africa.

B.C. 147.

B.C. 147.

Destruction of Carthage. — Scipio pushed the siege with energy and consummate skill. First, he closed the harbor by a mole ninety-six feet wide; and when the Carthaginians cut through a new passage, he invested the city completely by new earthworks on the land side. The next spring he

B.C. 146.

DESTRUCTION OF CARTHAGE.

proceeded to the assault. The Romans fought their way into the city; but, even when they were within the walls, it took six days to fight their way through the streets to the foot of the citadel. Less than 60,000 out of a population of half a million were now left to surrender. The lives of all but Roman deserters were spared; but the city, by command of the Senate, was burned. As Scipio gazed upon the fire which raged for seventeen days — the work of his own hands, but which he detested — he thought to himself that such might one day be the fate of his own city; and he repeated thoughtfully the lines of Homer:

> "Yet come it will, the day decreed by fate,
> The day when thou, imperial Troy, must bend,
> And see thy warriors fall, thy glories end." — *Iliad*, vi. 448.

The territory possessed by Carthage at the time of its fall was made the Province of Africa, with Utica as its capital.

Colony of Carthage. — The plough was passed through the soil, and the spot was solemnly cursed. Nevertheless so favorable a situation for trade did not long remain deserted. A few years later Gaius Gracchus sent a colony to the spot, which now received the name Junonia. It did not prosper at first, but was renewed by Augustus, who sent there three thousand new colonists; and under the empire it again became a seat of commerce and civilization. In the later empire Carthage was once more the chief city of Africa.

B.C. 122.

The Roman Empire. — The dominion of Rome in the Mediterranean was now complete. Besides the territory of Carthage, its empire embraced the entire peninsulas of Greece, Italy, and Spain. There remained independent upon the coasts of the Mediterranean (besides the barbarous tribes of Africa, Gaul, Thrace, and Asia Minor), only the kingdoms of Egypt, Syria and Pergamus, the republic of Rhodes, and in the West the republic of Massilia (*Marseilles*). This was a Greek colony of the best type, worthy to be compared with Rhodes, a seat of wealth and culture, ruling over a large tract of territory on both sides of the mouth of the Rhone. But all these states, even if they could have been united, were no match for the power of Rome. East of Syria, the Parthian empire had now pushed its conquests to the Euphrates and the Arabian Desert, and was preparing to take its historical place as rival empire to that of Rome.

Province of Asia. — A few years after the conquest of Greece and Carthage, Attalus III., the last king of Pergamus, died, by his will bequeathing his dominions to the Roman people. As these dominions comprised all the western portion of Asia Minor, including the most fertile and populous regions of that peninsula, together with the great Greek cities upon the coast, Smyrna, Ephesus, Miletus, and others, this was a step of the first importance in building up the empire of the Roman republic.

B.C. 133.

SUOVETAURILIA.

PERIOD OF CIVIL DISSENSIONS.

CHAPTER XII.

THE GRACCHI.

I. THE SOCIAL AND ECONOMICAL CONDITION OF ITALY.

Decay of Republicanism. — It is a sign of the decay of genuine republicanism in Rome, and the approach of autocratic government, that from this time on its history centres about the names of individuals. Scipio Æmilianus was the last great Roman who embodied the spirit and the traditions of the republic; and he cannot be taken as a type of the corrupt and greedy age in which he lived. The century which still remained of the life of the republic can be best related in connection with six names, with which we may successively associate the events of their times. These are: the Gracchi, Marius, Sulla, Pompey, Cæsar, and Octavian.

Causes of Decay. — During the half century that had passed since the overthrow of Hannibal at Zama, there had been a rapid deterioration of the Roman people, and a rapid growth of misgovernment and social injustice. From these causes there now broke out civil dissensions of the most bitter character, speedily resulting in bloodshed, riot, civil war, and at last the destruction of the republic itself. The causes of these evils may be described under three heads, — the government of the provinces, the government of Italy, and the occupation of the land.

I. **The Government of the Provinces.** — It has been already shown that the Roman provincial system was a fruitful cause of mischief. It could not, in the nature of things, be otherwise. Power, joined with effective responsibility, sobers its possessor, and makes him cautious and conservative; but irresponsible power always produces recklessness and corruption. Now the Roman people were the irresponsible masters of the provinces, and they vested their governors with a practically irresponsible authority over the persons and property of the inhabitants of the provinces. The provinces were looked upon only as mines, from which the Romans should derive profit. The revenues derived from them not only made it possible to relieve the Roman people from taxation, but even to support them in idleness. From the time of the Second Macedonian War no tribute, or land-tax, was levied upon Roman citizens until the very close of the republic; and distributions of corn, either gratuitous or at a reduced rate, became more and more common. This was the lawful revenue of the state, even if gained by extortion and used for corruption; but besides this the governors made it their object, during their terms of office, to enrich themselves with unlawful plunder.

Abuses of Administration. — For these abuses the provincials had no redress, because cruelties and extortions exercised upon them were not regarded as crimes by the Roman law, while their own courts of justice had no authority over their foreign rulers. Lucius Flamininus, the brother of the victor at Cynoscephalæ, when commanding an army in Cisalpine Gaul, caused a noble Gaul, a fugitive in his camp, to be beheaded, not for any offence, but to gratify with the spectacle one of his favorites, who, to follow him to the camp, had been obliged to miss the gladiatorial shows. Flamininus was removed from the Senate by the censors for immorality, but the courts had no power to punish him.

B.C. 149. **Establishment of the Court of Repetundae.** — At last the abuses of administration became unbearable, and at the time of the Third Punic War a special court was organized in Rome for the trial of provincial governors for oppression and extortion. This was called the court of *Repetundae* (trial for extortion). Something was accomplished by this; but as the judges of the court were taken from the Senate, and the provincial governors were also members of the Senate, — that is, of the ruling nobility, — class interests stood, for the most part, in the way of any effective administration of justice.

II. **The Government of Italy.** — The government of Italy was no better, except that the Italian states were not placed under Roman governors, and were not called upon for contributions of money; but the arrogance and greediness of Roman officials were seen everywhere, and there was no effective machinery for bringing them within reach of the law. On one occasion, when the consul with his wife was on a visit at Teanum, a free town of Campania, the wife took a whim to bathe in the men's baths, which were consequently prepared for her use. But as she complained that she was kept waiting over long, and that the bath was not sufficiently clean, the magistrate of the town, its leading citizen, was stripped and flogged in the market-place. A young official, passing in a litter through the territory of Venusia, — a Latin colony, and therefore a free town, — was met by a herdsman, who asked jestingly whether they were carrying a corpse. The young man, inflamed at the insult, ordered the litter to stop; and the unfortunate herdsman was flogged to death. These two incidents, narrated in a speech of Gaius Gracchus, show the temper in which Italy was now governed, and enable us to understand how it was that the loyalty which had steadfastly resisted Hannibal was by degrees changed into hostility. The principal Latin colony, Fregellæ, was driven at length to revolt, was captured by treachery, deprived of municipal rights, and reduced to   B.C. 125. the rank of a village.

III. **The Land Question.** — During the period just passed a great change had taken place in the social condition of the Italian people. Before the wars with Carthage Italy was a country of small peasants, simple, industrious, living by the labor of their hands. It was now transformed into a country of great landed estates, owned by rich noblemen, and cultivated by slaves. In the mountain regions, especially in the territories of the allies, there still existed a peasantry of the old stamp; and the municipal towns were the seat of vigorous self-government. But in the

Roman domain and in the territories of many of the allied cities the rule of the nobles was unrestricted, and all independent proprietorship was being rapidly swallowed up in their plantations. The change is well illustrated in the contrast between Cato, the peasant statesman of the present period, and Curius, the peasant statesman of the century before. Curius was a yeoman, Cato was a planter. He owned large estates of land, which he cultivated with the labor of hard-worked slaves; and when his slaves were old and broken down with toil, he remorselessly sold them for what they would bring, that he might not be burdened with the care of their maintenance.

Slavery in Italy. — A new type of slavery had come into existence, and a new system of agriculture. In the old days the slave, a captive from some Italian nation, of the same race as his owner, was a member of his household, and worked by his side in the fields. There was no large market, and no large profits were expected; but every household earned its own livelihood. The greed of gain had now seized upon all classes. When the peasants were crowded out of their homesteads, the great plantation that took the place of these was cultivated purely for the profit of its owner, and with little care for the interests of the cultivators. Slave labor cost the planter less than free labor; his slave could not be called away for military service as a hired laborer could; and it was no concern of his what became of the free peasants who had been superseded by slaves. It is a well-established truth that free labor cannot exist by the side of slave labor, any more than good money can circulate by the side of bad; and no nation has illustrated this truth more fully than the Roman republic.

Causes of the Change; 1. War. — The process of building up great estates at the expense of the small freeholds no doubt began very early, and was held somewhat in check by the Licinian laws (p. 75), which regulated the amount of public land that any person could occupy, and required the employment of a certain proportion of free labor. The rapid economic changes and rise of prices at the time of the First Punic War (p. 101) gave a fresh impulse to the movement, and inspired a spirit of reckless speculation. But the change must have been greatly hastened by the devastations of the Second Punic War, when Hannibal traversed the lands of Central Italy year after year, burning and destroying wherever he went. Hannibal did not destroy the power of Rome, as he expected; but he did her a vital injury in annihilating the peasantry, and reducing great districts of territory to a condition in which they easily fell into the hands of capitalists and speculators. Within a very few years after the close of this war we find slave revolts in Apulia, showing that here B.C. 185. the prevalence of slave labor was already complete. In 135 there was a formidable insurrection of slaves in Sicily, which lasted until 132.

2. Force and Fraud. — It was not merely as a result of the devastations of war that the peasant freeholds vanished. There were of course voluntary sales, the small farmer not being able to compete with his wealthy neighbor in the present speculative system of husbandry. But a great proportion of the changes were wrought by force and fraud. In the secluded parts of the peninsula it was not easy for a peasant to hold his own against the chicanery, and even the positive violence, of the nobleman who wished his land. The story of Naboth's vineyard was repeated again and again in these rural communities; and even more than a hundred years later Horace describes, in glowing language, the rapacity of the proprietor who tears up the boundary stones of his neighbor, and drives from their home the husband and wife and ragged children, carrying with them the images of their household gods.[1]

The Public Domain. — This process was assisted by the continued occupation of the public lands, in the neglect of the restrictions imposed by the Licinian legislation (p. 75). It is true a large part of the conquered territory was employed in the establishment of colonies, both Latin and Roman. But

---

[1] quid quod usque proximos revellis agri terminos et ultra
limites clientium salis avarus? pellitur paternos
in sinu ferens deos et uxor et vir sordidosque natos. — OD. ii. 18, 23.

what remained became the prey of wealthy nobles or of capi-talists. In the Second Punic War the state had to borrow large sums from capitalists; and when they pressed for their pay, there was no resource but to mortgage to them all the public lands within fifty miles of Rome.[1] Public lands which had once in this way come into the hands of private persons were not likely ever to be redeemed.

B.C. 200.

The Grazing Industry. — It soon appeared that the great estates which had been thus built up could be more profitably employed in grazing than in agriculture. A single slave could guard the herds and flocks, over an extent of land which had contained many homesteads of free peasants. Cato, when asked what was the most profitable branch of industry, answered, "Successful cattle-raising." What next? "Moderately successful cattle-raising." What next? "Unsuccessful cattle-raising."[2] When the sole object was pecuniary profit, it was easy to see that, as slave labor was cheaper than free labor, so a few slaves, engaged in herding flocks, were more profitable than a large number engaged in cultivating the soil. So there took place an eviction of householders, a levelling of cottages, and an annihilation of agriculture, such as, for the same objects, took place in England in the time of the Tudors, and, for the sake of game, in Northern Scotland during the present century. This abandonment of agriculture was made possible by the foreign conquests. The provinces were required to contribute corn to the capital, and the Roman people were able to live upon the forced tribute of foreign nations.

The City Proletariat.[3] — From this we learn what became of the dispossessed peasants. Having no longer any home, they had nothing to do but to throng to the city, where they helped to swell

---

[1] Livy, xxxi. 13.

[2] Cic. de Off. ii. 25, 89.

[3] The term *proletarius* (producer of children) was given to those citizens who, by the smallness of their property (under 1500 *asses* = $15.00) were exempted from taxes, and served among the light-armed troops.

the rapidly increasing throng of the idle and worthless. They lived now, not upon the honest labor of their hands, but upon the plunder of the provinces. It was the provincial system which made it possible to turn Italy into pastures and pleasure grounds. From the time of the Second Punic War distributions of corn to the people, either gratuitously or at reduced rates, became more and more the practice.

The Publicans. — The proud aristocracy of Rome was, therefore, now given up to the eager pursuit of gain, by methods which undermined the well-being of the Italian people. By the side of this land-holding aristocracy there had grown up a body of rich capitalists, which formed a second aristocracy, even more sordid than the first, for their capital was not employed in productive labor, but in speculation and financiering. These capitalists, uniting in joint stock companies, and called *publicani*, contracted for the construction of public works and the collection of indirect revenues, such as salt works, mines, and public pastures. This was all very well; but in certain of the provinces the system of collecting direct taxes, through the instrumentality of these companies was adopted. This wasteful and oppressive system of "farming the revenues," as it was called, was in use in France in the last century, and was a leading cause of the French Revolution. The publicans contracted for a round sum to be paid into the treasury, and then squeezed out of the people all that they could, putting the surplus into their own coffers; it is easy then to understand the hatred with which they were regarded by the people of Judea, as expressed in the New Testament. As early as the close of the war with Hannibal, we find contractors of this class punished for B.C. 196. fraud; and it is easy to see, as time went on, that the unfortunate provincials would suffer as severely from the greedy publicans as from the oppressive governors.

II. Tiberius Gracchus.

The Family of Gracchus. — Tiberius Sempronius Gracchus was a young man of a noble plebeian family, distinguished for ability, honor, and public spirit. His father had been governor of Spain for two years, and had not only strengthened the Roman dominion in that country, but had gained the entire confidence and affection of the natives by his justice and humanity. Before this, as tribune, he had defended the two Scipios against their assailants (p. 140), and had afterwards married Cornelia, the daughter of Scipio Africanus, the well-known "mother of the Gracchi." Of their large family only three grew to maturity, two sons, Tiberius and Gaius, and a daughter, Sempronia, who was married to her cousin, Scipio Æmilianus. She was unattractive and ill-tempered, and they did not live happily together.

B.C. 179.

Wars in Spain. — The young Tiberius had served in the armies of Spain, a country which, by the turbulence of its natives and the atrocious misrule of its Roman governors, was a seat of almost constant warfare. There had been a formidable uprising among the Lusitanians (in modern Portugal) headed by Viriathus, a man of heroic character, who maintained himself against the power of Rome for eight years, until he was assassinated. Before the war with Viriathus was at an end the city of Numantia revolted, and withstood a siege of ten years, when it was at last reduced by Scipio Æmilianus, the conqueror of Carthage. It was at the siege of Numantia that Tiberius Gracchus, then quæstor, first distinguished himself, and showed that he possessed his father's high qualities.

B.C. 139.

B.C. 133.

Plans of Gracchus. — On his return to Rome Gracchus had occasion to pass through Etruria, and was impressed by the condition of things described in the last section, — the disappearance or impoverishment of the peasantry, the growth of enormous estates, and the prevalence of slave labor. It was plain to him, as to all clear-sighted Romans, that if this went on the republic could not endure; but where others were content to mourn the degeneracy of the times, Gracchus determined to seek a remedy. It favored his purposes that he was a plebeian, for he was thus able to hold the office of tribune, an office which made him the especial representative of the people, and which more than any other put it in his power to embody his ideas in legislation. He was elected tribune for the year 133.

The Agrarian Law. — It appeared to Gracchus that the public lands which were in the occupation of individuals might be made the agency for creating anew an Italian peasantry; in this reviving the policy of Spurius Cassius (p. 48). The Licinian law, which limited the amount of these lands to be occupied by any individual (p. 75), had fallen into oblivion; and the great estates which had been built up were largely composed of lands of this class, which were legally the property of the state. It was the plan of Gracchus to enforce this law, reduce the occupations to the lawful amount, and make use of the public lands thus resumed in providing households for landless citizens. In order, however, that his measure might not bear too hard upon those who had present possession of the lands, he provided that each of these might retain, in addition to the five hundred *jugera* permitted by the earlier law, two hundred and fifty for each son — not, however, to exceed one thousand in all. The lands thus resumed were to be divided into lots of thirty *jugera* (15 acres), and granted to both citizens and Italians in perpetual lease; it was feared that if they could be sold, they would soon be swallowed up in the great plantations, as the original homesteads had been.

The Tribunate. — This project of law came near being thwarted by one of the most absurd and mischievous features of the Roman constitution. The tribunes, ten in number, were originally appointed in order to protect individual citizens against magistrates who were disposed to abuse their enormous power (p. 43). For this purpose each of the ten was enabled, by his simple intervention, to block the action of any magistrate, even of his colleague. This had been a salutary power during the contest of the orders; but now that the tribunes had ceased to be the representatives of an order, and were, like the rest of the magistrates, regular organs of the government and agents of the Senate, — the requirement of plebeian birth having now no real meaning or object, — such a power as this was a mere instrument of anarchy, enabling a single factious member of the board to block the wheels of government.

Passage of the Law. — On this occasion Marcus Octavius, a colleague and old friend of Gracchus, interposed his veto, and thus brought the plan of legislation to nought. Gracchus employed all his powers of persuasion, but to no effect; and, desperate at the threatened failure of his cherished scheme, he, like many other impatient reformers, felt that he could not wait for a more favorable opportunity, but must attain his end by a violation of law. The Roman constitution made no provision for removing a magistrate from office, except the voluntary act of abdication. Impeachment, which with us must be brought against a person while in office, could not in Rome be brought until the offender had retired from office: even if, like the Decemvirs and the Censor Claudius (p. 59 and 89), a magistrate continued in office after his term had expired, there was no legal remedy. Gracchus, however, made up his mind to remove from office his contumacious colleague. This was done by a vote of the tribal assembly. The law relating to the public lands was then passed, and its execution entrusted to a board of three commissioners, — Tiberius himself, his younger brother Gaius, and his father-in-law, Appius Claudius. It did not seem safe to trust the execution of a law so vital, and an object of such fierce opposition, to any but those who ardently desired its success.

Death of Gracchus. — A violation of law in the interest of personal ambition is very likely to be successful, because the interested party is bound by no scruples as to how far he may push his encroachments; but a violation of law for good ends is almost sure to fail, because it at once shows inconsistency, and excites suspicion of personal motives. Gracchus' illegal act had placed him in the wrong, and he soon found himself helpless. Nothing could

DEATH OF TIBERIUS GRACCHUS.

save him from impeachment but to continue in office a second year, and that too was illegal. He presented himself for reelection, with the offer of new favors to the people; among them that the recently acquired treasures of King Attalus (p. 146) should be given to the new land-holders for the purchase of stock and tools. But it was to no avail; the nobles were determined to have his life. A "mob of gentlemen," headed by Scipio Nasica,[1] grandson of the one who had been, seventy years before, pronounced the best Roman (p. 129), attacked Gracchus, and beat him to death with the fragments of broken benches.

End of the Commission. — Nevertheless the commissioners proceeded to their work, took possession, in the name of the state, of such lands as were clearly held in contravention of the law, and divided them among actual settlers. But soon questions of title were raised. There were many estates in which, from the length of occupation and the variety of modes of acquisition, it was impossible to decide readily what was public land and what private. The functions of the commissioners were not only administrative, in assigning lands, but judicial, in determining titles. Complaints were raised against them; and, on the proposition of Scipio Æmilianus, who had now returned from the capture of Numantia, the right to decide questions of ownership was taken away from them, and vested in the consuls. As B.C. 129. the consuls had enough to do, in their regular duties, without undertaking the settlement of these delicate questions, this was equivalent to abolishing the commission. Its work was at an end, because no more land was given it to distribute.

Result of the Reforms. — Nevertheless, the reform of Tiberius Gracchus did not perish with its author. His place upon the commission had been filled, and by its action about eighty thousand citizens and allies had been provided with homesteads. Thus Italy was redeemed, so far as, under the circumstances, it

---

[1] This Scipio Nasica, nicknamed Serapio, is in his youth one of the characters in Ebers' *Sisters;* the characterization is good, but the incidents improbable.

could be redeemed. It is probable that any further resumption and distribution of lands would have worked more mischief than good. However that may be, the man who had arrested the proceedings, Scipio Æmilianus, at once lost his popularity, and was shortly after found dead in his bed.[1] It was suspected that Gaius Carbo, a member of the commission, and a profligate demagogue, was his murderer.

III. Gaius Gracchus.

B.C. 123. **Gaius Gracchus.** — Ten years after his brother, Gaius Gracchus entered upon the office of tribune, which he held for two years, it having now been made legal to hold this office in successive years. He was superior to Tiberius in intellect and in eloquence, more vehement in nature, and more inclined to violent measures, while his naturally fiery disposition had been further inflamed by his brother's tragical death. The two years of his tribunate were marked by a bitter contest with the party of the aristocracy, by sweeping measures of reform, — some of them very questionable in policy, — and at last by an end even more tragical than that of his brother.

Reforms of Gaius Gracchus. — The reforms of Tiberius Gracchus had worked great benefit to the Italian people, by placing a check to the growth of great properties, and bringing into existence a numerous peasantry of the ancient type. But they were reforms which did not go far below the surface. The causes of decay, in the selfishness and unbridled power of the nobility, the destructive system of slave labor, the corrupting influence of the provincial system, and the entire inadequacy of the Roman constitution, were still in full operation; and temporary remedies, like those of Tiberius, could work only temporary benefit. Gaius Gracchus saw that what was needed was a fundamental change

[1] Scipio, who sympathized with the motives of Tiberius, but disapproved of his actions, had, on hearing of his death, exclaimed in the words of Homer: "So perish whoever else may act in like manner."

in the organic life of the community, and his legislation was devised for this end. In this clearness of vision, and in the singleness of purpose with which he set about his end, consists his greatness as a statesman; but he had the limitations of his age, as well as of his personality, and was guilty of fatal mistakes. Some of his measures were wise and salutary, others only aggravated the evils they were designed to remedy.

The Evils to be remedied. — He saw, no doubt, as others had done long before him, that slave labor was ruinous to the interests of the free population; but slave labor was so completely ingrained in ancient society that it would have been impossible to be rid of it, even if such a thing had occurred to them. The provincial system too had now become fastened upon the Roman people, and Gaius does not appear to have recognized that it was an evil; some of its worse features he even exaggerated. The fundamental defects of the political system of the Romans he does not seem to have noticed any more than his countrymen in general. Inspired with a bitter hatred towards the nobility, which had murdered his brother, he bent all his energies to the task of overthrowing their power. The domination of Rome over the subject nations seemed to him right; the clumsy and incongruous machinery of government which had by successive steps been created gave him no concern; his aim was to shift the balance of power, and deprive the oligarchy at once of the administration of the government at home and the rule of the provinces abroad.

Political System. — We have already spoken at some length of the growth of the plantation system, the disappearance of the free peasantry in the presence of slave labor, the government of the provinces, and the disqualification of the Italians. It remains to speak of the inadequacy of the political system of the Romans, an evil which for the first time manifested itself, now when the city upon the Tiber had become the controlling power, not only within the peninsula of Italy, but in the Mediterranean circle of lands.

The Ancient City. — Rome was in its origin a city, like the other cities of Greece and Italy, and its government, now that it had become a great empire, was still the government of a city. The city (πόλις, *civitas*) of the ancients was not, like our modern cities, a place set apart from the surrounding country, and distinguished from it by special privileges and a more highly organized government. The ancient city, as a body politic, included the territory about it, and the inhabitants of the surrounding territory were not dependent upon, or subject to, the inhabitants of the walled town, but were themselves fully qualified citizens. Indeed, ownership of land, rather than residence within the walls, composed the qualification for citizenship, and the *rus*, or rural territory, formed as essential a part of the *civitas*, or city, as did the *oppidum*, or walled town, where were the temples and other public buildings, the seat of residence and trade. The boundaries of one city were also the boundaries of the neighboring cities,[1] and the whole of Italy — with perhaps the exception of some rocky mountain-tops or uncultivable morasses — was divided up into the territory of its several cities.

The City Government of Rome. — We have seen how Rome, in its territorial growth, had step by step annexed and incorporated into its body politic a large part of the Italian peninsula.[2] The free inhabitants of all this immense area were Roman citizens, and — except so far as they were disqualified for political reasons — were entitled to vote in the Roman assemblies, and hold the offices of state. So far as their Roman citizenship secured them in their rights of property and of personal liberty, it was a great advantage to them, distinguishing them favorably from the inhabitants of the Latin colonies and the allied towns; but it will be readily seen that as an agency of government this Roman citizenship could

[1] See, to illustrate this, the map of Italy in the time of the Second Punic War (p. 118), in which, for example, are shown approximately the territorial extent of Ardea and Laurentum as adjoining cities.

[2] The map (p. 118) shows approximately the Roman domain at this period. The *City of Rome* (*civitas Romana*) comprised all the territory thus designated.

have been of very little efficacy, either to the people themselves or to the state. All public assemblies must be held within the city, and, of course, as a rule none but the residents of the city itself or of its immediate neighborhood could be present at them.[1] There were no good roads except the military highways — the Appian, leading to Capua, the Flaminian to Ariminum, and two or three others; few but women and children rode in carriages; and the Sabine or Campanian peasant who wished to vote in the election of magistrates or the passage of laws must trudge on foot or ride on horseback, and spend several days on the journey to and fro. The elections, moreover, were not all held on one day, as with us, but each class of magistrates (consuls, prætors, etc.) were elected on a separate day: and legislative *comitia* might be held in any part of the year.

The Municipalities. — The Romans had established, in these outlying parts of the peninsula, an admirable system of municipal government, by which all local affairs were managed directly by the inhabitants of the several localities (p. 99); but for lack of the modern principle of representation, there was no machinery to enable the inhabitants of these municipalities to take part in the government of the republic. This fundamental defect in their political system the Romans were never able to remedy. They could not conceive of any form of government except the free city of Greece and Italy, and the despotically governed empire of the Orient; and when the city type broke down, they could do nothing but establish the autocracy.

Constitutional Defects. — An equally serious defect, and one which showed itself more and more as the city grew to great proportions, was in the machinery of government itself, which was inconsistent and incoherent in the highest degree. In the early republic the consul, whose power was derived from that of the kings, was the sole magistrate, the Senate being his council, and the popular

[1] In the independent cities of Greece and Italy it was a tacitly accepted rule that the territory (*pagus*) should not exceed in extent the distance to which a citizen might go in the morning to cultivate his fields, returning at night.

assembly the organ of the popular participation in the government. As the business of state grew more burdensome and complicated, a number of inferior magistrates (prætors, censors, etc.) were established from time to time, with functions derived from those of the consuls. At the present time the consuls were left with hardly more than executive and military powers, all their other functions being distributed without order or symmetry among a multitude of inferior officers and assemblies. By the necessity of the case, the Senate, as a permanent body of experienced statesmen, had taken the government in hand, and superintended and controlled the action of all the magistrates and assemblies. As long as the Senate was "an assemblage of kings" (p. 98), this work of co-ordination was done wisely and efficiently; and the inherent evils of the form of government were not perceived. Now that the Senate was an assembly of tyrants and speculators, the government of Rome became more and more weak and incompetent.

Attack upon Senatorial Government. — It was, therefore, with a clear judgment of the needs of the situation, that Gaius Gracchus directed his attack against the government of the Senate, as the chief obstacle to any permanent remedy for the economical and social evils of the time. But it was not so easy to find a substitute for the Senate, as the supreme power in the state, and here was the principal weakness of his plan of reform. To place an autocrat at the head of the state would have been to break violently with Roman tradition. To create an effective system of republican administration, so long as the city type of government was preserved, was a problem beyond the capacity or ideas of classical antiquity.

The Plan of Gaius Gracchus. — The plan of Gaius Gracchus seems to have been to get into his own hands a controlling influence in the state, similar to that which Pericles had possessed in Athens, not as a permanent chief magistrate of monarchical character, but as an influential citizen: his authority partly resting upon moral ascendency, partly associated with the tenure of the regular magistracies. For this purpose the tribunate was well fitted. It could be held continuously, it gave the power of controlling all the other magistracies, and also the right to summon the legislative assembly and convoke the Senate. As long, therefore, as he could persuade the people to elect him to this office, and he was protected by its sacred character, he was master of Senate, people, and magistrates. But if he once should lose this moral ascendency, — and he lost it the second year, — his power was gone. We shall see, when we come to the establishment of the Empire by Augustus Cæsar, how this fertile idea of the tribunician power as the foundation of supreme authority was revived, and was supplemented by being joined with the military power, — the point in which the plan of Gaius Gracchus was weak.

Reform of the Senate. — Gracchus did not propose to abolish the Senate as the supreme power in the state, but undertook to overthrow the nobility, as the power that controlled the Senate and through it the state. He proposed to restore the dignity and character of the Senate by adding to it an equal number of *Knights*, or persons of so-called equestrian families ; that is, families that were wealthy, but not noble.[1] Of course the new members thus added would soon have been merged in the nobility, but in the meantime a better public sentiment might have been created. And, while leaving this enlarged Senate in the possession of the government, Gracchus deprived its members of one source of profit and corruption by a law requiring that the judges in the court of *Repetundae* (p. 148) should be no longer taken from the Senate, but from members of the equestrian order.

Miscalculations of Gracchus. — Here again his calculations were at fault. The new judges proved no less corrupt than the old, for they were exposed to equal temptations. If the provincial governors were taken from the Senate, the publicans — quite as intolerable a scourge to the provinces — were of the equestrian

---

[1] They were called *equestrian* because they were qualified by their property to serve in the cavalry, and it was from them that the *equites equo privato* (p. 70) were taken.

order, and were quite as well disposed as the senators to shield delinquents of their own order. That he might still further gain the Knights to his support, he extended to the newly acquired province of Asia, the system of farming the revenues by companies of publicans, thus still further sacrificing the provincials to the supposed interests of Rome. But while sacrificing the provincials, he favored the Italian allies, whom he proposed to admit to citizenship — a proposition which lost him the support of the selfish mob of Rome.

Popular Measures. — By these measures he expected to establish a control over the Senate. For continuance in his office of tribune he must look to the people, and here again he favored the Romans at the expense of the provinces. Sales of corn, the contribution of the provinces, at a much reduced price, had been occasionally made. Gaius Gracchus made them regular, thus establishing the principle that the sovereign people were to be fed at the public expense. The agrarian legislation of his brother was revived and extended in some way, as to the details of which we are ignorant; and besides this the policy was established of planting colonies in the provinces. The available land in Italy had been now for the most part taken up. What public lands still remained were either unsuitable for homesteads, or were retained by the state to be rented as a source of public revenue. He proposed, therefore, to establish twelve colonies in the provinces, and himself carried a body of settlers to the abandoned site of Carthage, where he founded the colony of Junonia (p. 145), the first Roman colony outside of Italy. A second colony,

B.C. 120.
Narbo (*Narbonne*), was founded shortly after his death, and at about the same time the territory between the Pyrenees and the Alps was made into the province of Transalpine or Narbonese Gaul.[1] The rest of his colonial plan was abandoned.

Overthrow of Gaius Gracchus. — But the ascendency of Gaius

[1] This included none of the sea-coast, except the town of Narbo itself, the rest of the coast being in the possession of Massilia.

DEATH OF GAIUS GRACCHUS.

Gracchus, resting upon the selfish interests of the citizens and the precarious tenure of an annual magistracy, was easily overthrown. Another tribune, Marcus Livius Drusus, outbade him for popular support by proposing twelve colonies in Italy, with lands in full ownership; and the fickle people hastened to support their new leader. The excitement reached a tremendous height. Gracchus lost his election, and became a private citizen. In January, B.C. 121, the new consul, Lucius Opimius, took active measures against him. Gracchus and his coadjutor Flaccus entrenched themselves on the Aventine Mount, where they were attacked and routed by the consul. A bloody battle followed in the streets of Rome. The two insurgent leaders were killed, and it is said that three thousand of their party were afterwards strangled in prison. The consul Lucius Opimius, by a grim irony, to commemorate this restoration of order, built a temple to Harmony (*Concordia*) at the head of the Forum, which was thereafter one of the principal temples of the city, used as a museum of art, and a frequent place of assemblage for the Senate.[1]

---

[1] It was probably a restoration, on a larger scale, of that vowed by Camillus, B.C. 367 (p. 75). It was again rebuilt by Tiberius, and its remains are now to be seen between the Tabularium and the Arch of Septimius Severus.

CHAPTER XIII.

MARIUS.

I. THE CONTEST OF PARTIES.

Parties in Rome. — The Roman people were now divided into two hostile parties, — the *optimates*, or party of the nobility, and the *populares*, or party of the people. These parties were not merely divided by a difference of opinion upon public policy, but by personal and pecuniary interests; and this gave the contest a degree of bitterness which, as we have seen, had already led to bloodshed. What incited the nobles to the murder of the Gracchi was not the question whether the landless should receive land, but the fact that the land so bestowed was to come out of their possessions, — that they were assailed in their vested interests. In the party contest which now ensued the equestrian order — the wealthy citizens who were not noble — sided for the present with the *populares;* but the ascendency of the *optimates*, which had been established by violence, was maintained by the votes of their clients and dependents.

Party Questions. — The principal questions in dispute were, first, that of the law courts, which Gaius Gracchus had taken from the senators and given to the knights; secondly, the admission of the Latins and the Italian allies to the privileges of citizenship. For a long time there had been no real difference between Romans and other Italians, except that the Romans were the ruling power, and the Italians were subjects. All power went with Roman citizenship, and along with the power went social superiority and pecuniary privileges. The Gracchi had begun the movement for the enfranchisement of the Italians, and one cause of their failure was the unwillingness of the Romans to give up any share of their privileges to the despised Italians. Here lay the strength of the *optimates*, for the poorest Roman felt that he had his special rights to defend.

Territorial Relations. — The land question was for the present at rest, inasmuch as all the available land in Italy had been disposed of; and the lands occupied by the nobles, as well as those assigned to settlers by the Sempronian laws, B.C. 111. were shortly after given to the occupants in full ownership. From this time there was no longer any *ager publicus* in Italy, except certain tracts rented to publicans, chiefly as pastures.[1] The scheme of colonies in the provinces too, after the planting of Junonia (Carthage) and Narbo, was allowed to drop. But the occupation of Narbo brought after it the establishment of the province of Transalpine or Narbonnese Gaul (p. 164), and the possession of this new province was attended with important consequences.

War with Jugurtha. — The first event of importance during this period of the revived ascendency of the nobility was a long and obstinate war with Jugurtha, king of Numidia. Jugurtha was grandson of Masinissa, and had obtained his throne by the murder of his cousins, the rightful heirs, aided by the corrupt connivance of Roman senators. When public opinion at last forced the Senate to make war upon Jugurtha, the first com- B.C. 112. manders who were sent against him, equally greedy, incompetent, and corrupt, only left matters in a worse condition than they found them. It was not until the B.C. 109. command was taken by Quintus Cæcilius Metellus, known as Numidicus, a nobleman of ability and high character, that affairs began to mend. Metellus was perhaps the best Roman of his generation; but the Roman type had fallen far below the standard of Fabricius (p. 94), who had delivered up the physician of King Pyrrhus when he came to him with an offer to poison his

[1] The most important of these tracts, the *ager Stellatinus* in Campania, became again the subject of agrarian agitation in the time of Cæsar; but this was just before the collapse of the republican institutions.

master. Metellus had no scruple in bribing the servants and officers of his enemy, and would have regarded as justified any treachery which should get Jugurtha into his hands. He was, moreover, offensively proud and arrogant.

Gaius Marius. — The best officer in Metellus' army was Gaius Marius, a peasant of Arpinum, who had risen purely by merit from low birth to high position, and had held all grades of honor except the highest, the consulship. When Marius asked leave of absence from the army, in order to present himself as a candidate for the consulship, he received the contemptuous answer that it would be time enough for him to seek the consulship when he could do it in company with the son of Metellus, then a young man of about twenty. As the legal age for the consulship was forty-three, this meant a delay of about twenty years. Marius never forgot the insult. Shortly after, however, Metellus grudgingly granted the leave of absence. Marius was elected consul by a large B.C. 107. majority, and assigned to the command in Numidia by a vote of the people, thus superseding his old commander. B.C. 106. The next year Jugurtha was taken prisoner by a young officer named Sulla, and carried to Rome, where he was put to death. Part of his territory of Numidia was annexed to the kingdom of Mauritania (*Morocco*), whose king, Bocchus, had assisted in the overthrow of Jugurtha; part remained under native princes until the time of Cæsar.

The Cimbri and Teutones. — During the war with Jugurtha a still more formidable danger had threatened the Roman power in the advance of the German tribes, the Cimbri and the Teutones, upon the new province of Transalpine Gaul. This was the commencement of that series of invasions and migrations which, five hundred years later, broke the Roman Empire to fragments. From this date the relations with the Germans seldom ceased to be a source of perplexity and danger. The nations of the Teutonic race had been, we must suppose, for hundreds of years slowly moving towards the west from their original seat in the far east. When at last they reached the Rhine, they found themselves no longer in the presence of savage tribes, occupying wild forests and dreary steppes, but saw before them a rich and well-cultivated land in the possession of a people, the Gauls, well advanced in civilization and prosperity. At this point the onward movement of the Germans was necessarily checked, and they passed by slow degrees into the customs and institutions of settled life.

The Cimbric Invasion. — It was in the invasion of the Cimbri and Teutones that this great wave of Teutonic migration reached the Roman dominions. These tribes did not pause at the barrier of the Rhine and the possessions of the Gauls, but passed over the bounds, and made their way towards the fertile fields of Italy. Army after army of the Romans was defeated by these new enemies, who at last, in the year 105, gained a victory at Arausio (*Orange*) upon the Rhone, almost as complete as those at the Allia and at Cannæ. In terror the Romans elected as consul for the next year Marius, the hero of the Numidian war; and when by some caprice the victorious Germans turned away from Italy, and roamed through Gaul and Spain for two or three successive years, they re-elected him in four successive years, in order to be ready for the coming danger. It was an illegal act,[1] but the safety of the state prevailed against the letter of the law.

B.C. 113.

Victories of Marius. — At last the invaders again set their faces towards Italy; but the two nations had separated, and each moved by itself. In the year 102 the Teutones were met at Aquæ Sextiæ (*Aix*) in Southern Gaul, not far from the battle-field of Arausio, and annihilated by Marius. Their companions, the Cimbri, made their way across the Alps to the valley of the Po in Northern Italy, where the following year, 101, they were cut in pieces at the Raudian Fields, not far from Vercellæ, by the colleagues, Marius and Catulus. In this battle Catulus, one of the best members of the nobility, did good service; but the chief merit belonged to

---

[1] The order in which and the age at which the several magistracies could be held were fixed by the Villian law (B.C. 180). Ten years must by law elapse before any magistracy could be held a second time.

Marius, and it was his victory of the year before that made this victory possible. For the present, therefore, danger from this source was averted.

Military Reforms of Marius. — Marius was an unlettered peasant, a man wholly without political abilities or statesmanship, of violent and unforgiving temper; but he was personally honest, and his military abilities were of a high order. To him is attributed the re-organization of the legion, the most important military reform since the introduction of the manipular order in the time of Camillus (p. 69). The division of the legion into thirty maniples, breaking up the phalanx into small divisions capable of independent action, led naturally to the practice of giving more and more scope to the individuality, both of the division and of the soldier. The first step was the formation of the three lines, advance (*hastati*), main line (*principes*), and reserves (*triarii*), which came successively into action as they were needed. It then became customary to combine three or more maniples into larger temporary divisions, called cohorts. Scipio, at Zama (p. 127), by leaving larger spaces between the three lines, and thus allowing more independence of action, took the final step in the manipular organization. The legion, as thus organized, showed its superiority over the Greek phalanx at Cynoscephalæ and Pydna (pp. 133, 136).

MARIUS.[1]

Marius' Military Organization. — The decay of the Italian peasantry, from which the Roman infantry had been chiefly recruited, made the old method of a citizen soldiery composed of men of substance no longer available. Marius, therefore, introduced the custom of taking soldiers from all classes of citizens,[2]

---
[1] This bust passes as that of Marius, but is of very doubtful authenticity.
[2] Citizenship was at all times a requirement for service in the legions; and

principally men of no property. Thus the character of the army was fundamentally changed, and it was henceforth composed of a low class of professional fighters. The distinction in equipment and service, which had been observed when every soldier was a citizen of standing, was no longer befitting. The system of three permanent lines was abolished, and every maniple provided with the same equipment, and employed in the same service.[1] The threefold order of battle was still the usual one; but, now that the permanent lines were abolished, the several cohorts were drawn up as seemed fit at the time — the best troops generally in the front line. The cohort, which had until now been an occasional grouping of maniples, now became a regular and permanent division, being one-tenth of a legion, and consisting of three maniples. The cohort, as well as the maniple, now had a standard of its own; and a new standard, the silver eagle, was introduced for the legion.

Saturninus and Glaucia. — The great work which Marius accomplished for his country was the defeat of the Teutonic invasion, but the Roman politicians of the popular party conceived the design of using the simple-minded soldier for the furtherance of their political schemes. The leaders of this party were Saturninus and Glaucia, the successors of the Gracchi, but men of a much lower type. For the year 100 they procured the election of Marius to his sixth consulship, while Glaucia was elected prætor and Saturninus tribune of the people. This formidable combination proposed to take the government of Rome in hand just as Gaius Gracchus had done, but with a more complete organization, and with less scruple as to means.

Sedition of B.C. 100. — The propositions made by these confederates aimed in general to carry out the policy of Gaius Gracchus, — the creation of new colonies in the Po valley and the

when, under the empire, non-citizens were recruited into them, they received citizenship at the time of enlistment.

[1] The names *triarii*, *principes*, and *hastati* were still used, but only for the centurions of the maniples, to distinguish them in rank.

provinces (in these colonies Italians were to have equal rights with Romans), the confirmation of the judicial power of the knights, and larger distributions of corn to the people. By the unblushing use of violence these laws were carried, and all members of the Senate required to take oath to support them. Metellus Numidicus alone refused to take the oath, and was by consequence obliged to go into exile. Marius, who was already beginning to shrink from the more radical measures of his associates, took the oath with a mental reservation, — "so far as the laws were really valid."

Victory of the Nobility. — As in the case of the Gracchi, an armed collision followed between the reformers and the adherents of the Senate; and Marius, as chief magistrate of the state, found himself at the head of an armed force, opposed to his old associates. A battle was fought on the Forum, in which the revolutionary party was wholly crushed. Saturninus and many others were taken prisoners, and confined in the Senate-house, where they were stoned to death by the young nobles, who climbed upon the roof, and stripped off the tiles for this purpose. Glaucia was also found and put to death. Their laws were abrogated, and for another ten years the rule of the nobility was confirmed; but Marius, through whom the victory had been obtained, was thoroughly discredited with both parties, and remained for several years in obscurity.

II. THE SOCIAL WAR.

The Italian Question. — The burning question at Rome was now that of the Italian allies, who were becoming more and more impatient in their demand to be placed upon an equality with the Romans. Upon this question the leaders of the popular party had a true sense of the needs of the situation. The movement begun by the agitation of Gracchus did not stop until, A.D. 212. by the famous edict of Caracalla, citizenship was extended to provincials as well as to Italians. The selfish ambition and violence of Saturninus and Glaucia had only delayed the

THE REFORMS OF DRUSUS.

reform. In the consulship of the great jurist, Scævola, and the great orator, Crassus, both of them moderate as well as upright members of the aristocracy, a law was passed prohibiting, under severe penalties, the citizens of allied towns from claiming the privileges of Roman citizenship. The passage of this law hastened the crisis. B.C. 95.

Drusus. — The question came to an issue in the year 91. The tribune Marcus Livius Drusus, son of the rival of Gaius Gracchus (p. 165), and one of the most prominent members of the nobility, came forward as champion of the Italians. With the proposition to grant citizenship to the allied cities he combined other reforms, — the reorganization of the Senate by the admission of three hundred new members, and the restoration of the courts to this body; he proposed to secure the support of the common people by distributions of corn and grants of land. His principal supporter in this reform was Lucius Licinius Crassus, the leading orator of the time. Crassus had, as chief magistrate, rigidly enforced the laws against the allies; but now, as a statesman, he used all his efforts to advance their interests. Even this moderate measure of reform, emanating from their own body, met with the determined opposition of the nobility. After a stormy debate Crassus suddenly died, and Drusus was shortly after assassinated. His propositions of law died with him.

The Varian Commission. — The fate of Drusus and his measures taught the Italians that they had nothing to expect, either from a sentiment of justice or from a policy of wise statesmanship, and they at once rose in rebellion. The first uprising was premature, and only incited the Romans to severity. A commission of investigation was appointed, upon the proposition of Quintus Varius, the supposed murderer of Drusus; and by this commission a number of the associates and sympathizers of Drusus were banished. B.C. 90.

The Uprising of the Italians. — The insurrection, however, went on. It found little support in the northern regions, — Etruria and Umbria, — where the plantation system was most fully developed, and the middle class had nearly disappeared. Its strength was in the vigorous tribes of Central and Southern Italy, the Samnites, and kindred nations of Italian stock, among whom a numerous peasantry still survived, and kept up the traditions of the simple and healthful social system of earlier times. The Latin colonies remained loyal, as in the war with Hannibal, and many cities of the allies did the same.

Italia. — The insurgents were inspired by no mean ambition. They aimed at nothing less than the complete destruction of Rome, and the establishment of a new empire, which should embrace the whole peninsula. In the form of government which they established, they did not rise above the conceptions of their age. The only type of free government of which they could conceive was the City (p. 160); they proposed to found a new city to take the place of Rome, — not as capital of the confederacy, according to our modern notions, but as itself the State, with a territory embracing all Italy, and a body politic coextensive with the territory. For this purpose they selected the city of Corfinium, situated as nearly as possible in the centre of the peninsula, and gave it the name of Italia; this city was to be henceforth *Italy*. But while the new city was to embrace the whole of Italy, on the other hand its ambition was to be limited to Italy; the selection of this spot among the high Apennines was in itself a surrender of all possibility of universal dominion. The poverty of the confederates in political ideas is shown by the fact that they slavishly copied the Roman constitution in all essential details; they do not appear, however, to have adopted the tribunate, its worst feature.

Italian Coin in the Social War.

(The Italian ox goring the Roman wolf.)

The Social War. — The war was an unequal one. The well-trained armies of centralized Rome, supported by the wealth of all the provinces, and led by such experienced leaders as Marius and Sulla, and younger leaders of promise, like Lucius Cæsar, Metellus Pius, and Gnæus Pompey, were more than a match for the resources of the loosely knit confederacy. The contest was heroically kept up for two years, with successes on both sides; but the Romans, by adroit policy, succeeded at last in dividing the confederates, by the offer of favorable terms of submission. The Julian law, proposed by the consul Lucius Cæsar, gave citizenship to all communities which had remained loyal; and the Plautian-Papirian law, shortly after, made the same offer to all which should return to allegiance. Thus, as in the case of the Latins (p. 80), the citizenship which had been churlishly refused before the war, was after all granted as its result.

B.C. 90.

The Municipal System. — All Italy was now brought within the territorial limits and political organization of Rome. But the name Italy was not at this time applied to the regions north of Umbria and Etruria; here was Cisalpine Gaul, a province in which there were a number of Roman and Latin colonies, but which did not receive citizenship as a whole until about forty years later. All the cities of Italy, south of Cisalpine Gaul, now formed municipal towns,[1] the citizens of which were also fully qualified citizens of Rome, with magistrates and assemblies of their own, in which all purely local matters were managed. This admirable system, the foundation of our modern political system, was the creation of the political genius of the Romans; and its complete adoption — of course as the gradual work of several years[2] — was the fruit of the Social War.

---

[1] From this time the distinction between *colonies* and *municipia* (p. 99) is practically effaced; but the colonies, both Roman and Latin, looking to Rome as their metropolis, retained their distinctive appellation, and were regarded as ranking a little higher in dignity.

[2] The municipal system received its final shape in the *Lex Julia Municipalis*, of Julius Cæsar (B.C. 45), and was afterwards extended into the provinces.

CHAPTER XIV.

SULLA.

I. THE FIRST CIVIL WAR.

Mithradates[1] VI., of Pontus. — Just as the Social War was finished, a new war, of formidable proportions, was brought upon Rome by an antagonist only second to Hannibal in ability, and perhaps more violent in his antagonism; while his savage and unscrupulous temper made him an even more dangerous enemy. This was Mithradates VI., king of Pontus. Pontus was one of the petty states of Asia Minor, which had gained their independence when the empire of the Seleucidæ began to break up (p. 132). Situated upon the southeastern shore of the Pontus Euxinus (*Black Sea*), from which it derived its name, it had extended its territory so as to embrace all the eastern coast of that sea, as well as the Crimean peninsula, upon the north, where a prosperous Greek community had existed for many generations. The king of Armenia, Tigranes, had married the daughter of Mithradates, and added the resources of his kingdom to that of his father-in-law.

MITHRADATES VI.

Schemes of Mithradates. — Having thus established his empire in the east of Asia Minor, Mithradates prepared to expel the Romans from their province of Asia (p. 146), which embraced its western portion, and to extend his dominion over the entire peninsula.

---

[1] This is shown by coins to be the correct spelling of the name; it is associated with the cult of the oriental god Mithras.

BEGINNING OF THE CIVIL WARS.

He rapidly overran the country, got the Roman governor, Manius Aquillius, into his hands, and put him to death by pouring molten gold down his throat, in derisive allusion to the Roman thirst for gold. Then, from his headquarters at Ephesus, he issued orders for a massacre of all the Italian inhabitants of Asia in one day: eighty thousand, at the lowest computation, were thus murdered.

B.C. 88.

Sulla. — The Romans at once declared war, and committed its conduct to the consul, Lucius Cornelius Sulla.[1] Sulla was a member of a noble patrician family, a man of extraordinary ability, both as a general and as a statesman, but cruel and vindictive, even beyond the measure of his age and nation. He had been Marius' best officer in the war against Jugurtha, and it was he that had brought the war to an end, by capturing the Numidian king (p. 168). Since that time the two men had become rivals and personal enemies. Sulla's cold, conservative nature, governed by a keen and far-seeing intellect, was in every way a contrast to the hot temper and democratic sympathies of his old commander; and now political differences intensified and gave direction to their animosity. Sulla was as completely identified with the party of the *optimates* as Marius with the *populares*.

The Sulpician Laws. — The popular leaders were uneasy at so great military authority being entrusted to a leader of the aristocracy; and the veteran Marius, whose services in the late war had not added greatly to his reputation, craved new opportunities for distinction. The Social War, like most wars, had been followed by economic disturbances; and a young leader of the popular party, Publius Sulpicius Rufus, a brilliant orator and a sincere patriot, had brought forward some propositions of reform.[2] These measures were carried; and Sulpicius now took the rash step of bring-

---

[1] See article on *Lucius Cornelius Sulla*, in second series of Freeman's Historical Essays.

[2] Among others, to remove from the Senate all senators who were deeply in debt, and to admit the new citizens to the tribes on an equality with the old.

ing in another proposition, — to take the command from Sulla and give it to Marius. This was a revolutionary measure, for the public assemblies had never been accustomed to deal with such matters, and the command had been lawfully given to Sulla. Its passage led by a fatal necessity to civil war. Sulla refused to obey, marched upon Rome and captured it, put Sulpicius and many of his associates to death, and promulgated a new set of laws of a conservative tendency. Marius escaped capture.

First and Second Mithradatic Wars. — Having repealed the laws of Sulpicius, and established matters in Italy upon an aristocratic basis, Sulla immediately proceeded to the East, and in a war of three years brought Mithradates to terms, forcing him to surrender all his conquests in Asia Minor, and to pay a heavy indemnity. At the same time he punished severely the adherents of Mithradates and the agents of his massacres. He then returned to Italy in B.C. 83. After his departure from his province, there was a brief renewal of hostilities between his successor Murena and King Mithradates, which is known as the Second Mithradatic War. Its incidents are of no importance.

B.C. 88.

B.C. 83-2.

Escape of Marius. — Marius had escaped from the slaughter of his partisans, and making his way along the coast, concealed himself in the marshes of Minturnæ, where he was arrested and thrown in prison. The town executioner, a Cimbrian slave, was ordered to dispatch him in prison; but when he recognized the conqueror of his nation, and heard him ask, in a stern voice, "Darest thou kill Gaius Marius?" he fled from the apartment, crying, "I cannot kill Gaius Marius!" By the connivance of the magistrates of Minturnæ, Marius again escaped, and passed over to Carthage, where, as is said, he was found by an officer of the governor, who ordered him to leave the province. "Return," said Marius, "and tell him that thou hast seen Gaius Marius sitting an exile on the ruins of Carthage." It would have been well for his memory if he had died with these heroic words upon his lips.

Revolution of Cinna and Marius. — The next year, 87, a counter-revolution took place in Rome. The two consuls, Octavius and Cinna, were of opposite parties, and their dissension soon came to an open rupture. A battle was fought upon the Forum, in which Cinna, the champion of the Marian party, was defeated and driven from the city. He soon, however, gathered adherents from the Italian population, called Marius back from exile, and entered the city in triumph. All the worst qualities of Marius' character had been stimulated by the disappointments and disgraces of the last years, and he entered Rome in a transport of vindictive fury. His associate Cinna, a patrician of base mould, was his ready agent, and the victorious party commenced a massacre of their opponents, which continued for five days and five nights. The first victim was the consul Gnæus Octavius; others were Lucius Cæsar, the commander in the Social War (p. 174); Quintus Catulus, the colleague of Marius in the victory over the Cimbri (p. 169); and Marcus Antonius, the rival of Lucius Crassus as an orator, and, since the death of Crassus, without a question the head of the Roman bar. When Marius was entreated to spare the life of his old colleague Catulus, he coldly answered, "He must die."

Rule of Cinna and Carbo. — The next year Marius entered upon his seventh consulship, with Cinna as his colleague; but his vital powers were exhausted, and he died on the thirteenth of January, B.C. 86, having by his actions of the last few weeks effaced the memory of his great services against Jugurtha and the Cimbri. For three years the revolutionary party remained in possession of the government, under Cinna, Carbo, and the son of Marius; it was then overthrown by Sulla, on his return from the East.

Renewal of the Civil War. — In the year B.C. 83 Sulla returned from the East, full of honors, and marched with his victorious army against his enemies in the city. He had exhibited great self-control and patriotism, remaining steadily at his post of duty, and carrying on the wars of his country, while his enemies were running riot in the capital. But he had confidence in his own resources, and on his side was the memory of the outrages perpetrated by his opponents. Upon his landing at Brundisium he was promptly joined by Quintus Metellus Pius, Marcus Crassus, and Gnæus Pompey, — young men who afterwards attained great distinction, — and before the year closed his cause was decidedly in the ascendant. Early in the following year the consuls, Carbo and the young Marius, were obliged to evacuate Rome. Carbo proceeded to the north of Italy, where his forces gradually fell to pieces. Marius made his head-quarters at Præneste, and a last desperate struggle was made under his command.

B.C. 82.

Battle of the Colline Gate. — Before abandoning Rome, Marius had ordered another massacre, of such nobles as had survived the former reign of terror. In this massacre, which was perpetrated by the prætor Damasippus, the most illustrious victim was Quintus Scævola, the most distinguished lawyer of Rome, the consul of B.C. 95 (p. 173), and the founder of the scientific study of jurisprudence. The struggle reached its crisis when an army of Samnites, under Pontius Telesinus, marched upon Rome to co-operate with Marius, and encamped in front of the Colline Gate, upon the north side of the city. The memory of the Samnite and Social wars rankled in the mind of the leader, and "he called out to his followers that, in order to get rid of the wolves which had robbed Italy of freedom, the forest in which they harbored must be destroyed."[1] Rome was to be burned. But Sulla followed close upon him, and the victory at the Colline Gate saved the city from destruction. Præneste shortly afterwards surrendered.

Sulla's Proscriptions. — Sulla, like Marius, stained his brilliant record of patriotic services by vindictiveness and cruelty in his hour of triumph. And if Sulla was inherently a greater man than his rival, and showed a better balanced character and a higher statesmanship, it must be admitted that the cold-blooded atrocities of his victory excite even greater horror than the massacres

[1] Mommsen.

of Marius. He introduced the policy of proscription. Every morning a list was posted (*proscriptum*), of the names of those whose lives were forfeited, and who might be put to death by any one with impunity. As the property of the proscribed was confiscated, the proscription was an invitation to crime, very acceptable to private enemies, or to those who hoped to buy the estates of the attainted at a low rate. The number thus put to death amounted to nearly five thousand, and the amount of confiscated property to three hundred and fifty million sesterces ($17,500,000). It was by purchases of these confiscated estates that Marcus Crassus, the richest Roman of his time, and the political confederate of Cæsar and Pompey in the First Triumvirate, built up his immense fortune.

II. THE CONSTITUTION OF SULLA.

Character of Sulla. — Sulla was now master of Rome, with his legions behind him, and he had it in his power to establish a monarchy on the ruins of the republic. But nothing is more remarkable about this remarkable man than his disregard of vulgar personal ambition, at the same time that he displayed a savage hatred of his personal enemies who were also his political antagonists. In his refusal to surrender his army to Marius, when ordered to do so by the Sulpician law (p. 177), he might be regarded as vindicating that principle of the constitution which placed the command in the hands of the consuls, and gave no authority over it to the popular assembly. In the years that followed he remained steadily at his work in the East, while Cinna was massacring his friends in Rome, — this in the face of bitter opposition and even

SULLA.[1]

[1] This bust, in the Vatican, has been named Cicero, which is certainly incorrect; Bernoulli (*Römische Ikonographie*) thinks it probably that of Sulla.

personal danger. All the while his passions had been burning fiercely, and when at last he had Rome in his power he took cruel vengeance upon his enemies, even causing the tomb of Marius to be broken open, and his ashes to be thrown into the river.

Sulla made Perpetual Dictator. — Sulla's temper was thoroughly conservative, and he was careful to respect the forms of the constitution. Under the violent shocks of the civil war, the machinery of government had, as we may say, run down. The consuls of 82 were both dead, and there was no legal authority competent to restore order, for Sulla's authority as pro-consul would cease the moment he entered the city. In circumstances like these, it was, as we have shown (p. 20), the duty of the patrician senators, in whom resided the ultimate sanction of the constitution, to come together, and by the appointment of an *interrex*, or provisional chief magistrate, to set again in operation the wheels of government. Therefore Lucius Valerius Flaccus, a patrician of ancient stock, was made interrex, and on his proposition Sulla was created perpetual dictator, with complete power to revise the constitution and to govern the state until the new order of things should be established.

Restoration of Senatorial Government. — Sulla's plan, consistently with his conservatism of opinion, was, so far as possible in the changed condition of things, to restore the system of government which had in former days carried Rome to her height of prosperity and power, — the Senate possessing supreme authority and exercising control over the magistrates and the assemblies. The Gracchi, acting upon the lines marked out by Flaminius, had rudely broken with this traditional order, and had made the assemblies, instead of the Senate, the ruling power in Rome. The change had worked no advantage. Bad as the Senate was now, the people were no better; and as long as the Italians were prevented, by their distance from Rome and the absence of representative machinery, from taking any active part in the government, it was no doubt safer to have the power in the hands of the oligarchy than of the mob. The misfortune of Rome at this juncture was that there survived no elements of a healthy free government. Sulla's aristocratic reconstruction was perhaps the best framework of government possible, of a republican type. How completely it collapsed, from causes inherent in the state of society, we shall see.

The Senate. — For a restoration of the senatorial government the first thing necessary was a restored Senate. It is easy to conceive how the Senate had suffered in numbers and in character by the prosecutions, massacres, and proscriptions of the last few years. Of the experienced statesmen of the period before the Civil War hardly one survived; the new generation of public men entered upon their task without experience or example. The first step to the restoration of the Senate was the election of about three hundred new members, chiefly from the equestrian order. For the future supply of members it was provided that every person elected to the quæstorship, the lowest of the regular magistracies, should become a member of the Senate for life. The age at which the quæstorship could be held was thirty, and as twenty quæstors were elected every year, and they had an expectation of perhaps thirty years of life on an average, it follows that the Senate after this time averaged between five and six hundred members.

The Magistrates. — The prætors were increased in number from six to eight, and were to be employed exclusively in judicial functions, two having the administration of civil cases, the others presiding over the newly organized criminal courts. The consuls were also confined to purely civil functions, being required to remain, during their term of office, in Italy, where no exercise of military authority was allowed except on extraordinary occasions. Both consuls and prætors, after their terms of office had expired, went into the provinces as governors. The office of censor was tacitly dropped.

The Tribunes of the Plebs. — It was Sulla's policy to reduce the overgrown power of the tribunate. The holding of this office was made a disqualification for the curule offices, and the tribunes were deprived of their right to initiate legislation, except by the previous authority of the Senate. This was a wise provision, giving to Roman legislation some of the advantages which we derive from our modern system of two legislative chambers. Moreover, the legislative power of the tribunes was the principal agency for the mischievous work of demagogues. For these very reasons the restoration of the power of the tribunes immediately became the popular demand, and in only about ten years Sulla's restrictions upon it were abolished. This was the only material point in which his legislation was short-lived.

B.C. 70.

The Permanent Courts. — The reorganization of the system of criminal justice was one of the most important of Sulla's reforms. The court of *Repetundae* (p. 148), for the punishment of extortionate and oppressive governors of the provinces, afforded a model for this reorganization. One or two other courts had already been added to that of *Repetundae*,[1] and now the whole range of criminal offences was arranged in groups and assigned to permanent courts (*Quaestiones perpetuae*), composed of senators and presided over by the several prætors and other officers. The system itself was a clumsy one and rested upon no well-considered principles of criminal jurisprudence; but this reform at any rate removed the trial of offences from the tumultuous public assemblies, and established some deliberation and order in the administration of criminal justice. Civil cases continued to be tried by the two principal prætors, *urbanus* and *peregrinus*.

Permanent Advantages of Sulla's Constitution. — The conservative provisions of Sulla's constitution were for the most part permanent, and might have been expected to work material advantage if the Roman constitution had not had defects incapable of remedy, and if the governing class had not been too deeply corrupted to be safely trusted with power. The reorganization of criminal justice, and the regulation of the government of the

[1] A court for the trial of murder (*de sicariis et veneficis*) had been organized by Gaius Gracchus; as to others there is no certainty. The whole number of courts established by Sulla was somewhere from eight to twelve.

provinces, were salutary provisions, which continued in operation until they were suspended by the institutions of the empire. But it was too late for any reform in administration to check the downward course which was carrying the republic rapidly to its destruction.

The Aims and Methods of the Rival Parties. — Neither party in the state was capable of working any real and permanent reform. Sulla, the leader of the aristocratic and conservative party, made salutary changes; but they were wholly on the surface, improving the machinery of administration, but not touching the real disease from which the body politic was suffering. The popular party saw deeper. Its ideal was higher, its policy nobler and more generous; but it was thoroughly discredited by the misrule of Marius, Cinna and Carbo. Julius Cæsar was the first Roman statesman who possessed at once broad and sound statesmanship, and an administrative capacity equal to that of Sulla; and when he rose to the leadership of the state the republic was too far diseased to be capable of preservation.

Abdication and Death of Sulla. — After having held the dictatorship about three years, and reorganized the government, as he supposed, on a permanent basis, Sulla abdicated his office, and retired to his villa near Puteoli, where the next year he died from the rupture of a blood-vessel. B.C. 78.
But hardly had he retired from power when his institutions were subjected to a critical test. The consuls of 78 were Marcus Æmilius Lepidus, a member of the popular party, and Quintus Lutatius Catulus, son of the victor of Vercellæ. The attempt of Lepidus to set aside Sulla's constitution led to a short civil war, in which Lepidus was defeated, and shortly after died.

CHAPTER XV.

POMPEY.

I. THE ROMAN PEOPLE.

Changed Condition of Society. — The Civil Wars of Marius and Sulla were, as we may say, a gulf, separating two distinct epochs. There was no longer among the Romans any sentiment of unity as a people, any community of interest, hardly any genuine patriotism or public spirit. They were divided into two opposing factions, each hating the other, and struggling only to secure its own advantage. It is not that there was no virtue or morality left. It is easy to exaggerate the vices and corruptions of any period or any people, and it is certain that Rome still contained many men and women of noble and exalted character; but, from the intensity of party spirit and the defective machinery of government, the best elements of society were powerless against the influences of corruption. Public life was therefore worse than private life, and, while steadily growing worse, dragged down private character with it.

Structure of Society. — We have already become acquainted with the principal obstacles to good administration, so far as these consisted in the organic law, or framework of government, — the illogical and inefficient distribution of powers among the several magistrates and assemblies, and the inadequacy of the city type of constitution. Even more fatal to a free government was the constitution of society, as it existed in the last century of the republic. The people of the early republic had been a homogeneous peasantry: patricians and plebeians, divided from one another by rights and privileges, were alike Italians of the same stock and the same type. Now society was divided between rich and luxurious nobles and the dependent populace. There was no longer any middle class; the peasantry had disappeared as a political factor, and there was no other industrial class to take its place.

Industry in Rome. — Here we touch upon the fatal and irremediable defect of ancient society — the absence of industry as a social power, a necessary consequence of slave labor. The economic changes through which Rome had passed are in certain particulars strikingly like those of modern England — in the disappearance of peasant properties and the building up of a great landed aristocracy. What has saved England from the fate of Rome has been the absence of slavery and the marvellous development of new forms of productive industry, the great manufacturing and commercial interests of modern society. In ancient times this was impossible. Most articles of household necessity were produced by the labor of slaves; manufactures, as a distinct branch of industry, did not exist. With commerce it was different. The great commercial republics, like Rhodes and Massilia, were among the best governed of the states of antiquity, and the patricians of early Rome had been a commercial aristocracy. But Rome at the present day had no true commerce, if by commerce we mean a free exchange of products. It lived upon the spoils of conquered nations, and its only large industries were farming the revenues, carrying on speculative operations and dealing in money.

The Debtors. — In the century which we have reached, as in the early republic, private indebtedness had grown to vast proportions, and society was convulsed by contests between debtors and creditors. But it was a contest of a wholly different character from the former. The debtors of early Rome were peasants who had fallen into the clutches of creditors armed with the oppressive powers of the law. For the relief of these, laws had been passed regulating the rate of interest, and the oppressive features of the law of debt had at last been abolished (p. 41). The debtors of the present time were speculators who could not meet their engagements, and aristocratic young men who had squandered their patrimony; the debts were not incurred for the benefit of honest industry, or the relief of distress, but to furnish means for extravagance, dissipation, and speculation.

The Demand for "New Accounts." — Nevertheless, the debtors made themselves out to be an oppressed class, and appealed for protection to the sympathies and the obsolete laws of the early republic. Usurious interest had been prohibited by an old law, and now the debtors persuaded the prætor Asellio to put this law in operation, and punish the creditors to whom they had been paying unlawful rates. The creditors were no more scrupulous than the debtors: they banded themselves together under the leadership of one of the tribunes, and attacked the prætor and murdered him, just as he was assisting at a sacrifice in his priestly robes. From this time the cry of the debtors was "new accounts" (*novae tabulae*), that is, a general abolition of debts, such an abolition as, in whole or in part, had been effected by the laws of Solon and of Licinius, but for the benefit of a wholly different class. This now became a party cry, not embodying any principle of public polity, but the selfish demands of the worst and most dangerous elements of society.

B.C. 89.

Divorce. — Nothing struck such fatal blows at the welfare of society as the increasing frequency of divorce, by which the institution of the family, the very foundation of society among all nations of the Aryan race, was assailed and vitally weakened. Among the Romans marriage had been regarded with peculiar reverence, and family relations had been pure and rigorous. By the usages of primitive society, as they survived in the early republic, divorce was freely permitted; but such was the strength of the family sentiment and the purity of morals that the power was very rarely exercised in early times. The first instance of divorce is said to have been in the time of the Punic wars. But the moral check which had been sufficient in those days wholly failed in the growing license and immorality of the present age, and divorce was now an every-day occurrence. Cato divorced his wife in order to accommodate a friend who wished to marry

B.C. 231.

her. Cæsar divorced his because of certain gossip, saying that "Cæsar's wife must be above suspicion." Cicero divorced Terentia, with whom he had lived through a long life in apparent harmony. Augustus fell in love with the wife of a nobleman and took her from him; he afterwards, in order to secure a succession to the throne, compelled her son Tiberius to divorce a wife to whom he was much attached, and married him to his dissolute daughter Julia, to the misery of both parties.

Gladiatorial Shows. — Another cause of demoralization was the passion for gladiatorial contests, which was becoming more and more the leading taste among the Roman people. The Romans were not originally a cruel or brutal people, but they were a warlike people, and early acquired a fondness for contests which exhibited military skill and prowess. The first exhibition of gladiators was at a funeral celebration in the first year of the First Punic War. From this time the number and   B.C. 264. magnitude of the contests rapidly increased. Schools were established for training the gladiators, who were slaves selected for their qualities as fighters; and the spectators soon ceased to be satisfied with exhibitions of skill, but demanded bloodshed and death. Thus the populace were brutalized, and the spectacle of human suffering became a keen source of enjoyment. Fights between gladiators were not enough for their depraved taste, but a new zest was added to the sight by the introduction of savage wild beasts into the arena.

Religion. — There was plenty of religious sentiment in Rome, but not of a kind to be of much value in the promotion of morality. The native Roman faith held its ground in the rural districts, but in the city its temples fell into neglect and ruin, until rebuilt by Augustus. The popular forms of worship in Rome were the more showy rites of the oriental religions — that of the Great Mother, already described (p. 129), and particularly of the Egyptian goddess Isis, whose temples were thronged with women, particularly of the lower class, but whose cult was associated with superstitions and gross indecencies.

The Auguries. — One branch of the Roman religion, however, was never kept up with more care and assiduity than in this age, and we may add, was never more devoid of reality; that is, the Auguries, the organ of communication between the state and the gods. The Romans had at one time believed that through the auspices[1] the gods expressed their will to the magistrates (p. 20); and they continued now to pretend to the same belief. But from the time that Publius Claudius had thrown the sacred chickens into the sea (p. 108) the belief in the auguries had sunk more and more to a mere form, only to become more and more essential as a form. By their power of interpreting the auspices, the Augurs — a board of fifteen noblemen — had little difficulty in controlling the action of magistrates and assemblies; while the rule of augury, that the assembly must disperse if thunder was heard, enabled the magistrate to break up an assembly by merely announcing that he intended to watch for signs from heaven — for it stood to reason that what he sought for he would find. The only remedy was the lamentable one of prohibiting, on certain occasions, the will of the gods to be consulted.

Greco-Roman Religion. — Among the higher classes the more dignified and elegant gods of Greece had been merged in thought into those of Rome in such a way that the Pantheon now consisted of a multitude of deities, some purely Greek, like Apollo, some purely Roman, like Janus; but for the most part an incongruous combination — Roman names, as Mercury, Mars, Minerva, associated with myths and attributes which belonged only to the Grecian Hermes, Ares, and Athena. The worship of these gods was maintained with pomp and solemnity; but it had no reality in the belief or the conscience of the worshippers.

Philosophy. — What influence there was to counteract vice and inspire to a better life came from the study of the Greek philosophers. But even here the good was by no means unmixed. The

---

[1] These two terms designate the same thing, from different points of view; the *auspices* being the signs by which the will of the gods was manifested, *auguries* the science of interpreting them, as a public institution.

philosophy of Epicurus, in its origin a lofty speculative system, of healthy and tonic power, had sunk to be a mere systematizing of pleasure, although its poet Lucretius, the noblest in tone of all the Roman poets, still represented it in its best phase. The Stoic philosophy was its chief rival, and the power of this was wholly good and ennobling, for it appealed to the best qualities of human nature. It had its limitations; but for three hundred years the Stoic philosophy was the healthiest and best influence in Roman society. A third school of philosophy, the Academic, was speculative and sceptical in tone, and its votaries were confined to a few persons of intellectual habits.

Literature. — It is remarkable, in the face of the facts here recorded, that at just this time literature makes great advances. During the century which followed the Second Punic War there is almost a complete dearth of original literature in Rome. In the period with which we are at present engaged there was a throng of writers, most of whose writings, to be sure, were either insignificant or have perished, but who prepared the way for the great literature of the generation which followed. Sulla himself wrote his memoirs; Quintus Scævola, the founder of scientific jurisprudence (p. 180), and Lucius Stilo, the founder of Roman philology, lived at this time. Above all, amid the turmoil of the civil wars and the collapse of society which followed, there was growing up that group of writers whose works have cast a glory upon the closing days of the republic — Cicero, the greatest orator and philosophic writer of Rome; Lucretius, its noblest poet, and Catullus, its most brilliant; Cæsar, a model of military narration; and Sallust, an historian of great and graphic power.

II. THE CONQUEST OF THE EAST.

The War with Sertorius. — The Civil War was, after all, not completely ended by the defeat and death of Lepidus (p. 185). The Spanish provinces were still in the hands of Quintus Sertorius, a leader of the Marian party, who had been sent thither in the time of Cinna to take command. Sertorius was by far the best man of his party, and its best general after the death of Marius; he had, moreover, a power of personal attraction which attached the Spanish population warmly to him. This personal attachment was strengthened by his practice of having with him a pet fawn,

POMPEY. (From a Statue in the Spada Palace at Rome.)

which followed him everywhere, and which the superstitious people believed to be his medium of intercourse with the gods. Under the rule of Sertorius Spain was wisely and justly governed, and general after general was sent against him without result.

SERTORIUS AND SPARTACUS.

Gnaeus Pompeius Magnus. — At last the government sent against Sertorius its ablest officer, the young Gnaeus Pompey. He was the son of a commander of some distinction in the Social War, and had himself held command under Cinna and Carbo. When Sulla landed in Italy on his return from the East, Pompey was one of the first to join him, with a large and well-organized army. He was in consequence peculiarly favored and trusted by Sulla, who bestowed upon him the surname Magnus, *the Great*. His sympathies were no doubt in general with the conservative, aristocratic policy, represented by Sulla. He was, however, no politician, and is identified with no large policy of statesmanship; his political career is marked with strange inconsistencies and changes. But he had military abilities of a high order, and was personally a humane man, less stained by crime than perhaps any of his contemporaries of equal prominence. For nearly thirty years he was the most conspicuous personage in Rome. [B.C. 82.]

Death of Sertorius. — The predecessor of Pompey in the command against Sertorius was Quintus Metellus Pius, son of Metellus Numidicus (p. 167). Metellus, too, was a man of more than average character and ability; but neither he nor Pompey was able to accomplish anything against an antagonist who was at once so able as Sertorius, and possessed such an ascendancy over the people whom he governed. But although Sertorius was loved and trusted by the Spaniards, there were traitors among the degenerate Romans in his own camp. He was assassinated at a banquet by one of his own officers, and the Spanish insurrection speedily collapsed. [B.C. 72.]

War with Spartacus. — While Pompey was absent in Spain, a formidable uprising of slaves had occurred in Italy. It began among the gladiators in Capua. These were slaves, captives in war or kidnapped from barbarous nations, and trained to entertain the Roman populace by their bloody combats. Under the leadership of Spartacus, a Thracian by birth, they escaped from the gladiatorial school at Capua, ensconced [B.C. 73.]

themselves in the wild recesses of Mount Vesuvius, and held their pursuers at bay. They were joined in their retreat by fugitive slaves from the plantations, and soon Spartacus was at the head of a powerful army, with which he long resisted the Roman power.[1] But it was not in the nature of things that a hastily gathered band of slaves should hold out against the most warlike nation in history. The insurrection soon began to weaken, and after about two years the insurgents were defeated and dispersed by the new commander, Crassus. Some scattered remnants were met by Pompey, on his triumphant return from Spain, and by cutting them to pieces he added to his laurels.

B.C. 71.

Consulship of Pompey and Crassus. — For the next year, B.C. 70, the two successful generals were elected consuls, and the year is memorable for the overthrow, in some important particulars, of the Sullan constitution. Marcus Licinius Crassus was, like Pompey and Metellus Pius, one of the younger generation of nobles, who had come into prominence since the Civil War; but he was the least reputable of his class. His chief ground of distinction was his wealth, which he had acquired by very questionable means (p. 181). He was a politician of a sordid type. Like Pompey, he had been a prominent adherent of Sulla, and it does not appear that either of them was less an aristocrat now than then; but to favor a restoration of popular privileges was at this time the road to political success.

Democratic Legislation. — The reactionary legislation of Pompey and Crassus consisted of three principal measures: First, the power of the tribunes was restored, and this office became again, what it had been before the time of Sulla, the chief instrument of discord and sedition. Secondly, the question of the criminal courts, which had been the political issue most hotly contested, received a final and rational settlement. These courts were originally composed of senators; Gaius Gracchus had given them to the equestrian order (p. 163); Sulla had restored them to the senators (p. 184); now, by the Aurelian Law, they were to be

[1] *Prusias*, by Eckstein, deals with the story of Spartacus.

divided between the two orders: that is, they must be composed exclusively of wealthy citizens — one-third senators, one-third officers of the tribes, and one-third selected at large from the equestrian order.[1] The third measure was the restoration of the censorship. This magistracy formed no part of Sulla's scheme. He had given its financial and administrative functions to the consuls, and had made regular provision for admission to the Senate by election to magistracies, while its third power, the inspection and regulation of morals, was dropped. This office was now re-established.

Third Mithradatic War. — Meantime affairs in the East had again become threatening.[2] The war with Mithradates broke out again, and the Roman dominion in the Mediterranean was seriously menaced by a commonwealth of pirates. The war against Mithradates was entrusted to Lucius Licinius Lucullus, a typical nobleman of the time, — brave and skilful in war, rich and luxurious, arrogant to the degree that his troops refused to obey him. He gained many brilliant victories, but no decisive one, as he had not the moral ascendency to conquer a peace.   B.C. 74.

War with the Pirates. — Even more formidable at the moment was the piratical state which had its headquarters upon the rocky coast of Cilicia. Mithradates threatened the Roman power in Asia, but the pirates rendered insecure every part of the Mediterranean, cutting off the supplies of food upon which Rome depended for sustenance, and even kidnapping Roman magistrates and wealthy merchants from the coast of Italy, and holding them for ransom. To meet the emergency, a law was passed, giving to Pompey extraordinary powers for three years over all the coasts of the Mediterranean, and thirty miles into the interior. This law broke with constitutional usage, both in the manner in

---

[1] The census, or property qualification, of the equestrian order was 400,000 sesterces (= $20,000): there was no fixed requirement for the Senate, until the time of Augustus, when it was established at 1,000,000 sesterces (= $50,000).

[2] These times are depicted in *Two Thousand Years Ago*, by A. J. Church.

which the power was granted (by vote of the people), and in the extent and duration of the power; but the safety of the people is the highest law, and the result justified the extraordinary measure. In less than fifty days Pompey had cleared the sea of pirates, captured their strongholds in Cilicia, and brought this country into the power of Rome. It was organized as the province of Cilicia, to which was shortly afterwards annexed the island of Cyprus.

B.C. 67.

End of the Mithradatic War.—The brilliant successes of Pompey, contrasted with the resultless victories of Lucullus, had, as their natural effect, the passage of a law which added all the countries of the East to Pompey's previous province.[1] He displayed the same energy and military genius in this broader field of operations as in the campaign against the pirates. In two years he had overrun the territories of Mithradates, and driven him into exile in the countries north of the Euxine, where he was put to death by his own son. His kingdom was divided: part of it remaining until the time of Nero under native princes, and the most important part being annexed to the Roman province of Bithynia.[2]

B.C. 65.

Annexation of Syria. — From the conquest of Pontus Pompey proceeded to regulate the affairs of Syria, as his commission warranted him. The mighty empire of the Seleucidæ had shrunk, as we have seen (p. 135), to a petty kingdom; and in these narrower dominions the degenerate sovereigns of the dynasty had lost all capacity of government. The country was in a state of utter anarchy, and it was a welcome boon to its inhabitants to be brought under even the severe and extortionate rule of Rome. It was made into the province of Syria, B.C. 64. The principal resistance which Pompey met was among the Jews; but Jerusalem was captured, and the conqueror was admitted into the temple, even into the Holy of Holies, looking with wonder upon a temple and a

---

[1] The *Manilian Law*, advocated by Cicero in a well-known speech.

[2] Bithynia, in Asia Minor, was bequeathed to the Roman people by its last king, B.C. 74.

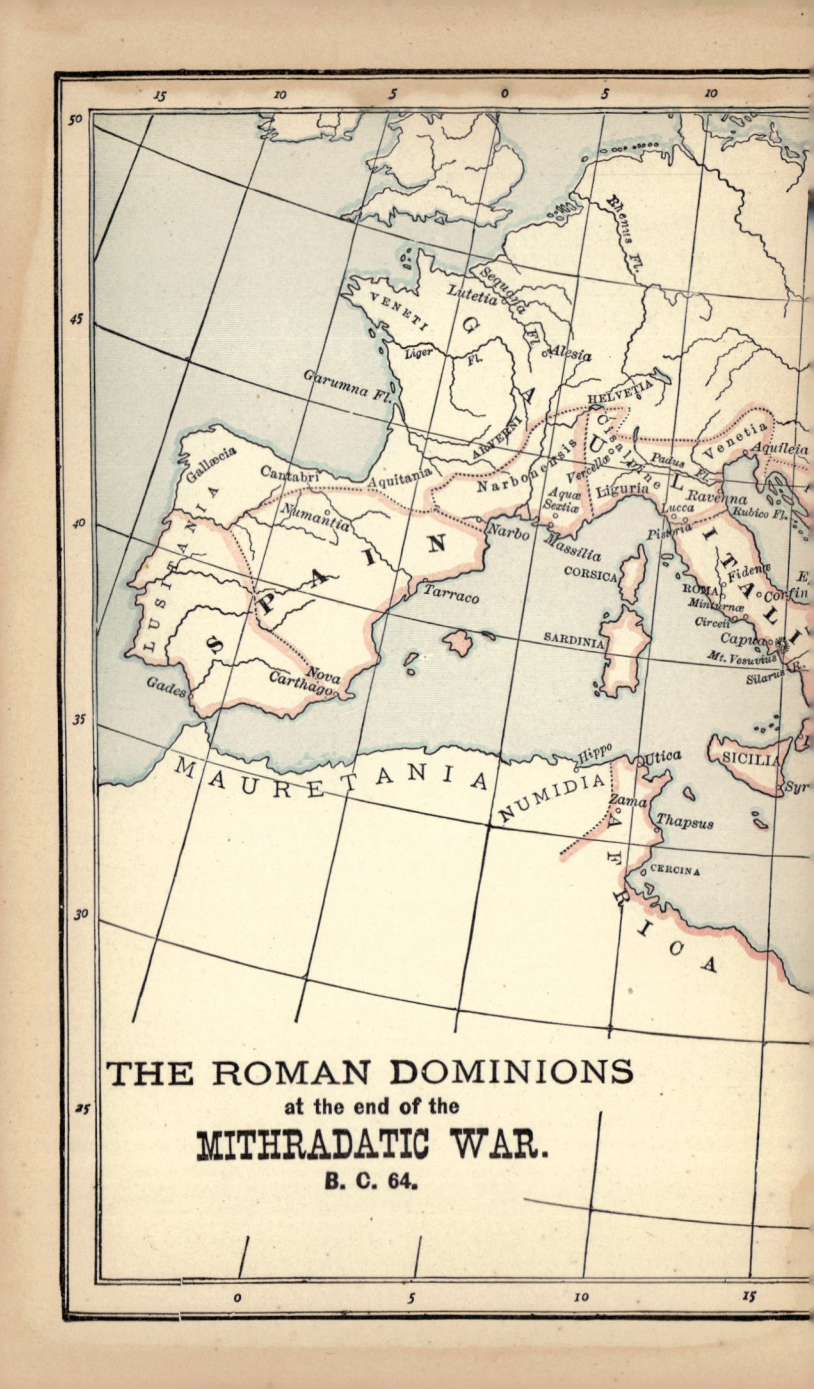

THE ROMAN DOMINIONS
at the end of the
MITHRADATIC WAR.
B. C. 64.

SCYTHIA
Danubius Fl.
THRACE
Byzantium
Sinope
PAPHLAGONIA
PONTUS
Zela
Nicomedia
BITHYNIA
PARTHIAN
EMPIRE
MACEDONIA
Dyrrachium
Brundisium
Philippi
Thessalonica
Pharsalus
Actium
Corinth
ACHAIA
Athenæ
Megalopolis
ASIA
Pergamus
Smyrna
Ephesus
LYCIA
RHODUS
Xanthus
CILICIA
Tarsus
Antiochia
SYRIA
Palmyra
CYPRUS
CRETE
CŒLE-SYRIA
JUDÆA
Cyrene
CYRENAICA
Alexandria
EGYPT

ritual with no statue of a god. Having set in order the affairs of the East, he returned home with a higher military reputation than any Roman before him, except Scipio, had gained.

III. THE FIRST TRIUMVIRATE.

Cicero. — In the year B.C. 63, the consulship was held by Marcus Tullius Cicero,[1] the most illustrious name in the annals of Roman literature. He was, like Marius, a native of the municipal town of Arpinum, where he was born B.C. 106. Like many ambitious young men from the country towns, Cicero established himself at Rome, where his eloquence, learning, integrity, and skill as an advocate soon placed him at the head of the Roman bar. He even ventured to present himself for office in competition with members of the noble families; and, notwithstanding his low birth, he achieved the almost unprecedented distinction of being elected to each of the principal offices in succession at the very earliest age permitted by law.[2] It was in his prætorship that he B.C. 66. argued for the law giving Pompey the command against Mithradates; and as soon as the necessary two years' interval had elapsed, he was elected to the consulship.

CICERO. (From a bust at Madrid.)

His Writings. — Cicero was master of a Latin style remarkable alike for vigor, elegance, and purity; and in every branch of literature, except poetry, which he essayed with no brilliant suc-

---

[1] His life by Trollope is a book of high merit.

[2] The quæstorship could be held at 30, the ædileship at 37, the prætorship at 40, and the consulship at 43.

cess, he reached the highest eminence. His orations are models of eloquence; his correspondence, very voluminous, is genial and entertaining, and crowded with information and illustration as to Roman life;[1] his rhetorical writings combine the ripe fruits of his own rhetorical labors; and his philosophical works present, in a lucid and attractive form, without much originality, but with high power of appreciation, the doctrines of the Academic or Platonic school of philosophy (p. 191), to which he was attached.

His Public Life. — Cicero's unquestionable ability in administration secured him, as we have seen, rapid success in public life; and in better times, with a higher standard of political morality, he might have been an influential and distinguished statesman. It was his misfortune that his best qualities, his integrity and patriotism, had no scope in these evil times, while he was not sufficiently daring and unscrupulous to earn the kind of success which the times offered. As a result, his reputation with posterity has suffered from a melancholy absence of consistency and disinterestedness, while he missed the rewards which his own generation had to bestow. His life after his consulship was spent in fruitless efforts to make himself a place in political life, in the face of contemptuous rebuffs from the practical politicians. Twice in his life he rose above the standard of the self-seeking politician, — at the beginning, when he boldly defied the creatures of the tyrant Sulla,[2] and at the end, when he led the Senate in opposition to the schemes of Mark Antony. His efforts were defeated by the perfidy of the young Octavian, and he surrendered his life with a dignity and nobility which had been wanting in the greater part of his career.

B.C. 82.
B.C. 43.

Conspiracy of Catiline. — The year of Cicero's consulship was marked by an event very significant of the times, — the conspiracy of Lucius Sergius Catilina[3] to take possession of the

[1] Read Miss Preston's charming papers upon Cicero's life, as exhibited in his letters, in the *Atlantic Monthly* for 1888 and 1889.

[2] This was in his speech for Roscius of Ameria.

[3] Catiline is defended by Professor Beesly in *Catiline, Clodius, and Tiberius*. Herbert's *Roman Traitor* depicts this period.

government. Catiline was a young patrician of brilliant abilities and great physical powers, but debauched life, over head and ears in debt, like so many of his class, from which he saw no way to extricate himself but by throwing society and government into confusion, with the expectation that he would be able to seize the power into his own hands. It is not to be supposed that Catiline himself had any plans of reform, or any object but the gratification of his own passions and ambition; but it is believed that Gaius Julius Cæsar, another young patrician, of equally dissolute life, and equally overwhelmed with debt, was associated with him. And Cæsar, with all these faults, was humane and clear-sighted, and perhaps already cherished enlightened plans for the re-organization of the state.

The Conspiracy. — It was Catiline's intention to gain the consulship, and use the authority of this office in furtherance of his plans. When defeated by Cicero, he determined to obtain by force what he had failed to secure by lawful means. The conspirators organized a secret association, composed of discontented men of various classes in all parts of Italy; and when the autumn approached one of their adherents, Marcus Manlius, set up his standard at Fæsulæ (*Fiesole*), in northern Etruria, and gathered about him a considerable force, part a rabble, part well-trained soldiers. For some time it was not known with certainty, although it was suspected, that this army was in league with the conspirators.

Suppression of the Conspiracy. — The conspirators within the city were planning, in secret meetings, to excite an uprising, massacre the magistrates and leading citizens, seize the government, and then unite themselves with the army in Etruria. But the watchful consul outwitted them. By his secret emissaries he informed himself of all their movements; and just as the time agreed upon for the outbreak was approaching, he made their plans known to the public. Catiline left the city, and united with the insurgents under Manlius. His accomplices were then arrested, and put to death. The suppression of the conspiracy within the city was speedily followed, in January of the next

B.C. 62. year, by the defeat of the insurgent army in Etruria. In this battle Catiline himself perished.

The Coalition of Party Leaders. — Pompey returned to Rome in the year 61 B.C., and celebrated a magnificent triumph for his various victories and conquests. The triumphal celebration lasted two days. He was now at the height of his glory; and there was no place of greater dignity or power to which, in the ordinary course of Roman politics, he could rise. He was anxious, however, to have the regulations which he had made in the East confirmed by lawful authority; and with this intention he entered into a coalition with the two most prominent political leaders, each of the three agreeing to advance the political interests of the others. This coalition, or "ring," is known as the *First*
B.C. 60. *Triumvirate*, an incorrect use of the term, inasmuch as a triumvirate was properly a legal commission or board of three men, while the agreement between Pompey, Cæsar, and Crassus was a purely personal arrangement, with no legal character and no binding force.

Crassus and Cæsar. — The associates of Pompey in this coalition were Publius Licinius Crassus and Gaius Julius Cæsar. Crassus we have already met, a man of noble family, who had broken up the army of Spartacus, (p. 193), and had held the consulship with Pompey (p. 194). He, as well as Cæsar, was suspected, and probably with justice, of complicity in the plots of Catiline. Cæsar was a younger man, and a man of far greater ability and stronger character than either of his confederates, although his abilities were not yet fully known. He was of a patrician family, but was connected by marriage with Marius, and had himself married a daughter of Cinna, whom he refused to divorce at the command of Sulla. The dictator had with difficulty been induced to pardon him for this obstinacy, saying to his friends that there was many a Marius in that young man. Cæsar lived the dissolute and extravagant life of young men of his class, and seems to have looked to the "new accounts" promised by Catiline's revolution as the only escape from his overwhelming indebtedness. The next year he held the prætorship, B.C. 62. and the year following went to further Spain as governor, returning from thence in the year 60 in season to enter into the coalition with Pompey and Crassus.

Cæsar's Consulship. — In the bargain now made Pompey contributed his military reputation, Crassus his wealth, as the richest Roman, and Cæsar his ability and influence as a political leader. The three influences united were irresistible. Cæsar was elected consul for the year 59, and a popular vote gave him, as proconsul, the government of the two provinces of Cisalpine Gaul and Illyricum for five years, and to these the Senate added Transalpine or Narbonnese Gaul. Pompey's arrangements in the East were legally confirmed, and the popular leaders who had supported Cæsar received their pay in being allowed to send their enemy Cicero into exile.

Banishment of Cicero. — The demagogue Publius Clodius was a member of the patrician family of the Claudii, who had suffered himself to be made a plebeian, in order that he might hold the office of tribune of the plebs. He was a bitter enemy of Cicero, and, with Cæsar's connivance, carried a law which declared the banishment of any person who had put to death a Roman citizen without trial. This Cicero had done in the case of Catiline's accomplices. He went into exile therefore, with piteous and unmanly lamentations; his house was torn down in his absence, and the spot on which it had stood was consecrated. It was not for long, however. A reaction followed, and two years later he was recalled with great honor, and was recompensed B.C. 57. for his losses from the public treasury.

The Conference of Luca. — The year following his consulship, Cæsar took command in his provinces, and B.C. 58. commenced a series of military operations which will be narrated in the next chapter. But he soon found that the five years allotted to him would be insufficient for completing the work which he had undertaken, and as the end of the term approached a conference of the three confederates was held at Luca, at which there were present some two B.C. 56.

hundred senators, and so many of the higher magistrates that there were counted one hundred and twenty fasces upon the ground.[1] At this meeting it was agreed that Pompey and Crassus should hold the consulship for the next year, and should then receive each a command for five years — Pompey in Spain, Crassus in Syria; further, that Cæsar's command in the Gauls should be extended for another term of five years. These agreements were all carried out by law.

B.C. 55.

Pompey in Italy. — Pompey did not go to his province, however, but remained in the neighborhood of Rome, watching the political movements in the city, and administering his government through *legati*, or deputies, — a method adopted afterwards by the emperors. The alliance between him and Cæsar had been cemented by his marriage to Julia, Cæsar's daughter; but the death of Julia the next year dissolved the alliance, and gradually the two confederates passed through the stages of coolness and unfriendliness to that of open enmity.

B.C. 54.

The Parthian Empire. — While Pompey remained in Italy, Crassus proceeded to the East, hoping there to rival the exploits of Cæsar in the West. This province of Syria bordered upon the great Parthian empire, which now divided the world with that of Rome. Parthia, the mountain region southeast of the Caspian Sea, had achieved its independence about the middle of the third century before Christ (p. 132); about a century later (p. 135) Mithradates the Great had converted his petty kingdom into a powerful empire, which stretched from the Euphrates to the Indus, thus inheriting the glories of the Persian and Macedonian empires.

Crassus in the East. — A revolution in Parthia, which made Orodes king in place of his brother Mithradates III., and was followed by the murder of Mithradates, gave Crassus a pretext for intervening in the affairs of the East. Impatient to gather the treasures of the Orient, as well as the laurels which he be-

[1] The consul was attended by twelve lictors, each carrying *fasces* or bundles of rods, the prætor by two; but the prætor or pro-prætor who governed a province had six.

lieved were awaiting him, Crassus left Rome even be- B.C. 55.
fore the year of his consulship had expired. But once
arrived in his province, the gold seems to have attracted him more
than the glory: he dallied through the year, adding new sums to
his enormous fortune, and it was not until the year 53 that he
crossed the Euphrates. Then, while traversing the desert under
the guidance of a pretended ally, he was suddenly betrayed into
an ambuscade. His army was surrounded by swarms of cavalry,
armed with bows and pikes, against whom his heavy-armed legions
contended in vain. His army was cut to pieces, and shortly after
Crassus himself lost his life. This disastrous battle was fought a
few miles from Carrhæ.

The Poets: *Lucretius.* — During the period which we have
just traversed, Roman literature was made illustrious by perhaps
the two most original of its poets, and two of its best historians.
Titus Lucretius Carus, while inferior to Virgil in grace and finish,
far surpassed him in originality and sublimity. If he had chosen
a more popular theme, it may be believed that he would easily
have ranked as the greatest of Roman poets; but he chose to
elucidate the Epicurean system of philosophy, so that a large part
of his poem is occupied with curious and abstruse discussions,
to which the poetic character is wholly wanting. Many of his doctrines come very near to the modern theory of evolution. Even
the philosophical portions, however, are often rich with beauties,
and his introductions and digressions mark the highest point which
Roman poetry reached.

Catullus. — Quintus Valerius Catullus was as distinguished for
grace and poetic fancy as Lucretius for sublimity. His works,
many of them of exquisite beauty, occupy a very moderate space.
Among them are some in which he attacks Cæsar with great
vehemence and scurrility.

The Historians: *Sallust.* — Gaius Sallustius Crispus ranks, for
vigor and picturesqueness of narration and powerful delineation of
motives, among the greatest historians. He was, like most of the
ancient historians, wholly devoid of the critical faculty, and his

descriptions of military campaigns and localities are almost worthless. But the insight which he gives into the politics of Rome is invaluable, and to him we owe our most complete knowledge of the war with Jugurtha and the conspiracy of Catiline. His principal work, which would have been of priceless value in narrating the history of his own time, is lost, except for a few fragments.

Cæsar. — A complete contrast to Sallust was Julius Cæsar. Cæsar's account of his wars in Gaul — the "Commentaries" — is concise and dry, wholly lacking in the liveliness and passion of Sallust; but in its clearness and exactness it is a model of military narration, and contains valuable information upon the nature of the country, its inhabitants, manners and customs and institutions. Without making any parade of philosophical analysis, Cæsar nevertheless has the intuitive insight of a man of genius into the connection of events with one another, and the relations of cause and effect. In his account of the Civil War, in which personal and political passions were violently excited, he loses the impersonal coolness of his earlier work; but even here he possesses the same great qualities as an historian. It must be added, that when he is telling the story of his own actions, he sometimes passes lightly over his own shortcomings, whether moral offences or military blunders. In general, however, he is eminently fair and impartial.

CHAPTER XVI.

CÆSAR.

I. The Conquest of Gaul.

The Province of Narbonese Gaul. — Gaul, *Gallia*, was the name given by the ancients to that country which extended from the Pyrenees to the Alps and Rhine, embracing the modern France and Belgium, with part of Holland and Switzerland, and a small portion of Germany. The southwestern part was inhabited by Aquitanians, a people of the same race as the Iberians of Spain, represented by the modern Basques[1]; in the north some German tribes had crossed the Rhine; but with these exceptions the inhabitants were of the Celtic race. We have seen (p. 167) that, shortly after the time of Gaius Gracchus, the Romans had taken possession of all the territory between the Pyrenees and the Alps, except that which belonged to the Greek republic of Massilia, and had founded the colony of Narbo, from which the province had its name, Narbonensis. West of the Rhone the province was separated from free Gaul by the Cevennes Mountains; east of these mountains the Rhone and its tributary, the Arar (*Saône*), afforded a direct passage into the heart of Europe (p. 2). It was by this natural route that Cæsar, the new governor of Gaul, advanced in his schemes of conquest.

The Gauls. — The Gauls had reached a tolerably advanced stage of civilization, but their form of government was still the primitive one of the tribe, an outgrowth of the family (p. 18). There were about sixty of these tribes among the free Gauls. Their government was aristocratic, and they were divided into factions

---

[1] The Basques are a people who inhabit a small mountain district at the head of the Bay of Biscay. They are not of Aryan race.

bitterly hostile to one another, — tribe opposed to tribe, and factions within the tribes. It was at all times the policy of the Romans to attach to themselves one party in any country where they wished to obtain influence; and finding that two neighboring tribes, adjoining the province, were arrayed against each other, they allied themselves with the Æduans, in the modern Burgundy, against the Sequanians, who lived east of the Æduans, separated from them by the river Saône.[1] The region of these two tribes upon the river Saône was, as we have seen, the natural entrance to Gaul.

The Helvetian Migration. — It was not difficult for any Roman governor who wished to interfere with the affairs of some foreign nation to find a pretext. In the present case it was the restlessness of the Helvetians, who inhabited modern Switzerland, just east of the Sequanians. The Helvetians, dissatisfied with their rugged and limited territories, proposed to migrate in a body across the country to the shores of the Bay of Biscay. This they undertook in alliance with the Sequanians, their nearest neighbors, through whose territories they received permission to pass. The Æduans of course objected, and Cæsar alleged that, although their proposed course was north of the Cevennes, wholly outside of his jurisdiction, yet their new locality upon the Bay of Biscay might be a menace to the colony of Narbo; he consequently marched against the Helvetians, defeated them in a bloody battle, and obliged them to return to the homes which they had abandoned.

B.C. 58.

Expulsion of the Germans. — Cæsar's next enterprise, the same year, was one of extreme interest and historical importance. A German king, Ariovistus, with his followers, had crossed the Rhine to assist the Sequanians in their feud with the Æduans, and had settled forcibly in their territories. This was another chapter in the great German migration of which we have already spoken (p. 168). The Cimbri and Teutones had been cut to pieces by Marius; but in the north of Gaul the Germans had obtained

---

[1] This was the modern province of Franche Comté.

a foothold, and now the settlement of Ariovistus was but an advance guard of the hordes that were pressing forward to occupy the rich fields of Gaul. The defeat of Ariovistus placed a decisive check upon this migration, and was therefore an event of great moment in the history of the world. The onward movement of the Germans was arrested by this defeat; and it was held in check

ROMAN RIDER AND SUEVE.

for nearly five hundred years. Then, when the Germans had grown stronger and the Romans weaker, the Teutonic tribes swept in an irresistible current over the provinces of the Empire.

Cæsar's Visits to Britain. — Cæsar continued in Gaul for eight years, and reduced the entire country to submission. In the fourth year and again in the fifth, he passed over B.C. 55, 54.

to Britain, an island until then known to the Romans only by the reports of chance travellers and traders. His visits to Britain were only reconnoissances, perhaps with a view to a possible conquest in the future, but he never had the opportunity to follow them up; and it was nearly a hundred years before Britain was formally reduced to a province. As is natural, in so short and incomplete an expedition, the account which Cæsar gives of Britain is brief and incomplete.

A.D. 43.

Cæsar in Germany. — He visited Germany, as well as Britain, and has given us the earliest and most authentic information which we possess with regard to the country and its inhabitants. Although brief, it is remarkable for accuracy and lucidity, — a model of vigorous and condensed statement. His natural history is, however, of less value than his account of institutions. The war between the Roman empire and the German tribes, commenced by Cæsar, was kept up with hardly an interval until the end of the Roman Empire of the West.

Revolt of Vercingetorix. — At the close of his sixth campaign Cæsar appeared to have completely accomplished his task, and to have established the Roman dominion from the Pyrenees to the Rhine. But the next year he was confronted by a formidable insurrection under the Arvernian chief, Vercingetorix, which soon embraced nearly all the tribes of Gaul, even the Æduans, formerly the stanchest friends of Rome. Many times during this campaign the Roman cause seemed irretrievably lost; but Cæsar, often rash and inconsiderate in plunging into difficulties, was unsurpassed in fertility of resources and indomitable resolution. These qualities were never more brilliantly displayed than in the war with Vercingetorix.

B.C. 52.

Siege of Alesia. — The campaign culminated in the siege of Alesia, an almost impregnable fortress on the summit of a steep hill, where Cæsar succeeded in shutting up his antagonists within a continuous line of works. The city was converted into a fortress, and all non-combatants were relentlessly thrust out, where they perished miserably between the contending forces. An immense army was sent to the succor of the besieged; and it seemed for a moment that it would succeed in raising the siege, and that the work of seven years would be brought to nought. But by a sudden and well-directed attack the relieving army was defeated and scattered, and the fortress soon fell into Cæsar's hands. Its heroic commander, Vercingetorix, was kept in custody for five years, to be exhibited in Cæsar's triumphal procession, and was then beheaded.

Conquest of Gaul. — All resistance was soon at an end, and the conqueror held his victorious armies ready for the civil contest which was evidently approaching. The newly conquered territory was divided into three districts for financial and administrative purposes, which were afterwards regularly organized as independent provinces. These districts were *Belgica* in the north, *Aquitania* in the southwest, and *Lugdunensis* in the centre. The latter took its name from the city of Lugdunum (*Lyons*), shortly afterwards founded at the junction of the Rhone and Saône, the most important natural centre in Gaul. This became the seat of administration of the three provinces, which for the present were known as the Three Gauls (*Tres Galliæ*), and placed under one governor.

Importance of the Conquest. — The conquest of Gaul was perhaps the most important which the Romans had yet made outside of their natural boundaries. It was not a large source of revenue, and that was well; for the tributes of Asia and Africa worked no good to Rome. But it was a broad, fertile land, occupied by a people who readily adopted Roman institutions and civilization, and who speedily became Romanized. The sixty Gallic tribes were organized into sixty municipalities.[1] The language, customs, and culture of the Romans became those of the native inhabitants; and no part of the empire was more homogeneous and contented. Gaul became a seat of flourishing trade and of well-conducted schools. Above all, its situation, giving access at once to Britain and to Germany, made it in the later empire the centre of civilization and power in western Europe.

[1] These were afterwards, probably by Tiberius, increased to sixty-four; and they were the basis of the territorial divisions of mediæval France.

II. The Second Civil War.

The Situation in Rome. — At the very moment that the revolt of Vercingetorix seemed upon the point of overturning the Roman authority in Gaul, Rome itself was upon the verge of anarchy. The triumvirate had been broken in pieces. Crassus was dead, Cæsar was absent, and since the death of Julia (p. 202) he and Pompey, though still nominally friends, had been gradually drawing apart. Everything now pointed to Pompey's ascendency. As proconsul of Spain (p. 202), and as commissioner of the corn supplies, he was invested with the highest military authority; and, although he was prohibited from entering the city while in possession of this authority, he remained in its neighborhood, where he could make his influence promptly and decisively felt. When needful, the Senate was convened in some temple outside of the city walls,[1] in order that the great man might be present at its deliberations.

B.C. 52.

The Death of Clodius. — An event now occurred which raised Pompey still higher in power and influence. The year 53 had passed in contention and disorder: party dissensions had been so violent and unscrupulous that no magistrates could be elected for the year following. When New Year's Day arrived, there were no consuls to be inaugurated; the machinery of government had come to a stand-still, and, according to constitutional usage (p. 20), an *interrex* had to be appointed by the patrician senators, to set the wheels in motion again.

B.C. 52.

In this condition of things, it happened that two notorious bullies, the demagogue Clodius (p. 201) and Milo, a champion of the senatorial faction — "the Achilles and the Hector of the streets" — met upon the Appian Way, a few miles from the city, each at the head of a company of gladiators and roughs. In the fight that ensued, Clodius was killed. His body was carried

---

[1] More correctly the *pomœrium*, or sacred enclosure of the city, which did not at all points run parallel with the city walls. As the Campus Martius was outside of the *pomœrium*, he could remain there freely.

to Rome, and his funeral made the occasion of a disorderly political demonstration. The funeral pile was made in the Senate-house, and the building itself was consumed in the flames. Anarchy ran riot, and order was not restored until Pompey, without being required to lay down his other offices, was appointed sole consul — an unconstitutional authority and a meaningless term.[1] Milo was brought to trial, and Cicero was engaged as his counsel; but the howls of the mob intimidated the orator, and the splendid speech which he had prepared was never delivered. Milo went into exile at Massilia.

Attitude of Pompey. — The course of events had thus separated Pompey from his democratic associates, and brought him into alliance with the senatorial party. This was not a surprising change, for he had never been at heart a democrat. But neither was he at heart attached to the aristocratic constitution of the state. He was for himself, first and always. Although no statesman, he was clear-sighted enough to see that the supreme power in Rome would be the prize of the man who had the courage and ability to seize it. The senatorial leaders, for their part, saw with equal clearness that Cæsar was their most dangerous adversary, and were ready to make Pompey their leader, and the nominal champion of the republic. It was a hollow coalition, no less than that between Cæsar and Pompey had been; for each party sought its own ends, and neither trusted the other, but each hoped to make of the other a means of victory over their common enemy Cæsar. Armed with such extraordinary powers, and with the support of the Senate, Pompey seemed all-powerful; and if he had had political abilities equal to his ambition, and to his unquestioned military capacity, it would seem that, in the absence of Cæsar, he might easily have made himself master of Rome.

Situation of Cæsar. — Cæsar's situation, meanwhile, was embarrassing, and even perilous. His legal term of office, as governor

---

[1] "Consul without colleague (*sine collega*)": but the very word *con-sul* means colleague. After a while Pompey appointed as colleague his father-in-law, Metellus Scipio.

of the three provinces, would end March 1, B.C. 49. After this date the Senate might send a successor to supersede him, but it was usual to allow the provincial governors to continue in command until the new year, and Cæsar had reckoned upon this. It was his plan to be elected consul for the year 48, and thus to pass at once from his proconsulate to the consulship. That he should do this was almost necessary for his personal safety, as his enemies made no secret of their intention to impeach him for various irregularities and misdemeanors, as soon as he should become a private citizen; for no magistrate could be impeached during his term of office. If he could obtain the consulship he would be safe, and would be sure of a new provincial governorship afterwards.

Impediments in Cæsar's Way. — But there was an impediment in the way. The election regularly took place in July, and there was a law requiring candidates for office to present themselves in person at the election. This Cæsar could not do without giving up his proconsular command, and becoming a private citizen; but the law had on several occasions been suspended, and it was part of the bargain between the triumvirs that it should be suspended in Cæsar's case, and that he should be allowed to offer himself as a candidate without leaving his province. By forgetfulness or trickery on Pompey's part, this privilege had not been legally obtained for Cæsar, and now, as the close of his command approached, he found himself without any security for the future.

Negotiations between the Parties. — On the other hand, when the terms of Pompey's threefold authority had expired,[1] his command in Spain was continued for five years, and he was placed by the Senate over Italy and all its resources. He felt so confident of his strength that he asserted openly that Cæsar was no more likely to resist the Senate than a child to give a blow to his parent; and when questioned as to his forces, he said he had but to stamp his foot, and Italy would swarm with soldiers. The year 50 passed with fruitless negotiations; the Senate, coming under the influence

[1] He was consul (B.C. 52), proconsul of Spain (54–49), and commissioner of corn supplies (57–52).

of the compromise or peace party, ordered both rivals to lay down arms. Cæsar declared that he was ready to do this, if Pompey would do the same; but Pompey stubbornly refused.

Beginning of the Civil War. — With the new year B.C. 49. the war party regained the ascendency in the Senate, and peremptorily ordered Cæsar to give up his command; and when two tribunes, Mark Antony and Quintus Cassius, tried to use their legal right of intercession and stop the proceedings, their sacred character was violated, and they were obliged to escape in disguise to Cæsar's camp at Ravenna. Cæsar acted with his usual promptness and decision. Declaring himself the champion of the constitution, which had been violated in the person of the tribunes, he put his army in motion; exclaiming "the die is cast," he led his troops over the little river Rubicon, which was the boundary between his province and Italy, and the civil war was begun.

Retreat of Pompey. — Cæsar's prompt action in crossing the Rubicon threw his opponents into distraction and panic. No soldiers sprang from the ground at Pompey's call; he found himself destitute of resources, and was compelled to take refuge beyond the Adriatic Sea. The greater part of the magistrates and Senate accompanied him, and the government of the republic was set up at Thessalonica, on the coast of Macedonia. There were thus two rival governments, at Rome and Thessalonica, each claiming to be the legitimate one.

Cæsar's Conquest of the West. — It was necessary for Cæsar to secure himself in the West before following his enemy into the East. He first set things in order in Italy, then proceeded to Spain, and brought it under his authority. On his way back to Italy, he besieged and captured the rich city of Massilia, which had ardently espoused the cause of the republic. He left it in possession of its independence, but deprived it of the principal part of its territory; and it continued for some years longer to exist as an inferior power, nominally independent of Rome. In the meantime Cæsar had sent Curio, one of his officers, to take possession of Africa; but Curio was defeated and killed by Juba,

King of Mauritania, and Africa remained in possession of the senatorial party, while Cæsar's authority was supreme in Italy, Gaul, and Spain.

Cæsar's Dictatorship. — During Cæsar's absence in the West he was appointed dictator, which office he held for only eleven days, using its machinery to procure his own election to the consul-

JULIUS CÆSAR. (From a Bust in the Museum of the Louvre.)

ship for the next year, B.C. 48. He also procured the passage of an important act giving the citizenship to the inhabitants of Cisalpine Gaul.[1] This was in the line of the policy of the early

[1] As the communities which obtained the franchise by this law were almost entirely north of the Po, it is generally known as a law giving citizenship to the *Transpadani*.

CÆSAR AS DICTATOR. 215

democratic leaders, who had procured the citizenship for the Italian allies (p. 175). Cisalpine Gaul had been made subject to Rome before the war with Hannibal (p. 111), and had been governed as a province. Cæsar had for many years been the champion of its inhabitants, and almost his first act, when in possession of supreme power, was to procure them the suffrage. As a result, Cisalpine Gaul ceased to be reckoned as a province, and now became a part of Italy.

Financial Legislation. — Cæsar's most important legislation at this period was for the relief of financial embarrassments. We have seen how the unbounded extravagance of the young nobles had plunged them hopelessly into debt (p. 188), and how the demand for "New Accounts" had led to an attempt to revolutionize the government, in the conspiracy of Catiline. Cæsar himself was deeply involved in debt, and it was believed that he had secretly been an accomplice of Catiline; every one expected, therefore, that now that he was in possession of the power, he would follow out the programme of his party, and proclaim "new accounts." But he disappointed these expectations, and promulgated instead a moderate measure for the relief of debtors, deducting the interest already paid from the principal, and requiring property to be taken in liquidation of the debts at the valuation before the outbreak of the war. The revolutionists were keenly disappointed by this law, and attempted, in Cæsar's absence, to carry more sweeping measures of relief; but by his moderation in this respect, as well as by his unexpected clemency, Cæsar gained the confidence and support of quiet and conservative citizens.

Cæsar in Greece. — Having thus secured himself in the West, and assumed the consulship for the year 48, Cæsar followed Pompey into the East. His forces were much inferior to those of his antagonist, and Pompey still ranked as the greatest soldier of his generation. Moreover, Cæsar's first operations were far from promising. By a rash and hasty attempt to capture Dyrrhachium, upon the coast of Illyricum, he came near being ruined. Even his extraordinary fertility of resources scarcely rescued him. He escaped with great difficulty into Thessaly, where the two rivals encountered one another upon the plains of Pharsalus, just south of Cynoscephalæ (p. 133).

Battle of Pharsalus. — The armies were very unequal in numbers: Pompey had 47,000 infantry, Cæsar barely 22,000. In cavalry there was a still greater disparity: Cæsar had not much over 1000, against Pompey's 7000. The armies were drawn up in such a manner that Cæsar's left flank and Pompey's right were protected, while the other flanks stretched into the open plain. Pompey therefore made his attack upon Cæsar's right, where his powerful cavalry speedily routed Cæsar's handful of horsemen, and drove them in flight, designing then to take Cæsar's infantry upon the flank. But in the rear of the fleeing horse they suddenly encountered a body of 2000 infantry, picked veterans of the Gallic army, who charged impetuously upon the victorious cavalry, using their javelins as pikes, and thrusting them in the faces of the enemy.[1] This infantry charge decided the battle; Pompey's army was broken in pieces, and he himself, losing heart, fled in all haste to Egypt.

Cæsar in the East. — Egypt was at this time ruled by the boy-king, Ptolemy Dionysus, who had expelled his sister and consort, Cleopatra. When the defeated Pompey arrived on the shore of Egypt to seek a refuge, the ministers of Ptolemy, unwilling to receive him, and yet not daring to leave him at large, had him perfidiously assassinated; and his dissevered head was the first sight that greeted Cæsar when he arrived at Alexandria in pursuit. A few months were spent by Cæsar in ordering affairs in Egypt, where he restored Cleopatra to her throne and suppressed a dangerous revolt; and in Asia Minor, where Pharnaces, son of Mithradates, ventured to oppose him. The rapidity of his victory over Pharnaces was expressed in his laconic missive: *Veni, vidi, vici;* "I came, I saw, I conquered."

B.C. 47.

---

[1] The order to strike in their faces was, says Mommsen, in order to secure the greatest efficacy of their weapons, — not, as is often alleged, to disfigure the faces of the dandies.

END OF THE REPUBLIC.

War in Africa. — The year of Cæsar's operations in the East had been energetically spent by the republican leaders in preparing to resist the conqueror in Africa, the only part of the empire which now remained to them. They were under the command of Metellus Scipio, a zealous aristocrat, but a man of mean character, and Cato, the true leader and the best representative of his party, an honest man, but narrow in opinions and prejudices. Cato held Utica, the capital of the province, while Scipio commanded the army in the field.

Mutiny of the Troops. — After the victory of Pharsalus, Cæsar was appointed to a second dictatorship, and before proceeding against Scipio and Cato, made a brief visit to Italy, whence he prepared to transport his army to Africa. But a dangerous mutiny threatened to defeat all his plans. The soldiers in Campania, tired of their long warfare and disappointed as yet in their expectations of plunder and vengeance, refused to move until certain promised rewards should be paid them, assaulted their officers, and marched to Rome, demanding discharge. To their unutterable surprise it was promptly granted; and when their general proceeded to address them, no longer as "fellow soldiers," but as "fellow citizens" (*Quirites*), they at once submitted, and begged him to receive them again into his service. This he did, punishing the ringleaders, however, by depriving them of a large part of their donatives. Cæsar's genius was never more conspicuous than in the suppression of this mutiny.

Battle of Thapsus. — The decisive battle, fatal to the republic, was fought the next year, B.C. 46, at Thapsus in Africa. The army of the republic was commanded by Metellus Scipio, a soldier quite incapable of meeting Cæsar on equal terms. The mutiny of the year before had displayed the lawless spirit of Cæsar's soldiers; and at Thapsus they showed this again, rushing impetuously forward without waiting for the word of command, but forcing their general to fall into line with them. Scipio's array of elephants was thrown into disorder, and his army was swept away with them. The victors refused to give quarter. Fifty thousand of the republican army were slaughtered, while only about fifty of Cæsar's troops fell. At the news of the defeat, which he had expected, Cato put himself to death at Utica, determined not to survive the republic.

Cæsar's Triumphs. — On his return to Rome Cæsar celebrated a fourfold triumph for his victories: over the Gauls, King Ptolemy of Egypt, King Pharnaces of Pontus, and Juba of Mauritania. The sentiment of nationality and patriotism was still too strong to permit a triumph over fellow-citizens; the victories over Pompey and Scipio received no commemoration.

Cæsar's Third Dictatorship. — At the news of the battle of Thapsus a third dictatorship, for ten years, was bestowed upon Cæsar, together with the censorial power (*praefectura morum*) for three years, and the right to nominate all magistrates. The tribunician power he had already received in the year 48; and to the office of *pontifex maximus*, or head of the Roman religion, he had been elected B.C. 63. He now entered upon a series of legislative acts of a far-reaching and beneficent character. Among these were laws which regulated the military service, the care of the streets, the government of the provinces, the evils of luxurious living, and the criminal courts; the provision of the Aurelian law (p. 195), by which one-third of the jurors in these were taken from the officers of the tribes, was abolished, and the juries were to be composed equally of senators and knights. The number who received donations of corn from the state was reduced from 320,000 to 150,000. The organization of the municipal system (p. 175) belongs to this group of laws. An attempt was also made to counteract the most dangerous tendencies of Italian society (pp. 150-2) by a law providing that one-third of the herdsmen should be freemen; another law seems to have regulated loans and mortgages. Large assignments of land were made to his veterans, and care was taken that they should neither be concentrated in a few localities, nor interfere with previous occupation. With Cæsar began also the regular coinage of gold; the *aureus*, of the value of 100 sesterces ($5.00), issued by him, was the standard of the early Empire, and retained its purity until the reign of Nero.

Reform of the Calendar. — The most important of these acts was the reform of the calendar, which he accomplished by his authority as *pontifex maximus*. The Roman calendar had probably been the clumsiest and most inconvenient that any civilized nation ever had;[1] and it had fallen so completely out of relation with the seasons that in the year 49 the vernal equinox came in May. Cæsar established the calendar which, with some slight improvements, still continues in use.[2] It went into operation on the 1st of January, 45. To make the new year correspond with the season, it was necessary to make so large an intercalation that the year 46 consisted of fifteen months of four hundred and forty-five days.

Battle of Munda, B.C. 45. — One more military exploit remained. The battle of Pharsalus had dissolved the connection between the party of Pompey and that of the republic. The sons of Pompey, Gnæus and Sextus, escaped their father's fate. They did not join the republican leaders in Africa, having no interest in the preservation of the Republic, but repaired to Spain, where their father had many adherents, and here set up an independent power. Cæsar followed them the year after Thapsus, **B.C. 45.** and by a final victory at Munda established his undivided authority over the Roman empire. Gnæus shortly after lost his life, but Sextus continued an active career for several years.

The Empire. — The battle of Munda was followed by new grants of honor and power to Cæsar, chief of which was the bestowal of the title *Imperator*, to be held for life, and transmitted to his heirs.

---

[1] It consisted of four months of 31 days, seven of 29, while February had 28 every other year; in the alternate years an intercalary month of 27 days being inserted after February, which on these years had alternately 23 and 24 days.

[2] It is known as the *Julian Calendar;* as corrected by Pope Gregory XIII. in the sixteenth century (omitting the intercalation once in a century), it is called the *Gregorian Calendar.*

By this act an hereditary monarchy was formally established in Rome. The Republic had come to an end with the battle of Thapsus, and Cæsar had been invested with absolute power under the name of a republican magistracy. With the title Imperator a new magistracy, monarchical and hereditary in character, came into existence. Early the next year the dictatorship was made perpetual.

B.C. 44.

III. The Death of Cæsar.

Cæsar's Craving for the Royal Title. — With all his greatness, Cæsar was not free from the human foibles of vanity and ostentation, or from that craving for empty titles, which was afterwards the ruin of Napoleon, and from which even Cromwell was not exempt. He possessed the substance of kingly power, and it was made hereditary in his family; but he was not satisfied without the name of king. And yet he did not dare to assume the name in the face of the intense hatred in which it was held by the people of Rome. But he allowed himself to be the object of extravagant honors, and even to be worshipped as a god. He surrounded himself, so far as was possible in the presence of the memories of the Republic, with the ceremonial of oriental monarchies. When Mark Antony, his colleague in the consulship of B.C. 44, offered him a diadem in the presence of the people, at the festival of the Lupercalia (Feb. 15), he twice rejected it, but in such a way that, as Shakespeare puts it, "For all that, he would fain have had it."

Cleopatra, Queen of Egypt. — Thus Cæsar was king in all but name, and he took little pains to conciliate the feelings of the republicans by moderation of demeanor. He even received in Rome the visits of the dissolute Queen Cleopatra; and the proposition was made in the Senate, — it cannot be supposed that it was without his knowledge, — that he should be allowed to marry as many wives as he pleased, and whomsoever (that is, from whatever nation) he pleased. This was in order to enable him to marry

Cleopatra. The law in question would have abrogated the strict law of marriage, upon which Roman institutions rested (p. 61), and, what is worse, would have destroyed the very foundation of the Roman family, and set up the oriental harem in its place.[1] So far had Cæsar departed from the spirit of those institutions to which Rome owed its greatness.

Conspiracy for Cæsar's Death. — We need not be surprised, therefore, that a conspiracy was formed to put an end to a dominion which so outraged Roman sentiment, nor that the conspiracy included, not only friends of the Republic, but some of Cæsar's earlier adherents. It was not, however, wholly inspired by worthy and patriotic motives. Its leader, Gaius Cassius, was a peevish, disappointed man, who desired to avenge a personal slight.[2] His chief associate, Marcus Brutus, was a consistent upholder of the senatorial rule, a man of philosophical tastes and temperament, who brooded over the loss of public liberty, and weakly allowed himself to be made the tool of Cassius and other schemers. The identity of his name with that of the traditional founder of the Republic, although there was probably no relationship between the two, was used as a powerful incentive upon a mind incapable of broad statesmanship. He could not see that the Republic had really perished, that Cæsar's rule had established peace and order, and that his death would be the signal for new disturbances and bloodshed. The leader next in importance was Decimus Brutus, whose share in the event was even less creditable; for he was neither a fanatic, like Marcus, nor had he, like Cassius, any grievances, real or fancied, against Cæsar, from whom he had received peculiar favor and friendship.[3]

---

[1] It is related that King Ptolemy of Egypt offered marriage to Cornelia, the mother of the Gracchi. We are not told how the offer was received, but such a marriage was not possible by Roman law.

[2] Cæsar had withheld from him the consulship, to which he thought himself entitled.

[3] It was Decimus Brutus, not Marcus, who engaged Cæsar's personal affection. Shakespeare is mistaken in this.

Plans of the Conspirators. — The conspirators vainly imagined that if the "tyrant" should be removed the Republic could be easily restored, and that the populace would gather enthusiastically about the champions of liberty. But the Roman populace had long ceased to have any real interest in the institutions of the Republic. They hated the name of king, but for the substance of monarchical power they cared little. So long as they had their distributions of corn and free exhibitions in the circus and amphitheatre (*panem et circenses*), they were satisfied. Cæsar's humanity, liberality, and justice had won their hearts; and the conspiracy proved a melancholy, almost a ridiculous, failure.

Their Preparations. — There were in all some sixty accomplices; and for nearly a month they succeeded in keeping their designs secret: not so secret, however, but that Cæsar received more than one warning, to which he heedlessly refused to pay attention. It was debated among the conspirators whether Cæsar's colleague in the consulship, Mark Antony, and his master of the horse, Marcus Lepidus, should also be slain; but Brutus urged that it would pollute their sacred cause if any should be put to death but the tyrant himself. It was proposed to admit Cicero to a knowledge of their plans; but this too was judged unadvisable. The assassination was fixed for the Ides of March (March 15), B.C. 44, on which day a regular session of the Senate was to be held. At this meeting a new consul was to be nominated to take Cæsar's place for the remainder of the year.[1]

The Assassination. — The Senate sat, on this occasion, in a hall attached to the theatre of Pompey, on the Campus Martius, not far from the Capitoline.[2] A statue of Pompey stood in the hall, and it was at the foot of this statue,[3] "which all the while ran

---

[1] This was the plan regularly followed under the empire, that the first, or *eponymous*, consuls of each year retired after some months. In some cases there was a succession of several pairs during the year.

[2] This was the first stone theatre erected in Rome.

[3] The statue from which the illustration is taken (p. 192) was found in this neighborhood, and is believed to have been the one at whose base Cæsar fell.

blood," that "great Cæsar fell." One of the conspirators detained Mark Antony out of doors, in order that there might be no interruption of the deed. Another, presenting a petition, grasped Cæsar's robe, to impede his movements, while "the envious Casca" struck him from behind in the neck. For a moment he defended himself; then, seeing that he was hemmed in by a circle of armed enemies, and that resistance could avail him nothing, he covered his face with his toga, at the same time dropping its folds so as to cover his feet, and died without a struggle.[1] The conspirators then, holding aloft their bloody daggers, rushed into the street and proclaimed the restoration of liberty.

Events following the Assassination. — It soon appeared how wofully they had deceived themselves. The senators had fled in terror. The people, instead of flocking to their support, shrank from them in bewilderment. They saw the fatal mistake they had made in suffering Antony and Lepidus to live; for, had these been removed, Brutus, as *prætor urbanus*, would have been the chief magistrate of the state. As it was, these two friends of Cæsar were armed with all civil and military power, as lawful rulers, and Brutus and Cassius were nothing but conspirators. Lepidus was a man without weight or influence; but Antony, far from being the trifler that they had fancied him, showed himself possessed of lofty ambition, ready in resources, prompt and resolute in action. He at once possessed himself of Cæsar's papers and treasures, and was master of the situation.

Cæsar's Funeral. — Meanwhile the conspirators, disappointed in their expectations, had taken refuge in the Capitol, protected by the gladiators of Decimus Brutus. Weeks passed in bargaining and intriguing. The passions of the people were easily excited against the conspirators by Antony's adroit eloquence; and when

---

[1] There is no classical authority for the famous *Et tu Brute!* When Tillius Cimber pulled his robe, he cried, *Ista quidem vis est!* at the first stroke he exclaimed angrily to Casca, after which he appears not to have uttered a word, although some reported that when he saw Marcus Brutus among the assassins, he said, καὶ σὺ τέκνον!

Cæsar's will was read, which gave liberal donations to the people, their gratitude and affection were roused to a high degree of enthusiasm.[1] They seized Cæsar's body, carried it into the Forum, to a place opposite his residence, and burned it upon a funeral pile constructed of benches and other chance timber. On this spot a temple was afterwards erected to the deified Cæsar (*Divus Julius*), the ruins of which have been lately discovered.[2]

Domination of Mark Antony. — Antony now had everything his own way, and ruled with vindictiveness and arrogance. The conspirators found themselves powerless, and were fortunate in being allowed to depart in safety from the city. Provinces for the next year had been assigned to the leaders before Cæsar's death, and now they proceeded to take possession of them. Decimus Brutus assumed command in Cisalpine Gaul, where he was attacked by the consul Antony; Marcus Brutus became governor of Macedonia, and Cassius of Syria. In July Cicero left Italy, to spend at least the rest of the year in the East, but was driven back by unfavorable winds, and plucked up courage to return to Rome, where he arrived about the end of August, and at once placed himself at the head of the opposition to Antony. The six months that followed are the noblest in his life.

Character of Cæsar. — The character of Cæsar[3] and his influence upon the world are subjects upon which it is not easy to form a positive opinion. He was one of those men of lofty genius, like Napoleon, who believe themselves, and are tacitly admitted by their admirers, to be exceptional beings, not bound

[1] Shakespeare's account of these occurrences, as ususal in his historical plays, has many inaccuracies of detail, but seizes the spirit of events with remarkable truthfulness.

[2] Cæsar's residence, the *regia* (the official residence of the *pontifex maximus*), was on the Sacred Way, just east of the Forum, where its remains have recently, as is believed, been identified.

[3] Froude's life of Cæsar is the best, and is characterized by genuine historic insight, but is one-sided and not always accurate in detail. See also Mr. Ropes' paper on the portraits of Cæsar, in *Scribner's Monthly* for February, 1887.

by the rules of conduct which govern human relations in general. His early life is admitted to have been dissolute; his mature life was not controlled by any considerations of right and wrong. But his impulses were generous and humane; he saw clearly the evils of society and government, and possessed an intuitive perception of the means to check them. With all his kindness of heart, he was capable of gross bad faith and wholesale slaughter, when it served his purposes. His premature death makes it impossible for us to judge what his reconstruction of the state might have accomplished for society, especially seeing that his successor, Augustus, adopted a plan of government widely at variance with his. His measures in themselves were eminently wise, and his organization of the municipal system shows that he realized the value of local self-government (p. 175). But the eagerness with which he pursued the phantom of royalty, which caused his downfall, leads us to question whether, if he had lived, he would not have made the mistake of so many men of genius, and constructed a scheme of government which no one was capable of administering but himself.

GLADIATORS. (From an Ancient Mosaic.)

CHAPTER XVII.

OCTAVIAN.

The Young Octavius. — Soon after Cæsar's assassination, his grand-nephew, Gaius Octavius, returned to Rome from the East, where he had been sojourning. He was a young man of nineteen, and as Cæsar left no legitimate descendants, he adopted Octavius by will, and made him his heir. As the law required, he took the name of his adoptive father, Gaius Julius Cæsar, from whom he is usually distinguished by the surname Octavian.[1] The delicate health of the young Cæsar had kept him out of a military life, and, as "the nephew of his uncle," he seems to have been regarded with some degree of contempt. He was, however, long-headed and astute, cool and sagacious, devoid of passion or affection, and proved himself a match for the most experienced politicians of Rome.

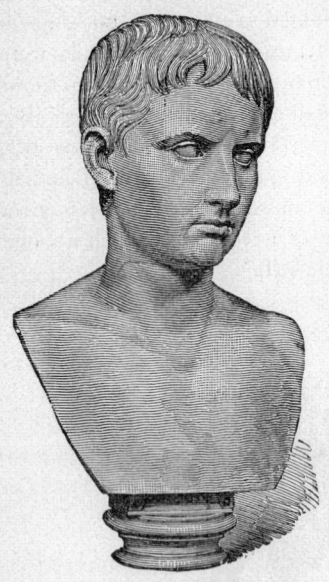

THE YOUNG CÆSAR.

Octavian as the Champion of the Senate. — The relations of Octavian with Antony were not at first friendly. Antony had taken possession of Cæsar's property, and when the young heir demanded

[1] He does not appear to have used this name himself, but it is employed by most modern historians.

his inheritance, he was told that it had been already expended for public purposes. Without hesitation Octavian, with the assistance of his relatives, but chiefly from his own fortune, paid Cæsar's legacies, and thus gained permanent popularity with the populace. He now joined the party of the Senate, which invested him with extraordinary powers; and during the autumn and winter that followed he was its leading champion in the field. It was during this winter that Cicero delivered his last series of speeches, — his fourteen invectives against Antony, which are known as *Philippics*.[1] B.C. 44.

Octavian's Treachery. — The consuls for the following year were Hirtius and Pansa, former adherents of Cæsar, but who now held with the Senate. Antony was engaged in besieging Decimus Brutus at Mutina (*Modena*), and the consuls, with Octavius, advanced to raise the siege. Two battles followed in April, in which Antony was decisively beaten, and retired across the Alps, where he joined Lepidus; in these battles both consuls lost their lives. Octavian had done good service to the Republic, and now demanded the vacant office of consul. But the Senate distrusted him, and it was not until the end of the summer that the consulship was reluctantly granted to him. It was too late. He was already alienated, if, indeed, he had ever been sincere in his support of the Senate. He now united himself with Antony and Lepidus, and the city fell again under military rule. B.C. 43.

The Second Triumvirate. — The three conspirators, masters of the city and all its military forces, had themselves appointed *triumvirs*,[2] with full authority to govern and reorganize the state. The power was granted for five years, and was afterwards extended for five more, after which time the triumvirs did not think it necessary to seek any legal foundation of their authority. They commenced their rule by a proscription even more cold-blooded than

[1] So called from their resemblance to Demosthenes' Philippic orations (against Philip of Macedon).

[2] This was the name given by the Romans to the members of a board of three (p. 200).

that of Sulla, in which each member of the trio gratified his resentment by procuring the sacrifice of his personal enemies. Lepidus conceded the death of his brother, Antony that of his uncle, while Cicero fell a victim to the enmity of Antony, whom he had attacked most bitterly during the past winter. The number who perished was said to surpass the victims of Sulla's proscription, and to have included 300 senators and 2000 knights.

Battle of Philippi. — In the meantime Brutus and Cassius had organized an army in their provinces of the East, while Sextus Pompey, with a strong naval force, was master of a large part of the Mediterranean. The triumvirs proceeded first against the republican leaders, whom they met at Philippi in the year 42. The battle here fought was the most considerable in the Roman annals up to this time; the army of the Republic counted some 80,000, that of the triumvirs 120,000. There were two battles at Philippi. In the first, Brutus, upon the right wing, drove the forces of Octavian, while upon the left Cassius was routed by Antony. Cassius, in a fit of unmanly despair, slew himself, and twenty days later Brutus in his turn was defeated by the united forces of the triumvirs, and took his own life. With the deaths of Cassius and Brutus ended the attempt to restore the Republic by assassination.

Rule of the Triumvirs. — The triumvirate lasted for more than ten years, during which time, however, the incompetent Lepidus was set aside by his more energetic colleagues. In this interval, too, Sextus Pompey was overthrown and slain. Having rid themselves of all rivals, the two remaining triumvirs divided the Empire between them, Octavian taking the West and Antony the East. Here Antony associated himself with the voluptuous Cleopatra, and undertook a war against the Parthians, in which he himself gained only dishonor, while all the success and reputation went to his lieutenant Ventidius.

B.C. 36.

B.C. 35.

War between Octavian and Antony. — An effort was made to cement the bond between the triumvirs, and to wean Antony from

his infatuated love for Cleopatra, by marrying him to
Octavia, the sister of Octavian. But the fascinations of   B.C. 40.
Cleopatra were too powerful; he resigned himself to
luxury and idleness in her court, and at last, for her sake, divorced
his faithful wife Octavia, with brutal disregard of her dignity, and
of public opinion. This disgraceful conduct aroused the Roman
people, and war was declared against Egypt — not a civil war
between the Roman triumvirs, but a war in which Antony, now a
traitor, was associated with a foreign enemy against the lawful
government of his native country.

Battle of Actium. — The contest was decided by a naval battle.
The fleets met Sept. 2, B.C. 31, in the Bay of Actium, west of
Greece. Hardly had the fight begun, when Cleopatra hoisted sail,
and hastened to leave the line of battle, followed immediately by
Antony. But their followers fought with desperation until their
fleet was destroyed. The cause of Antony and Cleopatra was lost.
When Octavian followed them the next year, they were found
unprepared. First Antony, in despair, put himself to death, and
Cleopatra followed his example, in order to escape the ignominy
of being carried in the conqueror's triumphal procession. Octavian was master of the world.

Establishment of the Empire. — The conqueror, well assured
of his strength, made no haste to return to Rome, but employed
his time in establishing affairs in the East upon a permanent basis.
Egypt was annexed to the Empire, which now embraced the entire
circuit of the Mediterranean lands with the exception of the wild
regions of Thrace and Mauretania, and the free republics of Lycia,
Rhodes, and Massilia. Octavian returned to the city in the year
B.C. 29, and celebrated a threefold triumph, — one over the Dalmatians, one for the victory of Actium, and a third for the final
subjugation of Egypt. The gates of the temple of Janus[1] were now

---

[1] This was an arched passage east of the Forum, the gates of which were
opened in time of war. Between the mythical reign of Numa (p. 15) and the
present time, they had only once been closed, at a time between the First and
Second Punic Wars.

closed, and peace reigned through the world. Two years later, Jan. 16, B.C. 27, Octavian laid down the extraordinary power of triumvir, which he had continued to exercise until this time without any formal extension of authority, and received from the Senate the name of Augustus. This was the commencement of the Empire.

LICTORS.

PERIOD VI. — THE EARLY EMPIRE.

CHAPTER XVIII.

AUGUSTUS.

I. THE REIGN OF AUGUSTUS.

The Dyarchy. — The Empire established by Augustus was not a pure monarchy, such as Julius Cæsar had planned, and Diocletian established three hundred years later. The government was still called a Republic; and the Emperor (or, as he was more properly called, the Prince) was a magistrate, all whose powers were derived from those of republican magistrates. The constitution of the early empire has been called a *Dyarchy*,[1] — that is, a government of two powers, — the old republican constitution still continuing in operation, and a new magistrate, the Emperor, exercising an independent authority by its side. It may be compared to a constitutional monarchy like that of England, where the substantial power belongs to Parliament, while the sovereign continues to possess some remains of his original monarchical authority. In Rome the relations were reversed. It was the republican institutions which had lost their vitality, and only survived as a shadow; while the real power was, to all intents and purposes, in the hands of a monarch, the Emperor.

Prince and Senate. — The title Prince designated the Emperor as first citizen;[2] and Augustus took pains to appear with the republican simplicity of a citizen, not, as Julius had done, with

---

[1] This name is given by Mommsen to the system of government now established.

[2] This title had nothing to do with the republican dignity of *princeps senatus*, although this too was enjoyed by Augustus.

the ceremonial of royalty. But exclusive authority over the armies of the Republic was given to him for a term of ten years, and then renewed; while the tribunician power, granted for life, placed him in possession of the most important civil functions. The possession of this twofold authority made him the supreme power in the state, so that the Senate, the organ of the republican institutions, nominally his equal, was practically subject to his will. What survived of the republican institutions was now vested in the Senate. The assemblies gradually lost all effective participation in public concerns, and at last disappeared entirely; but the Senate never, until the time of Diocletian, ceased to have a share in the government, and on various occasions it made itself the organ of an active opposition to the monarchical power.

Division of Power. — The division of power between the Prince and the Senate is seen most distinctly in the government of the provinces. As the Emperor had the exclusive command of the armies, it was natural that those provinces which required a military force should be assigned to him. He governed them as Pompey had done in the case of Spain (p. 202) by deputies (*legati*), residing himself at Rome, or visiting the various parts of the Empire from time to time. The rest of the provinces, about ten in number (the division varying from time to time), were governed by proconsuls appointed by the Senate, as in the time of the Republic. The senatorial provinces were, as was natural, the oldest and most orderly, — Sicily, Africa, Achaia (Greece), Macedonia, Asia, Further Spain, Narbonnese Gaul.

The Imperial Præfects. — In the government of the city (which now comprised the whole of Italy) there was more danger that the two authorities would clash. Here the Emperor was represented by Præfects, whose powers were not easily distinguished from those of the republican magistrates. One præfect had charge of the supplies of corn, another of the City, while a third had command of the emperor's body-guard, the Prætorian Cohorts, — a corps of nine thousand troops, stationed in Italy, and after the death of Augustus concentrated in Rome.

It followed, as a matter of course, that the City Præfect became in reality the municipal chief magistrate; and that the Prætorian Præfect, having command of the military forces in Italy (where no divisions of the regular army were stationed), became the chief support of the emperor's authority, and rose to be the most powerful subject. These two præfects drew into their hands almost all judicial authority, and before long the magistrates were as powerless and shadowy as the assemblies.

The Family of Augustus. — Augustus had climbed to supreme power by bloodshed and bad faith; but the disappointments that he experienced in his family relations, and his failure to transmit his ill-gotten power to his descendants, may almost be regarded as a retribution. Falling violently in love with Livia, the wife of Tiberius Nero, he obliged Nero to divorce his wife, and then married her himself (p. 189). But Livia brought him no children, although her two sons by her former marriage, Tiberius and Drusus, were received into his family, and the elder was finally adopted as his successor. Augustus at first intended the succession for the young Marcellus, son of his sister Octavia; and upon the untimely death of Marcellus, he looked to his daughter's posterity. He had but one child, a daughter, Julia, whom he married to Marcus Agrippa, his ablest general and statesman. But the two eldest sons of this marriage, Gaius and Lucius, died young; while a third son, Agrippa Postumus, was so dull and boorish as to be unfit for the throne. When Agrippa died, the emperor married Julia to his step-son Tiberius, whom he required, for this purpose, to divorce his wife, the daughter of Agrippa. This marriage brought nothing but misery. Julia was vicious and bad-tempered, Tiberius proud and sensitive. To escape her he went to reside at Rhodes, where he remained several years; while she, after a lawless and dissolute life, was banished by her father, and died in exile. Tiberius was now adopted by Augustus, associated with him in his authority, and designated as his successor.

The Boundaries of the Empire. — The Roman Empire, at the accession of Augustus, comprised nearly all the lands which border upon the Mediterranean Sea, being confined within natural boundaries in three directions, — on the west by the Atlantic Ocean, on the south by the African Desert, on the east by the Arabian Desert and the upper course of the river Euphrates, beyond which was the Parthian Empire. Upon the north the boundaries were still unsettled, and it was here that they were most exposed to assault. It was the great work of Augustus to establish a frontier upon the north as secure and permanent as were those in the other directions. At the very beginning of his reign he annexed the territory upon the lower course of the Danube (the modern Servia and Bulgaria), organizing it as the province of Mœsia. As Julius Cæsar had conquered up to the lower Rhine, this left an uncertain boundary only between the lower Rhine and the lower Danube.[1]

AUGUSTUS. (From the Statue in the Vatican.)

[1] See Map of the Roman Dominions at the end of the Mithradatic War The Roman color should be given also to Egypt, Numidia, Cyprus and Gaul.

The Danube Frontier.

The next task of Augustus was to occupy this intervening territory north of Italy, as far as the Danube, — a difficult task, because the hardy mountaineers of these regions made an obstinate and determined resistance. The command was given to his two step-sons, Tiberius and Drusus, able and energetic young men, who in a few years subdued the country from the Alps to the Danube, organizing it as the provinces of Rætia and Noricum. This task accomplished, the brothers were separated, Tiberius being sent to complete the occupation of the Danube, while Drusus should extend the empire east of the Rhine. The task of Tiberius was soon accomplished. Northeast of Italy a low and practicable pass by the Julian Alps (p. 1) connects the lands upon the Adriatic with the valley of the Save, the principal confluent of the Danube from the south. This valley was made into the province of Pannonia, which was gradually extended to the north, so as at last to reach the Danube and include all the lands, now Western Hungary, west and south of the great bend of that river. The conquest of Pannonia was completed rapidly; but after some years, a formidable revolt called Tiberius to that quarter, and occupied him for three years. B.C. 15.

B.C. 10.
A.D. 6.

The German Frontier.

In Germany it was the policy of Augustus to make the Elbe, instead of the Rhine, the boundary of the Empire. By this the great mountain-chains of Bohemia and Moravia would serve as an insurmountable barrier against invasion in that direction; and the northeastern frontier of the Empire would extend in almost a direct line from the mouth of the Elbe to the great turn in the course of the Danube, above Buda-Pesth. These mountain regions were occupied by the German nation of the Marcomani (*frontiersmen*), who were generally friendly to the Romans. The country further north, between the Rhine and the Elbe, was, on the other hand, occupied by warlike and hostile nations, who presented a determined resistance to the Roman advance. While still engaged in the work of conquest, Drusus died; and Tiberius, who had   B.C. 9.

now accomplished the conquest of Pannonia, took the place of his brother, and completed his work. Germany from the Rhine to the Elbe was a Roman province.

Check to the Roman Advance. — The conquest was of course a superficial one, consisting only in the occupation of a few military posts. It would require years of warfare and administration, as had been the case in Spain, to convert this military occupation into a secure possession; and this result was not destined to be attained. At this point the Roman Empire was forced to take its first step backward. In the year 9 A.D. the governor of Germany was Lucius Varus, a brave man and good officer, but wholly incompetent to govern a people like the Germans, of indomitable courage and a proud spirit of independence. He had somewhat the same arrogant contempt for the irregular warfare of a half-civilized nation that General Braddock had for his Indian antagonists. He was warned of an impending insurrection, but he could not believe that the unconquered Roman legions had anything to fear from the undisciplined levies of barbarians.

The Fight in the Teutoburg Forest. — The leader in the uprising was a young chief of the Cherusci, called by the Romans Arminius, which is supposed to be their way of putting the German name *Hermann*. He had served in the Roman armies, and knew their strength and weakness. He had made formal submission to the Romans, and was favored and trusted by Varus. When all his preparations were ready, he caused the news of a revolt among the German tribes to be brought to the Roman commander, who at once broke up his camp upon the Weser, and proceeded by an unfamiliar route to suppress the uprising. While the army was making its way through the wilderness, it was suddenly assaulted by its concealed enemies. The fight lasted three days, and ended with the complete annihilation of the Roman army, and the overthrow of the Roman dominion in Germany. A few years

A.D. 14-16. later, Germanicus, the son of Drusus, invaded these regions for three successive years, inflicted vengeance for

THE ROMAN EMPIRE
AT THE DEATH OF AUGUSTUS
A.D. 14.

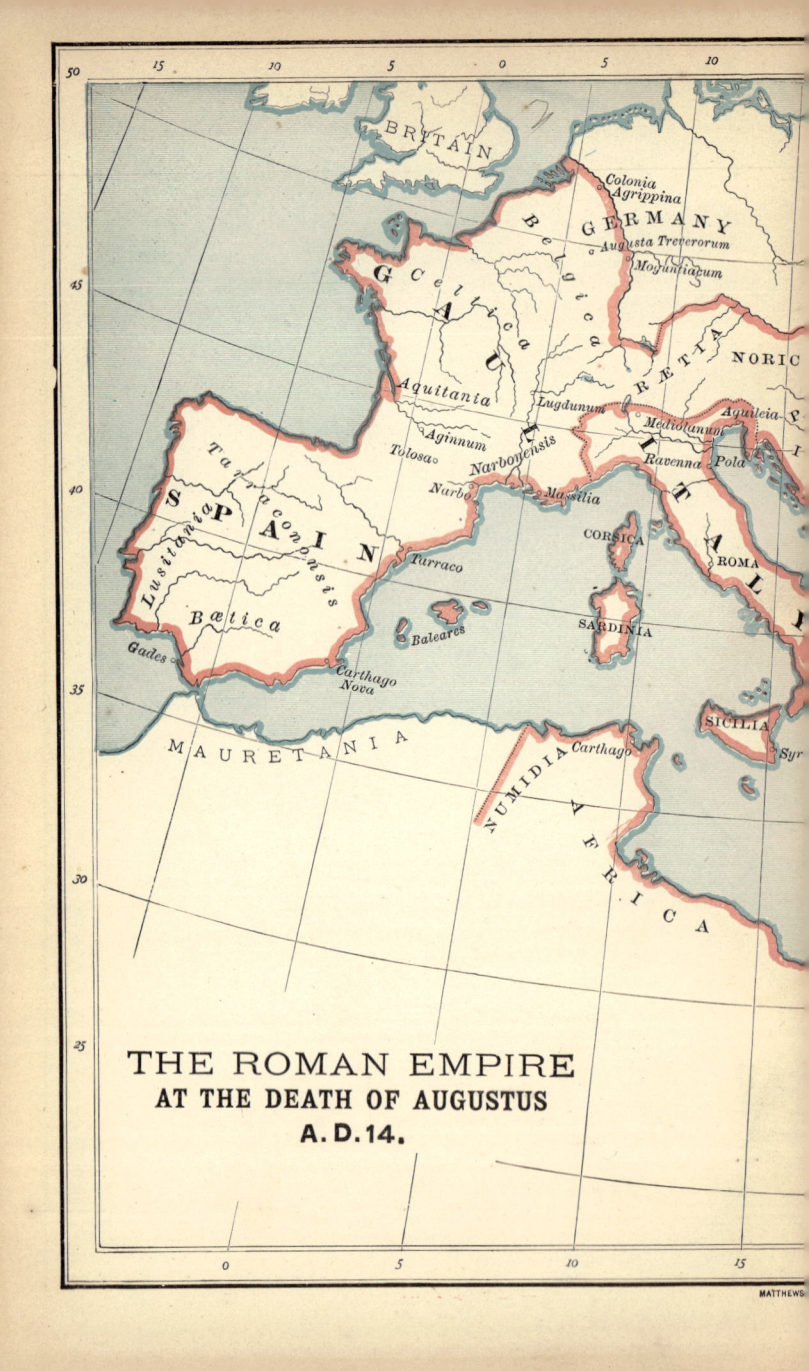

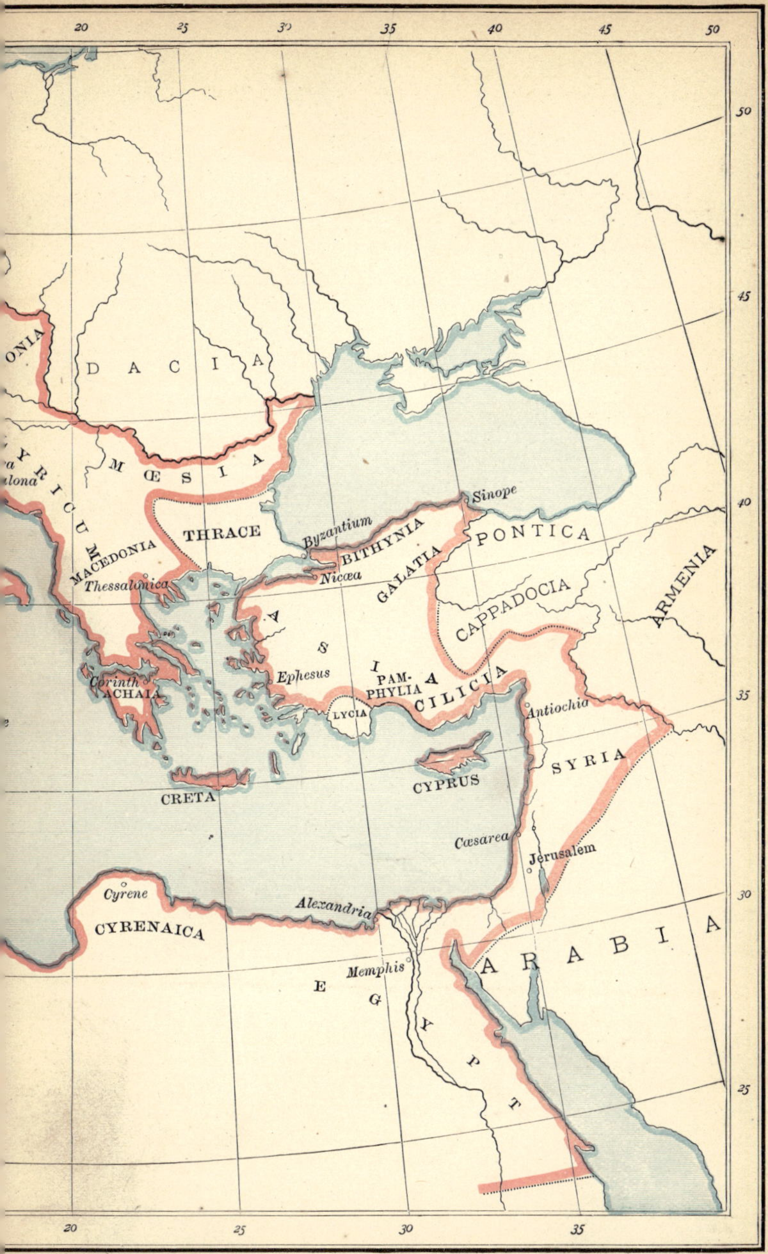

UP & CO., ART-PRINTING WORKS, BUFFALO, N. Y.

the disaster, and recovered the lost ensigns of the legions. But the lost dominion was never regained.[1]

Death of Augustus. — This was the greatest disaster which Augustus ever sustained, not merely a defeat in battle, but a loss of empire, — the first retreat which the Romans ever made from territory which they had once occupied. The aged emperor was broken down by so terrible a reverse at the close of his life, suffered his beard and hair to grow, — a mark of mourning, — and cried again and again, "Quintilius Varus, give me back my legions!" He died five years afterwards, asking his friends in his last moments whether he had not played his part well in the comedy of life.[2]

A.D. 14.

His Work. — The work of Augustus was a great and enduring one. He did not found a permanent dynasty; and the emperors of his own household, who succeeded him, have not as a whole left a happy memory. Moreover, there were defects in his political system, which at last brought it to ruin. But it had a long and successful life, and for the time it solved perfectly the political problem. Bringing order out of disorder, inaugurating a period of peace after a long and bloody civil war, ruling with remarkable tact and sagacity, Augustus impressed his contemporaries powerfully with the feeling of his greatness. It seemed that it was only to Divine Providence that they owed such blessings; and while he never, like Julius, allowed himself to be worshipped as a god, it is not to be wondered at that a form of worship, devoted to the deity incarnate in the emperor, gathered about him, and soon became the principal cult of the provinces, and a chief agency for maintaining the imperial power.[3]

[1] There is no direct evidence as to the locality of this battle-field, the Teutoburg Forest; but it was probably just north of the river Lippe, about half-way between the Rhine and the Weser.

[2] *Ecquid iis videretur mimum vitae commode transegisse* (Suet., *Aug.* 99).

[3] This worship of the Emperor, hardly known except from inscriptions, may be regarded as the distinctive religion of the Empire.

II. The Augustan Age.

The Age of Augustus. — The reign of Augustus was made illustrious by a group of writers, in prose and poetry, and by a splendor and activity in art, such as have seldom existed in the history of the human race. This period marks the culmination of the Roman genius in art and literature; and although the Emperor had little to do personally with these achievements of the human mind, yet their association with his reign fitly gives to the period the name of the Augustan Age.

Architectural Works. — The hand of Augustus was chiefly seen in the buildings with which he adorned the city. He himself enumerated twelve temples which he had built, besides repairing eighty-two which had fallen into decay, and building or restoring aqueducts, theatres, and porticos. This work of construction had been begun by Julius Cæsar, and was continued by his successor — a policy which reminds us of the great public works of the Tarquins, and still more of the rebuilding of Paris by Napoleon III. The architectural display of Julius and Augustus Cæsar was one of the marks of the new autocratic power. His example was followed by other noblemen, so that he could boast with good reason that he "had found Rome of brick and left it of marble."

The Public Squares. — The Forum, or market-place, had become too narrow for the world-empire. It is true, the less elegant and savory branches of trade had found a home in new market-places upon the banks of the river (p. 83), and now the business of the Forum was confined to bankers, brokers, and goldsmiths. But the public business encroached more and more. Special halls of justice (*basilicae*, p. 142) had been built along its sides, to relieve the open space, and now the Forum was nearly surrounded by magnificent edifices. The most important of these was the *Basilica Julia*, on the south side of the Forum, where its foundations are still to be seen; it was begun by Julius and finished by Augustus. Julius Cæsar also commenced that noble series of public squares to the north of the Forum, which was continued by his successors, ending in the Forum of Trajan, the remains of which still exist. For the purpose of laying out the new *Forum Julium*, he was obliged to move the Senate-house to a point somewhat nearer the great Forum, thus making the *Comitium* somewhat narrower; at the same time he moved the *rostra*, or speaker's platform, from its old position between the Forum and the Comitium, to a spot near the upper end of the Forum, where it has recently been uncovered.

The Campus Martius. — The Campus Martius, north of the Capitoline, and outside of the walls — the old parade-ground and field for military exercises — was also encroached upon by the new building activity. The theatre of Pompey, the first stone theatre in Rome, stood here: it was in one of the apartments of this that Cæsar was assassinated. In the northernmost portion of the field Augustus constructed a mausoleum for himself, a circular building, some remains of which are still in existence. The principal building in this space was the Pantheon, or temple of all the gods, built by Agrippa, and still in almost perfect preservation as a Christian church and burial place for distinguished men.

Roman Art. — The distinctive feature of Roman architecture was the Arch (p. 30), which we now find developed into the Dome; this noble architectural form was employed in the construction of the Pantheon of Agrippa, and was common in the later Empire. The Greek architectural orders, like other forms of Grecian art, were introduced into Rome, and most of the temples and other public buildings erected at this time were in Greek style. But the taste of the Romans was too crude and superficial to enjoy the simple grandeur of the Doric style, which satisfied the more highly cultured people of Athens; the elegance of the Ionic and the profuse ornament of the Corinthian orders pleased them better; and they even tried their clumsy hands at inventing a mixed style, known as the Composite, which has the merits neither of the Greek nor of the genuine Roman style. In other branches of art the Romans showed high appreciation, but little creative power.

Virgil. — In the field of literature, the foremost name of this period, and one of the most distinguished poets of all time, was

Publius Vergilius Maro, better known as Virgil. This poet has been in former ages the subject of extravagant admiration, and is at the present day perhaps unduly depreciated. He is not a great creative poet; he must be placed distinctly in the second rank. He is not only deficient in originality, but in spontaneity, and in truth and profundity of insight. The reader often feels that his descriptions of nature and delineations of human passion are not drawn from his own experience or observation, but are artificial, — copied from earlier poets or deduced from theory. But his execution is exquisite, the narration spirited, the national sentiment strongly maintained, and the tone of thought elevated and inspiring. By his lofty ethical tone and his earnest patriotism he was an efficient coadjutor with Augustus in his efforts for the restoration of national life and character.

Horace. — By the side of Virgil stands Horace, perhaps the most popular poet who ever wrote, the most perfect master of poetic expression. Nothing can surpass the grace and felicity of his style. His songs, most varied in spirit, — gay and pensive, devoutly religious and earnestly patriotic, expressing simple affection or the wildest passion, epicurean indolence, bacchanalian frenzy, or even stoical virtue, — are the models of lyric poetry for all time: while his satires and epistles are equally models of shrewd, every-day wisdom, — by no means commonplace poetry, but what we may call the poetry of the commonplace.

Ovid. — Far below Virgil and Horace is Ovid, a poet with a great gift of narration, but whose easy flow of verse is apt to betray him into a prosaic diffuseness. The poetry of his early life was luxurious in style and often sensual; his chief work, the *Metamorphoses*, contains in graceful form many mythological narratives which otherwise we should have lost, and his *Fasti*, a poetic calendar of the year (only six months are extant), have preserved from destruction many details of the native Roman religion. For some unknown reason he was banished by Augustus, and spent his last days in exile on the western shore of the Black Sea; from this place of exile he sent home some of his tenderest and truest verses.

Propertius and Tibullus. — The works of two other poets of this period are extant, small in amount and limited in style; they are exclusively in the elegiac measure. Propertius rose at times to a high degree of dignity and power; but he was over-fond of metaphysical obscurities, in imitation of the Greek poet Callimachus. Tibullus is simple, elegant, tender, a writer of genuine merit in these qualities, but with no range or variety of style. There were other poets, but their works have been lost.

Prose Writers. — Of the prose writers of this period — orators and historians in considerable number — there remain only portions of the works of two. Livy was the greatest of Roman historians, considered simply from the point of view of literary excellence. He was as far from the modern standard of historical criticism as the other historians of his nation. But for picturesqueness of style, grace of narration, and sustained interest, there are few historians of any age who compare with him. Only about one-third of his works are preserved, — containing the early period through the Samnite wars, and the Second Punic and Macedonian wars; for the rest we have bare and unsatisfactory abstracts. Of Nepos, a voluminous biographer of this reign, we have only a few short lives, dull in style and of little worth.

Mæcenas. — If this age is the Age of Augustus, its literature is almost equally associated with the name of Gaius Cilnius Mæcenas, a wealthy knight of an ancient Etruscan family, a chosen counsellor of the Emperor, and a munificent patron of literature. Mæcenas, although a counsellor of the Emperor, had no taste for public life, and preferred to live in elegant retirement, surrounded by men of his own tastes. Horace and Virgil owed to him much of the encouragement which induced them to devote themselves to literary composition, and his name is so indissolubly associated with their poetic productions, that it has come down to us as a synonym for a patron of literature.

Statesmen and Orators. — The most influential statesman of the reign of Augustus was Marcus Vipsanius Agrippa, a man of inferior birth, but of sterling qualities. He was so highly esteemed by the

Emperor, that he married him to his daughter Julia (p. 233), designing for him or his posterity the succession to the throne; the Emperor Caligula was his grandson, and Nero his great-grandson. The most distinguished orator of the time was Gaius Asinius Pollio, whose versatility of talent displayed itself also in the fields of arms and of literature; he was a poet of considerable merit, but none of his works are extant. In public life he was characterized by a strong spirit of independence, and his attachment to the memories of the Republic prevented him from very active support of the new Empire. More eminent as a general than either Agrippa or Pollio, and also a friend of literature, was Marcus Valerius Messalla; he was especially the patron of the poet Tibullus.

STREET IN POMPEII.

CHAPTER XIX.

THE JULIAN AND CLAUDIAN EMPERORS.[1]

I. THE JULIAN CÆSARS.

The Succession to the Throne. — As the Roman Emperor was in theory not an hereditary monarch, but a republican magistrate, it followed as a matter of course that the office could not be held by a woman. The hereditary principle, inherent in its monarchical feature, made it easy to transmit the crown to any male member of his family; but Augustus at his death left no male descendant capable of taking up his work. His granddaughter, Agrippina, was a woman every way qualified for it — by ability, character, and ambition; and in a true monarchical government she might have made a Semiramis, a Zenobia, or an Elizabeth.

AGRIPPINA.
(From a Coin in the Berlin Museum.)

Her husband, Germanicus, son of Drusus, the conqueror of Germany, was a man of many imperial qualities, but still young and inexperienced. It seemed to Augustus expedient on the whole to give the succession to his step-son Tiberius, designating as next in the succession the young Germanicus, together with his cousin of about his age, Drusus, son of Tiberius.[2] For this purpose Germanicus was to be adopted as a son by Tiberius.

[1] Tiberius and Caligula were, by adoption, descendants of Julius Cæsar in the male line, and therefore compose, with Julius and Augustus, the Julian house.

[2] The following genealogical table of the Julian and Claudian emperors, will show these relationships.

GENEALOGICAL TABLE OF THE JULIAN AND CLAUDIAN EMPERORS.

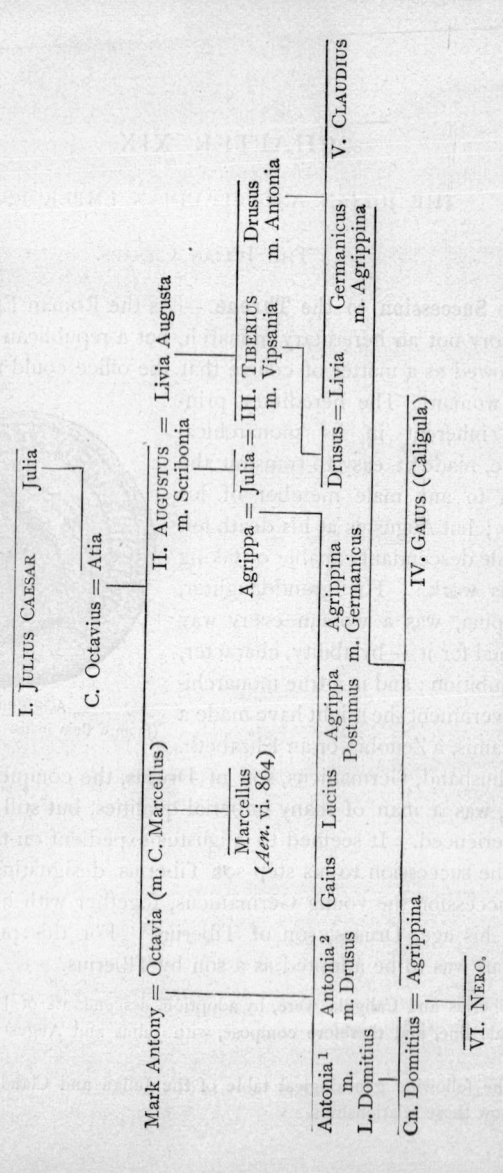

```
I. JULIUS CAESAR    Julia
        |
C. Octavius = Atia
        |
        ├─────────────────────────────────────────────────┐
                                                          |
                              II. AUGUSTUS = Livia Augusta
                                    m. Scribonia
                                         |
                        ┌────────────────┤
                        |                                    Drusus      V. CLAUDIUS
                 Agrippa = Julia = III. TIBERIUS           m. Antonia
                              m. Vipsania                        |
                                         |                       |
                    ┌────────┬────────┬──────────┐    Drusus = Livia   Germanicus
                 Gaius   Lucius   Agrippa    Agrippina                m. Agrippina
                         Postumus  m. Germanicus
                                                                         |
                                                            IV. GAIUS (Caligula)

Mark Antony = Octavia (m. C. Marcellus)
                        |
           ┌────────────┼────────────┐
      Antonia¹      Antonia²       Marcellus
      m.            m. Drusus      (Aen. vi. 864)
      L. Domitius
           |
      Cn. Domitius = Agrippina
                        |
                    VI. NERO.
```

Character of Tiberius.

Tiberius, 14-37. — Tiberius Claudius Nero therefore ascended the throne in the year A.D. 14. He was a man of fifty-six, who had shown the highest qualities as a military commander in Rætia, Pannonia, and Germany, and whose life until this time had been, if not irreproachable, yet without any serious blemishes. He showed himself as able upon the throne as in the field, and for

TIBERIUS. (From a Bust in the Capitoline Museum.)

nearly fifteen years ruled the Empire with consummate ability and sagacity, consolidating and systematizing the administration, and earning the credit of having given their permanent shape to the institutions of the empire. But he lived too long for his own reputation. He was by nature of a somewhat moody, suspicious disposition, and these qualities were aggravated by the dissensions with his wife Julia (p. 233), and afterwards with Agrippina, the widow of Germanicus. By degrees, as his mind lost its vigor, his temper became gloomy and suspicious, and he ended his life as a cruel and revengeful tyrant.

The Delations. — The tyranny of Tiberius was exercised under the forms of law. He was a scrupulous and rather pedantic observer of forms, and the rules of legal procedure in Rome lent themselves to great abuses, which crept in by slow degrees, until the administration of justice became a powerful engine of injustice. The Romans had no public prosecuting officer; it was left to the interest or public spirit of individuals to bring criminals to justice, and the private prosecutors were rewarded for their services by a share of the property of their victims. Hence it became a trade, and a very lucrative one, to hunt up offences and bring them to justice. This was called *delation*, and the prosecutors *delators*.[1] Now the laws for the punishment of treason were lax, and lent themselves readily to the practices of the delators. The person of the emperor being sacred, it was interpreted as treason even to subject his effigy upon a coin to any indignity, to flog a slave in the presence of his statue, and other acts as trifling as these. Hence trials for what we may call *constructive treason* became more and more common. Tiberius at first took pains to pardon the offenders and mitigate their punishment; but as the practice became more rooted, and his moral sensibilities became blunted, he ceased to oppose this miscarriage of justice, and even seems to have encouraged it. The activity of the delators is the greatest blot upon his reign.

Germanicus. — At the beginning of the reign of Tiberius his adopted son Germanicus was governor of Gaul and Germany, and was engaged for three years in inflicting vengeance upon the Germans for the defeat of Varus, perhaps with the expectation of recovering the lost territory. At the end of the third

A.D. 16. year's campaign, the Emperor wisely decided that this was a hopeless task, and the Elbe frontier was definitively

---

[1] From *deferre*, to bring information.

given up, the Rhine being now made the boundary of the Empire. Germanicus was transferred to the government of the East, where the relations with Parthia made it important that there should be an able officer in command. Here he shortly died, and the circumstances of his death, accompanied by a violent quarrel with Piso, his officer next in command, inspired his wife Agrippina with

GERMANICUS.

a suspicion that he had been poisoned by Piso, with the connivance of Tiberius. From this time her sentiments towards the Emperor became more and more unfriendly, until at last she made herself suspected of treasonable designs, and was involved in ruin, together with her two eldest sons. A younger son and daughter, the emperor Gaius (Caligula) and Agrippina, mother of the emperor Nero, were afterwards of bad eminence.

Sejanus. — Tiberius had a favorite minister, Sejanus, præfect of the prætorian guards. He was an able, unscrupulous man, of daring ambition, and, to further his own ends, he took pains to foment the quarrel between Tiberius and Agrippina. The Empire had not been long enough established to have a well-recognized hereditary succession, and Sejanus appears to have conceived the design of securing the throne for himself. With this end in view he procured the murder of Drusus, son of Tiberius, and brought about the overthrow of Agrippina and her sons; he then aspired to marry Livia, the widow of Drusus, who had been his agent in her husband's murder. He had already persuaded the Emperor to retire to the island of Capri,[1] where he spent the last eight years of his life in seclusion, leaving the government in the meantime wholly in the hands of Sejanus. At last the knowledge of his schemes and crimes came to the ears of the Emperor. The situation was a difficult and embarrassing one; for the reins of power were in the hands of Sejanus, and any sudden or incautious steps against him might throw him into open rebellion. By a secret commission, appointing Macro as Prætorian Præfect in his place, and by a long and obscure letter to the Senate, only by slow degrees opening to that body his desire to be rid of Sejanus, the Emperor succeeded in accomplishing the hazardous task.

A.D. 31. Sejanus was seized and strangled in prison, and his body was thrown into the Tiber.

Reign of Terror. — The alleged plots of Agrippina, and the narrowness of his escape from the treason of Sejanus, threw the aged Emperor into a paroxysm of terror. The partisans and friends of Sejanus were promptly and severely punished; and even with this his trepidation did not end, but he continued year after year, banishing and putting to death all upon whom

A.D. 37. his jealous suspicion lighted. At last he died, and there

---

[1] *Neæra*, by Graham, describes the life in Capri.

was a momentary gleam of hope and joy at the succession of the young son of the beloved Germanicus.

Caligula, 37–41. — Gaius, the successor of Tiberius, was the son of Germanicus and Agrippina. As a young child, he had lived with his parents in the camp in Gaul and Germany, and had been a pet of the soldiers, who called him *Caligula*, — the name of a coarse shoe worn in the army. This nickname has clung to him. But whatever good qualities he may have inherited from his parents were lost in the corrupting life of the camp and the court, and a youth passed in the expectation of absolute power. If Tiberius, in his last years, was a gloomy tyrant, Caligula was a capricious and wanton one.[1] His head was turned by his greatness, and indeed his acts would almost show insanity. Divine honors, which Augustus accepted with reserve, and Tiberius constantly rejected, Gaius eagerly demanded, sometimes presenting himself in the temple in the guise of a god, and demanding worship. He delighted in bloodshed. In a fit of passion he wished that the Roman people had only one neck; and at a banquet burst into laughter at the thought, as he explained, how speedily he could have the heads of all his guests. This grotesque humor was displayed in many of his acts of cruelty. He craved the excitement and notoriety of grand achievements. He built a bridge from the Palatine, where he resided, to the Capitoline, in order to have readier access to the Capitoline temple. Another bridge, three and a half miles long, he constructed from Baiæ to Puteoli, in order to falsify the prediction that he would no more be emperor than he would drive over the water at Baiæ. At the dedication of this bridge he caused numbers of people to be upset in the water, and then thrust them off with poles, so that they should not rescue themselves. Four years of this mad tyrant were all that could be endured. He was at last assassinated by an officer of his guard, whom he had goaded to fury A.D. 41. by constant insults.

---

[1] Tiberius had said of his subjects, "Let them hate me, provided they respect me" (*oderint dum probent*). Caligula said, "Let them hate me, provided they fear me" (*oderint dum metuant*).

II. THE CLAUDIAN CÆSARS.

Claudius, 41-54. — The death of Caligula threw everything into confusion and uncertainty. The constitution of the Empire had made no provision for a successor; and the Senate hastily convened to consider whether the Republic should be restored, or an emperor chosen from some other family. But while the Senate was deliberating, some soldiers of the prætorian guard, who were engaged in plundering the palace of the late Emperor, dragged out from a place of concealment a middle-aged member of the imperial family, so insignificant that everybody had forgotten his existence. Recognizing in him the brother of the popular Germanicus, they proclaimed him emperor; and the Senate had no choice but to accept him. Under the name of Claudius he reigned for thirteen years; and, notwithstanding his physical and mental deficiencies, his rule affords a refreshing contrast to the misrule of Caligula, who came before him, and that of Nero, who followed him.

Rule of Claudius. — Claudius was a well-meaning prince, and his mental capacities were by no means despicable; but they were not such as to make him a good ruler. In some respects he resembled James I. of England. He was, like him, a man of learning and acumen, but with moral qualities which made him an object of contempt. He had from childhood been neglected and despised, even by his parents; and by this his natural timidity and weakness of will had been morbidly exaggerated. As emperor he was the slave of two wicked women, — first of his wife, Messalina, whose name has become a synonym for female depravity, and then of his niece, Agrippina, whom he married after the death of Messalina, and who at last poisoned him to make way for the succession of her own son. Whatever crimes rest upon his memory are for the most part to be attributed to the imperious desires of these women, to whom he had not the power to say, "No."

His Public Works. — Like Caligula, Claudius had grand ideas, and projected magnificent public works; but, unlike Caligula, his plans had in view public utility rather than self-indulgence or vain display. The most beneficent of these works was the new harbor, which he constructed at the mouth of the Tiber. The accumulations of sand had so choked up the mouth of this river that the old harbor of Ostia had become worthless; and the supplies for Rome had to be landed at distant ports — principally at Puteoli (*Pozzuoli*) in Campania — and hauled by land at great expense. By cutting a new channel to the north of the river, building out a couple of jetties, and dredging the space between, Claudius constructed a harbor which served for several centuries. He also secured the water supply of the city[1] by repairing the aqueducts, and drained the superfluous waters of the Fucine Lake by a subterranean passage, thus redeeming a large tract of land for cultivation.

Conquest of Britain. — The most important undertaking of his reign was the conquest of Britain, which he annexed to the Empire shortly after his accession. A.D. 43.
The conquest of this island met with a determined resistance, as is shown by the well-known stories of Caractacus and Boadicea; and for the present the occupation did not extend much beyond the southern half of England. The subjugation of England, Wales, and the southern part of Scotland was completed by the distinguished general Agricola, about forty years later. This province remained subject to Rome for nearly four hundred years, and the numerous remains of Roman houses and villas found in England testify to the completeness of the occupation; but the people of Britain did not assimilate Roman manners and customs and modes of thought as thoroughly as those of Gaul. When the troops of Rome were withdrawn, its civilization speedily disappeared.

Nero, 54–68. — Claudius had by his wife Messalina a son of great promise, named Britannicus; but the ambitious and unscru-

---

[1] Caligula, to be sure, had commenced, but Claudius completed, the great Claudian aqueduct, the ruined arches of which now form the most conspicuous feature of the landscape in the Roman Campagna.

pulous Agrippina (daughter of the elder Agrippina and Germanicus) determined to secure the throne for her son by a former marriage, whom she caused to be adopted into the imperial family, so that he is henceforth known by the family name, Nero. This young prince was of illustrious ancestry, being descended from Augustus, Mark Antony, and Drusus[1]; but he appears to have inherited only the bad qualities of his ancestors. The tyranny of Tiberius had its root in the deterioration of a sensitive and suspicious nature; that of Caligula can be regarded as the mad freaks of an unbalanced mind; that of Nero was pure wickedness. Among his victims were Britannicus, whom he had supplanted, his mother Agrippina, his wife Octavia, his tutor, the philosopher Seneca, and the poet Lucan. His reign of fourteen years, except the five years at the beginning, is an almost uninterrupted carnival of crime.

Character of Nero. — The most conspicuous mental quality of Nero was vanity. He piqued himself upon his ability as a poet and an artist, and was not ashamed to exhibit his skill in public: by this, more perhaps than by anything else, offending the public sentiment of Romans, for no people has ever insisted upon personal decorum so strongly as the Romans. His vanity was not confined to these higher realms of art; he even entered the lists, and drove a chariot round the course in the Circus Maximus. He had always had a passion for the games of the circus, and under his patronage the craving of the populace for these exhibitions was gratified to the full. Thus while he incurred the contempt of the nobles, he was popular with the masses, whose demand for donations and exhibitions was never more lavishly gratified than now.

Rule of Tigellinus. — In the first year of his reign Nero was under the influence of the philosopher Seneca, and Burrhus, the Prætorian Præfect; and during this period his administration was good, although it is not to be supposed that the credit of it belongs to him. The turning point in his career, as in the case of

---

[1] The wife of Drusus, mother of Germanicus and Claudius, was Antonia, daughter of Mark Antony and Octavia. See p. 243.

Henry VIII., was his falling in love with a fascinating woman, Poppæa Sabina, for whom he neglected and at last put to death his wife. From this moment all his worst qualities came to the surface. Burrhus and Seneca were succeeded, in their influence over him, by the freedman Tigellinus, who during the rest of Nero's reign was the real ruler of the Empire. This infamous creature, who maintained his ascendency and amassed riches by pandering to the worst vices of his master, was the first example of a class of favorites who obtained a bad notoriety under the Empire. The slaves, in antiquity, as we have seen (p. 89), were often the superiors of their masters in education and ability. When manumitted, they did not become entirely free, but remained the "clients" of their late masters, often performing for them services of a personal and confidential nature, as steward, secretary, etc. The tyrants among the Roman emperors, finding no cordial support among the nobles, their natural counsellors, made use of freedmen, who were by necessity wholly subservient to them, as agents in their misgovernment.

The Fire in Rome. — In the year 64 Rome was laid waste by a terrible conflagration, which consumed about one-half of the city, including the most central and populous portions. Although Nero was absent from the city when the fire broke out, and used all efforts to extinguish it, he was nevertheless suspected of having himself kindled it, in order to enjoy the spectacle. Either to pander to a popular prejudice, or to turn suspicion from himself, he accused the Christians, who were a small sect, mostly of the lower classes; and they were punished with horrible tortures. He indulged his taste for spectacular displays by placing them in the arena, covered with pitch, and letting them be burned as torches.

Rebuilding of the City. — The city had already been burned once, at the invasion of the Gauls, more than four hundred years before; and by a curious coincidence this fire broke out B.C. 390. upon the anniversary of the defeat of the Romans at that July 18. time. After its first burning the city had been rebuilt hurriedly and without system or order (p. 72); the work of rebuilding was now placed under the direction of skilled architects, and the work was done thoroughly, elegantly, and conveniently. The emperor indulged his passion for luxury and display by taking an immense tract of land from the heart of the city — extending from the Palatine to the Esquiline Mount — for a private palace and park. The palace, the "Golden House," upon the Esquiline, was planned upon an enormous scale, and surrounded by a colonnade a mile in extent. In front of it was a colossal statue of Nero, 110 feet high.

Revolution. — The misgovernment of this monster was brought to an end in the year 68. In this year an insurrection under Vindex broke out in Gaul, and the governor of Hither Spain, Galba, was forced by the suspicions and unfriendliness of the emperor to associate himself with the insurrection and proclaim himself emperor. Soon Verginius, the governor of Upper Germany, one of the noblest characters of the age, lent his support to the insurrection, and the Senate took courage to proclaim Nero a public enemy, and condemn him to be put to death "after the manner of the ancestors" — scourging to death, followed by beheading. He fled from the city to take refuge in the villa of a faithful freedman, but hearing the sound of the horsemen who were in pursuit, he ordered his freedman to slay him. Among his last words were a lamentation that such an artist should perish.[1]

Literature in Nero's Reign. — The period between the "Golden Age" of Augustus, and the revival of literature which is known as the "Silver Age," a century later, is illustrated by few productions of importance in literature. The historical works produced in these years have nearly all perished. Of the philosopher Seneca we have already spoken. As an ethical writer he has high qualities, but is verbose and inelegant. There were two poets of some eminence. Lucan, nephew of Seneca, was author of an epic of great brilliancy, entitled *Pharsalia*, marked by a strong republican sentiment. He was one of the victims of Nero's tyranny. Persius was a satirist, heavy and obscure, often dull, but pure and moral in tone.

---

[1] *Qualis artifex pereo!* (Suet., *Nero*, 49).

CHAPTER XX.

THE FLAVIAN HOUSE.

Year of Revolutions. — Galba, who succeeded to the throne by this revolution, was a member of an old patrician family, a man of the genuine Roman stamp, — a brave soldier, an honest man, but advanced in years, and parsimonious. His strict discipline and the meagreness of his donations excited the dissatisfaction of the prætorians (p. 232), who soon murdered him, and placed Otho upon the throne, a young man of dissolute character, a boon companion of Nero, but brave and able as a commander. But Otho did not reign without a rival. The army of Lower Germany had already proclaimed its commander, Vitellius, who, after some hesitation, assumed the purple, marched to Italy, and defeated the army of Otho in a battle near Placentia. After his defeat Otho slew himself; and Vitellius, an ignoble and gluttonous man, although a good soldier, occupied the throne. A.D. 68. A.D. 69. A.D. 69.

Vespasian, A.D. 69-79.[1] — The elevation of Galba to the throne had shown that emperors could be made elsewhere than at Rome; and now the East came forward with a claimant, who was of the type of Galba, and whose professed object was to avenge him and dethrone the unworthy occupant of the throne. Titus Flavius Vespasianus was engaged as commander in the war against the revolted Jews when he was proclaimed emperor by his soldiers. Judæa had, since its conquest by Pompey (p. 196), been reckoned a part of the province of Syria, although usually administered by an independent procurator, or imperial agent. The spirit of independence and nationality among the Jews was very strong, and was

[1] Freeman's article, *The Flavian Emperors*, in the second series of his historical essays.

systematically outraged by the Roman officials. At last A.D. 66. they were driven by their wrongs to rise in rebellion, and Vespasian was entrusted with the command against them.

Vespasian Emperor. — Vespasian was, like Galba, a blunt soldier, but was younger, had more administrative capacity, and more popular manners, although he was ruder and less humane. A better man could not have been found for the emergency, for the utter incapacity of Vitellius was already manifest. Vespasian was fortunate, moreover, in having the support of the governor of Upper Germany, Verginius (p. 254), and the active co-operation of Mucianus, governor of Syria, who acted throughout as his lieutenant. Leaving Vespasian to settle the affairs of the East,

COIN OF VESPASIAN.[1]

Mucianus pushed on with his army into Italy. Vitellius was overthrown and put to death after disorders in the city, in the course of which the capitol was burned; and Mucianus administered affairs until the arrival of the new Emperor. Vespasian, leaving the Jewish war in charge of his son Titus, followed leisurely to Rome, and assumed the reins of government.

Capture of Jerusalem. — The ten years of Vespasian's rule were a period of peace and good government at home. Abroad, his reign was disturbed by the formidable insurrection of Civilis in Gaul, and by the capture and destruction of Jerusalem. The

[1] The letters *S. C.* show that it was coined by the Senate, which retained the right to coin copper, while to coin silver and gold was the prerogative of the Emperor.

Emperor had, during his three years' command in Judæa, reduced the whole country into his power, except the capital. Titus, left in command on his father's accession to the throne, invested the city in the beginning of the year 70, and reduced it after a siege of over five months, attended with unutterable horrors of bloodshed, famine, and conflagration. The fanatic party among the Jews, the *Zealots*, had massacred the moderates of their nation, and now confronted the invader with relentless obstinacy. At

INTERIOR OF ARCH OF TITUS.[1]

first they intrenched themselves within the temple; and when this was captured and burned, they withdrew to the heights of Mount Zion, where they continued the defence of the holy city. When this, too, fell, and its buildings were destroyed by fire, Jerusalem had ceased to exist. In the course of time a handful of the survivors returned to their old home, and built for themselves humble dwellings among its ruins. The memories and

[1] Showing the golden candlestick among the spoils of Jerusalem.

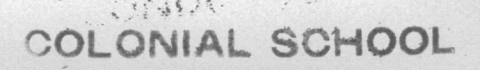

aspirations of the race were kindled afresh; and after two generations had passed, they even ventured to measure their strength again with that of imperial Rome. This was in the reign of the Emperor Hadrian; and when the rebellion was crushed, as it was certain to be, it was decided that the very name of the sacred city must disappear. A Roman colony was founded upon its site, named *Ælia* from the family name of the Emperor, to which was added *Càpitolīna* in allusion to the Capitoline Jove.

A.D. 132.

Architectural Works. — On his return to Rome Titus celebrated a triumph for his hard-won victory; and a few years later a triumphal arch was built upon the highest spot in the Sacred Way, on the walls of which was carved — still to be seen — a representation of that sacred candlestick of the Jewish temple which had been carried among the trophies in his triumph. The greatest architectural work of this reign was the Flavian Amphitheatre, better known as the Colosseum, to this day the most magnificent of the remains of ancient Rome.

Titus, 79-81. — Titus succeeded his father upon the throne in the year 79, and in his short reign of two years won all hearts by his justice and humanity. He had his father's military gifts, joined with a milder and more kindly disposition. His saying is well known, when any day had passed without an action of kindness, "I have lost a day." The only event of importance in the reign of Titus was the sudden renewal of volcanic activity in Mount Vesuvius; the tremendous eruption overwhelmed an immense area of ground, including the two populous cities of Herculaneum and Pompeii. Great portions of these cities have been disinterred within the last century, affording an instructive view of the streets and buildings of an ancient city, as well as bringing to light an innumerable number of remains of art and utensils of every-day life.

Pliny. — In this eruption perished the elder Pliny, the most conspicuous writer of the day. His history of the Germans has perished; but his Natural History, an ill-arranged cyclopædia of scraps of information of every kind, is preserved, and is a work of very great value, in spite of its confused arrangement and unscientific spirit, — less his fault, no doubt, than that of an age which was not accustomed to the orderly and scientific arrangement of modern treatises. That Pliny was a genuine student, who was not satisfied with hearsay, but wished to study phenomena at first hand, is shown by the circumstances of his death. He left the safe retreat from which he could have quietly observed the eruption at a distance, and went boldly to its near neighborhood, where he was suffocated by its vapors.

Domitian, 81-96. — The happy period of the reign of Titus was soon passed; and he was succeeded by his brother Domitian, a youth whom the possession of unlimited power, joined with a naturally cruel disposition, soon converted into a tyrant of the worst type. He began his reign as a reformer, professing himself — and perhaps sincerely — anxious to correct the immoralities of the time; but he seems to have derived so much enjoyment from the act of inflicting punishment, that he lost sight of the ends of punishment. In his reign the system of *delations* (p. 246), which had been a source of such suffering and misery under Tiberius, was revived, and reached its extreme height. In the year 96 he was murdered by a conspiracy.[1]

His Foreign Policy. — Nevertheless Domitian had some good qualities as an administrator, and some events of his reign show a certain degree of statesmanlike insight. We have already spoken of the brilliant campaigns of Agricola in Britain (p. 251), which, it is true, owed little to the Emperor's support, and which were even unseasonably cut short by his suspicious jealousy. We may more properly place the rectifying of the German frontier to the credit of Domitian. Upon the upper Rhine, between the provinces of Rætia and Upper Germany, was a wedge-shaped tract of land, — the modern Baden and Würtemberg, — which had never been brought under the authority of the Empire. Domitian, by

[1] Eckstein's *Quintus Claudius* describes this period.

constructing an earthwork and line of fortified posts from the Rhine, near Mentz, to the Danube, near Ratisbon, brought this large tract within the boundary of the Empire. By this narrowing of their territory, the Germans were forced, with greater rapidity, to adopt a more settled agricultural life, and were hastened in their progress towards civilization. These *tithe-lands* (*Agri Decumates*), as they were called, were, about two hundred years later, conquered by the Alamannians, and severed from the Empire.

The Twelve Cæsars. — The twelve emperors from Julius Cæsar to Domitian are known as the Twelve Cæsars, merely for the reason that Suetonius, a writer of this period, wrote their collected lives under this title. The name Cæsar, being assumed by every emperor, became a general appellation for them, and has come down to the present day with that meaning as the German word *Kaiser*.

ROMAN SOLDIER.

THE ROMAN EMPIRE UNDER TRAJAN A.D. 117.

CHAPTER XXI.

THE FIVE GOOD EMPERORS.

I. Trajan.

Nerva, 96-98. — Upon the death of Domitian the Senate bestowed the imperial title upon an elderly man, one of its own members, by the name of Nerva. The only important act of his short reign was the designation of his successor. For this purpose he selected Marcus Ulpius Trajanus, the most eminent soldier and most capable administrator in the realm, adopted him as son, and associated him as colleague. The example thus set by Nerva was followed by his successors; and in each case the choice fell upon a person of such high character and qualifications, that it has been said that the history of the world presents no example of a period of time of equal length so distinguished for the happiness and prosperity of mankind. The last and most distinguished of the "five good emperors," Marcus Aurelius, unfortunately had a son, to whom he gave the succession; and the line of good emperors was terminated by a besotted tyrant.

Trajan, 98-117. — Trajan was a warlike emperor, the first since Augustus who extended the bounds of the Empire by conquest, if we except the occupation of Britain by Claudius. For some years the Dacians north of the Danube, in the mountainous region in the eastern part of Hungary, had given great annoyance to the Romans, and had endangered the provinces upon the Danube. Trajan subjugated this country in two campaigns, exterminated the population, and created the province of **Dacia**, which he peopled with colonists from the Empire. A.D. 106. Dacia continued to be a Roman province for about one hundred and fifty years, when the advance of the Goths in this region obliged the Emperor Aurelian to withdraw his troops to the south of the Danube, and give up the province; but the Roman language had obtained such a foothold that a language derived from it is still the prevalent tongue in large parts of this region.[1] During the course of the Dacian wars Trajan also annexed Arabia Petræa, a country which afforded an important route of communication between Egypt and Syria. His later enterprises were of less permanent value, although in appearance more splendid. He invaded

TRAJAN.

the Parthian empire, now seriously weakened by internal decay, and annexed the territory as far as the river Tigris and beyond; but these distant regions formed no natural part of the Roman dominion, and Trajan's successor, Hadrian, wisely gave them up. Portions of them were afterwards regained.

[1] The origin of this "Rumanian" tongue is still a matter of controversy; but even if the province was completely evacuated by Aurelian, which is hardly possible, it cannot be doubted that the Rumanians of the Balkan peninsula are in part at least descended from Trajan's colonists.

The Empire at its Height. — The Roman Empire was, under Trajan, at the height of its power. It never again reached the extent of dominion to which he carried it by his Dacian and Assyrian conquests. Its government, moreover, was never before or after so humane and equitable as under Trajan and his three successors; and the morals of the people, under these happy influences, steadily improved. Society was tired of the beastly debauchery which characterized the first century of the Empire, and there seems little doubt that there was less vice at the end of this period than one hundred or two hundred years before.

Economic Decay. — Nevertheless, even as early as this, we begin to see indications of an economic decay of society. The most distinct sign of this is in the financial distress of the Italian cities at this date. The cities, as we have seen (p. 159), were not scattered and isolated municipalities, like those of modern times, but were territorial divisions of the entire country. The whole population of Italy was, therefore, contained in these municipalities; and when it is said that the municipalities had fallen into financial embarrassment, this means that the whole population of Italy was in a condition of economic distress. The extravagance of the early Empire and the collapse of native Italian industry (p. 149), which went on under the Empire with increased rapidity, were having their natural effects. The worst feature of this was, however, that the municipal governments showed themselves so incapable of dealing with these financial difficulties that the Emperor was obliged to appoint commissioners (*curatores*) to inspect and regulate their accounts. In this way some degree of prosperity was restored, but self-government had proved a failure.

Decay of the Peasantry. — An effort was made to check the decay of the free peasantry by a system of poor relief, called *alimentationes*, introduced at this period. In order to relieve the embarrassments of the land-owners and the municipalities, loans were made to them by the state, which took mortgages of their lands. Through this agency provision was also made for the support of poor children of the neighborhood. In this way it was hoped to protect the peasantry from the encroachments of capital. But the scheme, beneficent no doubt for the time and in individual cases, could not check a tendency which was the inevitable consequence of slave labor and the degradation of industry. The peasantry steadily sank in status until, in the century following, it is found reduced to a condition of "predial serfdom"; that is, a condition in which, without legally ceasing to be freemen, they were held under an hereditary obligation to labor upon certain lands to which they were bound (*ascripti glebae*).[1]

The Silver Age. — The reign of Trajan not merely marks the highest degree of power and dominion reached by the Roman Empire, but presents that unerring mark of national vitality, a strong and original literature. The style of composition and the forms of language had changed considerably since the time of Augustus, as must necessarily be the case where there is a genuine national life. The age of Trajan has been called the "Silver Age," to distinguish it from the "Golden Age" of Augustus; but for originality and vigor and many of the best qualities of style, the writers of this period are not unworthy to rank with those of a century before. The busy and practical Silver Age excelled in prose writers: its poets were for the most part of inferior type.

Tacitus. — The greatest literary name of this period is that of the historian, Tacitus, whose writings contained an account of the events of the Empire from the death of Augustus. Only about a third of them, however, are extant. His most marked characteristics as an historian are his wonderful picturesqueness and his intense moral earnestness, qualities in which few historians of any age have equalled him. It cannot be denied that the strength of his moral convictions, joined with the lack of critical acumen which belonged to his age, make him often prejudiced and unjust; but there is no reason to impugn his motives. His account of

[1] The serfs of the later Roman Empire were known as *coloni*, and their condition as *colonatus*. The origin of this institution is very obscure; the best discussion of the subject (although still not wholly satisfactory) is found in Coulanges' *Recherches sur quelques problèmes d'histoire*.

the reigns of Tiberius and Nero and of the disturbed events which followed the death of Nero are priceless treasures of literature.

The Younger Pliny. — A contemporary and intimate friend of Tacitus was the younger Pliny, whose published correspondence places before us a picture of the times, unequalled in ancient history except for the correspondence of Cicero. It is from two of his letters that we derive our information of the death of his uncle in the eruption of Vesuvius (p. 258); and his official correspondence with Trajan, when he was governor of the province of Bithynia, contains a complete picture of the administration of a province of the second rank. The broad humanity and modern spirit of Pliny contrast him with almost all other writers of pagan antiquity.

A.D. 79.

Quintilian. — A prose writer, somewhat earlier in time and of great and enduring influence, was Quintilian, whose treatise upon rhetoric is one of the soundest and most complete in existence. In the deterioration of literature and of intellectual life which followed shortly, the influence of Quintilian was soon lost; but his book has in modern times been an exhaustless mine of sagacious criticism.

Juvenal. — The greatest name in the poetry of this period is that of Juvenal, the satirist. His works are not voluminous; but as satire was the most original branch of Roman literature, and Juvenal was the greatest Roman writer of satire, he may in a certain sense rank as the most distinctive Roman author. There is a marked contrast between him and his greatest forerunner, Horace (p. 240), whose satire was genial, good-natured, in keeping with the easy epicureanism of its author. Far surpassing Persius (p. 254) in poetic merit, Juvenal was inspired with an equal ethical passion; his writings fairly burn with indignation and intensity of conviction. It is easy to believe that writers of so strongly moral tone as Tacitus and Juvenal had a large share in raising society to that higher moral plane in which we find it a generation or two later.

Lesser Writers. — Of the writers of less reputation we need say only a few words. Frontinus, a statesman and general of great merit, has left two short works, containing much information and practical knowledge, — one is an account of the Roman aqueducts, the other a scrap-book of military anecdote. The epigrammatist Martial is brilliant and witty, often indecent. His writings are of great value as a picture of society; only the reader must bear in mind that it was Martial's aim to find objects of entertainment and ridicule, and that his delineations, like those of Juvenal, present only one phase of life, and that the worst. Statius was a court poet of great popularity, but showy and inflated in style. Silius Italicus wrote a poem upon the Second Punic War, rather a dull performance, but containing some acceptable information.

SIEGE OF A DACIAN STRONGHOLD. (From Trajan's Column.)

Art. — Art, too, in this century had a vigorous life. There was no great school of art, perhaps there were no artistic creations of the highest merit. But the taste and the technical skill, inherited from earlier periods, kept the art of the second century at a high standard. This is especially marked in the bas-reliefs of this period, which are numerous and well preserved. The most significant monuments of the time are the columns of Trajan and Marcus Aurelius. The reliefs which clothe these columns from top to bottom are not only admirable works of art, but an inexhaustible mine of information, in their graphic representations of the actions of war and peace.

The Christians. — One of the most interesting of the letters of Pliny is one in which he consults the Emperor as to the treatment of the Christians, who had now become somewhat numerous in the East. The Romans were not intolerant in religion. They readily accepted the religion of every people with whom they came in contact, and incorporated it with their own. We have seen this in the case of Æsculapius (p. 95), the Great Mother (p. 129), etc. As the Empire had become a world empire, gathering in all nations under its organization, it aspired to make its religion a world religion, embracing all national religions. But Judaism and Christianity could not be thus incorporated. Their fundamental tenet, the unity of the divine nature, was incapable of accommodating itself to the loose polytheistic notions of the Romans. Their God could not be placed on the same footing with Jupiter, Mars, and Apollo. But even this need not have led to persecution, because the easy-going faith of the people took little notice of strange and individual forms of religion. There were large numbers of Jews residing in Rome during the Republic, and their worship was not disturbed. It was not until the deification of the Emperor (p. 237), and the insistence upon his cult as the duty of a patriotic citizen, that there was any motive to persecute. The man who would not sacrifice at the altar of the Emperor was no good citizen. A Christian could not so sacrifice, and was punished, — not as a Christian, but as disloyal.

Policy towards the Christians. — As a rule, the government took little notice of these sectaries. It was not until they became numerous, organized, and self-assertive, that the arm of the law was stretched out against them. The Jews were few and quiet; and they were generally let alone, as were also the Christians, unless there was special reason to molest them. For the most part, the policy pursued was the compromise prescribed by Trajan in his answer to Pliny. The governor had testified to the harmlessness and good character of the Christians, but also to their obstinacy and impiety. The Emperor tells him not to make any effort to trace them out and bring them to justice; but, if they are brought before him, the law must take its course. The law under which the Christians were punished at this time was that which forbade unlicensed associations.[1] It was in Trajan's reign that A.D. 115. occurred one of the earliest and most noted of the Christian martyrdoms — that of Ignatius of Antioch, who was thrown to the lions in Rome.

Hadrian, 117–138. — Hadrian,[2] the successor of Trajan, was a ruler as strongly contrasted as possible with his predecessor, but perhaps of a type more needed by the age. His reign was a period of peace. While Trajan carried his arms with restless activity and brilliant success to all parts of the frontier, Hadrian displayed as unwearied an activity in traversing the Empire from one end to the other, personally examining its situation, and putting it in the best condition for administration and protection. He seems to have felt, what proved to be the case, that the attitude of the Empire after this time would be one of defence. No emperor after Trajan attempted, with any success, to enlarge the bounds of the Empire. Hadrian surrendered the three new provinces upon the East, and made the Euphrates and the desert again the boundary in this direction;[3] and after a brief period of peace, under Hadrian and his successor, the series of aggressions by foreign powers commenced, before which the Empire finally succumbed.

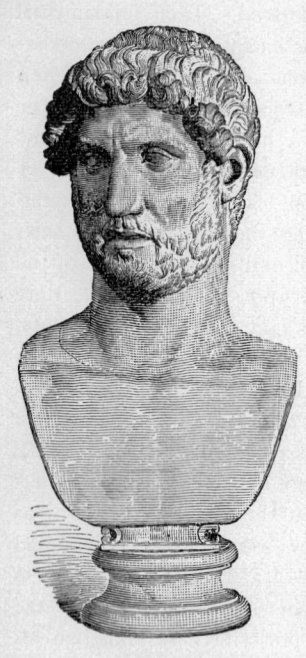

HADRIAN.

---

[1] See Hardy's *Correspondence of Pliny and Trajan* (p. 243).
[2] Ebers' *The Emperor*.
[3] These territories were partly regained by Marcus Aurelius, see p. 270.

Hadrian's Wall. — The most interesting work of defence which we associate with Hadrian is a wall and line of fortified posts across the narrow part of Britain, similar to that which Domitian had constructed in Germany. The remains of this great work, extending from the Tyne to the Solway, at nearly the modern boundary between England and Scotland, are still to be traced in nearly their whole extent. Hadrian's successor, Antoninus Pius, extended the frontier, and built a new wall between the Clyde and the Forth.

II. THE ANTONINES.

Antoninus Pius, A.D. 138-161. — Antoninus Pius was a man of noble and benign countenance, and his character corresponded to his features. His reign of twenty-three years is marked by no striking events; but in its unvarying justice and humanity, it affords, perhaps, the best illustration in history of the familiar saying, "Happy is the people whose annals are uninteresting."

ANTONINUS PIUS.
(From a Coin in the Berlin Museum.)

Marcus Aurelius, A.D. 161-180.[1] — Marcus Aurelius, the adopted son and successor of Antoninus Pius, was equal to his predecessor in virtue, and perhaps even superior to him in conscientious devotion to duty. His tastes were studious, and he delighted in the pleasures of family life; but he set aside his preferences, and devoted himself unremittingly to the duties of war and administration, which his station imposed upon him. His eminence in literature has given him the title of "the philosopher"; but when he was called from his books into active life, he showed himself equally able as a soldier and administrator. Philosophy was always his favorite pursuit; and at the very end of his life he composed a treatise upon practical morality, *The Thoughts*, which is to this

---

[1] Watson's *Marcus Aurelius* is the best account of this Emperor in English.

day read and valued for its lofty ethical teaching and tonic power.[1]

Reign of Marcus Aurelius. — It was a hard fate which associated this upright and conscientious prince with the most disturbed and calamitous events of the century, and has made his reign a critical moment in the downfall of the Empire. After the long period of quiet and prosperity under Hadrian and Antoninus Pius, the Empire suddenly found itself disturbed by war and rebellion, famine, pestilence, and religious dissensions; and in respect to each of these, the reign of Marcus Aurelius may be regarded as a turning-point in the history of Roman society. In three special fields, — the economic interests of society, the progress of Christianity, and the relations to the German barbarians, — we find here noteworthy and critical events.[2]

Lucius Verus. — In accordance with an arrangement made by the Emperor Hadrian, Marcus associated with himself as colleague a young man named Lucius Verus; but the selection was an unfortunate one, as Lucius was wholly unfitted for the responsibility and labors of the imperial throne. Fortunately he died

A.D. 169. within a few years, leaving Marcus in sole possession of the power. During the first portion of his short reign Lucius was nominally in charge of a war against the Parthians, the real command being in the hands of his lieutenant, Avidius Cassius. Cassius, a general of great ability, gained distinguished successes, capturing both the Parthian capitals, Seleucia and Ctesiphon, and forcing from the enemy the cession of the left bank of the Euphrates.

The Pestilence. — The victorious army, on its return

A.D. 166. to the West, brought with it that most dreadful of oriental scourges, the plague. This was the first, and perhaps the most destructive, of a long succession of such visitations from

[1] The religious life of this time is portrayed with remarkable truthfulness and delicacy in Pater's *Marius the Epicurean.*

[2] For these causes of decay, read the second of the lectures in Seeley's *Roman Imperialism.*

the East, the last being the oriental cholera, within the present century. Whether the present was the most destructive of the series or not, it was certainly the most fatal in its consequences; for the Empire never rallied from the losses which it now sustained. We have already noticed (p. 263) the loss of economic vigor in the second century. This does not appear to have been arrested, even during the long period of good government through which the Empire had just passed. Population could not increase, could barely hold its own, under such circumstances. In the reign of Marcus new causes of decline were at work. A few years before the pestilence an inundation of the Tiber, A.D. 162. unprecedented in extent and destructiveness, had been followed by distress and famine. To this were now added the horrors of the pestilence, which carried off perhaps half the population of Italy. And as, just at this time, the necessities and embarrassments of the government were greatly increased by the German invasions, it will be seen that this pestilence was a factor of the first importance in the downfall of the Empire. With a diminishing population and diminishing resources, the emperors of the third century found themselves called upon to meet constantly increasing dangers and difficulties.

The Christians. — In all times of great disaster the ignorant populace are disposed to throw the blame upon some obnoxious or unpopular class; and in the reign of Marcus Aurelius, it was easy to turn the popular suspicion against the growing sect of Christians. The gods, it was thought, must have sent these repeated calamities, — war, inundation, famine, pestilence, barbarian inroad, — as a punishment for some national guilt; and this could be nothing but the toleration of this impious and atheistic sect. For, it was reasoned, men who deserted the temples, and refused to worship the gods under whose protection the state had prospered, were of necessity impious and atheistic. The Roman religion was not by nature intolerant. As we have seen (p. 267), it permitted all forms of belief and worship, and readily received them into fellowship; but Christianity refused to be so received.

Persecution. — An outcry was therefore raised against this unpopular sect, and the mild and just Emperor had no choice but to carry out the laws against those who refused to worship the national gods; a religion which interfered with their duties as citizens could not be tolerated. The hatred against the Christians as an impious and unpatriotic class was intensified by the quarrels and dissensions among themselves, and by the discreditable shape in which the religion presented itself to observers. The Christianity which Marcus Aurelius knew was not a religion of peace and love, a sublime and intelligent theory of life and the unseen world; the Christian church was full of bickerings and jealousies, and its religion presented itself to him as a system of absurd and metaphysical speculations. It was with no misgivings, therefore, that he ordered the laws to be enforced, and made himself the agent of an active persecution.

The Martyrs. — The most distinguished victim of this persecution was Justin, known as the Martyr, one of the earliest of the extant writers of the church. Probably in the same

A.D. 166. year was the well-known persecution at Smyrna, in which perished Polycarp, the head of the church in that city. He was an aged man, who, as tradition asserted, had conversed with the apostle John; and when, as was regularly done, the opportunity was given him to recant by cursing Jesus, he answered: "Eighty and six years have I served him, and he never did me harm; and how can I now blaspheme my King who has saved me?" He was condemned to death, and burned

A.D. 177. at the stake. Some years later, a violent persecution broke out at Lyons, occasioned by the dissensions among the Christians themselves. The most conspicuous martyr in this persecution was a serving-maid named Blandina. When asked to deny her faith, she answered: "I am a Christian; there is no evil among us." She was put to death in the arena, with cruel tortures, after witnessing the sufferings of many of her fellow-worshippers.

The German Inroads. — These persecutions appear to have

been excited by a sudden outburst of popular fury at the calamities of this fatal year, 166. The year of the pestilence was marked also by the beginning of the Marcomanic War, the beginning, as we have said, of a long series of similar events which continued for centuries from this time. From this date the Empire was never free from peril from this source. Julius, and afterwards Augustus, had invaded Germany and attempted its conquest. Tiberius had withdrawn from the enterprise (p. 245), and since his time there had been almost a condition of equilibrium upon the frontier, the Rhine and the Danube separating the Empire from the barbarians. Domitian had even advanced the frontier at the angle between these rivers (p. 260), and Trajan had conquered the Dacians, north of the Danube. But now the balance was turned. In the reign of Marcus Aurelius the Germans began to be the aggressors, and the Empire to be upon the defensive until at last it fell under their repeated blows.

The Marcomanic War. — The Marcomani (*frontiersmen*) were a powerful nation inhabiting Bohemia and Bavaria, probably in their origin a group of tribes rather than a single tribe. In the early Empire they had been, as a rule, friendly to the Romans, or neutral in the great wars with the Germans farther north (p. 235). With them the great forward movement of the Germanic race now commenced. In the year 166 Marcus was called to resist a band of Marcomani who had advanced as far as Aquileia, upon the Adriatic Sea; and the remaining thirteen years of his reign were occupied with a succession of border wars, in which the Marcomani were aided by the Quadi (of Moravia) and other neighboring tribes. Rome was still the strongest power, and Marcus was an able commander, who carried on his campaigns with success; but he was still engaged in these wars when he died, probably at Vindobona (*Vienna*), A.D. 180.

Commodus, 180-193. — With Marcus Aurelius the line of "Good Emperors" came to an end. Great as he was, he had not the magnanimity to set aside his own son and adopt a successor to the throne; nor, considering the natural tendencies to

MARCUS AURELIUS RECEIVING THE SUBMISSION OF GERMAN CAPTIVES.
(From a Bas-relief in the Capitoline Museum, Rome.)

hereditary succession, is it likely that he could have succeeded if he had made the attempt. It was the misfortune of Rome that he was not childless, like his four predecessors; for his son Commodus was wholly unfit for the throne. As in the case of every one of the previous emperors who had been brought up in expectation of the crown, — Caligula, Nero, Domitian, — his moral nature was not capable of resisting the temptations of absolute power; and he speedily showed himself a gross and cruel tyrant. It was his delight to appear in the guise of Hercules, and himself take part

COMMODUS (as Hercules).

in gladiatorial games and other combats of the amphitheatre, — carefully protected, however, against danger, as when he sat safely in a gallery and amused himself by shooting the wild beasts in the arena. He could be brutal and severe, but had neither firmness nor vigor. Under his heedless administration military discipline was relaxed, and the army was demoralized by a spirit of insubordination and lawlessness. He was at last, A.D. 193, murdered by a conspiracy in his own household, and Pertinax, an able and experienced soldier, proclaimed Emperor.

PERIOD VII.—THE CENTURY OF TRANSITION.

CHAPTER XXII.

THE SEVERI.

I. THE DYNASTY.

Pertinax and Didius Julianus.— It would have seemed that Pertinax, the ablest and most experienced officer in the army, was the man pointed out by circumstances to hold the reins of government with a firm hand at this crisis. But the prætorians were too far demoralized by the license of the last reign to submit to the vigorous discipline of the new Emperor. He was murdered by them after a reign of three months, and his murderers then had the effrontery to offer the throne to the highest bidder. Two senators were willing to humiliate themselves and their office by competing for the empty dignity, which was at last given to Didius Julianus for a gratuity of twenty-five thousand *sesterces* ($1250) to each soldier. He promised at the same time that he would restore the good old times of license under Commodus. It is a satisfaction to know that both parties to this infamous bargain were deceived, as the new Emperor had not the means to pay the donation in full.

Septimius Severus, A.D. 193–211.— The news of the murder of Pertinax and of the sale of the imperial dignity to Didius Julianus excited indignation in all parts of the Empire; and the three armies of Syria, Britain, and Pannonia proclaimed each its own general as Emperor. Nearest and promptest of the three was Septimius Severus, commander of the legions upon the Danube. He declared himself the avenger of Pertinax, and was recognized

as Emperor by the Senate, which immediately condemned the unfortunate Julianus to death. The next A.D. 194.
year the Syrian pretender, Pescennius Niger, lost his
empire and life; and three years later the overthrow of A.D. 197.
Clodius Albinus left Severus in sole possession of the
throne.

Character of Severus. — The situation of Septimius Severus
was in many respects similar to that of Vespasian in 69 (p. 232).
Like him, he was a brave and capable soldier, who succeeded to
the throne after an interval of disturbance and civil war; like him,
the avenger of a good and capable prince, who had been the
victim of the prætorian guards; and as
Pertinax had followed the tyrant Commodus, so Galba had followed the tyrant
Nero. Like Vespasian, too, Severus founded
a dynasty; and the family of the Severi
occupied the throne, with the interval of
one year, for a period of forty-one years.
But Severus was a man of lower type than
Vespasian. He was cruel and without good
faith or magnanimity. His character is
reflected in his features, the vulgarity of

SEPTIMIUS SEVERUS.
(From a Coin in the Berlin Museum.)

which presents a strong contrast to the elegance of Augustus,
the manliness of Trajan, or the serenity of Antoninus Pius. His
sternness and vigor were, nevertheless, qualities needed by the
Empire at this juncture; and he may fairly rank among the able
and efficient rulers of Rome. The last years of his reign he spent
in Britain, where he died, at Eboracum (*York*), A.D. 211.

Caracalla, A.D. 211-217. — He was succeeded by his two sons,
Antoninus, better known by his nickname of Caracalla, and Geta.
But the very next year Caracalla murdered his brother, and reigned
alone until he was himself murdered, five years later, by Macrinus,
the commander of his guards, while engaged in a campaign in the
East. Caracalla was, like his father, an able soldier, but even
more cruel and vindictive. He is not counted among the worst

tyrants, with Caligula, Nero, Domitian, and Commodus; but his place is not much above them.

CARACALLA.

Elagabalus, A.D. 218-222. — The usurped reign of Macrinus was of short duration. The late Emperor had left two young cousins, sons of two sisters, Julia Soemias and Julia Mammæa. The son of Soemias was a priest in the temple of the sun-god, Elagabalus, at Emesa in Syria. His mother, giving him the name Antoninus, declared him the son of Caracalla; and soon he was at the head of an army, attracted by the popularity of his name and family among the soldiers. Macrinus was defeated in battle, and soon afterwards killed; and the young Antoninus was recognized as Emperor. The name Antoninus, however, associated with the virtuous Pius and Marcus, has escaped the discredit of being attached to Caracalla and his unworthy cousin. The new Emperor is always known by the name of the god, Elagabalus, whose priest he was. Elagabalus was the vilest of the Roman emperors, with all the vices of his worst predecessors, and with no sparks of manliness or sense of the responsibilities of his office, such as even they sometimes displayed. The corrupt priest of a corrupt religion, his life was given up to the grossest sensual enjoyments; and after a shameful reign of four years, he was slain, together with his mother, in a mutiny of the guards.

Alexander Severus, A.D. 222-235. — He was succeeded by his cousin, Alexander Severus, the last of his family, a prince whose reign of thirteen years, — a long one for this period, — brought back the good times of the Antonines. His mother, Mammæa, favorably contrasted to her weak sister Soemias by strength of character and worthy ambition, had trained him carefully, and prepared him well for the government of the world. But his vigorous reforms brought upon him the same fate that had befallen Pertinax. First, the able agent of his reforms, the prætorian præfect, the eminent jurist, Ulpian, was murdered in his presence by a body of mutinous soldiers. A few years later the Emperor A.D. 235. himself fell victim to a mutiny while on a campaign in Germany; and a gigantic soldier of Gothic descent, named Maximin, was proclaimed Emperor.

II. THE GOVERNMENT.

The Age of the Jurists. — The period of the Severi forms an important epoch in Roman history, marking as it does the close of the early Empire, and preparing the way for the reorganization of the Empire by Diocletian and Constantine a century later. The decay of society was now most marked. All independent art and literature ended with the Antonines. The age of the Severi was, to be sure, that of the jurists. Papinian, Paullus, and — greatest of all — Ulpian flourished at this time and completed that great work of scientific jurisprudence, which is the most illustrious monument of the Roman genius. But these great jurists only completed the work of many generations, and with them the Roman intellect seems to suffer a sudden eclipse. The age that followed the Severi was an age of barbarism.

Buildings. — The second century had been an age of magnificent building, and its architectural activity was continued by the princes of the house of Severus. Trajan had carried the system of public squares or forums (p. 238) to its northernmost extension, where he was obliged to level the hill to the depth of one hundred and seventeen feet in order to make room for his forum and the column which still marks the height of the hill which was removed. A similar column had been built still further to the north by Marcus Aurelius; and the bronze equestrian statue of this emperor upon the Capitoline Mount, one of the finest works of its class, is still one of the most striking monuments of modern Rome. The triumphal arch of Septimius Severus is familiar to all travellers, and the gigantic public baths erected by Caracalla still preserve his memory. But from this time building activity, as every other work of a high civilization, ceased, on any large scale, until revived by Diocletian and Constantine.

Military Rule. — The leading characteristic of this period is that it marks the end of the dyarchy (p. 231) or system of government by which power was divided between the Senate and the Emperor. The popular assemblies and the magistrates had long ceased to have any real power; and most of them had disappeared, even in name. The Senate had still continued to be in theory the seat of national authority, and even under the most despotic rulers it had been an essential part of the machinery of government. But this system was now outgrown, and Severus gave to it a rude blow. Owing his authority to his own right arm and to the weapons of his soldiers, he disdained to regard the Senate as its source. The century which followed witnessed several efforts on the part of the Senate to regain its lost authority, and was in this respect a period of transition from the republican empire of the first two centuries to the genuine monarchy of the fourth; but the transition began with the accession of Septimius Severus, who may fairly be regarded as the founder of the military monarchy. He put an end, however, to the insolence of the turbulent prætorians, dissolving this corps, and forming a new body-guard composed of legionary soldiers.

Assimilation of Italy and the Provinces. — In a second point of view this period marks an important transition in the history of the Empire. Until now it had consisted of two sharply contrasted portions — Italy, the ruling power, and the Provinces, which were subject. But this sharp line of division had long ceased to have any meaning, and it was now time it should be done away with. The municipal system had been extended to the provinces, which were divided into municipalities after the Roman plan; and many of these municipalities had received a complete or qualified Roman citizenship. Roman citizens had taken up their residence in the provinces, and the population was now thoroughly intermixed and pretty completely assimilated. Even Roman emperors, like Trajan and Septimius Severus, were natives of the provinces. The abolition of the prætorian cohorts was another step in this assimilation; for the rule that the legions could not legally be stationed in Italy was the excuse for the organization of this bodyguard.

Edict of Caracalla, A.D. 212. — The most important step in this direction, however, was taken by Caracalla, who in the year 212 issued an edict granting citizenship to all the inhabitants of the provinces. This famous act was not dictated by any enlightened statesmanship; its object was to extend the operation of certain taxes, which fell only upon Roman citizens, and thus to fill the coffers of the Emperor. It was, however, directly in the line of his father's policy, and it had beneficent and important results. The administrative system of the provinces was by degrees extended to Italy, and the revenue system of all parts of the Empire made uniform. The centralization of power in the hands of the Emperor, and the unity of the Empire under a single administrative and financial system, were the fruits of the policy of Septimius Severus.

Prætorian Præfect. — In abolishing the prætorian cohorts Severus did not, however, abolish the office of Prætorian Præfect. This officer, being now relieved of his especial military functions, became the chief minister of the Emperor, representing him in public business and clothed with authority hardly second to his. As the Emperor was the fountain of justice to whom all appeals in judicial proceedings were carried, it was natural that he should need an experienced jurist by his side, from whose trained intelligence should emanate the judgments which were nominally rendered by the Emperor. The office of Prætorian Præfect was therefore regularly given to some distinguished jurist; so that, from having originally been a purely military office, its duties were now principally civil, and at last exclusively so. It was as the incumbent of this office that Ulpian carried out his reforms and lost his life.

Finances. — The financial embarrassment which was the most menacing sign of decay in the preceding century now reached its height. To other causes of economic disturbances there was now added the depreciation of the currency, which had been begun by Nero and was pushed recklessly by Caracalla and Elagabalus. But Elagabalus, indifferent as he was to affairs of state, while paying his debts in debased currency was careful to have the taxes paid in good money.

III. The Religion.

Christianity. — The period of the Severi is an important epoch in religious history also. Until now the Christian church had been an obscure association of believers, with creed and organization in process of formation. The persecutions of Marcus Aurelius appear to have aroused the consciousness of the Christians, and to have at the same time attracted to them a more general attention. From this time their progress was rapid, and they became more and more active and conspicuous. The church had been a brotherhood of co-religionists, whose aims were essentially moral and social. Their doctrines began now to assume a more definite and dogmatic form, and unity of belief to be considered more essential. This was the age of Irenæus of Lyons, Clement and Origen of Alexandria, and Tertullian of Africa, — names of the first importance in the history of doctrine. The complete organization of the church, too, was the work of this century and chiefly of this period; and it was through these two instrumentalities — unity of belief and unity of discipline and administration — that it achieved its great triumphs in the following century. The organization of the church was based upon that of the state, and every city (p. 160) was made the seat of a bishop.

The Religion of the Severi. — The spirit of the age and of the dynasty were favorable to the progress of Christianity. The Severi were not, like the Antonines, earnest believers in the pagan system, and austere upholders of its faith. Even Elagabalus, the fanatic devotee of his religion, had not the moral earnestness to be a persecutor. And the women, who controlled the sentiments of this dynasty in a remarkable degree, — the sisters Soemias and Mammæa, their mother Julia Mæsa, and her sister Julia Domna, the wife of Septimius Severus, — were fully in sympathy with that religious philosophy, the controlling one at this age, known as Syncretism.[1]

Syncretism. — Syncretism is that development of pagan religion which recognizes the universality and identity of the religious sentiment, but has not yet advanced to the conception of a genuine unity of the divine nature, or monotheism. It is polytheistic, but a form of polytheism which embraces all countries and nations, seeing in their different systems of gods only varying names for the same beings. It was an act of Syncretism when the Romans identified their Minerva with the Greek Athena, and their Mercury with the German Woden. This sentiment controlled the popular religion of the early Empire, and in the time of the Severi it became formulated into a religious system, tolerant and humane, and moral in its tone, even if somewhat vague and lacking consistency in the form it took. Along with this reconstruction of the popular religion the old Greek philosophies were eagerly studied, revised in the light of recent thought, and thus invested with a new life. The Neo-platonism, or revised Platonic philosophy, thus constructed, was until the extinction of paganism the most dangerous rival of Christianity.

[1] For the religious thought of this period, read *The Mind of Paganism*, by J. H. Allen, Christian History, Vol. I.

Alexander Severus. — Syncretism reached its completest triumph in the reign of Alexander Severus, under the influence of his wise and tolerant mother, Julia Mammæa. Christianity was no doubt fully as hostile to the syncretic principle as to the older forms of paganism : but the Severi did not care to push these sectaries into opposition, but rather tried to win them by a tolerant policy; while the Christians of this age were too busily engaged in practical work to seek wilfully the crown of martyrdom. It is related of Alexander Severus that he had a chapel in his palace containing images of the saints of all religions, among them Christ, Abraham, Orpheus, and Apollonius of Tyana. But Syncretism had but a short career. It disappeared as an organic force in the disorderly times that followed, — vitality, earnestness of purpose, strength and coherence of organization were with Christianity.

IV. Foreign Relations.

The Northern Frontier. — This period is marked also by a distinct and important stage in the onward movement of the Germanic tribes. The operations of the Marcomanic war had occupied nearly the middle point upon the German frontier; that war was now past, and from this time we hear little more of the Marcomani.[1] Further to the east the Goths had already moved in a southeasterly direction from their old homes upon the Baltic, and were now established on the northern shore of the Black Sea. Here in the following century they were troublesome neighbors to the Roman province of Dacia, which at last had to be given up to them. At the western extremity of the frontier, upon the Rhine, we meet with a new and menacing condition of things in the time of the Severi.

The German Political System. — The Germans in earlier times, as they are described by Caesar and Tacitus, consisted of a num-

---

[1] This nation gradually disappears from history. The western portion of it became the Bavarians, while the territories to the east were gradually occupied by Slavic tribes.

ber of independent tribes, who were with difficulty brought to unite for special ends, and easily fell apart when the occasion had passed. But they had now begun to be conscious of their strength, and had learned that their strength was wasted by their disunion. We find them gathering together in loose confederacies, by which their resources were made more effective, while the independence and individuality of the several tribes were preserved. The Marcomani appear to have been the earliest confederacy of this type. Next to them came the Alamanni, — the *All-men*, — a body of tribes which gathered along Domitian's line of fortified posts (p. 260), extending from the middle Rhine to the Danube, and began to push their way across the bounds into the Empire. Here they were met and defeated by Caracalla; but before the end of the century they succeeded in their object, and took possession of the country along the upper Rhine. A few years later than the Alamanni, a similar association of tribes, known as the Franks,[1] are met upon the lower Rhine, principally in Belgium and Holland. Thus nearly the entire course of the Rhine was occupied by these new organizations.

A.D. 213.

A.D. 242.

The Western Germans. — The migrations of these western Germans are very different in character from those of the eastern nations, — the Goths, Vandals, and Lombards. These, as we shall see, swept rapidly and destructively over wide spaces of territory, taking military possession of all the countries of southern Europe. The Franks and Alamannians, on the other hand, consisted of tribes which had long been under the influences of Roman civilization, had learned to cultivate the soil, and had adopted other customs of civilized life.[2] They formed compact and permanent settlements, and only spread over as much territory as they could use. Forcing their way into the territories of the Empire, and occupying vacant lands which had become deserted and desolate in the disorders of these times, many of these in the course of

---

[1] The name of the Franks is barely mentioned a few years earlier.
[2] This important distinction was first pointed out by Dahn.

time came to an understanding with the Romans, recognized the superior authority of the Empire, and were allowed to occupy their lands on condition of military service, forming thus an important part of the military force of the Empire. Thus we shall have little more to do with either Franks or Alamannians during the period covered by this volume.

Revolution in the Orient. — During the reign of Alexander Severus a revolution took place in the far East, — namely, the establishment of a new and powerful empire in Persia — which was of the greatest importance in the world's history, and which exerted a great and direct influence upon the affairs of the Roman Empire ; but, as it had no immediate influence upon these affairs until some years later, its consideration may be postponed (see Chap. XXIV.).

PRÆTORIANS.

CHAPTER XXIII.

THE THIRD CENTURY.

The Empire in the Third Century. — It would be wearisome and useless to occupy our attention in detail with the reigns of the successive emperors who sat upon the imperial throne between the murder of Alexander Severus (A.D. 235) and the accession of Diocletian (A.D. 284). Many of these emperors were able and worthy, but the times were not favorable to their virtues. Death by battle, mutiny or assassination carried them off before they had an opportunity to display their qualities. The third century, from Septimius Severus to Diocletian, was occupied by the reigns of twenty-eight emperors (several of them in pairs), only five of whom (perhaps only four) died a natural death. It will be best therefore to present in tabulated form the names of these emperors, with the manner of their deaths, and any conspicuous events of their reigns.[1]

EMPERORS OF THE THIRD CENTURY.

A.D.
200. Septimius Severus: died 211.
211. Caracalla and Geta: Geta murdered by Caracalla, 212; Caracalla murdered by a conspiracy, April, 217.
217. Macrinus: defeated and killed, June, 218.
218. Elagabalus: killed by a mutiny, March, 222.
222. Alexander Severus: killed by a mutiny, February, 235.
235. Maximin: killed himself, May, 238.
238. Gordian I. and II.: killed in the same year.

[1] As these emperors were little more than military commanders, spending their lives in the camp, they are happily designated by Hodgkin the "Barrack Emperors."

THE THIRD CENTURY.

A.D.

238. Maximus and Pupienus Balbinus, declared emperors by the Senate: murdered by the soldiers in the same year.
238. Gordian III.: murdered 244.
244. Philip the Arabian: killed, October, 249.
249. Decius: 250, persecution of the Christians[1]; killed in battle against the Goths, November, 251.
251. Gallus and Hostilian: Hostilian died 252, Gallus murdered by his soldiers, February, 254.
253. Æmilian: murdered by his soldiers, May, 254.
253. Valerian: captured by the Persians, autumn, 260, and died in captivity.
260. Gallienus: dissolution of the Empire—the "Thirty Tyrants." Murdered, March, 268.

The Illyrian Emperors.[2]

268. Claudius Gothicus: victory over the Goths at Naissus, 269: died of pestilence, March, 270.
270. Aurelian: capture of Palmyra, 273[3]; Dacia given up to the Goths; killed by a conspiracy, March, 275.
275. Tacitus[4]: a Roman senator, killed by a mutiny, April, 276.
276. Florian[4]: his brother, killed by his soldiers, July, 276.
276. Probus: killed by a mutiny, autumn, 282.
282. Carus: killed by a conspiracy, December, 283.
283. Carinus and Numerian; his sons: Numerian died, September, 284; Carinus murdered, 285.
284. Diocletian.

---

[1] Cardinal Newman's *Callista* portrays the Christian life and thought of the age with remarkable truthfulness and beauty, but wholly fails to appreciate the contemporary pagan thought. Read also Mrs. John Hunt's *Wards of Plotinus*.

[2] Read Freeman's article "The Illyrian Emperors and their Lands," in the third series of his *Historical Essays*.

[3] William Ware's *Zenobia* and *Aurelian*.

[4] Tacitus and Florian were not natives of Illyricum.

CHAPTER XXIV.

AFFAIRS IN THE EAST.

Revolution in the East. — In the early part of this century the Parthian empire, which had shared the world with the Roman for nearly four hundred years, was suddenly overturned; and the new Persian empire took its place. The effete dynasty of the Arsacidæ gave way to that of the vigorous and ambitious Sassanidæ.

A.D. 226.

The Persian Empire. — In this event we see a repetition of the overthrow of the Median empire by Cyrus the Persian. Now as then the Persians, a vigorous people of the Aryan race, were dependent members of a great empire; and now the Parthian empire had lost strength and enterprise, as had been the case with the Median under Astyages. Artaxerxes, or Ardashir, the Persian prince who placed his nation for a second time upon the summit of power, was a worthy successor of Cyrus the Great; and now as then, but in a much higher degree, religious zeal was added to dynastic ambition; for Artaxerxes, like Cyrus, and still more like Darius, was the champion of a national religion of marked individuality and aggressive power.

B.C. 568.

Mazdeism, the Religion of Zoroaster. — The religion of Zoroaster, *Mazdeism*, is, in its pure form, the recognition of a dualism in the divine government of the world, — a good and evil spirit constantly warring against each other, an equilibrium of good and evil forces in the world as it is, but (in the best form of the religion), with a confident expectation of the final triumph of the good. In its best estate this religion had a positively moral character, and was wholly devoid of idolatrous or impure practices. The belief in a good god, Ormuzd, who will finally triumph over his antagonist, Ahriman, is hardly to be distinguished from monotheism;

and if this god was symbolized by the fire, so that his votaries came to be known as fire-worshippers, yet this was in reality only a symbol, not an object of worship.

Religion of the Sassanidæ. — The form of Mazdeism which now, after many centuries of eclipse, mounted the throne of Persia, was not the pure religion of Zoroaster. It was, nevertheless, a new and inspiring force, arming the soldiers of the Sassanidæ with religious fervor and the zeal of propagandism. The world had never before known a great empire and conquering armies whose

TRIUMPH OF SAPOR.

inspiration was so controllingly religious. This is what principally makes it an epoch in the world's history. The conquering zeal which characterized Islam and the Crusades was introduced into the world by the Sassanian monarchs. They were the first rulers in history who persecuted on purely religious grounds.[1]

The Sassanidæ. — The revolution which established the new Persian empire and the Sassanid dynasty took place in the year 226;

---

[1] This statement is made by Bryce (*Transcaucasia and Ararat*), and is, at any rate, approximately true. The religious propagandism of the early oriental monarchies was rather the extension of a national worship than of a distinctively religious faith.

and the empire now established continued as the principal rival of Rome, and far more bitter and obstinate in its rivalry than the Parthian had been, until overthrown by a new band of religious conquerors, the followers of Mohammed. After A.D. 641. a short reign Artaxerxes was succeeded by his son, Sapor, in whom the vigor, insolence, and cruelty of his A.D. 240. race culminated. It was he who captured the Emperor Valerian, and treated him with cruel indignity.[1] By his A.D. 260. arrogance Odenatus, Prince of Palmyra, was offended, and driven to alliance with Rome.

Reign of Gallienus, A.D. 260–268. — By the captivity of Valerian the Roman throne was left to be occupied by his son, Gallienus, a prince of many strong and amiable traits, but wholly unfitted for the stormy times in which he lived. The Empire seemed literally falling to pieces. What had occurred in the revolutionary years 68 and 193 in two or three provinces now took place in all directions. Everywhere the governors of single provinces or groups of provinces set up the standard of revolt, and there seemed every likelihood that the Empire would be resolved into its original elements. This period is known, very inappropriately, as that of the "Thirty Tyrants." To this internal dissolution there were added formidable dangers upon the frontiers. The Persians were incited to new arrogance by their victory over Valerian. Upon the north the German tribes were in a ferment. A company of Franks made its way through Gaul, plundering and A.D. 256. destroying, and even passed the Pyrenees, and ravaged portions of Spain. Some of them are said to have crossed to Africa. At about the same time the Goths north of the Black Sea possessed themselves of some swift galleys, and not only plundered the ports of that sea, but made their way into the Ægean.

---

[1] Of the details really nothing is known. Mommsen says, "That Sapor used him as a footstool in mounting his horse, and finally caused him to be flayed, is a Christian invention, — a requital for the persecution of the Christians ordered by Valerian." It is related that his skin was preserved by Sapor in a temple, but the body may have been flayed after death.

Palmyra. — Of all the fragmentary powers called into existence by the disruption of the Empire, Palmyra, the "City of Palms," was the strongest, most illustrious, and longest-lived. This city was an emporium of commerce upon an oasis of the Arabian Desert, at the junction of two caravan routes, a community of merchant princes, essentially Semitic in nationality, but very cosmopolitan in character. It was a city of great wealth and splendid architecture. The father of Odenatus had raised himself to a position somewhat similar to that of Lorenzo di Medici in Florence;

A.D. 264. and Odenatus himself, taking up arms for Rome, and defending the frontier against the menacing Sapor, had been recognized as colleague and even as "Augustus" by Gallienus, whose hands were so fully occupied with wars in every part of the Empire that he was glad to secure the loyalty of Palmyra by the concession of this title. Soon after

A.D. 267. Odenatus was murdered, and his throne occupied by his widow, Zenobia.

Aurelian, 270-275. — Claudius, during his short reign (268-270), had restored some degree of order; and his able and vigorous successor, Aurelian, re-established the imperial authority throughout the realm, and brought to an end the period of the "Thirty Tyrants." He was a coarse and uncultured peasant of Illyria, but his energy and native good sense have made his reign an epoch in the history of the period. The perils were great in every direction. In the East Zenobia had severed from the Empire a great portion of its Asiatic possessions. In the West a rival empire had been created, embracing Gaul, Britain, and a part of Spain, which, under a succession of "tyrants," had held the legitimate Emperor at defiance. At present this precarious throne was occupied by a pretender named Tetricus. In the North, where the German tribes had already pushed across the frontier, the emergency was even more pressing.

COIN OF AURELIAN.

Wars in the North. — Aurelian saw that the conquests of Trajan

- The Porta Capena, Esquilina and Collina mark the position of the Walls of Servius Tullius.
- Walls of Aurelian.

ROME

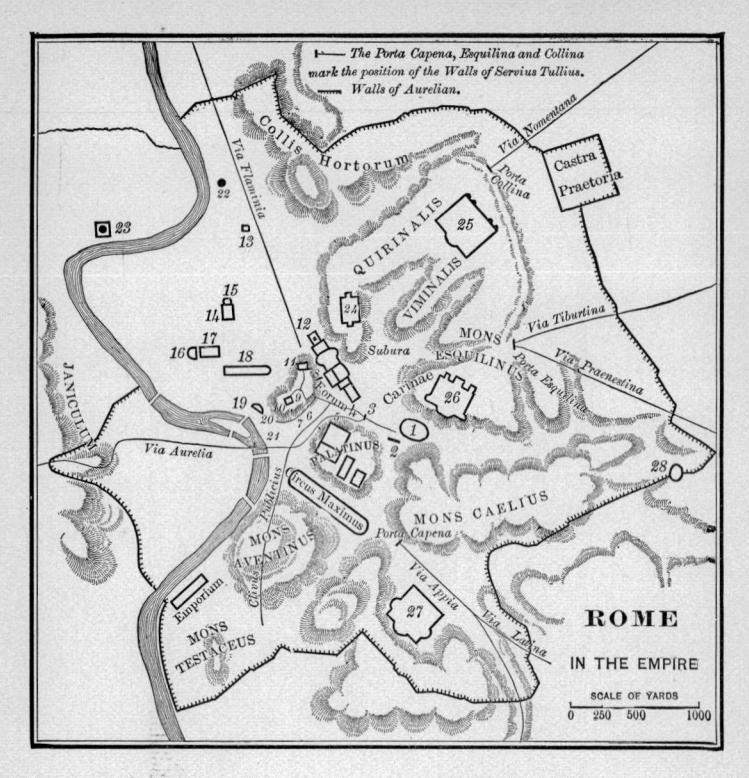

IN THE EMPIRE

SCALE OF YARDS
0   250   500   1000

1. Colosseum.
2. Arch of Constantine.
3. Arch of Titus.
4. Via Sacra.
5. Via Nova.
6. Vicus Tuscus.
7. Vicus Jugarius.
8. Arch of Septimius Severus.
9. Clivus Capitolinus.
10. Temple of Jupiter Capitolinus.
11. Arch.
12. Column of Trajan.
13. Column of Antonine.
14. Baths of Agrippa.
15. Pantheon.
16. Theatre of Pompey.
17. Portico of Pompey.
18. Circus Flaminius.
19. Theatre of Marcellus.
20. Forum Holitorium.
21. Forum Boarium.
22. Mausoleum of Augustus.
23. Mausoleum of Hadrian.
24. Baths of Constantine.
25. Baths of Diocletian.
26. Baths of Titus.
27. Baths of Caracalla.
28. Amphitheatrum Castrense.

beyond the Danube (p. 262) were a source of weakness rather than strength. He withdrew the garrisons and most of the colonists to the south of the Danube, and left the province of Dacia to be occupied by the Goths. A formidable invasion of the

RUINS OF TEMPLE OF THE SUN BUILT BY AURELIAN.

Alamannians had crossed the Alps, and was laying waste the regions about the Po. Aurelian defeated these barbarians, and freed Italy from this scourge. In order to secure the capital city more completely, he now proceeded to build a line of fortifications about it. The old walls of Servius Tullius had been long outgrown, and had fallen into ruin. Rome, in her days of greatness, needed, like Sparta, no walls except the shields of her legions. But these days had passed, and the walls of Aurelian are one among many signs of the approaching downfall of the imperial city. Having thus settled the affairs of Italy and the northern frontier, Aurelian proceeded against his rival in the East.

Zenobia. — Zenobia is one of the heroines of history. To great beauty and unblemished virtue she added a lofty ambition and, along with it, the power of ruling her subjects with combined mildness and justice. Herself a monotheist, she practised perfect toleration; Christian, Jew, Mazdean, and Pagan lived side by side in peace under her equable rule. The great Greek philosopher Longinus, the chief personage in Grecian literature in this century, and the most illustrious teacher of the new Platonism of the age, had been invited to Palmyra, and became her chief minister. But her ambition was not satisfied, like that of her husband, with a second place in the Empire, nor would even such a place have been conceded by a prince like Aurelian. She aspired to independence, — to rule a "middle kingdom" between the two great rival empires; and she had extended her bounds to the west so as to include Egypt and half of Asia Minor. But a middle kingdom such as she desired is sure, in an age of warfare, to be ground to pieces by its neighbors.

Fall of Palmyra, A.D. 273. — The campaign of Aurelian was rapid and successful. The armies of Zenobia were defeated in two battles, and then her capital city was besieged and taken. The captive queen had the weakness and meanness to throw upon her ministers the blame for her resistance; and they, including the illustrious Longinus, were put to death, while Zenobia was carried to Rome to adorn the conqueror's triumph. The city was spared; but an ill-timed revolt, when Aurelian was on his way home, called him back. This time he inflicted a terrible punishment. The citizens were massacred, the city was burned, and Palmyra rapidly fell from its wealth and beauty. It is now the seat of lonely and majestic ruins, visited by occasional travellers.

Subjugation of Gaul. — Having overthrown this powerful kingdom in the East, Aurelian found it an easy task to reduce his western rival (p. 292). Tetricus was tired of the mockery of state, and made only a feeble resistance. Like Zenobia, he was led in his victor's triumphal procession. But Gaul was in too serious a condition of social and economic decay to be speedily restored to order. Even before the conquest of this country by Cæsar, its peasantry had been a wretched and degraded class; they had sunk even lower in condition, as the demoralization which had seized upon the industrial relations of Italy spread to the provinces also. The depreciation of the currency, now at its height, fell — as it always does — with the greatest severity upon the laboring classes; and during the rest of the century Gaul was a hot-bed of discontent and revolution. A few years later (285), it broke out in the first, and one of the most formidable, of the peasant wars which have at various epochs laid waste this country. The *Bagaudæ* of the third century were the legitimate precursors, and probably the ancestors, of the *Pastoureaux* of the thirteenth, the *Jacquerie* of the fourteenth, and the insurgent peasantry of the French revolution. To suppress this insurrection was the first task of Diocletian, the greatest emperor of the third century, who succeeded to the throne in 284, and here as elsewhere re-established peace and order.

PERIOD VIII. — THE LATER EMPIRE (284-476).

CHAPTER XXV.

REORGANIZATION OF THE EMPIRE.

I. DIOCLETIAN.

Reforms of Diocletian. — In the century which we have just traversed, the Roman Empire appeared upon the point of falling to pieces from defects in its organization, decay of material prosperity, and the increased strength and aggressive spirit of foreign enemies. For the economic decay and the assaults from without there was no remedy, and they finally wrought the destruction of the Empire. The constitution, however, was capable of revision; and a statesman ascended the throne at the very close of the century who instituted a series of reforms which, while fundamentally changing its character, gave it a new efficiency, and prolonged its life for more than a hundred years. This was Diocletian, the last of the Illyrian emperors.

DIOCLETIAN.

Preparation for the Reforms. — The reform was not carried through at one stroke, nor was it entirely the work of Diocletian; it had been in preparation for a century, and was brought to completion by his more distinguished successor Constantine. But Diocletian was the first who saw clearly the logical consequences of earlier reforms, and carried them out to practical results. He was the man of ideas, Constantine the man of action, of this reform. Septimius Severus had put an end to the dyarchy (p. 280), but had not definitely established the monarchy; Caracalla had extended citizenship to the provincials (p. 281), but had not entirely effaced the distinction between Italy and the provinces. It was Diocletian who organized the entire Empire upon a uniform basis, and placed it under the irresponsible rule of a monarch. Free government was now at an end, even in name and semblance; but nothing but centralized despotism could hold society together under its present difficulties.

The Illyrian Emperors. — The reign of Gallienus (260–268) was the period at which the Empire was at the lowest point of weakness and disintegration. The Illyrian peasants who succeeded him — Claudius, Aurelian, Probus, Carus, all rulers of great merit — succeeded in holding the disruptive forces in check, and preventing any further dissolution; but they did not see just where the evil lay, nor were their reigns long enough for any matured policy of reform. The starting point in Diocletian's reforms was the observation that the Empire was too large and too varied in nationality to be efficiently administered by one chief. In the parts of the Empire where the Emperor could not be present in person, it was easy for the provincial governors, practically irresponsible and armed with both military and civil power, to set on foot rebellions which might perhaps become successful revolutions, placing their leaders upon the imperial throne. Vespasian, Septimius Severus, and numbers of others had been made emperors by *pronunciamentos;* why not Tetricus and his compeers?

Partnership Emperors.[1] — One of the first acts of Diocletian therefore was to associate with himself as "Augustus" a capable and trusted officer, although rude and harsh in character, named Maximian. They were colleagues, just as the consuls of the Republic had been, and all official acts were in their joint names; but they divided the administration upon local lines. Diocletian, residing

[1] This term, like that of "Barrack Emperors," (p. 287), is due to Hodgkin.

at Nicomedia, governed the East; Maximian, making Mediolanum (*Milan*) his capital, governed the West. A few years later the principle was extended further, and each "Augustus" associated with himself a "Cæsar," a younger man, who should have charge of the most exposed and laborious parts of his dominions. Galerius commanded upon the Danube, Constantius in Gaul and Britain; and it was the plan that when either Emperor should die or abdicate, his Cæsar should succeed to his vacant place. In this way it was thought that provision was made for a regular and peaceful succession to the throne,— the weakest point in the constitution of the Empire.

Oriental Despotism. — With four emperors at the head of affairs, there was no longer any danger that a successful rebellion would change the occupant of the throne at one blow. But Diocletian did not merely place the imperial office upon a new basis, — he gave it a new character and authority. The Senate now wholly ceased to be a part of the government, and from this time was hardly more than the municipal council of Rome. All authority and law emanated from the Emperor. But the Emperor's authority was not merely an actual autocracy, such as Julius Cæsar and Septimius Severus had exercised; it was remodelled after the type of oriental monarchs, and surrounded with oriental ceremonial and homage. The Emperor of the first century was *Prince*, that is, "first citizen"; the Emperor of the fourth century, as has been remarked, was a *Sultan*.[1]

Re-organization of the Provincial System. — The provincial system was also remodelled. In the time of Septimius Severus there were about forty provinces, all of them outside of Italy; and all were ruled as subject communities by governors sent from Rome. Italy was under a wholly independent administration, as being in law a part of the city of Rome (p. 175). Under Diocletian there were about a hundred provinces, Italy being now placed on the same footing as the other parts of the Empire; and these were all mere districts of territory for administrative, financial, and judicial

[1] Seeley's *Roman Imperialism*, Lecture 3.

purposes. In the Republic and early Empire it was a fundamental principle that the provinces, but not Italy, were subject to a land-tax or tribute. Now the land-tax, like other taxes, was made uniform in all parts of the Empire. Under the earlier system every province stood by itself, subject to Rome, but having no organic connection with the other provinces. Diocletian grouped them into larger divisions called *dioceses;* and this made the work of administration much simpler and easier, because the *Vicar*, or governor, of a diocese stood between the Emperor and half a dozen governors of provinces. Thus the administration was systematized, and the functionaries stood in successive grades from the Emperor to the lowest official. By this a regularity and efficiency like that of the modern bureaucracies was introduced into the public service.

Military System. — At the same time with this reorganization of the civil service, another reform of fundamental value separated the civil from the military authority. The governor of a province had been its absolute master, having command of its military forces and administering justice in it, as well as being its executive head; and it was this union of civil and military power in the same hands that made the rebellions of the provincial governors so formidable a danger during the third century. The military power was, by Diocletian, entirely taken away from the provincial governors, who now became merely civil functionaries; while the army was placed under a wholly different set of officers, responsible to the Emperor alone.

Permanence of Diocletian's Reforms. — By thus centralizing the executive power in the hands of two or four supreme rulers, invested with absolute power, and surrounded with a pomp and ceremonial wholly foreign to the earlier Roman government; by transforming the administrative system into an official bureaucracy, divested of all military power; and by establishing a uniformity of administration for all parts of the Empire; the government acquired a degree of vigor and efficiency which gave it a new life, and placed the name of Diocletian among those of the great lawmakers and organizers of history. Some parts of his scheme broke down in practice, and some were afterwards changed by Constantine; but, on the whole, the principles of absolute government now put in operation, not only held their own during the short remaining life of ancient Rome, but have been the controlling principles in the courts of Europe down to the present day.

Tenth Persecution of the Christians. — The name of Diocletian is chiefly associated, in most minds, not with his great work as an organizer and a ruler, but with the "Tenth Persecution" of the Christians, ordered by him in the year 303.[1] The cause of this would seem to have been dread of the growing strength and formidable organization of the Christians, for in the early years of his reign he was far from unfriendly to them. An edict of the year 303, followed by others of still greater severity, directed the Christian churches to be torn down, ordered their sacred writings to be given up and destroyed, and prohibited all their assemblies. Christians in public office were to be removed from their positions. Christians of low rank were to lose their civil privileges, and those of all ranks were to be subject to torture. The mildness and favorable disposition of Constantius Chlorus, the Western Cæsar, prevented or mitigated the execution of the edict in the regions under his rule. In the other parts of the Empire it was carried out with great severity, especially under Diocletian's successor in the East, Galerius, a bitter enemy of Christianity.[2]

CHRIST AS THE GOOD SHEPHERD.
(From the Catacombs.)

---

[1] The ecclesiastical writers have fixed upon this number, but it would not be easy to count exactly ten distinct persecutions.

[2] For this persecution read Cardinal Wiseman's *Fabiola, or the Church of the Catacombs*, a rather dull and very one-sided work, but containing an authentic and valuable account of the catacombs and their relation to the Church.

CIVIL WARS. 301

Abdication of Diocletian. — The year following this edict Diocletian was visited by a severe illness, which probably hastened the execution of a long-cherished purpose to retire into private life as soon as his scheme of government should be fully in operation. He and his colleague, Maximian, abdicated on the same day at their respective capitals. Diocletian retired to his splendid residence at Salona in Dalmatia, where he spent the remainder of his life in honorable leisure. Maximian, on the other hand, was drawn again into public life, with no great credit to himself, by the disorders of the following years. Diocletian's motive in this act has been the subject of many surmises. Possibly he had no further motive than to test the working of his scheme by actual experience.[1]

A.D. 305, May 1.

Failure of his Scheme. — Diocletian's abdication made evident the weak spot in his scheme, where his fondness for systematizing had resulted in an artificial and impracticable rule of succession. It took no account of human relations and personal ambitions or the accidents of life. Galerius and Constantius succeeded to the throne without opposition; but when Constantius died suddenly the next year, his troops refused to recognize the man of straw whom the scheme placed over them, in the person of one Severus, but proclaimed Constantine, the son of Constantius, as Emperor. From this time for a period of eight years there followed a dreary succession of civil wars between rival pretenders, — at one time there being six claimants to the imperial throne. The events of this period may be tabulated as follows: —

A.D. 306, July 25.

A.D. 307.

A.D.

305. Abdication of Diocletian and Maximian; *East:* Galerius (Augustus), Maximin (Cæsar) ; *West:* Constantius (Augustus), Severus (Cæsar).

306. Death of Constantius ; Constantine proclaimed ; Maximian and his son Maxentius assume the imperial title.

[1] This is the suggestion of the French historian, Michelet.

A.D.

307. Severus put to death by Maxentius; Licinius proclaimed by Galerius for the West.
310. Maximian put to death by Constantine.
311. April, edict of toleration; May, death of Galerius; Licinius and Maximin Emperors in the East.
312. Oct. 27: Maxentius defeated by Constantine in the battle of the Mulvian Bridge, and drowned in the Tiber; Constantine sole Emperor in the West.
313. April 30: Maximin defeated by Licinius at Adrianople; died shortly after; murder by Licinius of the families of Galerius, Severus, and Maximin; Licinius sole Emperor in the East.
314. Marriage of Licinius with Constantine's sister; war between Constantine and Licinius; peace; the Empire divided — Constantine in the West, Licinius in the East.

II. CONSTANTINE THE GREAT.

Constantine's Administration. — By the terms of the treaty of peace made after the war between Constantine and
A.D. 314. Licinius, Constantine received a large addition of territory, so that his dominions extended so far east as to comprise Greece and Macedonia. In commemoration of his victory a magnificent triumphal arch was erected by the Senate, which is still standing complete.[1] His Basilica, likewise, whose ruins are among the most conspicuous of those in Rome, was built at this period. Entire toleration was extended to the Christians, and great favor shown to them, although the Emperor did not yet declare himself a convert. The most important administrative act of this period was the reform of the currency, which had fallen into complete confusion. The depreciation of the currency had

[1] It must not be understood that this fine work represents the taste and technical skill of the age. Its plan and details are for the most part taken from earlier monuments.

begun in the time of Nero, and by the time of the Severi the silver coinage had sunk to less than half of its nominal value, while even gold was so uncertain in its standard that it was necessary to weigh the coins instead of counting them. Aurelian and Diocletian had effected some reform in the currency, but Constantine restored it completely to its purity of standard. With his coinage begins a new era in the history of currency; the *solidus*,

ARCH OF CONSTANTINE.

— whose name bespeaks its character, — a gold coin weighing one seventy-second of a pound, being the starting-point in all modern systems of money.[1]

---

[1] Its name appears in the French *sou* and the Italian *soldo*, whose present value (about one cent) shows the depreciation which the currency has again suffered in modern times, the original value of the *solidus* being about $3.00.

Bloodshed in the Imperial Families. — With the oriental type of monarchy had come in the oriental custom of securing the throne by political murder. Licinius, victor in the East, had put to death the families of Galerius, Severus, and Maximin, women and children inclusive; even the widow of Diocletian shared the fate of her daughter, the widow of Galerius. This wholesale bloodshed did not withhold Constantine from bestowing his sister in marriage upon its perpetrator; and when, notwithstanding, war had a second time broken out between the two Emperors, and victory had placed Licinius in the hands of his brother-in-law, Constantine, in violation of a positive promise made to his sister, caused Licinius to be strangled in prison. Thus, in the year 323, Constantine became sole Emperor, and ruled with unlimited power for fourteen years. In this period two events of special importance deserve to be mentioned — the establishment of Christianity, and the building of a new capital.

Adoption of Christianity. — The act by which Constantine is best known, and by which he earned the title of Great, is the adoption of Christianity as the state religion. His mother, Helèna, was a Christian; and we have seen that his father, Constantius, protected the Christians. But he does not appear to have been brought up in the Christian faith; at all events, he did not declare himself a Christian until near his death. But even as early as the year 311, his influence secured the edict of universal toleration, — the persecutor Galerius and the rude Licinius alike seeing the impossibility of crushing the new sect. When he

A.D. 312. marched the next year against Maxentius, he caused the Christian symbol[1] to be inscribed upon the standards and shields of the army; and it was believed that this was done in consequence of a vision. But the events which followed show that, even if he was a Christian in belief, which is hardly likely, he was not one in heart.

Policy of Toleration. — As Emperor, he held the old republican

---

[1] The monogram XP (*Christos*) on a banner of crimson silk called the *Labarum*.

CONSTANTINVS AVG

dignity of Pontifex Maximus, or official head of the state religion; and it was as Pontifex Maximus, — a title which his Christian successors also held for half a century longer, and which is now borne by the Roman Popes, — that he assumed authority over the Christian organization, making it the official religion; but the pagan worship was still tolerated until nearly the end of the century, when it was proscribed by Theodosius the Great (p. 315).

Christianity as an Organization. — Christianity had been, during the two first centuries of its existence, a spiritual faith and moral impulse, rather than a body of doctrines or an organized power. The work of the third century was that of organization (p. 282); and the persecution of Diocletian found the church a strong, coherent association, pervading every corner of the Empire. It was apprehension of the strength of this power within the state that incited Diocletian to persecute. Constantine, too, saw the immense power which the Christian church had gained, but instead of attempting to crush it, he determined to ally himself with it, and make it serviceable as an instrument of government.

Christian Doctrine. — Christianity had now advanced to a third stage in its development. Having been first a company of scattered believers, and having now become an organized church, it next proceeded to formulate its beliefs. The work of the church in the fourth century was to determine its creed, or authoritative set of doctrines. A series of controversies now began, which distracted the church for several centuries, and by the virulence of the debates which they excited, and the intolerant spirit which they engendered, exercised a baleful influence upon the spirit of Christianity. All the intellectual activity of the age concentrated itself in the field of speculative theology, and was busily engaged in determining questions of faith, many of which were upon points too subtle to be expressed in any language except Greek. Engaged in these polemics, the officers of the church lost that burning zeal for rectitude and purity of life which had been its great power in the earlier centuries.

The Arian and Athanasian Controversy. — At the time that

Constantine became sole Emperor, a violent controversy was raging, upon the most fundamental of these questions — the nature of Christ and his relation to the Father. The original seat of this controversy was Alexandria, the home of the subtlest intellects of this age, and the two parties were headed by two ecclesiastics of Alexandria, Arius and Athanasius. At first Constantine attempted to discourage what seemed to him idle discussion upon a question incapable of solution. He saw at last that no peace was possible without an authoritative decision of the question, and summoned for this purpose a general council of the rulers of the church, to be held at Nicæa, near his residence Nicomedia, in the year 325. It was the first of the great series of so-called Œcumenical Councils, held at intervals for the settlement of these controversies.

The Council of Nicæa, A.D. 325. — Although called a general council of the church, it was to all intents and purposes confined to the church of the East, where alone any real interest was felt in these subtilties. The church of the West concerned itself rather with practical matters. Of the 318 bishops who were present, only seven or eight were from the West; even Rome was only represented by two priests. The assembly was summoned and presided over by the Emperor, who, although not yet in name a Christian, was nevertheless, as *pontifex maximus*, the official head of religion. The debates were long and acrimonious. The Emperor had at first inclined to the party of Arius; but he changed his attitude, and at length threw the weight of his authority in the opposite scale. The doctrine of Athanasius, as formulated in the so-called *Nicene Creed*, was now made the orthodox or accepted doctrine, and was designated by the term *Homousian* (of the same substance with the Father), the opposing doctrine being known as *Homoiousian* (of like substance). But the Arian doctrine, now condemned as a heresy, and proscribed in the church of the Empire, had yet a history of great importance. When the German invaders of the Empire were converted to Christianity, it was in nearly every case the Arian form of this religion which they received. The historical consequences of this fact do not fall within the limits of the present work.

Death of Crispus. — Shortly after the Council of Nicæa, Constantine committed the greatest crime of his life, in putting to death his son Crispus. The cause of this act is a mystery, but it is supposed that he had conceived a jealous suspicion of this promising and popular young man, and that this suspicion was fomented by his second wife, Fausta, who wished to secure the succession to her own worthless sons. At any rate, the death of Crispus was soon followed by bitter remorse, and by vengeance inflicted upon Fausta. The only event of history to be compared with this tragedy is the execution of Alexis, son of Peter the Great, at his father's command; but Alexis was a turbulent and dangerous character, while Crispus was, according to all accounts, a worthy heir to the throne. It was not only a crime, but a public disaster; for by Crispus' death the crown passed to heirs as low in ability as in character.

Administrative Reorganization. — A year or two after the death of Crispus, Constantine accomplished the second great act of his reign, the establishment of a new capital. A glance at the map shows that the Empire, consisting of the countries which lie about the Mediterranean Sea, was excessively long from east to west in proportion to its breadth. This was a chief cause of the difficulties of administration, and we have seen that Diocletian endeavored to remedy it by having an Emperor reside at each end of the Empire (p. 298). This scheme was broken down by its complexity, but Constantine carried out its fundamental idea in a more practical way. As Diocletian had grouped the provinces into dioceses (p. 299), so Constantine united the dioceses into four large divisions, governed by prætorian præfects, who were all equally under the authority of the Emperor. Thus the unity of the imperial office was maintained, and in place of the two Augusti and their two Cæsars there were now four prætorian præfects, with only civil powers, at the head of the four great divisions of the Empire; each præfecture being divided into dioceses, thir-

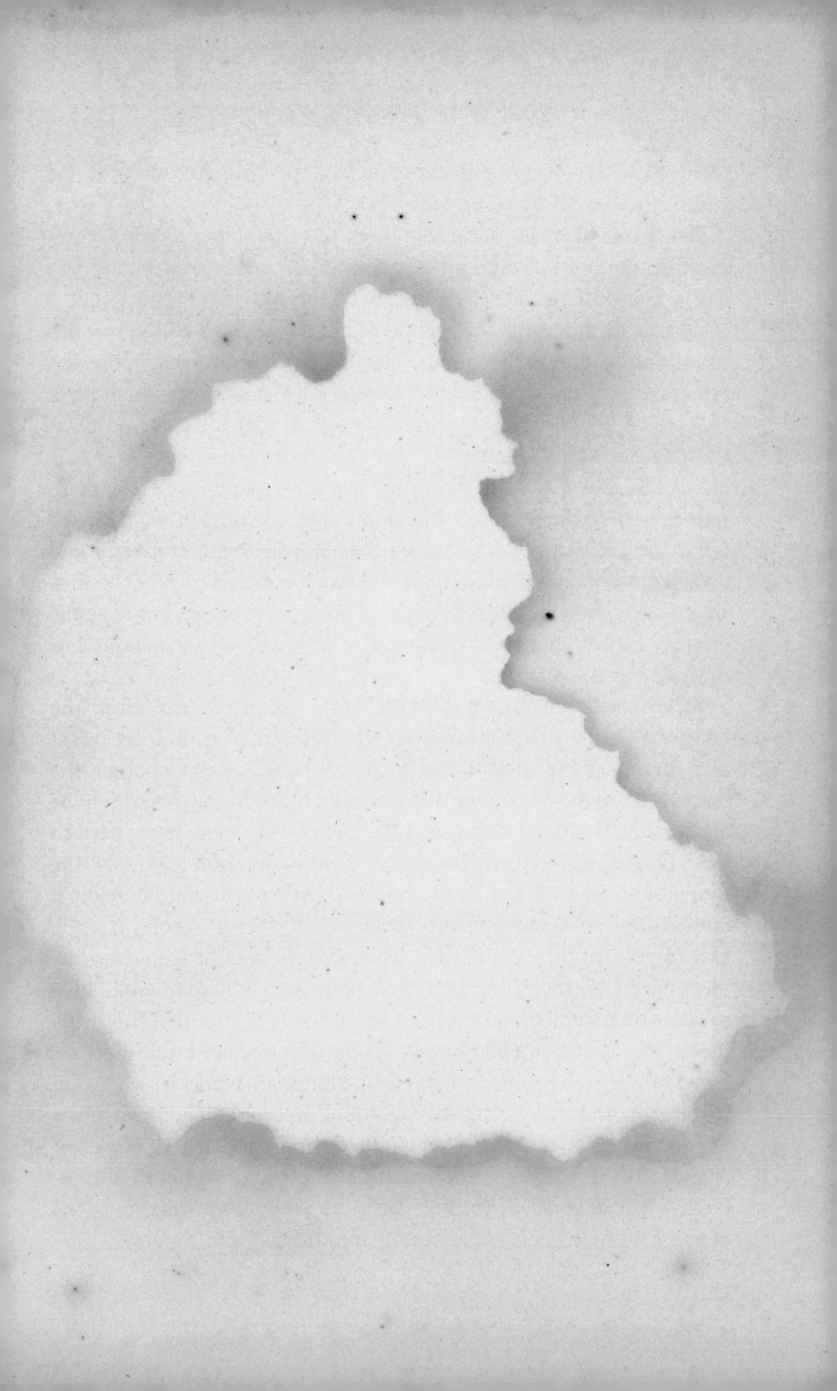

THE ROMAN EMPIRE

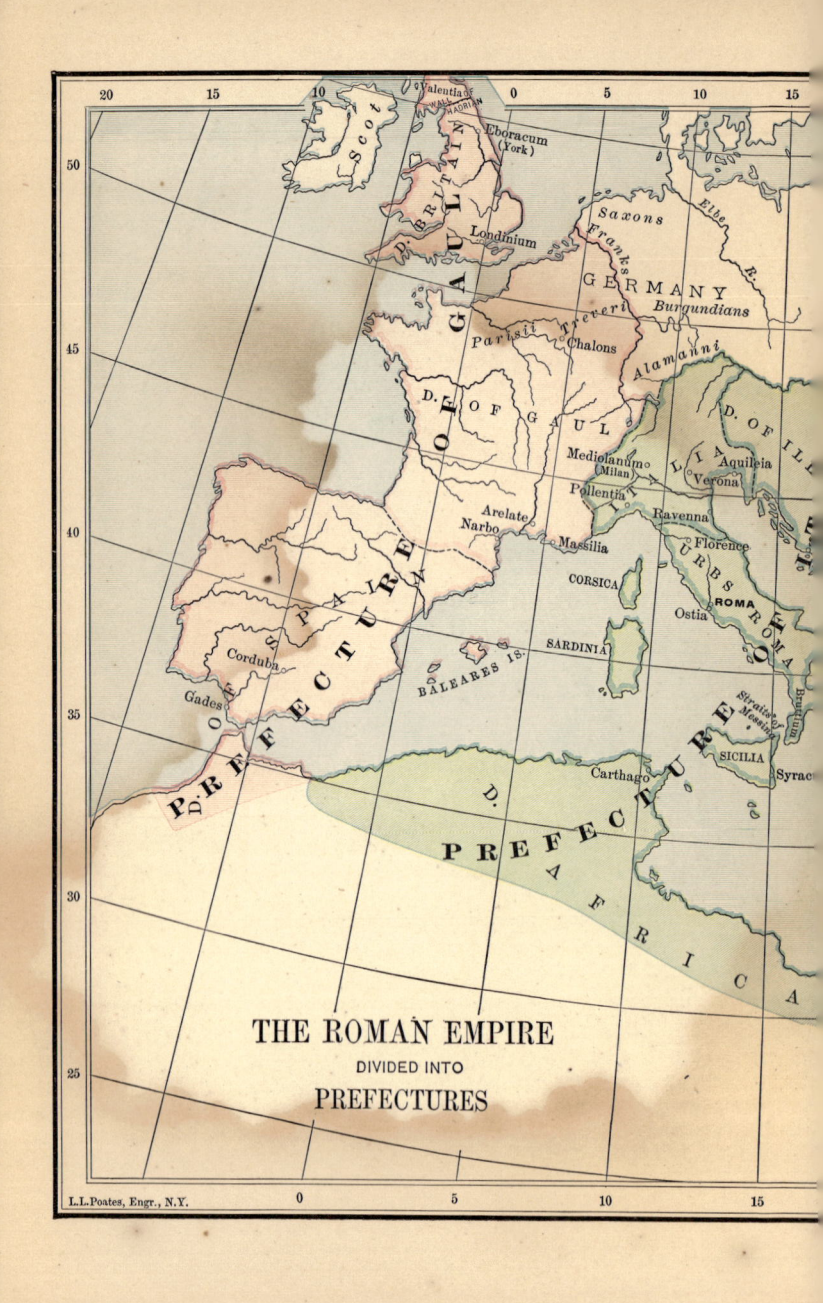

DIVIDED INTO

PREFECTURES

<!-- Map of the Eastern Roman Empire -->

- PREFECTURE OF ILLYRICUM
  - D. DACIA
  - D. MACEDONIA
  - D. THRACIA
- PREF.ced PONTUS
  - D. ASIA
- PREF.d OF THE EAST
  - D. OF THE EAST
  - D. EGYPT

Labels: Longobards, Goths, Huns, Danube R., Volga R., Euphrates R., Chersonesus, Theodosia, Adrianople, Constantinopolis, Bosporus, Nicomedia, Nicaea, Thessalonica, Thebes, Corinthus, Athens, Sparta, CRETA, CYPRUS, Antiochia, Nisibis, Edessa, Berytus, Tyre, Ptolemais (Acre), Caesarea, Palmyra, Cyrene, Alexandria, Ælia

teen in number in the whole Empire, and the dioceses containing an average of eight or nine provinces apiece.[1] The number of provinces was now one hundred and twenty.

Foundation of a New Capital. — Rome was no longer fitted to be the capital of this wide-extended Empire. It was too far from the centre and from the field of active operations. Diocletian, during his long reign, never visited his capital but once; he made his residence at Nicomedia, which was now the Eastern capital, while Milan became practically the capital of the West. But Nicomedia was neither accessible enough nor defensible enough. Constantine determined to build a new capital for the eastern half of his Empire, — a new Rome, which should be a worthy rival of the old. The spot which he selected for this purpose has been universally recognized to be of all within his reach the one possessing the most commanding situation and best fitted to be the capital of the world. And yet, although his decision seems to us self-evident, it was only after long and careful deliberation that he fixed upon the site of Byzantium.

Constantinople. — The Bosporus, the great stream of water which flows from the Black Sea to the Mediterranean, dividing the continents of Europe and Asia, broadens out about midway of its course into a sea of moderate extent, — the Propontis, or, as we call it, the Sea of Marmora. At just this point a deep inlet, the Golden Horn, runs up into the shore of Europe, and on the triangular space between the Golden Horn and the Propontis the Greeks had founded their colony of Byzantium. It was this city that Constantine determined to take as the nucleus of his New Rome. His new capital was a city of magnificent proportions. Its walls were laid out at a distance of two miles outside those of the old; and it was not easy, in an Empire which was not growing in wealth or population, to fill up so enormous a space with inhabitants. But the presence of the court, the commercial advantages of the situation, the magnificence of the new city, and the

---

[1] See map of *The Roman Empire divided into Præfectures.*

offer of extraordinary favors and privileges soon attracted settlers; so that even when the Empire did not flourish, the city of Constantine grew. The formal founding of this New Rome was on the fourth of November, 328.

The Municipalities. — One of the most significant signs of social decay in the later Empire is found in the condition of the municipalities. In the early Empire these had been the seat of a vigorous and healthy self-government, and their constitution rested upon the popular will. As early as the time of Trajan we note indications of loss of prosperity (p. 263), and in the disintegration of the third century a fundamental change in their government seems to have taken place. From this time they appear as narrow oligarchies, in which all power is vested in a few rich citizens, who composed the municipal Senate or *Curia*, and hence were called *curiales* or *decurions*. The fourth century marks another downward stage. This privileged class itself, the *curiales*, has now become rather the bearer of burdens than the possessor of power. The cities being territorial districts (p. 160), the regular subdivisions of the provinces, they were naturally made use of in the machinery of taxation; and as the taxes now became heavier and heavier with the increasing cost of government, the duty of collecting them, being placed upon the municipality, gave rise to a personal responsibility for the taxes on the part of its members, the *curiales*. The burdens thus laid upon them they of course shifted to others, and all classes of society were alike crushed by an unbearable weight of taxation. One of the great services which the emperor Valentinian rendered to the poorer classes was the creation of a new magistracy (A.D. 364), that of *Defensor Civitatis*, to protect them against the exactions of the *curiales*.

CHAPTER XXVI.

THE TRIUMPH OF CHRISTIANITY.

Death of Constantine. — Constantine the Great died May 22, 337, having been baptized a short time before his death. The death of Crispus was now bitterly avenged upon his house and his people. Fully aware of the unfitness of his three sons, Constantine, Constantius, and Constans, the Emperor did not venture to appoint either of them his sole heir, but divided the Empire between them, joining with them in the administration their two cousins, Dalmatius and Hannibalianus. But before the year was out, the three sons of Constantine brought about the murder of their cousins, and divided the Empire between themselves alone.

Constantius II., 337–361. — In a few years the death of his two brothers[1] placed the sole rule in the hands of Constantius, a prince with a great taste for theological controversy, but endowed with neither virtue nor capacity to govern. As the family of Constantine was near extinction, and the affairs of the Empire were steadily growing worse, Constantius associated in the rule his cousin Julian, with the title of Cæsar. This A.D. 355. able and energetic prince soon restored order and good government in the western provinces which were assigned to him, and to him belongs the distinction of being the last general of the Empire who placed an effectual check upon the impending advance of the German barbarians.

The Alamannians. — We have seen that the Germans upon the Rhine had gathered into two formidable confederacies, the Franks and the Alamannians, and had pushed across the frontier of the Empire to seek for themselves new homes. The strong Illyrian

---

[1] A.D. 340, death of Constantine II.; 350, of Constans.

emperors had held these invaders in check, and had even made of them a serviceable military force. But in the reign of the weak Constantius the Germans pressed forward again; the Alamannians already possessed the right bank of the Rhine, and now they began to cross that river, and take possession of the same country from which Ariovistus had been expelled four hundred years before (p. 206).

Battle of Strassburg. — Julian met the invaders at Strassburg in August, 357, and defeated them with great slaughter after a long and hard-fought battle. The "boar's head," the wedge-shaped battle column of the Germans, was pushed forward with energy, and for a while with success, but it could not withstand the discipline and effective armament of the Roman legions; and when both parties had brought up their reserves, the Romans were left masters of the field. We say *Romans;* but the Roman legions were now principally composed of German volunteers and auxiliaries. It was German against German, but Roman discipline against only half-trained courage. Thus the Alamannians were driven back for the present from the fields of Alsace, but it was only for a time. They were an orderly and industrious people, who were not in search of conquests but of homes; and before a century had passed they had again begun to spread over the left bank of the Rhine, through Alsace and Lorraine, where their descendants remain to the present day.

Julian Emperor, 360–363. — During three years Julian was engaged in settling the affairs of Gaul along the Rhine; but he was constantly menaced by the jealousy and hostility of Constantius, and in 360 he was proclaimed by his soldiers Augustus at Paris,[1] his capital. War was threatened, but Constantius died the next year, and Julian peacefully occupied the throne of the united Empire.

Julian's Apostasy. — Julian, like the rest of the family of Constantine, was brought up as a Christian; but his upright soul re-

[1] *Lutetia Parisiorum*, the chief town of the Parisii; as in numerous other cases, the name of the modern city is derived from that of the ancient tribe.

volted at the perfidies and cruelties of the imperial house, and his intellect was repelled by the metaphysical hair-splitting and the incessant bickerings of the Christian theologians. He was a man somewhat like Marcus Aurelius, but of a more robust nature, and with more taste for intellectual subtilties. The refinements of Neo-platonism, which tried to pour new wine into the old bottles of pagan mythology (p. 283), attracted his mind rather than the dogmatisms of Christian theology; and Christianity as a religion, as a moral force, seems never to have been presented to his mind.

Restoration of Paganism. — As soon as he was able to think for himself, therefore, Julian cast away the system of faith in which he had been trained, and ardently devoted himself to reviving the dead rites and beliefs of paganism. He was of a humane spirit, and did not institute any persecution of Christianity, but made it his effort to discourage it among his subjects. For this purpose he issued edicts ordering all municipal property which had been given to the churches by Constantine to be restored, and forbidding Christians to instruct in grammar and rhetoric, — thus cutting them off from the most effective means of propagating their faith. The shortness of Julian's reign gives this pagan reaction the appearance of a mere passing incident; if he had lived longer it is impossible not to believe that he would have been forced to a persecution of the Christians, probably the most relentless of all. A.D. 362.

Campaign in the East. — Affairs in the West were now quiet, but a storm was arising in the East. Sapor II. of Persia, an energetic and ambitious sovereign, had invaded the eastern provinces, and gained great successes. But Julian was an antagonist of a different type from Constantius. Crossing the Euphrates with a powerful army, he marched down the left bank of that river to the region of Babylon, opened a canal from the Euphrates to the Tigris, and through this conveyed his forces to attack the Persian forces on the Tigris. The Persians resisted with energy his passage of this river, but were routed in a decisive battle and forced to retreat to the highlands beyond. A.D. 363, May 27.

Here Julian undertook, in emulation of Alexander the Great, to follow them, but was obliged to turn back from lack of provisions. In a skirmish on the return march he was killed by a Persian arrow, June 26, 363. His chief officer, Jovian, was at once proclaimed Emperor in his place.

Valentinian I., 364-375. — After a reign of less than a year Jovian died, and was succeeded by Valentinian, one of the ablest emperors of the century and with many of the best qualities as a ruler. But his virtues were offset by an extreme of severity, even amounting to blood-thirstiness. He was chaste and just, but his justice was not tempered with mercy. Unfortunately for the Empire he associated with him his brother Valens as a colleague, assigning to him the Eastern præfecture, with Constantinople as a capital; and Valens was a wholly incompetent ruler. After a reign of eleven years, spent in energetic and unremitting efforts to hold together his fast crumbling dominions, a good ruler in most respects, but stained with many acts of ferocious

A.D. 375. cruelty, Valentinian died, and was succeeded by his two sons, Gratian and Valentinian II., — the latter an infant.

A.D. 378. Three years later, Valens was succeeded in the East by Theodosius, called the Great (p. 320).

Gratian, 375-383. — Gratian was a mild and cultivated prince, with the qualities of a good ruler and a good commander. He was a sincere upholder of the Christian faith, which he held in the orthodox form, — that which had carried the day in the Council of Nicæa, — while his uncle Valens was an adherent of the Arian heresy. In the ardor of his partisanship, Gratian took a step which led the way to the greatest evils and dis-

A.D. 376. graces of Christian history, by issuing an edict which forbade freedom of worship to all the heretical sects. This step is supposed to have been taken under the influence of the illustrious Ambrose, Bishop of Milan, the greatest ecclesiastic and probably the greatest man of his time, but whose uncompromising devotion to his faith coincided too well with his sentiment of the interests of his order to leave room for the policy of toleration. With this act the Christian church deliberately adopted the policy of persecution of other Christians on ground of difference in belief. Gratian was also the first Roman Emperor who laid aside the title of *pontifex maximus*, which had properly been borne by the pagan emperors, but was inconsistent with the present relations of church and state. It was afterward assumed by the bishops of Rome.

The Final Establishment of Christianity. — Within a few years both Gratian and Valentinian II. were murdered, and Theodosius, their Eastern colleague, now reunited the Empire and reigned as sole Emperor for three years. Theodosius completed the work of Gratian by the promulgation of an edict forbidding all exercise of the heathen rites of worship.[1] Orthodox Christianity was from this time the only lawful religion.

A.D. 383 and 392.

A.D. 391, Feb. 24.

---

[1] This edict was issued during the life of Valentinian II. ; but it will be remembered that in theory the authority of each Emperor extended over the whole Empire (p. 297).

CHAPTER XXVII.

THE BARBARIAN INVASIONS.

I. THE VISIGOTHS UPON THE DANUBE.

The Three Critical Events of the Fourth Century. — We have followed the fortunes of the Roman Empire from its foundation by Augustus, through its career of greatness and glory, and then of disintegration, to its reorganization and new life under Diocletian and Constantine. We have seen how the effort to infuse a new life into the religions of the pagan world had broken down (p. 284), and a new religion, possessing at once greater vital force, higher spirituality, and stronger moral power, had conquered society. We now pass to the third great series of events of the closing years of the Empire, — the infusion into the decaying population of the Old World of a new and more healthy element, in the German barbarians of the North. The conquest of the Empire by these peoples was not an unmixed benefit. The good as well as the bad of ancient society was ruthlessly trampled down. The new masters of the world were incapable of administering the elaborate system of government which had been worked out by the practical genius of the Romans, and society had to create a new set of institutions and a new social structure.[1] Nevertheless, these invasions were, in the long run, a good thing. Society did, after a long time, come out of the crisis better and stronger, under

[1] Under the rule of the Franks the financial system of the Empire gradually gave way to a species of *Naturalwirthschaft*, in which the obligatory services of individuals, and contributions in kind, took the place of taxes; while a crude militia system was substituted for the standing army, and civil, military, and judicial powers were all united in the same hands, as before the reforms of Diocletian and Constantine (p. 299).

the control of its new members; while it is a question whether ancient civilization had not sunk too low to be inspired with new life.

The Germans. — When we call the Germans *barbarians*, we use this word in its scientific sense, to designate a people by no means at the lowest social stage, but also not yet advanced to the stage of conscious civilization. The Greeks, as depicted by Homer, were barbarians, but with the capacity of unlimited progress. So the Germans, as described by Cæsar and Tacitus, and even when they conquered new homes for themselves within the limits of the Empire, were barbarians; but they possessed a healthy moral nature, pure domestic relations, systematic industry, and a well-ordered political system of remarkable efficiency and adaptability.

The Germans within the Empire. — The Germans were not new-comers at the period which we have reached. For years, even for centuries, they had been gaining a foothold within the limits of the Empire. The entire left bank of the Rhine was in the possession of German settlers (p. 285), and the Roman army was principally composed of German mercenaries. We shall even see Germans, within a very few years, occupying the highest places of government and administration, and at last by their will determining the destiny of the Empire. What was new at this period was the forcible entrance of organized nations within the boundaries of the Empire, sweeping over its entire extent, and carving out for themselves national kingdoms from the territories which they occupied. The Franks and Alamannians, in the West, had settled in the fields of the Empire by a gradual process of colonization. The Goths and Vandals, in the East, moved as hostile armies, conquered lands for themselves, and set up in them their already organized kingdoms. And yet they too entered the Empire as colonists; entire nations, — men, women, and children, with their flocks and herds and possessions of every kind, — traversing the countries of the Empire in long wagon-trains, fighting their way with the sword, and occupying by force lands which they might afterwards cultivate in peace.

318   THE BARBARIAN INVASIONS.

The Gothic Empire. — This new and most impressive
A.D. 376. series of events was commenced by the invasion of the
Visigoths. We have seen (p. 284) that the Goths had, in the second century, moved from their earlier seats upon the Baltic, and established themselves upon the shores of the Black Sea; and that even the conqueror Aurelian had found himself obliged to cede to them the province of Dacia north of the Danube (p. 293), so that their dominions now extended from that river to the Crimean peninsula. They were in two divisions, the East Goths (*Ostrogoths*), dwellers in the steppe, and the West Goths (*Visigoths*), dwellers in the forest. The Ostrogoths were recognized as the superiors, although they had no very well-defined authority or right of command over their brethren; and their great king, Ermanarich, was one of the most powerful sovereigns of his time. The Ostrogoths were still stoutly attached to their heathen faith; while the Visigoths, nearer to the Empire, had been in part converted to the Arian form of Christianity. Their bishop, the illustrious Ulfilas, had translated the Scriptures into their tongue; portions of this translation are still extant, an invaluable record of the early forms of Germanic speech.

The Invasion of the Huns. — A rude shock from a distant and unexpected quarter overthrew the Ostrogothic empire, and in its results forced both Gothic nations to seek new homes. This event was one of those rapid and resistless movements of savage hordes, — as unforeseen and unaccountable as a flight of locusts, — which at various times in history have swept from the regions of Central Asia, bringing terror and desolation among the inhabitants of the civilized West.[1] The Huns, of Tartar race, small, dark-hued, and hideous of feature, mounted on small, nimble horses, upon which they passed most of their lives, poured resistlessly over the steppes of Russia, prostrated the Ostrogothic power, and extended

[1] There have been at least six of these waves, — the Huns, in the fourth century; the Avars, in the sixth; the Magyars, or Hungarians, in the ninth; the Seljukian Turks (of whom the Ottomans were an offshoot), in the eleventh; the Mongols, in the thirteenth; and the Tartars at the end of the fourteenth.

their dominion over all Germany. The Visigoths, not exposed to the direct shock of the invasion, had time to take refuge upon the banks of the Danube, and there entreated per- A.D. 376. mission to cross and receive lands as subjects of the Empire. A few Ostrogoths were in their company.

Passage of the Danube. — There was vacant land enough within the limits of an empire which was losing every day in population; and it was for the interest of all that these vacant fields should be filled up with the healthy offspring of a people which was rapidly increasing in numbers, and needed homes. After some hesitation, therefore, Valens consented to grant to the Visigoths lands south of the Danube. It was agreed that they should give up their arms, cross the river peaceably, and be distributed in the unoccupied lands of the Balkan peninsula.

Battle of Adrianople. — But the well-devised plan was frustrated by the knavery of the Roman officials who had its execution in charge. By their corrupt connivance the Goths were allowed to keep their arms; by their greediness the newcomers were defrauded of promised supplies; and by their perfidy they were driven into open rebellion. The Emperor Valens hastened against the insurgents, but was totally defeated in the battle of Adrianople (Aug. 9, 378); and the Emperor lost his life after the battle.[1]

Theodosius the Great. — The young Emperor of the West, Gratian, was on his way to the assistance of his uncle, and had already reached the lower Danube, when Valens was driven by the impatience of his troops to engage in the disastrous battle, without waiting for the re-inforcements. Left in sole possession of the imperial power, for his brother Valentinian was too young to take any active part in the government, Gratian searched for a fit person with whom to share a task too great for his sole powers. He found the right person in Theodosius, one of his generals, a man of upright character and great ability, both as a general and

[1] It is generally stated, although not on very good authority, that he was burned alive in a cottage in which he had taken refuge.

A.D. 379, Jan. 19.
as a statesman. Theodosius was promptly proclaimed Augustus, and received the government of the East as his portion (p. 314).

Settlement of the Goths. — The new Emperor made Thessalonica the seat of his government while engaged in the arduous and perplexing task of restoring order in his provinces, and disposing of his troublesome guests. In the course of four years he had accomplished his task. The Goths received assignments of land, — the Visigoths in the provinces south of the Danube, their Ostrogothic auxiliaries in Phrygia, — as allies (*foederati*) of the Empire, upon the condition of receiving yearly presents, and rendering military service when called upon.

The Foederati. — The arrangement thus made with the Goths we find a common one in this last century of the Empire. They were settled within the limits of the Empire, and of course under its sovereignty, and yet were recognized as an independent nation, and bound to the imperial government by regular treaty provisions, as the word *foederati* indicates. It was an unnatural order of things, hard to reconcile with the idea of imperial sovereignty; but it has a certain analogy with the relations of the United States government to the Indian tribes, and may be illustrated by these. The Indian tribes, like the Visigoths, are independent nations under the sovereignty of the American government, with which they are connected by formal treaties; and, by the terms of these treaties, they occupy certain tracts of land, their *reservations*. The lands occupied by the Visigoths in Mœsia and Dacia were analogous to our Indian reservations.[1]

Character of Theodosius. — Theodosius, fitly called the Great, was the last great ruler of the Roman Empire. In the year 392, by the death of Valentinian II., the whole Empire was united under his rule, and continued so united for three years. Theodosius was not only an able ruler, but an upright and conscientious man. Apart from his religious intolerance, which was the expres-

[1] We might carry the analogy a step farther, and compare the dishonest officials of Valens with a certain class of Indian agents.

sion in that age of religious earnestness, there is only one stain upon his reputation. A garrison of Gothic soldiers in Thessalonica had been massacred by the mob for some trivial offence. It was not only an outrage in itself, but it embarrassed the Emperor in his earnest endeavors to establish peaceful relations with the Goths. He fell into a transport of fury, and inflicted upon the populace of Thessalonica the most fearful punish- A.D. 390. ment, gathering them into the circus to the number of seven thousand, and there having them massacred by a detachment of Gothic soldiers. His good faith was thus vindicated with the Goths, but at the expense of justice and humanity. The great Ambrose, bishop of Milan, appealed to by the bishop of Thessalonica, exhibited a dignity and courage, in his treatment of the offence, which have made this one of the significant incidents of history. Theodosius was forbidden entrance into the church until he exhibited a genuine repentance, and made complete submission, his penance continuing about eight months. He was required, moreover, to renew a law of Gratian, fixing an interval of at least thirty days between crime and punishment.[1]

Division of the Empire. — In the year 395 Theodosius died, leaving the Empire to his two young sons, Arcadius in the East and Honorius in the West: Arcadius received as his adviser the crafty and unscrupulous Rufinus; Honorius, the Vandal Stilicho, the most noteworthy personage of his time. This division, like that between Diocletian and Maximian (p. 297), was in theory one of administration alone, the two emperors being colleagues with co-equal powers. But as a matter of fact the two sections of the Empire steadily grew apart after their separation under the sons of Theodosius, and they were never again united except in name.

The Family of Theodosius. — The House of Theodosius sat upon the imperial thrones of Rome and Constantinople for two

---

[1] The humbling of Theodosius by Ambrose may rank with that of Henry IV. by Gregory VII.; but it was a far nobler act, inasmuch as Theodosius was a greater man than the penitent of Canossa, and no element of self-assertion or of ecclesiastical aggrandizement entered into the action of Ambrose.

generations.[1] The personality of the later emperors of this house was wholly insignificant. Events, however, of the most vital importance occurred in their reigns, and it will be well to append their names in a synchronistic table.

House of Theodosius.

East.	West.
379. Theodosius the Great.	392.
395. Arcadius.	Honorius.
408. Theodosius II.	
	423. Valentinian III.
450. Death of Theodosius II.	
	455. Death of Valentinian III.

II. Stilicho.

Stilicho, the Vandal. — Theodosius, at his death in 395, left the government of the Western Empire in the hands of Stilicho, as guardian of the nine-year-old Emperor Honorius. This German officer, who for thirteen years was the foremost character in the Empire, was now in the prime of life, and had earned the confidence of his patron by long and faithful services. He had bitter enemies, who at last compassed his downfall and death, and their enmity has left its mark in charges of bad faith in his public policy, — charges which the meagreness of our information does not allow us either to admit or to disprove. What can be asserted without question is that his policy was attended with entire success, that he defeated the enemies of the Empire in every engagement, and successfully maintained its integrity; while after his death disaster followed disaster, and no general or statesman was found competent to maintain the authority of the Empire.

Claudian. — The chief eulogist of Stilicho was the poet Claudian, a poet who, in these late days, is not unworthy to be compared with those of the great period of Roman literature, for genuine

---

[1] Hodgkin's *The Dynasty of Theodosius* is the best condensed history of this period.

poetic sentiment and elegance of style. His is the last great name in Roman literature. But the truest eulogy of Stilicho, and the real vindication of his character, are found in the history of his times.

Reign of Honorius, A.D. 395-423. — The death of Theodosius was the signal for all elements of discord to break into activity. The long reign of Honorius is the period in which the great barbarian invasions began in earnest, and the gradual dissolution of the Empire commenced. The first step was taken by the Visigoths, who, as we have seen (p. 320), had been established in the provinces of the Balkan peninsula.

Alaric. — In the year of the death of Theodosius, the Visigoths of the Danubian regions elected as their king the young Alaric, a high-spirited and ambitious youth, honorable in his personal relations, and not vindictive or inhuman on the whole, although goaded to vengeance by continued bad faith. For a number of years Alaric and his Goths traversed the provinces of the Eastern Empire, for the most part in the peninsula of Greece, where they committed great destruction and ravages. It is during this period that the relations between Stilicho and Rufinus, the minister of the Eastern Empire, excited suspicion of Stilicho's good faith. It seems probable, that in his dealings with the perfidious and vindictive Rufinus, Stilicho showed something of the wisdom of the serpent, and that his unscrupulous adversary found himself surpassed in his own cunning.

Victories of Stilicho. — After a number of years passed in devastating Greece and Epirus, Alaric was induced by Rufinus to carry his arms into the Western Empire. In this first invasion of Italy Alaric sustained two defeats at the hands of Stilicho — at Pollentia and Verona — and was obliged to depart from the peninsula and leave it unmolested for several years. A.D. 402-3.

Rhadagais. — In the year following the battle of Verona, a fearful danger threatened Italy in an invasion of Germans under the Ostrogoth Rhadagais. This was not the A.D. 404.

movement of a nation, like that of the Visigoths; the Germans of Rhadagais were soldiers of fortune gathered from all sources, and seeking plunder rather than homes. Rhadagais was a personal leader, not a national king like Alaric. These invaders too, like the Visigoths, came by the pass of the Julian Alps at the head of the Adriatic, and swept, two hundred thousand warriors in number, through the northern parts of the peninsula as far as Florence. Here they were met by Stilicho, and their army was annihilated. Rhadagais and thousands of his followers were slain, a large number were converted into serfs, and some twelve thousand were taken into the service of the Empire as soldiers.

A.D. 405.

Vandal Invasion. — The invasion of Rhadagais was a passing storm. The next year an even more serious disaster befell the Empire, although it did not touch Italy directly. The Vandals, a nation of the eastern Germans, who had been settled by Constantine in Pannonia, left their abodes upon the Danube, and, their number swollen by Sueves and Alans (these last of Hunnic stock), crossed the Rhine into Gaul, which they occupied for three years with fearful destruction and spoliation.

A.D. 406.

The Usurper Constantine. — The authority of the Empire was practically suspended in these western provinces, and their armies and officials looked in vain to the inert Emperor at Rome for relief. The task set to Stilicho was too great even for him. The armies of Britain, in this emergency, did again what had been done so many times before, — threw off the authority of the Emperor and set up an Emperor of their own, a common soldier by the name of Constantine — a name of good import.[1] This pretender soon brought all Britain and Gaul under his rule, and maintained his authority for four years. In this interval his officers induced the Vandals and their companions to abandon Gaul and pass into Spain, where they took into their possession nearly the whole peninsula, — the Suevi occu-

A.D. 409.

---

[1] Church, *The Count of the Saxon Shore.*

pying the northwest, the chief body of the Vandals the south (where they have left their name to the province of Andalusia), the Alans and the rest of the Vandals in Lusitania (*Portugal*). Thus the only region west of Italy which still recognized the authority of Honorius was the eastern portion of Spain.

Fall of Stilicho. — Stilicho was held responsible for disasters which no power could have averted. His faithful services to Theodosius and Honorius, and the successive defeats of Alaric and Rhadagais were forgotten, and his enemies prevailed upon the weak and inexperienced Emperor — he was not much over twenty years of age — to have him put to death. He was beheaded at Ravenna, August 23, 408.

Ravenna. — Ravenna had become the capital of the Western Empire. Rome had, as we have seen, long ceased to be the residence of the Emperors, although it still retained its prestige and dignity. Milan was the military centre of the western provinces; but Honorius had neither military abilities nor ambitions. When Rhadagais was laying waste the north of Italy, Milan was an unsafe refuge for his sacred person, and he sought a secure retreat in the city of Ravenna, which was protected from assault by the marshes of the Adriatic. This city continued for four hundred years from this time to be the seat of government, and still contains splendid remains of architecture dating from this period.

III. Alaric.

Second Invasion of Alaric. — The death of Stilicho was followed by cruel vengeance inflicted upon his adherents by his victorious enemies, and the massacre of the wives and children of the German soldiers in Italy. It was in a sense the revival of the sentiment of Italian nationality, in opposition to the impending domination of the German. These atrocious acts summoned Alaric a second time to Italy; and this time there was no Stilicho to meet him. He traversed the peninsula without opposition, and stood at length before the walls of Rome, — **A.D. 408.**

the first enemy since Hannibal who had looked upon them at the head of a hostile army.

Capture of Rome. — It was not Alaric's purpose to destroy or injure the world's capital. He invested it closely and reduced it by famine, after the Senate, in its frenzied hatred of the barbarians, had condemned to death Stilicho's widow, Serena, on the suspicion that she had invited the Goths in revenge for the death of her husband. When famine and pestilence had brought the citizens to submission, an embassy was sent to the conqueror to ask for terms on which they might surrender. The demand was for all their gold and silver, their movable property, and their slaves of barbarian origin. "What, then, do you leave to us?" was asked, and the answer, "Your lives." But the conqueror was after all satisfied with easier terms, and retired from Italy with immense treasures, the price of the city.[1]

Sack of Rome. — Twice again Alaric besieged Rome. A.D. 409. The first time it surrendered voluntarily, the second A.D. 410. time he took it by assault, and gave it up to plunder for three days. His patience was exhausted, and his soldiers had been too often disappointed of their prey. Much destruction and many outrages were no doubt wrought during these three days of rapine; but it is not probable that the city suffered nearly so much as from Geiseric, the Vandal, forty-five years later, or from the imperial troops of Bourbon's army in 1527. Alaric was of a finer and nobler nature than either of these.

Death of Alaric. — From the sack of Rome Alaric proceeded with his Goths to southern Italy, and there suddenly died in the same year, 410. His body received a unique and characteristic burial. The course of the river Busento was turned aside, the young chief was interred in its bed, and then the waters were suffered to flow back into their channel, so that his sepulchre might remain forever concealed.

Ataulf. — The successor of Alaric was his brother-in-law Ataulf (*Adolf*), a prince of mild temper and enlightened mind, whose

[1] Wilkie Collins' *Antonina; or the Fall of Rome*.

desire it was to bring his Goths into the current of civilization, and create a new race of men by uniting them with the citizens of the Empire — the result that has actually been wrought by the slow forces of time.[1] Ataulf departed from the policy of his brother-in-law, entered into negotiations with the court of Ravenna, and, in 412, led his people from Italy into Gaul, where the power of the usurper Constantine (p. 324) had just been overthrown.

Galla Placidia. — The story of Ataulf's short career is at once romantic and pathetic. The Goths had taken prisoner Placidia, the sister of the Emperor, and had refused to give her up, although they treated her kindly and honorably. The Gothic prince and the Roman princess, both noble by birth and of noble character, young, and of great personal beauty, became strongly attached to each other; but their marriage was forbidden by Honorius, and Placidia's hand was also sought by Constantius, the officer who had put an end to Constantine's usurped power, a favorite of Honorius, but a personal enemy of Ataulf. After long waiting, the lovers were united at Narbonne, A.D. 414. in spite of the Emperor's opposition; but their happiness was of short duration. Forced the next year by Con- A.D. 415. stantius to withdraw into Spain, Ataulf was murdered at Barcelona. Placidia then returned to her brother's court, where she was at last obliged to marry her husband's enemy, Constantius, by whom she became the mother of the wretched Valentinian III., the last of the family of Theodosius.

[1] The words of Ataulf were: "It was at first my wish to destroy the Roman name, and erect in its place a Gothic empire, taking to myself the place and the powers of Cæsar Augustus. But when experience taught me that the untamable barbarism of the Goths would not suffer them to live beneath the sway of law, and that the abolition of the institutions on which the state rested would involve the ruin of the state itself, I chose the glory of renewing and maintaining by Gothic strength the fame of Rome, desiring to go down to posterity as the restorer of that Roman power which it was beyond my power to replace. Wherefore I avoid war and strive for peace" (in Orosius; translated by Bryce).

Kingdom of the Visigoths. — After a brief interval Wallia, brother of Ataulf, was made king of the Visigoths. He led his nation back to Gaul, and received from the Emperor in the year 419 a formal grant of territory upon the Bay of Biscay, with Toulouse as his capital. By this act the Visigoths were established, as allies (*foederati*) (p. 320) of Rome, upon lands of their own. But these were not vacant lands, as those in Thrace had been, but were occupied by a numerous and wealthy people, over whom the king of the Visigoths exercised the authority of a Roman magistrate. Thus was established the first Germanic kingdom upon the soil of the Empire, soon to be followed by others; and with this act began that union of Roman and barbarian which had been the hope of Ataulf. Wallia died in the same year, and was succeeded by Theodoric, a grandson of Alaric.

A.D. 419.

St. Jerome. — The age of Alaric and Ataulf was made illustrious by the genius and literary activity of two distinguished fathers of the Church, one of them among the greatest men of all time, — Jerome and Augustine. Jerome had been educated in Rome, but had now lived for many years in Bethlehem of Judæa, where the news of the fall of Rome reached him and filled him with dismay and sorrow. He is best known as the author of the Vulgate, a Latin version of the Scriptures, which he translated from the Greek.

A.D. 420.

St. Augustine. — Augustine was an African by birth and residence. He had lived a wild life in his youth, but had been converted by Ambrose, and became a zealous and earnest Christian, devoting his great intellectual powers to the service of the Church. He was bishop of Hippo, where he died in 430. He, too, like Jerome, was powerfully impressed by the capture and sack of Rome, and was led by this event to the composition of his greatest work, *The City of God* (*De Civitate Dei*), the object of which is to show that the calamities of the Empire were not to be attributed to the change of religion; and that, though the city builded by men may perish, the city of God will abide forever. St. Augustine, in conjunction with Athanasius, was the founder of the great theological system which has held possession of the Church since his day.

CHAPTER XXVIII.

AETIUS.

The Age of Valentinian III. — Even in these days of degeneracy and dissolution, the Roman Empire and nationality did not cease to produce characters worthy of their best days; and in the reign of the good-for-nothing Valentinian III. there flourished two generals and statesmen of a high order, Aetius and Boniface. Unfortunately they were rivals. Each was by nature upright and loyal, and by himself would have done the Empire good service. But their rivalry and the unbalanced ambition of Aetius led both into treasonable conduct, which brought great calamities upon the Empire.

Count[1] Boniface. — Boniface was governor of Africa, that province which stood nearest to Italy, both in situation and importance; for here were the choice plantations of the Roman nobles, and from here came the most abundant supplies of grain for the capital. He was peculiarly favored and trusted by the Empress Placidia, who governed in the name of her son, Valentinian. This favor awakened the jealousy of Aetius, who occupied a position of trust in Italy, corresponding to that of Boniface in Africa, but who seems to have aspired to make himself to the present sovereign what Stilicho had been to Honorius, the supreme manager of affairs. In this he was successful, but only by base intrigue and perfidy, and to meet at the end a fate like that of Stilicho.

The Vandals in Africa. — Aetius succeeded, by false representations, in exciting Placidia and Boniface to suspicion and jealousy towards one another, even to the

A.D. 426.

---

[1] In the later Empire we meet with the term *Comes* (companion) as an official title, which may be rendered by the modern word "count," derived from it.

degree that Boniface was made to fear for his life; for under despotic rule there is only one step from suspicion to punishment. In his fear and resentment Boniface was tempted to commit a crime, less to be condemned morally than that of Aetius, but attended with the most disastrous consequences. He invited the Vandals of southern Spain to bring their forces to his aid, promising them as reward a tract of land in Africa. Hardly had he taken this treasonable step than he was made aware of the perfidy of Aetius and the true sentiment of Placidia. But it was

A.D. 429. too late. The Vandals were already on their way.

Geiseric. — The Vandal king, Geiseric,[1] was a man of mark, one of the most conspicuous among the German leaders of this century. He was not attractive and imposing in aspect, like Alaric and Ataulf, but of small stature and limping; neither had he their magnanimity and fineness of nature. He was shrewd and designing, and at the same time blood-thirsty and relentless. Boniface tried in his remorse to drive back his dangerous allies, but Geiseric carried everything before him; and Boniface was forced to return in discomfiture to Italy, where, the next

A.D. 432. year, he lost his life in a civil war with Aetius.

Aetius in Gaul. — Aetius was now, as he had aspired to be, in possession of undivided authority; and the services which from this time he rendered to the Empire are almost sufficient to wipe out the memory of his great crime. The scene of his activity during the twenty years which followed was chiefly Gaul, where the clouds were gathering fast over society. As long as Aetius lived, these perils were held in check, and the integrity of the Empire was maintained. As soon as his strong hand was removed, the Empire moved rapidly, and without hindrance, to its fall.

The Situation in Gaul. — By the withdrawal of the Vandals into Africa, Spain had been restored to the authority of the Empire, except for the occupation of the northwest of the peninsula by the Sueves. The Visigoths in southwestern Gaul were allies of the Empire, and nominally under its authority; and the vigorous

---

[1] This is the correct form of the name instead of the familiar *Genseric*.

AETIUS.

rule of Aetius maintained this authority sufficiently well. Along the Rhine the Alamannians and Franks were quietly pushing their way into the fields of Gaul, and between them a new nation had now thrust itself.

The Burgundians. — The Burgundians had made their appearance in western Germany in the century before, having moved thither from their old homes upon the Oder. In the disturbed reign of Honorius they had got a foothold upon the Rhine, making the city of Worms their capital, where their memory was long preserved, although it was their residence for only thirty years.[1] These people now began, like their neighbors, the Franks and Alamannians, but more turbulently and rapidly, to push further to the West; but they were defeated by Aetius, and transplanted by him to the high mountain region of Savoy, where they occupied a position similar to that of the Visigoths in Aquitania. These two nations, after the death of Aetius, gradually spread out from their lawful territories, and between them gained possession of nearly the whole of southern Gaul.

A.D. 413.
A.D. 435.
A.D. 443.

Attila, the Hun. — A new peril, the most menacing of all, now approached from the East. The Huns had remained in quiet occupation of the territories north of the Danube since their great migration of the century before (p. 318). From this seat of empire they had extended their authority as far as the Rhine, making tributary to themselves all the nations of free Germany, — the Ostrogoths, the Gepidæ, the Franks of the right bank of the Rhine, and other nations. Their king, Attila, was superior to his race in culture and humanity; but he was a Tartar, a man belonging to the class of Genghis Khan and Tamerlane, even if less savage than they.[2]

[1] The great German epic, the *Niebelungenlied*, has its scene at Worms in the time of the Burgundian rule.

[2] He appears under the name of *Etzel* in the *Niebelungenlied*, and is depicted as a humane and noble character, far nobler indeed than the Burgundian heroes of the poem.

Attila's Invasion. — Attila, master of all Europe north of the Danube and east of the Rhine, now conceived the mighty ambition of bringing the rest of Europe into subjection. In this plan he seems to have been secretly encouraged by the crafty Geiseric. Gathering the forces of all the nations which were subject to him, he crossed the Rhine with an army of at least five hundred thousand men, and made his way across Gaul as far as the river Loire, plundering and destroying as he went. He then laid siege to the city of Orleans; and his battering rams were already crashing against its walls, — according to some accounts his warriors had even entered the streets of the city, — when Aetius, with Theodoric, king of the Visigoths, appeared at the head of a great army, and the city was saved.

"Battle of the Peoples." — For some reason, unknown to us, Attila, in spite of the superiority of his forces, found himself obliged to retreat, and hastened towards the Rhine, pursued by Aetius and Theodoric. He was overtaken in his retreat, and brought to bay at a spot upon the river Seine, not far from the modern city of Troyes, about fifty miles south of Châlons.[1] The Roman general had under his standard all the forces of the Empire. Besides his legions, there were contingents from the allied Visigoths and Burgundians, as well as from the Alamannians and Salian Franks upon the left bank of the Rhine, who held their lands on the tenure of military service. All the nations of Europe were assembled on this great battle-field, — Roman against Hun, Visigoth against Ostrogoth, and Salian Frank against Ripuarian Frank. The battle is fitly called the "Battle of the Nations."

Defeat of Attila. — Aetius had skilfully taken possession of a ridge of ground, which the Huns vainly endeavored to storm; their horsemen, armed with bow and arrow, were ill-suited to this task. As Theodoric, king of the Visigoths, was rallying his men, he was pierced by a Hunnic spear. At this his people, excited to

---

[1] The engagement, called by contemporary writers "Battle of the Mauriac Plain," is usually known as the battle of *Châlons sur Marne*. But it is now generally admitted to have been fought at Méry upon the Seine.

fury rather than discouraged by his loss, rushed upon the enemy with irresistible force, and carried all before them. In the night which followed Attila retreated, leaving the victory to Aetius. In this fight it is said that a hundred and sixty-five thousand people fell. This great battle was fought in the summer of 451.

Results of the Battle. — The "Battle of the Peoples" is with good reason reckoned one of the decisive battles of the world's history. The Huns were not, like the Goths, the Franks, or the Vandals, a people of cognate race with the Romans and readily amenable to civilization; their aim was not to carve out for themselves a domain from the superabundant lands of the Empire, but to overthrow the very structure of the Empire, and destroy the fabric of Roman civilization and religion. The Empire did not long survive this victory, but when it fell it left its civilization as an inheritance to those who succeeded to its power. We cannot say that the Huns would not in time have developed the same high political aptitudes as their kinsmen the Magyars, but it is not likely. The times were different in the two cases. The Magyars fitted themselves into the scheme of an advancing civilization and a newly developed organization of society. In the time of Attila society was decaying, and the political structure just ready to fall. His triumph, and the overthrow of the Empire, would have led to a dominion like that of Genghis Khan, the enemy of humanity and of society itself.

A.D. 452. **Invasion of Italy.** — The year after this repulse, Attila advanced again upon the Empire, this time making his way into Italy by the old open route of the Julian Alps. The city of Aquileia, at the head of the Adriatic Sea, was taken and destroyed. The Venetian plains were laid waste, and a remnant of their inhabitants, seeking a refuge from the destroyer among the lagoons and marshy islands of the seashore, carried with them their national name. The scattered huts of these fugitives have grown into the stately palaces of Venice.

Death of Attila. — Advancing through the plains of northern Italy, Attila took up his residence at Milan, the military capital of the Western Empire. What were his plans, and in what manner Aetius proposed to meet them, cannot now be known. All we know is that Attila was here visited by an embassy from the Emperor, headed by Leo the Great, bishop of Rome, one of the most noteworthy men of his time, the one who laid the foundation of the temporal power of the popes. At his entreaties Attila consented to give up his schemes of conquest and return to his home beyond the Danube. The next year he sud- A.D. 453. denly died, and his immense empire crumbled to pieces. The Ostrogoths took possession of Pannonia, the Gepidæ of Dacia further east, while the more distant German tribes were left to their isolation and independence.

The Anglo-Saxons in Britain. — During these events Britain, too, began to be occupied by German tribes. This island had been practically severed from the Empire from the time of the usurper Constantine (p. 324). He had carried the Roman A.D. 407. troops with him to Gaul, leaving Britain defenceless; and after his fall there had been no disposition or opportunity to reoccupy the island. But the native Britons had, under the long Roman rule, lost all habit and capacity of self-government or self-defence. Harassed by their unruly neighbors at the north, the Scots and Picts, abandoned by their Roman protectors, they, as Boniface had done (p. 329), called in the A.D. 449. aid of auxiliaries from northern Germany, only to find at last that they had set a new master over themselves. For over a hundred years Angles and Saxons in successive companies flocked across the sea to Britain, and a new Germanic realm was established on its soil.

Death of Aetius. — As Stilicho's prestige had been destroyed by the disasters in Gaul (p. 325), so Attila's successes in Italy appear to have weakened the hold of Aetius upon the confidence of the Emperor. The year after Attila's A.D. 454. death Valentinian procured the assassination of his great general, and was himself assassinated the following year by the senator Maximus, whom he had grossly injured, and who now succeeded him upon the imperial throne.

CHAPTER XXIX.

THE FALL OF THE EMPIRE.

The Imperial System. — Aetius has been called "the last of the Romans": as long as he lived the authority of the Empire was maintained successfully against the assaults of the barbarians; after his death it soon succumbed to their blows. The establishment of the imperial government had given new strength to the Roman state in two ways; by knitting together its incoherent forces in a more efficient organism,[1] and by putting an end to the atrocious misgovernment of the provinces. The early emperors were tyrants towards the haughty Roman nobility, but to the provincials they gave some degree of peace and justice; while in the system of municipalities and that of provincial assemblies they possessed healthy institutions of local self-government.

Its Collapse. — But these forces were now exhausted. The unjust discrimination between Rome and the provinces had, it is true, been effaced (p. 280), and the reorganization by Diocletian and Constantine (p. 296) had still further centralized the government. But all internal life had perished. Wealth and population were every day diminishing; the enemies of the Empire were every day stronger and more audacious; the imperial court was every day more luxurious and more unscrupulous; the people were every day more incapable of meeting the demands made upon them by the government. Society could barely maintain its own existence; it had no surplus to hand down to posterity — taxation devoured all the fruits of industry. The municipal system was made an agency of taxation, and local self-government ceased to exist except in name. The peasants had become serfs, and the

---

[1] See, upon this point, the first of Seeley's lectures upon *Roman Imperialism*.

city population paupers. Even Christianity had no power against these principles of decay, and, benumbed by contact with a corrupt court, lost much of its tonic power. All capacity of progress being absent, society by necessity went backward; and there followed a complete collapse of civilization and social order.

Succession of Emperors. — During the years which followed a rapid succession of Emperors reigned in the West with only nominal power; their names may be best presented in tabular form.

	East.		West.
450.	Marcian.		
		455.	Maximus.
			Avitus, deposed 456.
457.	Leo I.	457.	Majorian.
		461.	Lybius Severus, d. 465.
		467.	Anthemius.
		472.	Olybrius.
			Julius Nepos.
		473.	[Glycerius, pretender.]
474.	Zeno.		
		475.	Romulus Augustulus.
		476.	Deposed by Odovacar.

Majorian. — Of all these Emperors of the West Majorian was the only one worthy of his dignity and rank. He vigorously maintained the authority of the Empire, especially against the Vandals, who were at this time its most formidable enemies. Those who succeeded him were mere shadows.

Geiseric in Rome. — The senator Maximus, who slew Valentinian III. and succeeded to the throne, laid claim A.D. 455. to the widow as well as the crown of his predecessor. Averse to the proposed marriage, Eudoxia called to her aid the powerful king of the Vandals, Geiseric, who promptly sailed from Africa with a strong force, and took possession of Rome. As he approached the city, he was met, as Attila had been on his approach to Milan, by the venerable bishop Leo, whose intercession availed now with the Vandal as it had with the Hun. He consented to spare the city and the lives and persons of the inhabitants, but demanded their treasures. He committed therefore no wanton destruction; no *sack*, in the true meaning of the word, was allowed; but the city was thoroughly plundered, and an enormous amount of wealth was carried away.

Empire of the Vandals. — The capture of the eternal city placed Geiseric upon the summit of renown, and his restless ambition incited him to new plans of conquest. The sentiment of patriotism was not yet extinct among the Romans, and for a short time they aroused themselves to oppose him. The year after his occupation of Rome he was defeated by Count Ricimer in a naval battle near Corsica, and the heroic Majorian, who now succeeded to the throne, held the Vandals at bay until his abdication and death. After this, Geiseric found no worthy opponent, and he speedily made himself master of Sardinia, Corsica, the Balearic Isles, and part of Sicily. He now ruled with undisputed sway over the western Mediterranean; but the greatness of the Vandal empire ended with the death of its great king.

A.D. 456.

A.D. 461.

A.D. 477.

Count Ricimer. — In these years the management of affairs at Rome had fallen into the hands of a Goth named Ricimer, a grandson of Wallia. This German, perhaps equal to Stilicho in ability, but far less disinterested, wielded for seventeen years an even more absolute authority, setting up and deposing emperors at his will. Majorian was the first who owed his crown to him; but when it appeared that the emperor of his creation would not be a puppet in his hands, Ricimer forced him to abdicate, and soon afterwards caused his death. Ricimer's domination lasted until his own death, eleven years later, after which the Empire rapidly fell to pieces. Selfish and unscrupulous as he was, Ricimer at least preserved it for a time from dissolution.

A.D. 457.

A.D. 461.

Disintegration of the Empire. — The fate which had so many times seemed impending over the Empire was now rapidly approaching. All central authority was lost, and the various provinces were becoming the seat of new kingdoms of German origin, independent in substance of power, although still nominally a part of the Empire.[1] The Vandals possessed Africa and the islands. The Burgundians had gradually advanced their boundaries, until now they occupied from the Alps to the Rhone, making Lugdunum (*Lyons*) their capital. Here, at the Rhone, their territories touched those of the Visigoths, who had on their part stretched out their hands from Toulouse to meet those of the Burgundians extended from the High Alps. The growth of the Visigothic empire was the work of King Euric, who came to the throne shortly after the death of Ricimer, and reigned for nineteen years. Euric carried his boundaries north to the Loire and east to the Rhone; then crossed the Pyrenees and reduced under his sway all Spain, except the Suevic state in the northwest; lastly he obtained from Odovacar the coast between the Rhone and the Alps, — the modern Provence, with Arelate (*Arles*) as its capital. The kingdom of the Visigoths, stretching from the Loire, the Rhone, and the Alps to the Straits of Gibraltar, seemed now destined to dispute with that of the Vandals the dominion of the West.

A.D. 466.
A.D. 475.
A.D. 478.
A.D. 480.

The North of Gaul. — Thus the whole Western Empire had fallen under the dominion of Germanic nations — Vandals, Sueves, Visigoths, Burgundians — except Italy itself and the northern portion of Gaul. Even here the Alamannians on the east and the Franks on the north had made themselves masters of a broad belt of territory; while at the West, in the modern Brittany, the Armoricans maintained a virtual independence. But in the great central region of northern Gaul, with Paris as his capital, the standard of the Empire was still ably defended by Count Ægidius, and after his death by his son Syagrius.

A.D. 464.

---

[1] For a vivid picture of these movements, read Dahn's *Felicitas*.

The Franks. — A new Germanic power was now gathering in this quarter. The Salian Franks, who inhabited the Netherlands under the authority of the Empire, consisted of a multitude of petty kingdoms gathered into a loose confederation like that of the Alamannians. The kingdom of Tournay, under the rule of the Merovingian[1] Childeric, had established a certain ascendency over the rest of the Salian Franks, an ascendency which, at his death, passed to his son Clovis,[2] a youth of sixteen. The disappearance of the imperial authority at this epoch left the king of Tournay, like the kings of Toulouse and of Lyons, in a condition of virtual independence; there was no longer any Emperor for them to obey,[3] and they reigned with no superior. As Euric had pushed his boundaries to the Loire and the Alps, and the Burgundian kings had advanced theirs to the Rhone, so Clovis now began to do the same thing, and entered upon that succession of conquests which built up the greatest and most enduring of the Germanic kingdoms. He had hardly been upon the throne five years when, by the defeat and overthrow of Syagrius, A.D. 486, he put an end to the last remains of Roman power in Gaul. The career of Clovis, the most illustrious of the Germanic kings, and the fortunes of his empire, the most enduring of all the Germanic kingdoms, do not fall within the limits of this work.

A.D. 481.

Fall of the Empire. — Before Syagrius fell, or Euric had conquered Spain, the Empire of the West had already ceased to exist. After the death of Ricimer the series of puppet emperors continued four years longer. Romulus, nicknamed Augustulus (the little Augustus), the last of the shadowy line, was a handsome and amiable youth, but with neither expe-

A.D. 472.

---

[1] This name is a patronymic, meaning the descendants of Meroveus, grandfather of Clovis.

[2] His name appears to have been *Hlodowig* (*Ludwig* or *Lewis*); the same guttural initial is found in the name *Childeric*, or *Hilderik*.

[3] After the extinction of the western line of emperors, the Emperor of Constantinople was nominally their sovereign, but with no real authority over them.

rience nor capacity as a ruler. In his reign the barbarian soldiers of Italy, tired of life in the camp, and of the uncertainties of their career, demanded to be treated as their brethren in the other provinces had been: to be no longer quartered in barracks, but to receive an assignment of land, — demanding one-third of the lands in Italy. When their petition was denied, they rose in mutiny, under the lead of Odovacar,[1] and took the government of Italy into their own hands. Romulus was allowed to retire to a pleasant villa near Naples, and Odovacar ruled the peninsula.

Odovacar. — Odovacar was not the recognized king of a nation of his own, like Alaric, Geiseric, and Clovis. His followers were not a nation, serving under its own head, like the Visigoths and Burgundians, but regularly enlisted soldiers of the Empire (p. 317), of varied and mixed nationality. Nevertheless, he was styled king by them, and ruled the German population of Italy as the kings of the Visigoths and Burgundians ruled their nations. At the same time he, like them, did not regard himself as an independent sovereign, but submitted himself to the authority of Zeno, Emperor of Constantinople, and received from him the title of *patrician*, in virtue of which he governed the native population of Italy, somewhat as a viceroy. A.D. 477.

Survival of the Empire. — The removal of Romulus Augustulus from the throne of Italy, with the submission of that country to Odovacar, was shortly followed, as we have seen, by the conquest of Spain by the Visigoths, and of northern Gaul by the Franks. Odovacar, Euric, and Clovis were contemporaries. Every portion of the Western Empire was now occupied and governed by kings of Germanic race. It is true, the sovereignty of the Emperor at Constantinople was still recognized in name, and the integrity of the Empire was still maintained in theory;[2] but, as a fact, the Roman Empire was at an end. The eastern half, the Empire of

---

[1] The name is commonly spelt *Odoacer*; his birth is uncertain, but he is usually ascribed to the petty tribe of the Heruli.

[2] See Bryce's *Holy Roman Empire* and Freeman's review of it in the first series of his *Historical Essays*.

Constantinople, still continued, in all its forms and with substantial power, another thousand years; and Charles the Great (*Charlemagne*), after three hundred years, re-established the Empire at Rome in a form which survived as a form until the present century.[1] But, however much the Empire of Charles owed to the memories and theories of the Empire of Augustus and Constantine, it was yet essentially a new creation, borrowing the style of the old Empire, and living on its traditions, but differing from it in organization, character, and composition.[2]

[1] It was formally dissolved in the reconstruction of Germany under Napoleon's influence in 1806; its last emperor, Francis II., had two years before saved his imperial dignity by assuming the title of Emperor of Austria.

[2] The period from the fall of the Empire to its renewal by Charlemagne can be best studied in Emerton's *Introduction to the Middle Ages*, a book which in an unusual degree combines exact scholarship with graphic power. See also Curteis' *History of the Roman Empire*, and Church's *Beginning of the Middle Ages* (Epochs series); for larger works Hodgkin's *Italy and her Invaders*, and (principally for the Eastern Empire) Bury's *Later Roman Empire*.

CHRONOLOGICAL SYNOPSIS OF ROMAN HISTORY.

PERIOD I.—THE MONARCHY.

B.C.		PAGE
753.	Traditional date of foundation of Rome. Patrician State; conquest of the course of the Tiber.	15
616.	Traditional date of Tarquinian dynasty. Empire over Latium. Great building activity.	29

PERIOD II.—THE EARLY REPUBLIC.

509.	The Republic; two consuls. War with Etruscans and Latins.	38
494.	Secession of the Plebs; establishment of the tribunate.	43
493-86.	Triple alliance with Latins and Hernicans; hegemony of Rome. Establishment of Latin colonies.	44
486.	Agrarian agitations. Death of Spurius Cassius.	49
471.	Publilian Law of Volero; establishment of plebeian assembly by tribes.	52
451-49.	The Decemvirate; codification of the laws.	58
445.	The Canuleian Law; intermarriage between patricians and plebeians.	61
444.	The military tribunate; 443, the censorship established; 421, the quæstorship thrown open to plebeians.	63
442.	Conquest of Ardea, followed by that of other towns.	65
406-396.	Siege of Veii. Military reforms of Camillus.	67
390.	Battle of the Allia; capture of Rome by the Gauls.	70
386.	Annexation of Pometia; 381, of Tusculum; 353, of Cære.	73, 78
384.	Sufferings of the poor; death of M. Manlius.	74
367.	The Licinian Laws; equalization of the orders; attempt to regulate the occupation and cultivation of the public lands.	75

PERIOD III.—ITALIAN WARS.

354.	Treaty with the Samnites; 348, with Carthage.	79
343.	First Samnite War; annexation of Capua.	79
340-38.	Latin War; dissolution of the Latin Confederacy. Establishment of municipal system and of maritime colonies (see p. 99).	80

CHRONOLOGICAL SYNOPSIS.

B.C.   PAGE

339. Publilian Laws of Philo; further gains of the plebeians.   77

327–304. Second Samnite War; The Roman army entrapped in the Caudine Forks.   85

312. Censorship and innovations of Appius Claudius.   89

311. War with the Etruscans; 310, expedition into the Ciminian Forest.   88

298–290. Third Samnite War; 295, battle of Sentinum. Annexation of the Sabine territory.   92

286. Sufferings of the poor. The Hortensian Law; legislative power of the plebeian assembly.   94

281–272. War with Tarentum and Pyrrhus; 280, battle of Heraclea; 279, of Asculum; 275, of Beneventum. Authority of Rome established over all Italy.   96

269. Coinage of silver; rapid rise of prices and depreciation of the currency.   102

PERIOD IV. — FOREIGN CONQUEST.

264–241. First Punic War: 260, battle of Mylæ; 256, invasion of Africa by Regulus; 249, defeat of Publius Claudius; 241, battle of the Ægates.   106

241. Peace made: conquest of Sicily; 237, of Sardinia and Corsica; 222, of Cisalpine Gaul. Establishment of provincial system.   109

218–201. Second Punic War: Hannibal passes into Italy; battle of the Trebia; 217, of Lake Trasimenus; 216, of Cannæ; surrender of Capua to Hannibal. 215, First Macedonian War. 212, surrender of Syracuse to Rome; 211, of Capua; 209, of Tarentum; 207, battle of the Metaurus; 202, of Zama; military reforms of Scipio.   116, 123

201. Peace made: acquisition of Spain.   127

200–196. Second Macedonian War: 197, battle of Cynoscephalæ; liberation of Greece.   132

192–190. War with Antiochus the Great: 191, battle of Thermopylæ; 190, battle of Magnesia; acquisitions of territory by Pergamus and Rhodes.   134

172–168. Third Macedonian War: 168, battle of Pydna; Macedonia divided.   136

167. Illyricum made a province.   136

149–146. Third Punic War: 146, capture and destruction of Carthage. Province of Africa.   143

146. Capture and destruction of Corinth. Province of Macedonia. Supremacy of Rome in the Mediterranean.   142

133. Annexation of Pergamus; province of Asia.   146

PERIOD V.—CIVIL DISSENSIONS.

B.C.

146–139. War of Viriathus in Spain; 143–133, siege of Numantia.   154

133. Legislation and death of Tiberius Gracchus. Creation of peasant freeholds.   154

123–121. Legislation and death of Gaius Gracchus; the Equestrian Order, an aristocracy of wealth, made the rival of the Senate; colony of Narbo.   162

120. Province of Transalpine Gaul.   164

112–106. War with Jugurtha.   167

105–101. War with Teutones and Cimbri: 102, the Teutones defeated by Marius at Aquæ Sextiæ; 101, the Cimbri at Campi Raudii. Military reforms of Marius.   168

100. Attempt at revolution by Saturninus and Glaucia.   171

95. Affront given to the Italian allies; 91, reforms and death of Drusus; the Varian Commission, to punish his adherents.   173

90–89. Social War: admission of the Italians to citizenship; extension of the municipal system over Italy.   174

88. First Mithradatic War conducted by Sulla; 83, Second Mithradatic War.   176

88. Civil War: banishment of Marius; 87, return of Marius; rule of Marius, Cinna, and Carbo.   177

83. Return of Sulla; aristocratic remodelling of the Roman constitution.   179

78. Death of Sulla; 78, attempt of Lepidus to undo his work.   185

74. Third Mithradatic War: victories of Lucullus.   195

73. Revolt of Spartacus; 71, suppressed by Crassus.   193

72. War with Sertorius finished by Pompey.   193

70. Consulship of Pompey and Crassus; democratic legislation.   194

67. Pompey appointed against the pirates; 66, against Mithradates; 65, end of the war; 64, expedition to Syria; its conquest.   195

63. Cicero's consulship; conspiracy of Catiline suppressed.   198

60. First triumvirate; coalition of Pompey, Crassus, and Cæsar; 59, Cæsar's consulship; banishment of Cicero; 57, his return.   200

58–49. Cæsar's proconsulship in Gaul; 56, conference of Luca; 55, Cæsar's visit to Britain; second consulship of Pompey and Crassus.   201

54. Crassus in the East: 53, battle of Carrhæ; his defeat and death.   202

52. Revolt of Vercingetorix in Gaul; anarchy in Rome.   208

49. Civil war of Cæsar and Pompey: 48, battle of Pharsalus; death of Pompey; 46, battle of Thapsus; overthrow of Republic; 45, battle of Munda; defeat of sons of Pompey.   213

B.C.		PAGE
49.	Cæsar's first dictatorship; 47, second dictatorship; 46, third dictatorship, for ten years; 45, Imperator; 44, perpetual dictator.	214
44.	Cæsar's assassination; civil war between the Senate and Mark Antony.	221
43.	Second triumvirate; Antony, Lepidus, and Octavian; 38, renewed; 36, Lepidus set aside; 35, death of Sextus Pompey.	227
42.	Battle of Philippi; defeat and death of Brutus and Cassius.	228
31.	Battle of Actium; Antony and Cleopatra defeated by Octavian.	229

PERIOD VI. — THE EARLY EMPIRE.

The Julian and Claudian Houses.

B.C.		
27.	Establishment of Empire; Octavian takes the name Augustus. The Golden Age of Literature.	231
15.	Conquest of Rætia and Noricum; 10, of Pannonia; of Germany to the Elbe.	235

A.D.		
9.	Defeat of Varus; the Danube and Rhine frontier.	236
14.	Tiberius Emperor: rule of Sejanus.	245
37.	Caligula.	249
41.	Claudius: conquest of Britain.	250
54.	Nero: rule of Tigellinus; 64, fire in Rome; first persecution of the Christians.	251

The Flavian House.

68–69.	Galba, Otho, Vitellius.	255
69.	Vespasian: siege and destruction of Jerusalem by Titus.	255
79.	Titus: destruction of Pompeii and Herculaneum.	258
81.	Domitian: conquest of Britain completed.	259

The Five Good Emperors.

96.	Nerva.	261
98.	Trajan: conquest of Dacia, Arabia Petræa, Assyria, etc.; the Silver Age of Literature.	261
117.	Hadrian.	268
138.	Antoninus Pius.	269
161.	Marcus Aurelius: conquests in the East; great pestilence (166); persecution of the Christians; Marcomanic War.	269
180.	Commodus.	273

CHRONOLOGICAL SYNOPSIS.

PERIOD VII.—CENTURY OF TRANSITION.

A.D.		PAGE
193.	Pertinax. Didius Julianus.	276
193.	Septimius Severus: establishment of military monarchy; dissolution of the Prætorian Guards.	276, 280
211.	Caracalla [and Geta, d. 212]: citizenship granted to the provincials; war with the Alamanni.	277, 281
217.	Macrinus; 218, Elagabalus.	278
222.	Alexander Severus: 226, the Sassanian or New Persian Empire; murdered, 235.	279, 289
240.	First appearance of the Franks.	285
250.	Persecution of the Christians by Decius.	288
251.	Decius killed in battle with the Goths.	288
260.	Valerian captured by the Persians.	291
269.	The Goths defeated by Claudius.	288
270.	Aurelian: Dacia given up to the Goths; 273, capture and destruction of Palmyra.	292

PERIOD VIII.—THE LATER EMPIRE.

284.	Diocletian: reorganization of the Empire; absolute monarchy; bureaucratic government; new provincial system; tenth persecution of the Christians; 305, abdicated.	296
306.	Constantine the Great; 323, sole Emperor; adoption of Christianity; 325, Council of Nicæa; 328, founding of new capital (Constantinople); 337, death.	302
357.	The Alamannians defeated by Julian at Strassburg.	312
360.	Julian; apostatizes from Christianity; expedition into the East; 363, death.	312
364.	Valentinian I. and Valens.	314
376.	Crossing of the Danube by the Visigoths; 378, battle of Adrianople; death of Valens; the Goths brought to submission by Theodosius.	318
375.	Gratian, Emperor of the West; 376, edict against heresy.	314
378.	Theodosius the Great, Emperor of the East; 391, edict suppressing paganism; 392, unites the Empire.	319
395.	Death of Theodosius; division of the Empire.	321
395.	Honorius, Emperor of the West; Arcadius, Emperor of the East; Alaric, king of the Visigoths; 402, first invasion of Italy by Alaric, defeated by Stilicho; 404, invasion of Rhadagais; 406, migration of the Vandals into Gaul; 408, death of Stilicho, second invasion of Italy by Alaric; 409, the Vandals pass into Spain; 410, third invasion, sack of Rome; the Visigoths, under Ataulf, pass into	321

A.D.		PAGE
	Gaul; 413, the Burgundians established at Worms; 419, the Visigoths at Toulouse.	
429.	The Vandals take possession of Africa.	329
443.	The Burgundians transferred to Savoy.	332
449.	Beginning of the Angle and Saxon conquest of Britain.	335
451.	Invasion of Gaul by Attila, king of the Huns; defeated at *Méry-sur-Seine* by Aetius; 453, death of Attila, and dissolution of his empire.	332
455.	Occupation and plunder of Rome by Geiseric, king of the Vandals; Vandal empire in the Western Mediterranean.	337
476.	The Empire overthrown in Italy by Odovacar the Herulian; 480–4, in Spain by Euric, king of the Visigoths; 486, in Gaul by Clovis, king of the Franks.	339

FORMATION OF THE ROMAN EMPIRE.

B.C.		
486.	The Triple Alliance; hegemony in Latium.	44
396.	Conquest of Veii, followed by that of other cities.	68
338.	Dominion of Rome in Latium.	80
275.	Dominion of Rome in all Italy.	84
241–37.	First two provinces: Sicily; Sardinia and Corsica.	109, 110
222.	Conquest of northern Italy.[1]	122
201.	Provinces of Hither and Further Spain.	127
167.	Province of Illyricum.	136
146.	Provinces of Africa and Macedonia.	142, 145
133.	Asia; 120, Transalpine Gaul.	146, 164
89.	Citizenship extended to the Italian peninsula.	175
74.	Bithynia; 74, Cyrene; 67, Crete; 64, Cilicia and Cyprus.	196
64.	Province of Syria.	196
52.	Conquest of Gaul completed.	209
49.	Citizenship extended to northern Italy.	214
46.	Numidia conquered, and annexed to Africa.	218
31.	Conquest of Egypt.	229
29.	The Danube frontier: Mœsia; 15, Rætia and Noricum; 10, Pannonia.	234
29.	Galatia; Pamphylia.	
A.D.		
17.	Cappadocia; 40, Mauretania; 43, Britain; 46, Thrace.	251
105.	Conquests of Trajan: Arabia Petræa; 106, Dacia; 114, Armenia; 117, Mesopotamia. Assyria.	261

[1] Probably not organized as a province until 82.

DISRUPTION OF THE EMPIRE.

A.D.		PAGE
117.	Hadrian surrenders the provinces of Armenia, Assyria, and Mesopotamia.	268
270.	Dacia occupied by the Goths.	293
282.	The *Agri Decumates* occupied by the Alamannians.	317
—	Northern Gaul (*Belgium*) occupied by the Franks.	317
419.	Aquitania occupied by the Visigoths; capital, Toulouse.	328
429.	Africa occupied by the Vandals; capital, Carthage.	330
443.	Savoy occupied by the Burgundians; Lyons afterwards made their capital.	332
—	The Visigoths and Burgundians by degrees occupy all southern Gaul; the Alamannians, eastern Gaul (*Alsace and Lorraine*).	332
476.	The authority of the Empire overthrown in Italy by Odovacar; 480-4, by Euric in Spain; 486, by Clovis in Gaul.	341

INDEX OF PROPER NAMES.

ABBREVIATIONS: A., Aulus; App., Appius; C., Gaius; Cn., Gnæus; D., Decimus; K., Kæso; L., Lucius; M., Marcus; M'., Manius; P., Publius; Q., Quintus; Ser., Servius; Sex., Sextus; Sp., Spurius; T., Titus; Ti., Tiberius.

Achæ'an League: 132; receives territory, 134; ally of Rome, 134.
Achai'a: made province, 143.
Ac'tium: battle, B.C. 31, 229.
A-dri-an-o'ple: battle, 319.
Adriatic Sea: 3, 324.
Æ'du-i: Gallic tribe, 206; join Vercingetorix, 208.
Æga'tes, Id.: battle, B.C. 241, 109.
Æge'an: 291.
Ægid'ius, Count: 339.
Æ'lia Capitoli'na (*Jerusalem*): 258.
Æ'lius Seja'nus, L.: prætorian præfect, 248.
Ælius Sti'lo, L.: philologist, 191.
Æmil'ian: Emperor, 288.
Æmil'ius Lep'idus, M.: civil war, 185.
Æmilius Lepidus, M.: master of horse, 222; triumvir, 227; set aside, 228.
Æmilius Pau'lus, L.: killed at Cannæ, 120.
Æmilius Paulus, L., his son: commands at Pydna, 136; his son Scipio, 144.
Æne'as: 18.
Æ'qui: 11; wars, 43, 53, 56, 73.
Æscula'pius: 24; worship introduced, 95.
Æ'tius: relations to Valentinian III., 329; in Gaul, 330 ff.; defeats Attila, 333, 334; death, 335; work, 336.
Æto'lian League: 132; receives territory, 134; ally of Antiochus, 134.
Africa: Roman province, 145; held by Senate, 214, 217; Boniface governor, 329; Vandals, 329.

Agric'ola: see Julius.
Agrigen'tum: captured by Romans, 106.
Agrip'pa: see Vipsanius.
Agrippa Pos'tumus: 233.
Ag-rip-pi'na: wife of Germanicus: 243; ruin, 247.
Agrippina, her daughter: 250; death, 252.
Ah'riman (or Ahriman'): 289.
Alaman'ni: 285; cross Alps, 293; contest with Julian, 311, 312; settle in empire, 317; along Rhine, 332; against Attila, 333; in Gaul, 339.
Alans: 324, 325.
Al'aric: king of Visigoths, 323; in Greece, 323; in Italy, 323; second invasion, 325; captures Rome, 326; sacks Rome, 326; death, 326.
Alba Longa: 10; conquered, 17.
Alban Mount: 10; occupied by Rome, 29.
Ale'sia: city of Gaul, 208.
Alexander: 2; division of empire, 97, 131.
Alexander Seve'rus: Emperor, 279, 287; Syncretism, 284.
Alexan'dria, 2, 307.
Al'gidus, Mt.: important pass, 53, 56; victory of Postumius, 65.
Al'lia, R.: battle, B.C. 390, 70.
Alps: crossed by Hannibal, 116; crossed by Goths, 293.
Alps: Julian, important pass, 1, 3; passage of Visigoths and Ostrogoths, 324; passage of Attila, 334.
Alps: Maritime, 3.
Alsace: 312.
Ambarva'lia: 26.

INDEX OF PROPER NAMES.

Ambrose: bishop of Milan, 314; relations to Theodosius, 321; Augustine converted by, 328.

An'cus Mar'tius: king of Rome, 15; conquests, 17.

Andalu'sia: 325.

Androni'cus: see Livius.

Anglo-Saxons: in Britain, 335.

A'nio, R.: 17.

Anio Ve'tus; Aqueduct: 94.

An'nius Mi'lo, T.: 210.

Anthe'mius: Emperor, 337.

Antiochi'a: 2.

Anti'ochus III., king of Asia: 128; "the Great," 131; war with Rome, 134; cedes territory, 135.

An'tium: Volscian town, 53; Roman colony, 82.

Antoni'nus: see Caracalla, Elagabalus.

Antoninus Pius: Emperor, 269.

Anto'nius, M. (*Mark Antony*): tribune, 213; consul, 219-223; power, 224; relations to Octavian, 226; triumvirate, 227; joined with Cleopatra, 228; defeated at Actium, 229; death, 229.

Antonia, his daughter: 252.

Anxur: see Terracina.

Apennines, Mts.: 3.

Apollo: 24, 96, 190.

Ap'pian Way: built, 90; to Capua, 161; death of Clodius, 210.

Appulei'us Sat-ur-ni'nus, L.: attempt at revolution, 171.

Apu'lia: 4; pasture-lands, 9; Hannibal, 125.

A'quæ Sex'ti-æ: battle, B.C. 102, 169.

Aq-ui-lei'a: 2; attacked by Marcomani, 273; destroyed by Attila, 334.

A-quil'lius, M'.: governor of Asia, 177.

Aq-ui-ta'ni-a: 209.

Arabia Petræ'a: conquered, 262.

Arabian desert: 292.

Aran'sio (*Orange*): victory of Cimbri, 169.

Ar'ar, R. (*Saone*): route into Gaul, 205.

Arca'dius: Emperor of East, 321.

Archime'des: death, 124.

Ardashir': 289.

Ar'dea: Latin town, 18; colony, 65; exile of Camillus, 74.

Arela'te (*Arles*): 339.

A'res (*Mars*): 23, 190.

A'rian: controversy, 306, 307.

Aric'ia: Latin town, 18; chief of confederacy, 45; annexed to Rome, 80.

Arim'inum: Latin colony, 112; in Second Punic War, 119.

Ar-i-o-vis'tus: German king, 206.

A'rius: 307, 308.

Arme'nia: allied with Pontus, 176.

Armin'ius: German warrior, 236.

Armor'icans: 339.

Arnus, R. (*Arno*): 4; in Second Punic War, 119.

Arpi'num: birthplace of Cicero, 197.

Arre'tium: Etruscan town, 6; occupied by Flaminius, 119.

Arsac'idæ: 289.

Artaxerx'es: 289, 291.

Arver'ni: Gallic tribe, 208.

Ar'yan race: 4.

As'culum: battle, B.C. 279, 98.

Asia Minor: 2; war with Antiochus, 134, 135; war with Mithradates, 176-178; in power of Zenobia, 294.

Asin'ius Pol'lio, C.: orator, 242.

Astar'te: Phœnician goddess, 105.

Asty'ages: 289.

At'aulf: king of Goths, 326, 327; death, 327.

Ath-a-na'si-an: controversy, 306-308.

Athanasius: 307, 328.

Athe'na (*Minerva*): 190.

Athens: empire, 45; laws, 58.

Atil'ius Reg'ulus, M.: commander, 107, 108.

At'talus I.: king of Pergamus, 132.

Attalus II.: king of Pergamus; bequeaths his dominions to Rome, 146; his treasures, 157.

At'tila: king of the Huns, 332; invasion of Gaul, 333; Chalons, 333; invasion of Italy, 334; death, 334.

INDEX OF PROPER NAMES.

Au'fidus, R.: 4; in Second Punic War, 120.

Au'gustine: bishop of Hippo, 328.

Augus'tus: makes Achaia a province, 143; renews colony of Carthage, 145; tribunician power, 163; divorce, 189; returns to Rome, 226; triumvirate, 227-230; Emperor, 232; establishes Danube frontier, 235; death, 237; Age of Augustus, 238-242.

Aure'lian: Emperor, 288; reign, 292; campaign against Zenobia, 294; subjugates Gaul, 295; mentioned, 297; reforms in currency, 303.

Aure'lius, M.: Emperor, 269-274; persecution of Christians, 271; Marcomanic War, 273; statue, 280.

Av'entine, Mt.: enclosed, 31; temple of Diana, 34; assigned to plebeians, 57; secession, 59; temple of Juno, 68.

Avid'ius Cas'sius: general, 270.

Avi'tus: Emperor, 337.

Bacchus: 24; secret rites, 140.

Bagau'dæ: 295.

Bal-e-ar'ic Isles: taken by Geiseric, 338.

Baltic: Visigoths on, 318.

Barca: see Hamilcar.

Barcelo'na: 327.

Bel'gica: 209.

Bello'na: 23.

Ben-e-ven'tum: battle, B.C. 275, 98.

Bethlehem: 328.

Bi-thyn'i-a: independent, 132; ally of Rome, 134; bequeathed to Rome, 196; governed by Pliny, 265.

Black Sea: 1, 176, 291, 309, 318.

Blandi'na: martyr, 272.

Bocchus: king of Mauritania; aids Rome, 168.

Bola: captured by Rome, 67.

Bon'iface: governor of Africa, 329; invites the Vandals, 330; death, 330.

Bos'porus: 309.

Britain: 4; visited by Cæsar, 207; conquered, 251; part of rival empire, 292; commanded by Constantius, 298; ruled by the usurper, Constantine, 324; withdrawal of Roman troops, 335; Anglo-Saxons in, 335.

Britan'nicus: son of Claudius, 251, 252.

Brittany: 339.

Brutus: see Junius.

Burgundians: at Worms, 332; in Gaul, 332; against Attila, 333; dominions, 339.

Burrhus: prætorian præfect, 252.

Busen'to, R.: 326.

Byzan'tium: site of capital, 309.

Cæcil'ius Metel'lus, Q. (Numidicus): war with Jugurtha, 167; refuses oath, 172.

Cæcilius Metellus, Q. (Pius): commander in Social War, 174; joins Sulla, 180; commands against Sertorius, 193.

Cæcilius Metellus, Q. (Scipio): consul, 211; defeated at Thapsus, 217.

Cæcilius: dramatist, 114.

Cæ're: Etruscan town, 6; tomb of the Tarquins, 36; conquered by Rome, 78.

Cæsar: see Julius.

Cæsars: Twelve, 260.

Cala'bria: 5.

Calig'ula: see Gaius.

Callim'achus: Greek poet, 241.

Calpur'nius Pi'so, Cn.: quarrel with Germanicus, 247.

Camil'lus: see Furius.

Campa'nia: 4; Etruscans, in, 5.

Can'næ: battle, 121, 122; order of troops, 126.

Canu'sium: town near Cannæ, 122.

Cape'na: captured by Rome, 68.

Capit'oline Mount: 34; seized by Herdonius, 56; besieged by Gauls, 71; faced with stone, 73.

Capitoline Triad: 7, 23.

Cappado'cia: independent, 132.

Ca'pre-æ (*Capri*): residence of Tiberius, 248.

Cap'ua: 6; conquered by Samnites, 67, 79; received Hannibal, 122;

INDEX OF PROPER NAMES.

captured, 124; gladiatorial school, 193.

Car-a-cal'la (Antoninus): Emperor, 277, 287; baths, 280; edict, 172, 281; debasement of currency, 282; defeats Alamanni, 285.

Carbo: see Papirius.

Cari'nus: Emperor, 288.

Carna: 22.

Carrhæ: battle, B.C. 53, 203.

Carthage: 2; treaty with Rome, 35, 79; war with Pyrrhus, 98; first war with Rome, 104-109; revolt of Mercenaries, 109; second war with Rome, 115-128; third war with Rome, 143-145; colony, 145; chief city of Africa, 145; refuge of Marius, 178.

Cartha'go Nova: founded by Hasdrubal, 116.

Ca'rus: see Lucretius.

Carus: Emperor, 288, 297.

Caspian Sea: 132.

Cas'sius, Spu'rius: treaty with Latium, 44; agrarian laws, 46 ff.; death, 46, 49, 74.

Cassius, Q.: tribune, 213.

Cassius Longi'nus, C.: conspirator, 221; governor of Syria, 224; death, 228.

Castor: 36, 96.

Catili'na: see Sergius.

Cato: see Porcius.

Catul'lus: see Valerius.

Catulus: see Luta'tius.

Cau'dine Forks: defeat of Romans, 87.

Cau'dium: 87.

Cenoma'ni: sided with Rome, 117.

Ce'res: 24, 96; festival, 122.

Chalons: battle, 333, 334; site, 333.

Charles the Great (*Charlemagne*): 342.

Cherus'ci: German tribe, 236.

Chil'deric: 340.

Christianity: as an organization, 306; doctrine, 306; made the only lawful religion, 315.

Christians: persecuted by Nero, 253; by Trajan, 267; by M. Aurelius, 271; organization, 282; persecuted by Diocletian, 300; tolerated by Constantine, 302, 304; relations of Julian to, 313; edict of Gratian against heretics, 314.

Cicero: see Tullius.

Cilic'ia: war with pirates, 195; made province, 196.

Cil'nius Mæce'nas, C.: 241.

Cim'bri: invasion, 168-170.

Cimin'ian Forest: passed by Fabius, 88.

Cincinna'tus: see Quinctius.

Cin'eas: embassy to Rome, 98.

Cinna: see Cornelius.

Circei'i: colony, 35, 46.

Circus Maximus: 26, 252.

Civi'lis: insurrection, 256.

Clau'dian: poet, 322.

Clau'dius: Emperor, 250-251, 288; Rhodes loses independence, 135.

Claudius, Ap'pius: migrated from Sabines, 22.

Claudius, Appius: decemvir, 59.

Claudius, Appius, Cæcus: censor, 89-91; opposes propositions of Cineas, 98.

Claudius, Appius, his son: advises to receive Mamertines, 106.

Claudius Goth'icus: Emperor, 288, 292, 297.

Claudius Pub'lius: loses naval battle, 108, 190.

Claudius Marcel'lus, M.: commander in Second Punic War, 123-124.

Claudius Marcellus, M., son of Octavia: 233.

Claudius Nero, C.: gains victory at the Metaurus, 125; quarrel with Livius, 128.

Claudius Nero, Ti., husband of Livia: 233.

Clement: Christian father, 282.

Cleon: 112.

Cleopa'tra: Queen of Egypt, 216, visits Cæsar, 220; joins Antony, 228; death, 229.

Clo-a'ca Max'ima: 30.

Clo'dius, P.: 112; enemy of Cicero, 201; death, 210.

Clodius Albi'nus: 277.

Clo'vis: ascendency over Salian

INDEX OF PROPER NAMES.

Franks, 340; defeats Syagrius, 340.
Clu′sium: Etruscan town, 6; war with Rome, 35; attacked by Gauls, 70.
Cœ′lian Hill: 17.
Colli′na (tribe): 33.
Col′line Gate: (battle) 180.
Col-os-se′um: 258.
Colum′na Mænia′na: 83.
Comit′ium: 17, 83; narrowed, 239.
Com′modus: Emperor, 273.
Concor′dia, temple: renewed, 165.
Constans: 311.
Con′stantine: Emperor, 301; puts Maximian to death, 302; administration, 302–310; death, 311.
Constantine, son of Constantine the Great: 311.
Constantine the Usurper: 324; overthrown, 327.
Constantinople: site 309.
Constan′tius, Chlorus: 298, 300, 301, 304.
Constantius II.: 311.
Constantius: 327.
Consua′lia: feast of Consus, 26.
Cora: independent, 80.
Corcy′ra: alliance with Rome, 112.
Corfin′ium: capital of Italy, 174.
Corin′thus: congress, 133; destroyed, 142.
Co-ri-o-la′nus: legend, 56.
Corne′lia: marries Gracchus, 154; 221.
Corne′lius Scip′io Barba′tus, L.: sarcophagus, 103.
Cornelius Scipio, P.: consul, 116; in Italy, 117; in Spain, 119; death, 124.
Cornelius Scipio, Cn., his brother: 116; in Spain, 119; death, 124.
Cornelius Scipio, P. (Africa′nus), his brother: in Spain, 124–125; wins battle of Zama, 126–127; policy, 139; exile and death, 140; Greek culture, 140.
Cornelius Scipio, P. (Nasi′ca): the best Roman, 129.
Cornelius Scipio, L. (Asiat′icus): conducts war with Antiochus, 134; accused, 140.

Cornelius Scipio, P. (Africanus Æmilia′nus): commands in Third Punic War, 144–145; death, 158.
Cornelius Scipio, P. (Nasica Sera′pio): murderer of Gracchus, 157.
Cornelius Sulla, L.: captures Jugurtha, 168; commands in Social War, 174; against Mithradates, 177–178; Civil War, 179–181; legislation, 181–185; spares Cæsar, 200.
Cornelius Cinna, L.: rule in Rome, 179.
Cor′sica, Id.: 3; occupied by Etruscans, 6; trade with Rome, 79; seized by Rome, 110; Geiseric defeated, 338; taken by Geiseric, 338.
Corvus: see Valerius.
Cremo′na: Latin Colony, 112.
Crete: 348.
Crispus: death, 308.
Crispus: see Sallustius.
Ctes′iphon: Parthian capital, 270.
Cu′rio: see Scribonius.
Cu′rius Denta′tus, M.: controversy with Ap. Claudius, 91; finishes the war, 93; conquers Sabines, 93; character, 93; defeats Pyrrhus, 98; compared with Cato, 139, 150.
Cursor: see Papirius.
Cyb′ele: worship introduced in Rome, 129.
Cyn-os-ceph′a-læ: battle, B.C. 197, 132, 136.
Cyprus, Id.: conquered, 196.
Cyrus, the Persian: 289.

Da′cia: conquered, 261; troubled by Goths, 284; occupied by Goths, 293; by Gepidæ, 335.
Dalma′tia: 301.
Dalmatians: triumph, 229.
Dalma′tius: 311.
Dam-a-sip′pus: see Junius.
Danube, R.: territory conquered by Augustus, 234; Aurelian withdraws garrisons to south of, 293; Galerius commands on, 298; crossed by Visigoths, 319; site of Vandals, 324.

INDEX OF PROPER NAMES.

Dari'us: 289.
Decem'virs: 27.
De'cius Mus, P.: commander, 86; devotion, 92.
Decius: Emperor, 288.
De'los: confederacy, 45; gains commerce, 142.
Denta'tus: see Curius Sicinius.
Dia'na (or Dian'a): 24; temple on Aventine, 34.
Did'ius Julia'nus: Emperor, 276.
Diocle'tian: Emperor, 288; suppresses the Bagaudæ, 295; reforms, 296–301; abdication, 301; reforms in currency, 303; murder of widow of, 304.
Diodo'rus: 35.
Domitia'nus: Emperor, 259.
Drep'ana: attacked, 108.
Drusus: see Livius.
Drusus, son of Livia: 233; death, 235.
Drusus: son of Tiberius, 243; death, 248.
Duil'ius, C.: gains battle of Mylæ, 107.
Dyrra'chium: attacked by Cæsar, 215.

East Goths: see Ostrogoths.
Eb-o-ra'cum (York): 277.
Egypt: 2; ruled by the Ptolemies, 131; annexed to Rome, 229; taken by Zenobia, 294.
El-a-ga-ba'lus (or El-a-gab'a-lus): Emperor, 278; debasement of currency, 282; religion, 283.
El-eu-sin'i-an Triad: 96.
Em'esa: a city of Syria, 278.
En'nius, Q.: poet, 113.
Eph'esus: city in Asia, 146.
Ep-i-cu'rus: philosophy, 191.
Ep-i-dau'rus: worship of Æsculapius, 96.
Erc'te, Mt.: 108.
Erman'arich: 318.
Er'yx, Mt.: 108.
Esquili'na (tribe): 33.
Es'quiline Hill: 11.
Etru'ria (Etruscany): 5 ff.; dynasty of kings, 29 ff.; war with Rome, 35; influence, 36; loss of power, 67; war with Rome, 73, 88, 92; invaded by Hannibal, 119; Catiline's army, 199.
Eudox'ia, wife of Valentinian III.: 337; calls Geisericd to Rome, 337.
Eu'menes II.: King of Pergamus; ally of Rome, 134.
Euphra'tes, R.: 1; boundary of Parthian empire, 135, 268; crossed by Julian, 313.
Euric: King of Visigoths; extends boundaries of his empire, 339.

Fa'bian gens: war with Veii, 22, 51.
Fa'bius, K.: performs sacrifice, 71.
Fabius Maximus, Q.: commander, 86–88; conservatism, 90; commands at Sentinum, 92.
Fabius Max'imus, Q.: dictator, 120; conducts war, 123, 125.
Fabius Pictor, Q.: historian, 113.
Fa-bric'ius, C.: statesman, 94; censor, 101.
Fæs'ulæ (*Fiesole*): 6; camp of Manlius, 199.
Fausta, wife of Constantine: 308.
Fel'sina (Bologna): 6.
Fe-ti-a'les: 26.
Fi-de'næ: ˙Etruscan town, 17, 29; captured by Rome, 67.
Flaccus: see Fulvius, Valerius.
Flaminian Way: built, 112; to Ariminum, 161.
Flam-i-ni'nus: see Quinctius.
Flamin'ius, C.: divides Gallic land, 112; killed at Trasimenus, 119.
Fla'vius, Cn.: divulges legal forms, 91.
Flora: 23.
Florence: 292, 324.
Florian: Emperor, 288.
Fora of the Cæsars: 238.
For'mi-æ: annexed to Rome, 82.
Forum: 17; drained, 30; adorned, 83; basilica, 141; new edifices, 238.
Forum Bo-a'ri-um: 83.
Forum Holito'rium: 83.
Franks: 285, 291; confederacy, 311; settle in empire, 317; along Rhine,

INDEX OF PROPER NAMES. 357

332; relations to Attila, 332, 333; conquests, 339; rise under Clovis, 340.
Fra'tres Arva'les: 26.
Fregel'læ, Latin colony: revolt, 149.
Fronti'nus: author, 265.
Fuci'nus Lacus: drained, 251.
Ful'vius Flac'cus, M.: death, 165.
Fundi: annexed to Rome, 82.
Fu'rius Camil'lus, M.: capture of Veii, 68; military reforms, 68–70; commander in war, 73; character, 73; temple of Concord, 75.

Ga'bi-i: Latin town, 17; annexed to Rome, 34.
Ga'des: Phœnician colony, 104, 115.
Gai'us Cæsar, son of Julia: 233.
Gaius (Calig'ula): Emperor, 249.
Gala'tia: independent, 132.
Galba: Emperor, 255.
Gale'rius: Emperor, 298, 300, 301, 302, 304.
Gal-li-e'nus: Emperor, 288; reign, 291; relations to Odenatus, 292; character of reign, 297.
Gallus: Emperor, 288.
Gaul, Cisalpine: 4; governed by Cæsar, 201; receives citizenship, 214.
Gaul, Transalpine: province, 164; invaded by Cimbri, 169; governed by Cæsar, 201; conquered, 205–209; invaded by Franks, 291; part of rival empire, 292; subjugation by Aurelian, 295; commanded by Constantius, 298; invaded by Vandals, 324; ruled by Constantine the Usurper, 324; Aetius in, 330; Visigoths in southwest of, 330; Burgundians in, 332; Attila in, 333; under Syagrius, 339.
Gauls: 8; conquests in Italy, 67; capture of Rome, 70–72; wars with Rome, 78, 92; conquered by Rome, 111, 136.
Gei'seric: King of the Vandals, 326; character, 330; encourages Attila, 333; takes Rome, 337; power 338; defeated at Corsica, 338; becomes master of Western Mediterranean, 338.
Genghis Khan: 332, 334.
Gep'idæ: 332; in Dacia, 335.
German'icus: wars in Germany, 236, 246; adopted by Tiberius, 243; death, 247.
Germans: invasions, 168, 273, 291–293; Arians in religion, 307; invasions, 311, 312; within the empire, 317; characteristics, 317; invasions, 323–325; massacre, 325.
Germany: visited by Cæsar, 208.
Ge'ta: Emperor, 277, 287.
Glau'cia: see Servilius.
Golden Horn: 309.
Gor'dian: Emperor, 287, 288.
Goths: on Black Sea, 284; into Ægean, 291; occupy Dacia, 293; in the empire as colonists, 317; Gothic empire, 318; settlement under Theodosius, 320.
Grac'chus: see Sempronius.
Gra'tian: Emperor, 314–315; 319.
Greece: influence, 36; part of Constantine's dominions, 302.

Ha'drian: Emperor; destruction of Jerusalem, 258; reign, 268–269.
Hamil'car Bar'ca: commands in Sicily, 108; conquest of Spain, 115.
Han'nibal: Second Punic War, 115–128; death, 135; destruction of Italy, 151.
Hannibalia'nus: 311.
Has'drubal, son-in-law of Hamilcar: 116.
Hasdrubal, brother of Hannibal: leaves Spain, 124; defeated at Metaurus, 125.
Ha'tria: Latin colony, 93.
Hel'ena, mother of Constantine: 304.
Helve'ti-i: Gallic tribe, 206.
Her-a-cle'a: battle, B.C. 280, 97.
Hercula'neum: destruction, 258.
Her'cules: worship. 90.
Herdo'nius, Appius: seizure of capitol, 55.
Her'mes (Mercury): 190.

Hermodo′rus : 58.
Her′nicans : 11; alliance with Rome, 44; cut off from Rome, 53; confederacy dissolved, 85.
Hi′ero : King of Syracuse, 106; death, 123.
Hir′tius, A. : consul, 227.
Hono′rius : Emperor of West, 321, 322; reign, 323–325.
Horace : see Horatius.
Hora′tius, M. : consul, B.C. 449, 59.
Horatius Flac′cus, Q. : poet, 240.
Horten′sius, Q. : dictator, 94.
Hostil′ian : Emperor, 288.
Huns : invasions, 318–319; under Attila, 332–335; battle of Chalons, A.D. 451, 334.

I-be′rians : 5; subjects of Carthage, 104; in southwestern Gaul, 205.
Igna′tius : martyrdom, 268.
Illyr′icum : wars with Rome, 112; made a province, 136; governed by Cæsar, 201.
I-re-næ′us of Lyons: 282.
I′sis : 24.
Is′lam : 290.
I-ta′lia : city, 174.
I-u′lus : 18.

Jac′querie : 219.
Janic′ulum, Mt. : 12; enclosed, 31; secession to, 94.
Ja′nus : 24, 190; temple closed, 229.
Japyg′ians : 5.
Jerome, St. : 328.
Jerusalem : entered by Pompey, 196; captured by Titus, 257.
John, the Apostle, 272.
Jo′vian : Emperor, 314.
Juba : King of Mauretania, 213.
Judæ′a : part of Syria, 255; revolt, 256, 328.
Jugur′tha : King of Numidia; war, 167–168.
Julia, daughter of Julius Cæsar: 202.
Julia, daughter of Augustus: 189; married Agrippa, 233.
Julia Domna, wife of Septimius Severus : 283.

Julia Lœ′mias, mother of Elagabalus : 278, 283.
Julia Mæsa, her sister: 283.
Julia Mammæ, mother of Alexander Severus : 278, 283.
Julian, the Apostate : 311–314; death, 314.
Julius Cæsar, L. : commander in Social War, 174.
Julius Cæsar, C. : statesmanship, 185; divorce, 189; writings, 191, 204; associated with Catiline, 199; forms triumvirate, 200 ; conquers Gaul, 205–209; visits Britain, 207; breach with Pompey, 207 ; Civil War, 213; dictator, 214; war in Greece, 215; in the East, 216; suppresses mutiny, 217 ; war in Africa, 217; legislation, 218; battle of Munda, 219; ambition, 220; conspiracy for his death, 221–223; character, 224.
Julius Agric′ola, Cn. : conquest of Britain, 251.
Julius Ne′pos : Emperor, 337.
Junius Brutus, D. : conspirator, 221; governor of Cisalpine Gaul, 224; besieged, 227.
Junius Brutus, L. : 221.
Junius Brutus, M. : conspirator, 221; governor of Macedonia, 224; death, 228.
Junius Damasip′pus, L. : massacre, 180.
Juno : 23; temple in Veii, 68; Mone′ta, temple: 102.
Juno′nia (Carthage) : 145, 164.
Jupiter : 23.
Justin Martyr : 272.
Juvena′lis : satirist, 265.

Labi′cum : conquered by Rome, 67.
Lanu′vium : annexed by Rome, 80.
Latin Way : 4, 53.
La′tium : 4, 10 ; Tarquinian empire; 29, 34 ; alliance with Rome, 44; war, 80; confederacy dissolved, 80; name extended, 81.
Lauren′tum : Latin town, 18 ; independent, 80.
Leo I. : Emperor, 337.

INDEX OF PROPER NAMES.

Leo the Great: embassy to Attila, 335; intercedes with Vandals, 338.
Lep'idus: see Æmilius.
Li'ber: 96.
Lib'era: 96.
Lib'yans: subjects of Carthage, 104.
Li-cin'i-us: Emperor, 302; bloodshed, 304.
Licinius Crassus, L.: orator, 173.
Licinius Crassus, M.: joins Sulla, 180; buys confiscated property, 181; commands against Spartacus, 194; consul, 194; forms triumvirate, 200; war in the East, 202–203.
Licinius, Lucul'lus, L.: commands against Mithradates, 195.
Licinius, Mure'na, L.: Second Mithradatic War, 178.
Licinius Stolo, C.: laws, 74–76; punishment, 76.
Ligu'rians: 5; conquered, 136.
Lil-y-bæ'um: besieged, 108.
Li'ris, R.: 4.
Li-ter'num: death of Scipio, 140.
Liv'ia: marries Augustus, 233.
Livia, wife of Drusus: 248.
Livius Androni'cus: poet, 113.
Livius Drusus, M.: opposes C. Gracchus, 165.
Livius Drusus, M.: reforms, 173.
Livius, M.: pontiff, 92.
Livius, M.: gains victory at the Metaurus, 125; quarrels with Nero, 128.
Livius Patavi'nus, T.: historian, 241.
Loire, R.: northern boundary of Euric's empire, 339.
Longi'nus: see Cassius.
Longinus: philosopher, 294.
Longus: see Sempronius.
Loren'zo de Med'ici: 292.
Lorraine: 312.
Luca: conference, 201.
Luca'nia: 9; allied with Rome, 92.
Luca'nus: poet, 252, 254.
Lu'ceres (tribe): 17.
Lucius Cæsar, son of Julia: 233.
Lucre'tius Ca'rus, T.: poet, 191, 203.
Lugdunen'sis: 209.
Lugdu'num (*Lyons*): 209; persecution, 272; capital of Burgundians, 339, 340.
Luper'ci: 26.
Lusita'nia: occupied by Vandals, 325.
Luta'tius Cat'ulus, C.: victory at Ægates, 109.
Lutatius Catulus, Q.: victory at Raudian Fields, 169.
Lutatius Catulus, Q., his son: civil war, 185.
Lutit'ia Parisio'rum (*Paris*): 312.
Lyb'ius Seve'rus: Emperor, 337.
Lycia: independent, 229.
Lyons: see Lugdunum.
Ly-sim'achus: king of Thrace, 97.

Mac'cabees: independence of Jews, 136.
Macedo'nia: first war with Rome, 123; second, 132; third, 136; divided, 137; province, 142; part of Constantine's dominion, 302.
Macri'nus: Emperor, 277, 287.
Ma'cro: prætorian præfect, 248.
Mæan'der, R.: 135.
Mæce'nas: see Cilnius.
Mæcia (tribe): 129.
Mæ'lius, Sp.: treason, 74.
Mæ'nius, C.: adornment of Forum, 83.
Magna Græcia: 9.
Magne'sia: battle, B.C. 190, 134, 136.
Ma'go: work on agriculture, 141.
Magyars (Mod'jors): 334.
Majo'rian: Emperor, 337; holds Vandals in check, 338; death, 338.
Mam-er-ti'ni: Campanian mercenaries, 106.
Man'lius, M.: saves capitol, 71; treason, 74.
Manlius, M.: accomplice of Catiline, 199.
Manlius Torqua'tus, T.: fight with Gaul, 78.
Man'tua: Etruscan town, 6.
Marcel'lus: see Claudius.
Mar'cian: Emperor, 337.
Marcoma'ni: German nation, 235; war, 273; confederacy, 285.

INDEX OF PROPER NAMES.

Ma'rius, C.: conducts war against Jugurtha, 167–168; against Cimbri, 169–170; military reforms, 170; commander in Social War, 174; Civil War, 178–179.

Marius, C., his son: 179, 180.

Mar'mora: see Propontis.

Mars: father of Romulus, 14; Roman god, 23, 190.

Martia'lis: epigrammatist, 266.

Mas-i-nis'sa: king of Numidia, 126–128; aids Romans, 143.

Massil'ia: Greek city in Gaul, 116; commerce, 145; government, 187; captured by Cæsar, 213; independent, 229.

Mauritan'ia: enlarged, 168; independent, 229.

Maxen'tius: 301, 302, 304.

Maxim'ian: 297–298, 301, 302.

Max'imin: Emperor, 279, 287.

Maximin: Emperor in the East, 302.

Maximus: see Fabius.

Maximus: Emperor, 288.

Maximus: Emperor, 335, 337.

Maz'de-ism: 289, 290.

Me'dian Empire: 289.

Me-di-o-la'num (*Milan*): 9, 298; capital of West, 309, 325; occupied by Attila, 334.

Mediterranean Lands: 1.

Me-nan'der: dramatist, 141.

Mercury: 190.

Messali'na, wife of Claudius: 250.

Messal'la: see Valerius.

Messa'na: seized by Mamertines, 106; independent, 111.

Metau'rus, R.: battle, B.C. 207, 125.

Metel'lus: see Cæcilius.

Milan: see Mediolanum.

Mile'tus: city in Asia, 146.

Mi'lo: see Annius.

Minerva: 23, 190.

Mintur'næ: Roman colony, 82; capture of Marius, 178.

Mithrada'tes I.: king of Parthia, 135.

Mithradates III.: king of Parthia, 202.

Mithradates VI.: king of Pontus; first and second wars, 176–178; third war, 195–196.

Mœ'sia: conquered by Augustus, 234.

Mohammed: 291.

Mo'loch: Phœnician god, 105.

Mucia'nus: governor of Syria, 256.

Mu'cius Scæ'vola, Q.: consul, 173; death, 180; jurist, 191.

Mum'mius, L.: destroys Corinth, 142.

Munda: battle, B.C. 45, 219.

Mure'na: see Licinius.

Mus: see Decius.

Mu'tina (*Modena*): battle, B.C. 43, 227.

My'læ: naval battle, B.C. 260, 107.

Næ'vius, Cn.: poet, 114.

Nar, R.: 94.

Narbo: colony, 164.

Narbonne: 327.

Neo-Platonism: 283, 313.

Nep'e-te: Latin colony, 68.

Neptune: 22; Equestrian, 26.

Nero: see Claudius.

Nero Claudius, Ti.: Emperor, 251–254; debasement of currency, 282.

Nerva: Emperor, 261.

Netherlands: inhabited by Salian Franks, 340.

Nicæ'a: council, 307.

Nic-o-me'di-a: 298, 307, 309.

Nile, R.: 1.

Nodo'tus: 22.

Nomen'tum: annexed to Rome, 80.

Norba: colony, 45.

Nor'icum: conquered by Augustus, 235.

Numa Pompil'ius: king of Rome, 15.

Numid'ia: subject to Carthage, 104; in Second Punic War, 126; divided, 168.

Octa'via, sister of Octavian: 229; mother of Marcellus, 233.

Octavia, wife of Nero: 252.

Octavius, C.: see Augustus.

Octavius, Cn.: consul, 179.

Octavius, M.: tribune, 156.

Od-e-na'tus: prince of Palmyra, 291; his father, 292; aids Rome, 292.

INDEX OF PROPER NAMES.   361

Oder, R.: 332.
O-do-va'car: grants land to Euric, 339; rules Italy, 341.
Olyb'rius: Emperor, 337.
Opim'ius, L.: consul, 165.
Origin of Alexandria: 282.
Orleans: besieged by Attila, 333.
Or'muzd: 289.
Oro'des: king of Parthia, 202.
Ossipa'go: 22.
Os'tia: colony, 12, 82; reception of Great Mother, 129; harbor filled up, 251.
Os'trogoths: contrast with Visigoths, 318; prostrated by Huns, 318; in Phrygia, 320; relations to Attila, 332; into Pannonia, 335.
O'tho: Emperor, 255.
Ovid'ius Na'so, P.: poet, 240.

Pa'dus, R. (*Po*): 4, 5, 8, 116, 117, 169, 293.
Pal-a-ti'na (tribe): 33.
Palil'ia: festival of Pales, 25.
Palmy'ra: prince of, 291; city, 292; fall, 294.
Panno'nia: conquered by Tiberius, 235; Vandals in, 324; Ostrogoths in, 335.
Panor'mos: town in Sicily, 108.
Pansa: see Vibius.
Pan'theon: 239.
Papin'ian: jurist, 279.
Papir'ius Carbo, Cn.: revolutionary leader, 179.
Papirius Cursor, L.: dictator, 86.
Paris: 312, 339.
Parthians: independent, 132; extension of empire, 135; war, 202; invaded by Trajan, 262; overthrown, 289, 291.
Pastoureaux: 295.
Paulus: see Æmilius.
Paulus: jurist, 279.
Pe'dum: annexed to Rome, 80.
Pelas'gians: 46.
Per'gamus: allied to Rome, 129; independent, 132; war with Antiochus, 134; receives territory, 135; annexed to Rome, 146.
Per'i-cles: authority, 162.

Per'seus: king of Macedonia; war with Rome, 136.
Persians: new empire, 289-291; contest with Julian, 313-314.
Per'sius: poet, 254.
Per'tinax: Emperor, 276.
Pescen'nius Ni'ger: 277.
Pes'sinus: worship of the Great Mother, 129.
Pharna'ces: king of Pontus, 216.
Pharsa'lus: battle, B.C. 48, 216.
Philip V.: king of Macedonia; war with Rome, 123; Second Macedonian War, 132; ally of Rome, 134; disloyal, 136.
Philip: false, 142.
Philip the Arabian: 288.
Philip'pi: battle, B.C. 42, 228.
Phi'lo: see Publilius.
Pi-ce'num: annexed to Rome, 93.
Picts: 335.
Pi-na'ri-i: worship of Hercules, 90.
Pi'so: see Calpurnius.
Placen'tia: Latin colony, 112; in Second Punic War, 117; battle, A.D. 69, 255.
Placid'ia: marries Ataulf, 327; marries Constantius, 327; mother of Valentinian III., 327; regent, 329.
Plautus: dramatist, 114, 141.
Plin'ius Secun'dus: historian, 258.
Plinius Secundus, his nephew: 265.
Po: see Padus.
Polen'tia: 323.
Pol'lio: see Asinius.
Pollux: 36, 96.
Polyb'ius: Greek historian, 35.
Pol'ycarp: martyr, 272.
Pome'tia: conquered by Rome, 73, 79.
Pomo'na: goddess, 23.
Pompei'i: destruction, 258.
Pompei'us Mag'nus, Cn.: commander in Social War, 174; joins Sulla, 180; commands against Sertorius, 193; against Spartacus, 194; against Pirates, 195; against Mithradates, 195-197; forms triumvirate, 200; receives Spain, 202; breach with Cæsar, 210; Civil War, 213; defeated at Pharsalus, 216; death, 216; theatre, 222.

Pompeius, Cn., his son: defeated, 219.
Pompeius, Sex., his brother: defeated, 219; death, 228.
Pon'tius, C.: Samnite commander, 87.
Pontius Tel-e-si'nus: Samnite commander, 180.
Pontus: independent, 132; Mithradatic War, 176.
Poppæ'a Sabi'na, wife of Nero: 253.
Por'cius Ca'to, M.: character, 139; opposed to Greek culture, 140; works, 141; basilica, 141; persuades to destruction of Carthage, 143; compared with Curius, 150; recommends grazing, 152.
Porcius Cato, M. (the younger): commands at Utica, 217; death, 218.
Por'sena, Lars: king of Clusium, 35.
Porta Scel-e-ra'ta: 51.
Postu'mius, A.: dictator, 65.
Po-ti'ti-i: worship of Hercules, 90.
Prænes'te: Latin town, 53; independent, 80; siege, 180.
Pro'bus: Emperor, 288, 297.
Proper'tius, Sex. Aure'lius: poet, 241.
Propon'tis: 309.
Provence: 339.
Pru'sias: king of Bithynia, 135.
Ptol'emies: in Egypt, 131.
Ptolemy: king of Egypt, 221.
Ptolemy Di-o-ny'sus: king of Egypt, 216.
Publil'ius Phi'lo, Q.: 77.
Publilius Vo'lero: 53.
Pute'oli: port, 251.
Pydna: battle, B.C. 168, 136.
Pyrenees: 291.
Pyrrhus: war, 96–98.

Qua'di: associated with Marcomani, 273.
Quinc'tius Circinna'tus, L.: 55.
Quinctius K.: 55.
Quinctius Fla-min'ius, T.: gains battle of Cynoscephalæ, 132; Greek culture, 141.
Quintilia'nus: rhetorician, 265.

Quintil'ius Va'rus, L.: defeated, 236.
Quir'inal Hill: Sabine settlement, 15, 17; religious ceremony, 71.
Quiri'nus: 23.

Ræ'tia: conquered by Augustus, 235.
Ram'nes (tribe): 17.
Raven'na: Etruscan town, 6; Cæsar's camp, 213; becomes capital of the West, 325, 327.
Re-a'te: Sabine town, 94.
Red Sea: 1.
Regil'lus, Lake: battle, 36.
Reg'ulus: see Atilius.
Rhad'agais: 323 ff.
Rhe'gium: seized by mercenaries, 106.
Rhine, R.: conquests of Cæsar, 234; Alamanni on, 311–312; left bank held by Germans, 317; crossed by Vandals, 324; Alamanni and Franks, 332.
Rho'dus, Id.: republic, 132; war with Antiochus, 134; receives territory, 135; gains commerce, 142; government, 187; independent, 229; residence of Tiberius, 233.
Rhone, R.: route into Gaul, 2, 205; eastern boundary of empire of Euric, 339.
Ric'imer, Count, grandson of Wallia: defeats Geiseric, 338: rule, 338; death, 338.
Robi'go: 26.
Rom'ulus: 14.
Romulus Augus'tulus: Emperor, 337, 340.
Rostra: 83; removed, 239.
Ru'bicon, R.: crossed by Cæsar, 213.
Rufi'nus: 321, 323.
Rufus: see Sulpicius.

Sabi'ni: 11; seizure of maidens, 26; wars, 43, 53, 56.
Sacred Mount: 43.
Sagun'tum: captured by Hannibal, 116.
Sa'li-i: 23.
Sallus'tius Crispus, C.: historian, 203.

INDEX OF PROPER NAMES. 363

Salo'na: 301.
Sam'nites: 4; capture of Capua, 67; treaty with Rome, 79; First War, 79; Second War, 84-88; Third War, 92-94; uprising, 174.
Sa'por: 291, 292.
Sapor II.: 313.
Sardin'ia: 3; conquered by Carthage, 6; trade with Rome, 79; seized by Rome, 110; taken by Geiseric, 338.
Sassa'nian monarchs: prosecutions by, 290.
Sassan'idæ: 289-290.
Sat-ur-na'li-a: 26.
Sat-ur-ni'nus: see Appuleius.
Satur'nus: 23, 26.
Savoy: Burgundians in, 332.
Scæ'vola: see Mucius.
Scip'io: see Cornelius.
Scots: 335.
Scribo'nius Cu'rio, C.: defeated in Africa, 213.
Seine, R.: 333.
Seja'nus: see Ælius.
Seleu'cia: Parthian capital, 270.
Seleu'cidæ: kings of Asia, 131; collapse of empire, 135.
Seleu'cus Ni-ca'tor: king of Asia, 131.
Sempronius Longus, Ti.: consul, 116.
Sempro'nius Gracchus, Ti.: protects Scipio, 140; marries Cornelia, 154.
Sempronius Gracchus, Ti., his son: reforms and death, 154-156.
Sempronius Gracchus, C., his brother: reforms and death, 158, 162-165.
Se'na Gal'lica: 8.
Sen'eca, L. Annæ'us: philosopher, 252, 254.
Senti'num: battle, B.C. 295, 92.
Septim'ius Seve'rus: Emperor, 276, 287; arch, 280; provincial system, 298.
Seq'uani: Gallic tribe, 206.
Sere'na: wife of Stilicho: 326.
Ser'gius Cat-i-li'na, L.: conspiracy, 198-200.
Serto'rius, Q.: war in Spain, 191-193.

Servil'ius Glau'cia, C.: attempt at revolution, 171.
Ser'vius Tul'lius: king of Rome, 31.
Seve'ri: 276, 303.
Seve'rus: 301, 302, 304.
Sicily: 3; occupied by Carthaginians, 6; trade with Rome, 79; ceded to Rome, 109; province enlarged, 124; taken in part by Geiseric, 338.
Sicin'ius Denta'tus: 59.
Sig'nia: colony, 35, 45.
Sil'ius Ital'icus: poet, 266.
Sines'sa: Roman colony, 82.
Smyrna: city in Asia, 146; persecution, 272.
So'lon: laws, 31; abolition of laws of debt, 41.
Spain: 2; trade with Rome forbidden, 79; ceded to Rome, 127; wars, 136; war of Sertorius, 191; governed by Cæsar, 201; reduced by Cæsar, 213; ravaged by Franks, 291; part of rival empire, 292; occupied by Vandals, 324, 325; Visigothic kingdom, 339.
Spar'tacus: gladiator, 193.
Sta'tius: poet, 266.
Stil'icho: minister of Honorius, 321, 322-325; victories, 323, 324; death, 325.
Sti'lo: see Ælius.
Strassburg: battle, 312.
Subura'na (tribe): 33.
Sue'vi: occupy northwestern Spain, 324, 330, 339.
Sulla: see Cornelius.
Sulpic'ius Rufus, P.: propositions, 177.
Suovetauril'ia: 26.
Su'trium: Latin colony, 68; besieged by Etruscans, 88.
Sya'grius: 339.
Syn'cretism: 283.
Sy'phax: king of Numidia, 126, 127.
Syracu'sæ: aided by Pyrrhus, 98; independent, 111; captured, 123.
Syr'ia: kingdom, 136; conquered, 196.
Syrtis (Bay): 2.

INDEX OF PROPER NAMES.

Tac'itus, P. Cornelius: historian, 264.
Tacitus: Emperor, 288.
Tam'erlane: 332.
Taren'tum: city of Magna Græcia, 9; war with Rome, 96; spoils, 103; revolts, 123; captured, 124.
Tarquin'ian dynasty: 14, 29; expulsion, 39.
Tarquin'ii: Etruscan city, 6.
Tarquinius Priscus, L.: king of Rome, 15, 31; reforms, 29.
Tarquinius Superbus, L.: king of Rome, 29; Latin empire, 34; purchase of Sibylline books, 36.
Tartes'sus: Phœnician colony, 104, 115.
Ta'tius, T.: king of Rome, 15.
Tau'rus, Mt.: 135.
Teren'tia: wife of Cicero, 189.
Terentil'ius Harsa, C.: 54.
Teren'tius: dramatist, 141.
Terentius Varro, C.: commanded at Cannæ, 121.
Terraci'na: captured by Rome, 67; Roman colony, 82.
Tertul'lian of Africa: 282.
Tet'ricus: pretender, 292; captured, 295.
Teu'toberg Forest: battle, A.D. 9, 236.
Teu'to-nes: invasion, 168-170.
Teuton'ic race: 168.
Thapsus: battle, B.C. 46, 217.
Theod'oric: king of Visigoths, 328; attacks Attila, 333; death, 333.
Theodo'sius the Great: proscribes paganism, 306, 315; succeeds Valens, 314, 319-322; character, 320.
Theodosius II.: 322.
Thermop'ylæ: battle, B.C. 191, 134.
Thes'pis: 114.
Thessalon'ica: Pompey's government, 213; center of government under Theodosius, 320; massacres under Theodosius, 321.
Tiber, R.: 4.
Tibe'rius, Emperor: divorced, 189; son of Livia, 233; conquest of Pannonia, etc., 235; Emperor, 245.
Tibul'lus, Al'bius: poet, 241.

Ti'bur: Latin town, 17; neutrality, 53; independent, 80; refuge of pipers, 91.
Tici'nus, R.: battle, B.C. 218, 117.
Tig-el-li'nus: freedman of Nero, 252.
Tigra'nes: king of Armenia, 176.
Ti'gris: crossed by Julian, 313.
Tit'i-es (tribe): 17.
Ti'tus, Emperor: war against Jews, 256, 257; arch, 258; reign, 258.
Torqua'tus: see Manlius.
Toulouse: 339, 340.
Tournay: 340.
Traja'nus, M. Ulpius: Emperor, 261-268; conquests, 261, 262; persecution of Christians, 267; forum, 280; his conquests a source of weakness, 292.
Transpada'ni: receive citizenship, 214.
Trasime'nus, L.: battle, B.C. 217, 119.
Tre'bia, R.: battle, B.C. 218, 117.
Tre'rus, R.: 11.
Trifa'num: battle, B.C. 340, 80.
Tul'lius Cicero, M.: divorce, 189; writer, 191; consul, 197; character, 198; banished, 201; return, 201; speeches against Antony, 227; death, 228.
Tul'lus Hostil'ius: king of Rome, 15, 17.
Tus'culum: Latin town, 17, 45; aids Rome, 56; annexed by Rome, 73.
Tyrrhe'nian Sea: 3; enclosed by islands, 110.

Ul'filas: 318.
Ul'pian: prætorian præfect, 279, 282.
Um'brians: 4, 5; war with Rome, 92.
U'tica: Roman headquarters, 143.

Va'lens: receives Eastern præfecture, 314; grants land to Visigoths, 319; defeated at Adrianople, 319.
Val-en-tin'i-an: 310; Emperor, 314.
Valentinian II.: 314; death, 320.
Valentinian III.: 322; Age of, 329 ff.; assassinated, 335.

INDEX OF PROPER NAMES. 365

Vale′rian: Emperor, 288; captured, 291.
Vale′rius Catul′lus, Q.: poet, 203.
Valerius Corvus, M.: fight with Gaul, 78.
Valerius Flaccus, L.: interrex, 182.
Valerius, M.: consul, B.C. 449, 59.
Valerius Messal′la, M.: general, 242.
Valerius, P.: consul, B.C. 460, 56.
Vandals: colonists in empire, 317; invasion, 324; take possession of Spain, 324; in Africa, 329, 330; empire of, 338; in possession of Africa, 339.
Va′rius, Q.: commission, 173.
Varro: see Terentius.
Va′rus: see Quintilius.
Vei′i: Etruscan town, 6; wars with Rome, 11, 35; with the Fabii, 51; siege and capture, 67-70.
Veli′træ: Volscian town, 53; annexed to Rome, 80.
Venetians: 5; invade Gallic territory, 72.
Venice: foundation, 334.
Ventid′ius, P.: war against the Parthians, 228.
Venu′sia: Latin colony, 92; escape of Varro, 122; neighborhood of Hannibal, 125; incident, 149.
Vercel′læ: battle, B.C. 101, 169.
Vercinget′orix: Gallic chief, 208, 209.
Vergil′ius Ma′ro, P.: poet, 239.
Vergin′ius: governor of Germany, 254; supports Vespasian, 256.
Vero′na: the Cenomani, 117; Alaric defeated at, 323.
Ve′rus, L.: Emperor, 270.
Vespasia′nus, T. Flavius: Emperor, 255-258.

Vesta: 24.
Vesuvius, Mt.: retreat of Spartacus, 194; eruption, 258, 265.
Vib′ius Pansa, C.: consul, 227.
Vi′cus Tuscus: 37.
Vindex: rebellion, 254.
Vindobo′na (Vienna): 273.
Vipsa′nius Agrip′pa, M.: 233; built Pantheon, 239; statesman, 241.
Virgil: see Vergilius.
Virginia: 59.
Vis′igoths: invasion, 318-320; converted to Arian Christianity, 318; passage of the Danube, 319; in provinces south of Danube, 320; kingdom, 328; granted territory on Bay of Biscay, 328; in southwestern Gaul, 330, 332; against Attila, 333; dominions under Euric, 339.
Vitel′lius, A.: Emperor, 255.
Vol-a-ter′ræ: Etruscan city, 6.
Vo′lero: see Publilius.
Volscian Mts.: 35.
Vol′scians: 11; wars, 43, 53, 73.
Volsin′ii: Etruscan town, 6.
Vol-u-ti′na: 23.
Vulcan: 22.
Vultur′nus, R.: 4; boundary of Latium, 82.

Wal′lia: king of Visigoths, 328; leads Goths into Gaul, 328; death, 328.
West Goths: see Visigoths.

Za′ma: battle, B.C. 202, 126.
Ze′no: Emperor, 337.
Zeno′bia: 288; occupies throne, 292; character, 294; capture, 294.
Zoroas′ter: 289, 290.

INDEX OF ANTIQUITIES.

addic′tus: 41.
æ′diles: 62; cu′rule, 76.
æra′rius: 129.
A′ger Roma′nus: original extent, 17; embraces course of Tiber, 17; annexation of Gabii, 34; extension, 65, 73; annexation of Cære, 78; of Capua, 79; of Sabine territory, 93; composition, 99.
agrarian laws: of Cassius, 48; of Flaminius, 112; of Gracchus, 155; of Drusus, 165.
agriculture: Roman, 100, 149–152; Cato's treatise, 141.
A′gri Decuma′tes: 259, 260.
alimentations: 263.
alliance: triple, 44.
allies: 100; stand with Rome against Hannibal, 120; demand citizenship, 166, 173; Social War, 174.
alphabet: 36.
ambassadors: privileges, 70.
amphitheatre: 258, 275.
aqueducts: 90, 94; of Claudius, 251.
arch: 30, 239; of Titus, 258; of Septimius Severus, 280; of Constantine, 302.
architecture: Roman, 238–239, 258; of Ravenna, 325.
army: see military affairs.
art: 27, 102; of Augustan Age, 239; of Pompeii, 258; of Age of Trajan, 266.
as: 102.
ascrip′ti gle′bæ: 264.
assemblies: 62; powers, 112, 178; meeting, 161; loss of powers, 232; end, 280. See plebeian assembly, *concilium tributum plebis, comitia centuriata, comitia curiata, comitia tributa.*
assembly: plebeian, 44; its powers, 50, 62; organized by tribes, 53; powers enlarged, 77; legislative power, 95; restricted, 184.
assignment of land: 49.
Ater′nian Tarpei′an law: see law.
auguries: 190.
augurs: 20, 26; plebeian, 76.
Augustus: title under Diocletian, 298.
Aure′lian law: see law.
auspices: 20; disregarded, 108; meaning, 190.

Barrack Emperors: 287.
basil′ica: 141, 238, 302.
baths: of Caracalla, 280.
bishop: 283, 307.
building: by Tarquins, 30; after destruction of Rome, 72; by Augustus, 238; by Caligula, 249; by Claudius, 250; by Nero, 253; by Domitian, 258; under the Severi, 279–280; under Constantine, 302; at Ravenna, 325.
bureaucracy: 299.
burying: 96.

Cæ′ritan rights: 78.
Cæsar: general appellation for Emperor, 260; office created by Diocletian, 298.
calendar: 27; reform, 219.
Canulei′an law: see law.
capitol: 30.
Capit′oline Triad: 7, 23, 30.
cattle: for money, 57.
cavalry: see military affairs.
censors: appoint senators, 19; establishment of office, 64; plebeian, 77; office suspended, 183; restored, 195.
census: 64, 195.
centuriate assembly: see *comitia centuriata.*

INDEX OF ANTIQUITIES.

centuries: 32; military, 60.
Christianity: under Nero, 253; under Trajan, 267; under Marcus Aurelius, 271; under the Severi, 282-283; under Diocletian, 300; under Constantine, 304-307; under Julian, 313; final establishment, 314-315.
chronology: importance, 13.
church: complete organization, 282; theological system, 328.
citizenship: rights, 63; contest, 166, 173; granted to Italians, 175; to Transpadani, 214; to all provincials, 281.
city: ancient, 159; time of Trajan, 263; fourth century, 310.
civilization: Etruscan, 6.
civ′itas: 160.
civita′tes fœdera′tæ: see allies.
clans: 18; land, 19; serfs, 20; power, 21.
classes: of Servius Tullius, 32.
clients: 20; family worship, 25; joined with patricians, 50; rights of property, 60; freedmen, 253.
clip′eus: 70.
cohorts: 69, 170.
coinage: gold, 218; right of, 256; depreciation, 282; reformed by Constantine, 303.
collegiality: 89.
colo′ni: 264.
colonies: Greek, 9; Ostia, 12, 15; of Tarquin, 35; Latin, 45, 49, 73; Roman, 82, 99; Junonia, 145, 164; of C. Gracchus, 164; of Drusus, 165; Ælia Capitolina, 258; of Trajan, 261; German, 317.
Colosse′um: 258.
column: of Mænius, 83; of Duilius, 107.
comit′ia centuria′ta: instituted, 34; powers, 39, 60, 62; reform, 113. See assemblies.
comitia curia′ta: 19; in republic, 39, 62.
comitia tribu′ta: 62.
commerce: Italian, 9; of Rome, 12, 22; rights (*commercium*), 21, 63; decay, 39, 42; with Carthage, 79;
of Rhodes and Delos, 142; of antiquity, 187.
concil′ium tribu′tum ple′bis: 62. See assembly: plebeian.
confederacy: Latin, 10; under Tarquins, 30; relations of Rome to, 34; alliance with Rome, 44; dissolved, 80; name extended, 81; German, 285; Franks, 340.
constitution: patrician, 18-22; of Servius Tullius, 31; Roman, 61, 95; of Sulla, 181-185; of Augustus, 230 ff.; of Diocletian, 296 ff.
consula′ris: 63.
consuls: 38, 61; appoint senators, 19; privileges, 63; plebeian, 75; age, 168.
conu′bium: see intermarriage.
corn: see distributions.
council: of Nicæa, 307.
cremation: 96.
crucifixion: 105.
curato′res, to inspect accounts: 263.
cu′ria: 310.
cu′ri-æ: 18.
curia′les: 310.
currency: depreciation, 295; reform by Constantine, 302.
cu′rule chair: 37, 63, 65.
curule offices: 65 *n*. 1; disqualification for, 183.

debauchery, 263.
debt: law, 41; relief, 75; in last century of republic, 187; relief by Cæsar, 215.
decem′virate: 58.
decu′rions: 310.
Defen′sor Civita′tis: 310.
delation: 246; under Domitian, 259.
demagogues: 74; Flaminius, 112; Saturninus and Glaucia, 171.
dena′rius: 102.
despotism: system under Diocletian, 298.
dictator: 38; right of appeal, 59; perpetual, 220.
diocese: 299, 308.
distributions of corn: 148, 164, 173; reduced, 218.
divorce: 188, 233.

INDEX OF ANTIQUITIES.

dome: 239.
drainage: of Rome, 30, 96; of the Pontine Marshes, 101; of the Fucine Lake, 251.
drama: germs, 114; Grecian, 141.
dyarchy: 231; end, 280.

economic decay: 263.
Edict: of Caracalla, 281.
elections: 161; time, 212.
elephants: in warfare, 97.
empire of Rome: of the Tarquins, 29; of Augustus, 231; boundaries, 233, 235, 268, 293, 330–332, 335; at its height, 263; division, 321; collapse, 336, 337, 339; disintegration, 338; fall, 340; survival, 341. See *Ager Romanus*.
eponymous consuls: 222.
epulo'nes: 76.
equestrian order: 163, 166; census, 195.
eq'uites: equo pub'lico, 33; *equo priva'to*, 70, 163.
equum ven'dere: 128.
estates (*latifun'dia*): 101, 149.

family: worship, 24; law, 60.
festivals: 25; of Ceres, 122.
fe-ti-a'les: 26.
finances: 263, 282.
fines regulated: 57.
fla'men: 23.
fœdera'ti: 320.
formulas: published, 91.
freedmen: 21; in Senate, 89; in empire, 253.

games: 26.
gen'tes: see clans.
Genu'cian law: see law.
gladiatorial contests: 189, 193, 275.
gold coinage: 218.

hasta'ti: 70, 127, 170; centurions, 171.
hegemony of Rome: in Latium, 30, 34, 45, 80.
hills of Rome: 16.
history: its character, **13.**
hono'res: 63.
Horten'sian law: see law.

Icil'ian law: see law.
Ides: 222.
impera'tor: title, 219.
impe'rium: 62; *proroga'tum*, 110, 125.
industry: Italian, 9, 101; collapse, 149; defects, 187; effects of collapse, 263, 264.
insig'nia: royal, 37; of consuls, 63.
intermarriage: rights (*conubium*), 21; plebeians, 61; foreigners, 221.
in'terrex, interreg'num: 20, 76, 182.

ju'gerum: 75.
Julian law: see law.
Julian-Papir'ian law: see law.
jurists: under Severi, 279.
jurors: equestrian, 163; senatorial, 184; of both orders, 194; Cæsar's reform, 218.
jus auxil'i: 44, 62.
jus exil'i: 100.
jus ima'ginum: 65.
justice: criminal, 38, 60; permanent courts, 184; prosecution, 246.

Kalends: 27.
kings: Roman, 15; elective, 19; possessed auspices, 20; hatred of name, 222.
knights: see equestrian order.

land: held by clans, 19; private property, 33; public, 47; its aggregation, 149; grants by Gracchus, 155, 164; tithe-lands, 260; occupied on condition of military service by Germans, 286. See also *Ager Romanus*, agrarian laws.
law: Aternian-Tarpeian, B.C. 454, 57; Aurelian, B.C. 70, 194; Canuleian, B.C. 445, 63; Flaminian, B.C. 232, 111; Genucian, B.C. 342, 78; Hortensian, 94; Icilian, B.C. 456, 57; Julian, B.C. 90, 175; Julian-Papirian, B.C. 430, 58; Julian (*Municipalis*), B.C. 45, 175; Manilian, B.C. 66, 196; Plautian-Papirian, B.C. 90, 175; Publilian (of Philo, B.C. 339), 77; (of Volero, B.C. 471), 53; Sempronian,

B.C. 133, 155; B.C. 123, 163; Sulpician, B.C. 88, 177; Terentilian, B.C. 461, 54, 58; Villian, B.C. 180, 169. See agrarian laws.
laws: passage, 53; customary, 54; codification, 55, 58.
lec'tio sena'tus: 64.
lega'ti: governing provinces, 202, 232.
legion: 69, 127; opposed to phalanx, 133.
lictors: 37; of consuls, 38; of prætors, 202.
literature, Roman: beginnings, 113; of republic, 191, 203; of Augustan Age, 239; of Nero's reign, 254; elder Pliny, 258; Silver Age, 264–266.
literature, Greek: 140.
literature: patristic, 328.
locuple'tes: 32.
Luperca'lia: 220.
luper'ci: 26.
lus'trum: 64.

mænia'næ: 83.
magistrates: 38, 61; plebeian, 76; city, 161; age, 169, 197; loss of power, 232.
Manilian law: see law.
maniples: 69, 170.
maritime empire: of Carthage, 104.
martyrdom: of Ignatius of Antioch, 268; of Justin, 272; of Polycarp, 272.
master of horse: 86.
mausoleum of Augustus: 239.
migrations: commencement, 168, 273; of Western Germans, 285.
military affairs: situation of Rome, 12; early army, 20; reform of Servius Tullius, 32; service, 42; reform of Camillus, 68–70; of Scipio, 126; of Marius, 170; military rule, 280; incorporations of Germans into army, 286; Diocletian's reforms, 299.
money: 27; values, 58; silver, 102.
mortgages: 263.
municipalities: in Gaul, 209; economic distress, 263; under the later empire, 310.

municipal system: 99, 161; extended over Italy, 175; law, 218; failure of self-government, 263; oligarchies, 310.
municip'ium: 82, 99.
myth: 14; Roman 23.

navy: 106.
Neo-platonism: 283.
nexus: 41.
nobility: 63, 65; power, 138.
no'væ tab'ulæ: 188.
novus homo: 138.

occupation of land: 47; plebeian, 75; continued, 151.
op'pidum: 160.
optima'tes: 166.
orbis terra'rum veter'ibus no'tus: 1.

pa'gi: 33.
pa'nem et circen'ses: 222.
parties: 166, 186.
Partnership Emperors: 297.
pastures: 75.
pa'ter-famil'ias: 18; power lessened, 60.
pa'tres: 19.
pa'tria potes'tas: see *pater-familias.*
patricians: 18; power in republic, 38; occupation of land, 48; loss of privileges, 60, 77.
patrons: 21.
peasants: Roman, 40; property, 100; decay, 149, 154; Italian, 174; poor-relief to, 263; wars, 295.
peda'rii: 95.
persecution: cause, 267, 268; under Marcus Aurelius, 271, 272; under Diocletian, 300; of heretics by Gratian, 314, 315.
pestilence: time of Marcus Aurelius, 270.
phalanx: 69; Macedonian, 133.
philology: 191.
philosophy: Greek, 190.
pi'lum: 127.
pirates: 112, 195.
Plautian-Papirian law: see law.
plebeians: 21; civil rights, 31; in republic, 39; receive tribunes, 43;

receive the Aventine, 57; clans, 60; intermarriage, 61; organization, 62; equality of rights, 75. See also magistrates and assemblies.
plebisci'ta: 63.
pomœ'rium: 210.
pon'tifex max'imus: head of Roman religion, 218; residence, 224; imperial title, 306; papal title, 306; relinquished by Gratian, 315.
pontif'ices: 26; plebeian, 76.
poor-relief: 263.
popula'res: 166.
posses'sio: 47.
præfects: 232.
præfectures: under republic, 99; under Constantine, 308.
prætor: Latin, 45; administration of law, 48; office established, 76; additional, 110; courts, 141; by Sulla's laws, 183; *peregrinus*, 184; *urbanus*, 223.
Prætorian Cohorts: 232; sell throne, 276; dissolved by Septimius Severus, 280.
Prætorian Præfect: 232, 279; becomes chief minister of Emperor, 281; under Constantine, 308.
princeps: 231.
princeps sena'tus: 231.
prin'cipes (soldiers): 70, 127, 170; centurions, 171.
proconsul: 232.
procurator: 255.
proleta'rius: 152.
proprætor: 110.
proscription: of Sulla, 181; of the triumvirs, 227, 228.
provinces: Sicily, 109; Sardinia and Corsica, 110; Spain, 127; Illyricum, 136; Macedonia, 142; Africa, 145; Asia, 146; Transalpine Gaul, 164; Cilicia and Cyprus, 196; Bithynia, 196; Syria, 196; Cisalpine Gaul, 215; Mœsia, 234; Rætia, Noricum, Pannonia, 235; Germany, 236; Britain, 251; Dacia, 261, 284; Arabia, Petræa, 262; surrendered by Hadrian, 268; assimilation of Italy and the, 280;

provincial system: 110; its evils, 147; governors, 183; under empire, 232; edict of Caracalla, 280; reorganization under Diocletian, 298; under Constantine, 309.
publica'ni: 153, 164.
Publil'ian law: see law.

quæstio'nes perpet'uæ: 184.
quæstor: assistant of consul, 44; magistrate, 61; duties, 65.
quin'cunx: 70, 126.
quindecem'viri sa'cris faciun'dis: 36; plebeian, 75.
quin'quereme: 106.

races in Italy: 4.
re'gia: 224.
reg'imen mo'rum: 64.
religion: Etruscan, 6; Roman, 22–27; of Fabian *gens*, 71; innovations, 90; Carthaginian, 105; in last century of republic, 189; of Emperor, 237; Christian, 267; sun-worship, 278; under Severi, 282–284; of Zoroaster, 289; of Sassanidæ, 290; under Julian, 313; under Gratian, 314; under Theodosius, 315.
repetun'dæ: court, 148, 184; judges, 163.
roads: Appian, 90; Flaminian, 112; Latin, 4, 53.
rogation: 54.
Roma quadra'ta: 16.
rostra: 83; removed by Cæsar, 239.
routes of commerce: 2.

Sa'lii: 23.
satire: 113.
scu'tum: 70.
secession: first, B.C. 494, 43; second, B.C. 449, 59; third, B.C. 286, 94.
Sempro'nian law: see law.
Senate: 19, 62; governing body, 95; "assembly of kings," 98; government, 162, 182; appointment, 19, 183; census, 195; under empire, 232; under Severus, 280; municipal, 310.
sena'tus consul'ta: 62.

serfdom: predial, 264.
sester'tius: 102.
Sib'ylline books, 36.
silver currency: 102.
slave labor: 76, 101, 150; its fatal character, 187; regulated, 218; consequences, 264.
slaves: character, 89; revolt, 151.
so'cii: see allies
sol'idus: 303.
spo'lia opi'ma: 111.
standard: 171.
succession: rules, 243, 248, 261, 273, 301, 304, 311.
suffra'gium: 63.
syn'cretism: 283-284.

tab'ulæ: 59.
taxation: by Servius Tullius, 33: incident illustrating, 41; upon possessors of public land, 47-48; relations of censor to, 64; provinces relieved from revenues, 148; farming of, 153; effect of edict of Caracalla, 281; land tax made uniform, 299; in fourth century, 310.
temple: of Jupiter Capitolinus, 30; of Diana, 34; of Castor, 36; of Juno, 68; of Juno, on capitol, 71; of Concord, 75, 165; of Æsculapius, 96; of Juno Moneta, 102; of Cæsar, 224; of Janus, 229; built by Augustus, 238; Pantheon, 239.
Terentil'ian law: see law.
Theatre of Pompey: 239.
Thirty Tyrants: 291, 292.
timoc'racy: 31.
tithe lands: 260.
tor'ques: 78.

trades: centuries, 33.
tradition: 13, 57.
treason: law, 246.
treasury: 65.
treaty: with Latins, 34; with Gabii, 34; of Spurius Cassius, 44; with Carthage, 35, 79; with Gauls, 72; with Samnites, 79; with Tarentum, 97.
triar'ii: 69, 127, 170; centurions, 171.
tribes: patrician, 17; of Servius Tullius, 33; composed of landowners, 88; reorganized, 89; made basis of centuriate assembly, 113; German, 285.
tribunes: military, 20; with consular power, 63.
tribunes: of plebs, 43; usurpation of power, 50; number increased, 53; power to impose fines, 57; powers, 62; mischievous powers, 155; restricted by Sulla, 183; restored, 184.
tribu'tum: 33, 48.
trium'virate: 200, 227.
twelve tables: 59.

usury: 74; laws, 78; trials, 188.

Vestal Virgins: 25.
vicar: 299.
Villian law: see law.

walls: of Rome, 16; of Servius Tullius, 31; Cyclopean, 45; Hadrian's, 269; Aurelian's, 293.
worship: of Cybele, 129; of Bacchus, 140.

yoke: sending under, 87.

THE BEST HISTORIES

Myers's History of Greece. — For introduction, $1.25.

Myers's Eastern Nations and Greece. — For introduction, $1.00.

Myers's History of Rome. — For introduction, $1.00.

Myers's Ancient History. — For introduction, $1.50.

Myers's Mediæval and Modern History. — For introduction, $1.50.

Myers's General History. — For introduction, $1.50.

Myers and Allen's Ancient History. — For introduction, $1.50.

Allen's Short History of the Roman People. — For introduction, $1.00.

Emerton's Introduction to the Study of the Middle Ages. — For introduction, $1.12.

Emerton's Mediæval Europe (814-1300). — For introduction, $1.50.

Feilden's Short Constitutional History of England. — For introduction, $1.25.

Mace's Method in History. — For introduction, $1.00.

Channing and Hart's Guide to the Study of American History. — For introduction, $2.00.

Montgomery's Leading Facts of English History. — For introduction, $1.12.

Montgomery's Leading Facts of French History. — For introduction, $1.12.

Montgomery's Beginner's American History. — For introduction, 60 cents.

Montgomery's Leading Facts of American History. — For introduction, $1.00.

Montgomery's Student's American History. — For introduction, $1.40.

Cooper, Estill, and Lemmon's History of Our Country. — For introduction, $1.00.

Getchell's Mediæval History by Library Method. — For introduction, 50 cents.

GINN & COMPANY, Publishers,

Boston.   New York.   Chicago.   Atlanta.   Dallas.

TEXT-BOOKS ON HISTORY

FOR HIGHER SCHOOLS AND COLLEGES

By PHILIP VAN NESS MYERS
Professor of History and Political Economy in the University of Cincinnati, Ohio,
AND
WILLIAM F. ALLEN,
Late Professor of History in the University of Wisconsin.

Myers's General History. Half morocco. 759 pages. Illustrated. For introduction, $1.50.

Myers's History of Greece. Cloth. 577 pages. Illustrated. For introduction, $1.25.

Myers's Eastern Nations and Greece. (Part I. of Myers's and of Myers and Allen's Ancient History.) Cloth. 369 pages. Illustrated. For introduction, $1.00.

Myers and Allen's Ancient History. (Part I. is Myers's Eastern Nations and Greece. Part II. is Allen's Short History of the Roman People.) Half morocco. 763 pages. Illustrated. For introduction, $1.50.

Myers's Ancient History. (Part I. is Myers's Eastern Nations and Greece. Part II. is Myers's Rome.) Half morocco. 617 pages. Illustrated. For introduction, $1.50.

Myers's History of Rome. (Part II. of Myers's Ancient History.) Cloth. 230 pages. Illustrated. For introduction, $1.00.

Allen's Short History of the Roman People. (Part II. of Myers and Allen's Ancient History.) Cloth. 370 pages. Illustrated. For introduction, $1.00.

Myers's Outlines of Mediæval and Modern History. Half morocco. 740 pages. Illustrated. For introduction, $1.50.

A philosophical conception of history and a broad view of its developments, accurate historical scholarship, and liberal human sympathies are the fundamental characteristics of these remarkable histories. The hand of a master is shown in numberless touches that illuminate the narrative and both stimulate and satisfy the student's curiosity.

Schoolroom availability has been most carefully studied, and typographical distinctness and beauty, maps, tables, and other accessories have received their full share of attention.

GINN & COMPANY, Publishers,

Boston.   New York.   Chicago.   Atlanta.   Dallas.